C000100300

ELSEWHERE TEXTS

EDITED BY

GAYATRI CHAKRAVORTY SPIVAK AND HOSAM ABOUL-ELA

The series takes as its charge radical new directions in the engagement with the theoretical culture of the non-European. The point of departure here is the scandalous notion that the theorizing imagination of the Global South is as human as the European, complex, subject to the dynamism of history, fluid, unrepresentable, and impossible either to essentialize or reduce to any *counter* essentialism.

This series does not consider translation as producing a substitute, but rather as the first step in accessibility. As such, its problems are shared with the readers by the translator(s) of each text. The choice of text and the quality of the translation are peer reviewed. Our ideal reader is the engaged non-specialist, so that the circle of global criticality may expand beyond the North in the South.

SEAGULL
BOOKS
•
CELEBRATING
40 YEARS

ALSO AVAILABLE IN
ELSEWHERE TEXTS

RENÉ ZAVALETA MERCADO

Towards a History of the National-Popular in Bolivia, 1879–1980

Translated by Anne Freeland
With an introduction by Sinclair Thomson

SOFONIA MACHABE MOFOKENG

In My Heart

Translated by Nhlanhla Maake
With an introduction by Simon Gikandi

LUIS TAPIA MEALLA

The Production of Local Knowledge

History and Politics in the Work of
René Zavaleta Mercado

Translated by Alison Spedding
Edited by Anne Freeland and Sinclair Thomson

LONDON NEW YORK CALCUTTA

Seagull Books, 2022

Original published in Spanish by Muela del Diablo Editores, La Paz as
La producción del conocimiento local. Historia y política en la obra de René Zavaleta
© Luis Tapia Mealla, 2002

General Introduction © Gayatri Chakravorty Spivak, 2018

Preface © Luis Tapia Mealla and Sinclair Thomson, 2022

English translation © Alison Spedding, 2022

ISBN 978 0 85742 334 4

British Library Cataloguing-in-Publication Data
A catalogue record for this book is available from the British Library

Typeset by Seagull Books, Calcutta, India
Printed and bound in the USA by Integrated Books International

CONTENTS

ELSEWHERE TEXTS

General Introduction

Gayatri Chakravorty Spivak

'Theory' is an English transcription of the Greek *theorein*. Corresponding words exist in the major European languages. Our series 'Elsewhere Texts' works within these limits. 'Theory' has been creolized into innumerable languages. Yet the phenomenon of 'seeing or making visible correctly'—the meaning in Greek that will still suffice—does not necessarily relate to that word—'theory'—in those languages. This describes the task of the editors of a translated series on theory in the world. How does 'theory' look elsewhere from the Euro-US? Since our texts are modern, there is often at least an implicit awareness that 'proper' theory looks different as the 'same' theory elsewhere.

Heidegger thought that truth is destined to be thought by the man of 'Western Europe'.[1] Our series does not offer a legitimizing counter-essentialism. Take a look at the map and see how tiny Europe is—not even really a continent—but, as Derrida would say, a cap, a headland.[2] Such a tiny place, yet who can deny Derrida's description, which is an historical and empirical observation? Look at the tables of contents of the most popular U.K./U.S. critical anthologies, and you will see corroboration of the essentialist conviction that goes with the historical claim. The counter-essentialism is reflected in the choice of critics from 'the rest of the world', and today's espousal of 'the Global South'. Just being non-white is the counter-essence. An axiomatics for the other side, as Black Lives Matter points out.

The influential *Norton Anthology of Theory and Criticism,* for example, lets in only Maimonides before the modern university system kicks in.[3] But

---

1 Martin Heidegger, *What Is Called Thinking?* (Fred D. Wieck and J. Glenn Gray trans) (New York: Harper and Row, 1968).

2 Jacques Derrida, *The Other Heading* (Pascale-Anne Brault and Michael B. Naas trans) (Bloomington: Indiana University Press, 1992).

3 Vincent B. Leitch (ed.), *The Norton Anthology of Theory and Criticism* (New York: Norton, 2010). I have to tell my reader that I called my father "Maimonides" because he was born in Mymensingh in what is now Bangladesh! Comparative Literarure!

even if they had let in Khaled Ziadeh, Marta Lamas, and Marilena Chaui, the material would have been determined by the epistemological procedures of that system.[4] Norton lets in W. E. B Du Bois, the first African-American to get a doctorate from Harvard, the man who felt that 'of the greatest importance was the opportunity which my *Wanderjahre* [wandering years] in Europe gave of looking at the world as a man and not simply from a narrow racial and provincial outlook.'[5] Du Bois emphatically claimed that the African-American was the best example of the subject of the Declaration of Independence (the Founding Fathers were standing in). It is therefore significant that he claims here to inhabit the persona of Wilhelm Meister, Goethe's hero, with the trajectory not fully reversed. Meister came to the United States to act out the European Enlightenment in this new land—a trip described in Goethe's *Wilhelm Meisters Wanderjahre* [*Wilhelm Meister's Journeyman Years*]—a hope which Du Bois nuanced, perhaps as soon as his scholarship to the Friedrich Wilhelm University from the Slater Fund for the Education of Freedmen was canceled, the year after President Hayes' death, by a Standing Committee on Education chaired by a former Lieutenant Colonel in the Confederate Army, the army that had fought to retain slavery and the slave trade in the U.S. Civil War. (Hayes himself destroyed the possibility of Reconstruction by the 1877 Compromise with the Southern Democrats in order to retain the Presidency of the United States.) Du Bois as a young man was critical of his racism but probably not aware of political details, as he was later.

In the *Norton Anthology* we get Zora Neale Hurston (Columbia), Langston Hughes (Harlem Renaissance via Columbia), Frantz Fanon (University of Lyon), Chinua Achebe (University College, Ibadan; professor in the US), Stuart Hall (Oxford), Ngugi wa Thiong'o (Leeds; professor in the US), Taban Lo Liyong (Iowa), Henry Owuwor Anyuumba (Iowa), Spivak (Cornell), Houston Baker (UCLA), Gloria Anzaldua (UCSC), Homi Bhabha (Oxford), Barbara Christian (Columbia), Barbara Smith (Mount Holyoke), Henry Louis Gates, Jr. (Cambridge), bell hooks (UCSC). The point I am making is not that these writers have not challenged Eurocentrism. It is that they are sabotaging from within and this is a historical fact that must be turned

---

4 These authors were published by Palgrave in a series similar to this one, under the same editorial collaboration.

5 Cited in Henry Louis Gates, Jr., 'The Black Letters on the Sign: W. E. B. Du Bois and the Canon' in *The Oxford W. E. B. Du Bois* (New York: Oxford Univ. Press, 2007), VOL. 8, p. *xvi*.

around so that there is a chance for widening the circle. Fanon stands out because he is the only one who clearly operated outside the Euro-US, though he was what Du Bois would call a Black European, literally fighting Europe, also from within, located in a geographical exterior. Yet one cannot help suspecting that the certificate of violence granted him by the French philosopher Jean-Paul Sartre had a hand in this.

(In the next most influential anthology, the rest-of-the world entries are almost identical, but for Audre Lorde [Columbia], Geraldine Heng [Cornell], Ania Loomba [Sussex], Chidi Okonkwo [University of Auckland], Jamaica Kincaid [Franconia and New School].[6] Again, Fanon is the only working 'outsider'. I am sure the general pattern is repeated everywhere. I have myself been so tokenized through my long work-life as representing 'Third World criticism', that I am particularly alive to the problem.[7])

Our position is against a rest-of-the-world counter-essentialism, which honors the history-versus-tradition binary opposition. We recognize that a hegemonic Euro-US series can only access work abroad that is continuous with Euro-US radicalism.[8] To open ourselves to what lies beyond is another kind of effort. Within the limits of our chosen task we focus, then, on another phenomenon.

The history of the last few centuries has produced patterns of bilateral resistance. The formation is typically my nation-state, my region, my cultural formation over against 'the West'. These days there are global efforts at conferences, events and organizations that typically take the form of the Euro-US at the centre and a whole collection of 'other cultures', who connect through the imperial languages, protected by a combination of sanctioned ignorance and superficial solidarities, ignoring the internal problems when

---

6 Michael Ryan and Julie Rivkin, *Literary Theory: An Anthology* (Malden: Wiley Blackwell, 2004).

7 An example that has stayed with me over the years remains Diane Bell's excellent *Daughters of the Dreaming* (Minneapolis: University of Minnesota Press, 1993), which, in response to requests for inclusion of third-world material, put in Trin-ti Min-Ha and me, longtime faculty persons in prestigious United States universities!

8 This continuity and the discontinuous are beautifully staged in Bamako (2006) by Abderrahmane Sissako. Jean François Lyotard gave a clear articulation of the problem of discontinuity in *The Differend: Phrases in Dispute* (Georges Van den Abbeele trans.) (Minneapolis: University of Minnesota Press, 1988).

they are at these global functions.[9] The model is the fact and discipline of preservation. By the Nara document of 1994, it was insisted that preservation should be not only of built space but also of intangible cultural heritage. What started was the model that I have described above. It is now a tremendous capital-intensive fact of our world.

In and through our series, we want to combat this tendency. We want not only to present texts from different national origins to the US readership, but we want also to point out how each is singular in the philosophical sense, namely universalizable, though never universal. We are not working for area studies niche-marketing, though the work is always of specialist quality. In the interest of creating a diversified collectivity outside of the English readership, a long-term feature might be periodic conferences bringing the authors together.

The story begins for me in a conversation with the Subaltern Studies collective in 1986—asking them if I could arrange the publication of a selection from their work—because they were not available in the United States. A long-term preoccupation, then. To this was added Hosam Aboul-Ela's 2007 consolidation of a thought that was growing inside me: from the rest of the world literary editors wanted fiction, poetry, drama—raw material. Theory came generally from 'us'. Seagull Books, the only publishing house based in South Asia with direct world distribution, and, unlike most western conglomerates, uninterested in translations of theory not recognizable by the Eurocentric 'cosmopolitan' model, seems now the appropriate publisher.

In the intervening three decades a small difference has imposed itself—the one I have been emphasizing so far—the justification for 'elsewhere'. Earlier I had felt that my brief within the profession was to share and show that the work overseas was really 'theoretical' by Western sizing. (I use the word 'size' here in the sense of *pointure* in Derrida.)[10] Hence, 'strategic use of essentialism'. Now I also feel the reader must learn that 'theory' need not look the same everywhere, that, for the independent mind, too much training in pro-

---

9 My most memorable experience was to encounter a Maori activist-bookseller and an Indian feminist at such a convention, who had never heard of Frederick Douglass, where only in response to my questions did the South African participant admit to political problems with translation between indigenous languages, and the mainland Chinese participant to the barrier between Mandarin and Cantonese. Examples can be multiplied.

10 I have discussed this in 'Inscription: Of Truth to Size' in *Outside in the Teaching Machine* (New York: Routledge, 2009), p. 201–16

ducing the European model in stylistic detail might be a hindrance. In my teacher training work in rural India, it is the illiterate man who understands things best because his considerable intelligence has not been hobbled by bad education or gender oppression. The lesson here is not that everyone should be illiterate, but that strong minds should not be ruined by bad education or imperatives to imitate.

The caution would apply to *Neighborhood and Boulevard* by Khaled Ziadeh (belonging to our earlier series, see note 4)—not bad education, obviously, but the imperative to imitate 'French Theory'.[11] Ziadeh, in spite of his time at the Sorbonne, was not tempted. He theorizes by space and repetition; Hosam Aboul-Ela's Introduction to that book walks us through it. There are plenty of people writing in Arabic who produce work competitive with the best in European-style 'theory'. Reading Ziadeh, as Aboul-Ela points out, we have to learn to recognize 'theory' in another guise. My own work profits from his account of the de-Ottomanization of the city by the French into an 'Islamic' space; because I think de-Ottomanization, still active in our time, has a history as old as the Fall of Constantinople, and, re-territorialized, backward into Byzantium. Today's Khilafat movement can be read as an example of how imperial historical violence can produce a counter-violence of no return.

Our series is young. I have described our goal with appropriate modesty: to translate theoretical material operating outside the Euro-US, not readily available to metropolitan readership but continuous with the episteme, even as 'hybridity' keeps the local elsewhere. Yet there are also singular enclaves in many places where teaching and thinking apparently take place in less continuous epistemic formation. To acquire texts from these enclaves would require the kind of preparation, partly traditionalist, partly anthropologistic, that I do not possess. Perhaps, if our initial forays succeed, we will be able to fling our net wider: particularly important in the context of sub-Saharan Africa, where strong theoretical writing in the imperial languages (also languages of Africa, of course) flourishes and holds influence. For theoretical writing in the indigenous languages, not necessarily imitating the European model, contained within internal conflict, avoiding the anthropologist in the name of tradition will be on our agenda, I had written earlier. *Pelong ya ka* by

---

11 I use this phrase with the French nationalist irony reflected in François Cusset, *French Theory: Foucault, Derrida, Deleuze et Cie et les mutations de la vie intellectuelle aux États-Unis* (Paris: Découverte, 2003), translated as *French Theory: How Foucault, Derrida, Deleuze, & Co. Transformed the Intellectual Life of the United States* (Jeff Fort trans.) (Minneapolis: University of Minnesota Press, 2008).

Sophonia M. Mofokeng (1962), just completed in English translation as *In My Heart* by Nhlanhla Maake, is such a text. Our thanks to Njabulo Ndebele for this suggestion. *Towards A History of the National-Popular in Bolivia* by René Zavaleta Mercado was our inaugural text. The current volume is a passionate interpretation of Zavaleta's socio-historical, politico-theoretical journey. Luis Tapia Mealla is a political philosopher at the Development Sciences institute (CIDES) of the Universidad Mayor de San Andrés in La Paz. He is not only a commentator and interpreter but also an activist who takes forward Zavaleta's undertaking, reading his work as an open text, since Zavaleta died before completing his last major self-revising move, harboring epistemological change, one on one and collective, and the performative contradiction between politics and history.

Our series attempts to wrench the work outside its area studies context. Zavaleta's attempt as enhanced by Tapia—to honor local knowledge by wrenching it outside of the identitarian or merely Marxist impulse, to give it transhistorical validity—gave rise to his powerful concept of how to do a layered analysis of 'motley' societies, where the feudal co-exists with the capitalist and the democratic/modern. The need for such work today, when democracy is being destroyed by identity politics everywhere, is urgent. Important also is Zavaleta's understanding that each time this motley ensemble undergoes a conjunctural change, however minute, there is a 'primordial' new beginning. I prefer the word 'originary' but have respected the author's sense that 'primordial' is too strongly associated with Zavaleta's work to be jettisoned.

> The idea of the primordial form is not only a key for thinking local history but also for thinking the articulations of global history with attention to local histories, that is to say, its manner of thinking world or international history arises from the historical depth of each society and not from the surface of interstate articulations and data on the world economy on the level of exchange or the market.

My understanding, which of course is marked by the nomology that produces me, is that, by Zavaleta's reckoning, as each single or multiple strand(s) in the textuality produce(s) a perception of internationality, it is 'originary', rather than something to be referred to hierarchically to the 'original' development story of the idea of internationality. Let me share with you a class email I sent today regarding a translated text they are reading for a class:

> Dear Class: I forgot to give you another tremendous translation problem in the Derrida text, shared by many other translations. It is

the word 'primordial' used to translate *originaire* in French and *ursprünglich* in German. Many of us use 'originary' in English. Whereas 'primordial' has a lugubrious mysteriousness, originary simply means moves that have to be made each time a thing is started, for example, turning on the ignition in order to start a spontaneous combustion engine.

At our provocation in the Modern Language Association conventions, Tapia has himself provided a theory of how different 'local'-s might today connect through intermediary recognition of the globality nuanced differently in each case. That work will, we hope, be jointly forthcoming.

My hope is that this thinking will be itself wrenched into the gendered 'motley' by thinkers in the near future, without excuse/accusation—and the critique of 'postmodernism' will be thickened.

To begin with, my understanding of an activist 'Task of the Editor', was as I have outlined above: to combat the bi-lateralism—my place and your Euro-US—that legitimizes Eurocentrism by reversal. Today this is complicated by the confrontation between nationalism and globalism. Can an elsewhere text supplement both?

Down the line, a translation is well under way of the collected literary writings of Paik Nak-Chung, the brilliant Korean public intellectual. He is important for our world because he grasps the 'literary' in all its worldliness; and philosophizes the possibilities for a way out of gated nation-states. Translation has begun on *Mononer Modhu*, a philosophical text by Arindam Chakrabarti which, in the best comparativist tradition, deconstructs European philosophizing into ways of thinking that it otherwise ignores. Also underway is *Gender, Context and the Politics of Writing*, by Dong Limin from China, a powerful critic of many accepted social gender paradigms

Our translators share with us the problems of translation for each unique text, at least hinting to the reader that, although the activity of translating is altogether pleasurable, to accept translations passively as a substitute for the 'original' closes doors. We will not give up the foolish hope that a careful translation, sharing problems, will lead to language-learning.

Read our series as a first step, then. Come to the projected conferences if they happen, where all of the authors and translators will gather, to ask: what is it to theorize elsewhere, in our world.

Preface

Luis Tapia Mealla and Sinclair Thomson

The Production of Local Knowledge is fundamentally an epistemological reconstruction of the work of the major Bolivian political thinker René Zavaleta Mercado (1937–1984). Flowing conceptually from its very object of analysis, its composition might be likened to a snake biting its own tail. While the ouroboros image has sometimes been taken as a sign of cyclical return and ultimate stasis, here it represents more a bid for the dynamic self-renewal of theoretical knowledge.

The book was written in 1994-1997, and published in 2002, when Zavaleta's work was largely unavailable in Bolivia and could only be found dispersed in a range of Mexican and Latin American publications. It aimed to show the overall trajectory and spectrum of this body of writings, providing a panorama of Zavaleta's intellectual history and a view of the production of his conceptual strategy. The author embarked on this project of reconstruction in particular because Zavaleta's work helps us to understand the complex conditions of neocolonial modernity. The study was conceived originally as a methodological and explanatory strategy for Bolivian and Latin American social sciences in the early twenty-first century, and it prepared the analytical nucleus for the author's own subsequent work on internal colonialism and the state, popular struggle, social heterogeneity, and democracy.

Zavaleta's main conceptual proposition arises out of Marxist theory and seeks to advance it further. The distinctive epistemological feature of his project is that it elaborates an awareness of Marxism's own limits for thinking the social where capitalist relations are not fully consolidated and generalized. Zavaleta likewise writes with an awareness of the possibilities and limits for his own production of knowledge. He proposes to explain national histories starting from the autonomy of politics in each historically constituted social setting, while simultaneously asserting that the conditions for such explanation are shaped by the specific political configuration in each moment and each country. Thus, it is not possible to know any given thing in any given moment, but only those things that emerge out of the reflexivity allowed for by local and global historical processes.

Zavaleta's theoretical and explanatory strategy is the most mature, complex, and productive that has emerged in Bolivia insofar as it produces useful conceptual categories that make society intelligible and shed light on history. At the same time, it holds up Latin America as a horizon for comparison and for the mid-level generalization of categories, while it refers as well to the features introduced by capitalist expansion in the world.

The final chapter of *The Production of Local Knowledge* considers Zavaleta's relation to other theoretical currents at the turn of the century, including analytical Marxism, postmodernism, and hermeneutics. We would like to offer here a further note on Zavaleta's ideas in the world nearly two decades later and how they may be of use in other settings. The wider context involves a period of neoliberal reforms in academic and intellectual fields which have installed monocultural social and cultural theories. These have pretensions to universal validity, but are incapable of explaining colonialism's forms of reconstitution or of conceiving of modernity in greater depth and complexity. Two of the features of the neoliberal trend have been a reduction in the scope of historical and temporal awareness and an eclipse of the critique of capitalism and exploitation.

In response, in recent decades younger generations in Latin America—especially Argentines, Chileans, Ecuadorians, Colombians, and Mexicans—have begun to study, employ, and elaborate Zavaleta's ideas to examine new social patterns as well as the older structures of long-term historical development. One of the main motives for their interest is that Zavaleta is useful for conceiving of the social heterogeneity in their countries which exclusively monocultural theoretical models do not make intelligible. In countries that consider themselves totally or nearly modern, the social sciences have not elaborated conceptual strategies capable of adequately conceptualizing social heterogeneity, thereby rendering it invisible. This occurs in cases in which historical diversity resurfaces or, as in Europe, in which diversity arises with ex-colonial immigration.

Zavaleta's work can be put in dialogue with the project of subaltern studies generated in the South Asian context in the late twentieth century. Both draw on history as an axis of explanation for social forms and to identify the constitution of social practices and collective mentalities. Both strategies conceive of the colonial as a strong matrix for the determination of local social formations, which in certain moments and domains can also become internal determinations. Both approaches share a theoretical foundation that combines Marx and Gramsci to conceive of the instauration and globalization of capitalism and modernity. That same foundation also allows for understanding the articulation of different societies under colonial domination which renders hegemony impossible. Likewise, both examine the hierarchy of societies, social forms, and subjectivities shaped by external and internal colonial forces, and they attend to the historical experiences or processes that challenge them and attempt critically to build nation-states and create new communitarian structures in their wake. They also both analyze the colonial from the standpoint of the more or less autonomous political action of subaltern subjects.

Social knowledge is produced by reconstructing historical processes and not only applying general nomological models which act as methodological and explanatory structures. This requires reflexivity and criticism of sources as well as of the subjectivity of historical actors and their modes of mobilization, representation, and thought. Just as the interpenetration of ideas from Zavaleta and subalternist projects offers substantial potential for interpretation of colonialism, nationalism, and class or caste, Zavaleta's approach could combine with analysis of other critical issues—for example, involving gender or the environment—if we recognize the new parameters for knowledge production opened up by contemporary social and political movements. The conceptual strategy elucidated in the *Production of Local Knowledge* is capable of renewing itself by extending to additional dimensions of social reality, and does not seek to achieve closure by reducing explanation to a partial, static nucleus.

Zavaleta offers a fertile way to think through the relations between, on one hand, the dynamics of capitalist economic structures and colonial and modern political and cultural structures and, on the other, the forms of political action. For contemporary Marxism, his work provides a rich approach for connecting the law of value and the autonomy of politics with the problems of cultural heterogeneity. This allows us to link up the general tendencies of the age with local histories of multicultural societies and territories, some of which may challenge capital, in their processes of formation and decomposition.

In recent decades, social diversity has mainly been managed through the politics of recognition, especially in liberal and social-democratic contexts. Any politics or intellectual strategy that limits itself to recognition fails to provide a deeper understanding of social diversity and assumes it can resolve the historical contradictions through integration within the social, political, and economic institutions of the dominant culture. Zavaleta, by contrast, offers a deeper approach to the complexity resulting from the overlap of societies generated through colonialism and its modern reconstitutions. Recognition without this kind of historical and political knowledge, criticism, and self-criticism leads to assimilationism and integration that blocks transformation within the dominant society itself, including among subaltern subjects. What is required is to combine recognition, which is the horizon of liberal ethnocentric multiculturalism, with intersubjective social knowledge and transformation, which is cosmopolitan.

This reconstruction of Zavaleta's intellectual history and conceptual strategy served the author to elaborate a basic theoretical nucleus for his own later work, developing some of Zavaleta's own ideas. His *Pensando la democracia geopolíticamente* [Thinking democracy through geopolitics] (2009) and *Dialéctica del colonialismo interno* [The dialectics of internal colonialism] (2014) draw on the conceptual strategy that Zavaleta termed the 'primordial form' as well as other ideas concerning 'motley' (*abigarrado*) social formations. The author's analysis of the neocolonial state in *El Leviatán criollo* [The creole Leviathan] (2014) and *La hegemonía imposible* [Impossible hegemony] (2015), as well as in the more recent *Fuerzas sociales* [Social Forces] (2017) and *La historicidad de las luchas políticas* [The historicity of political struggle] (2018) draw from Zavaleta's notions of how seigneurialism is recreated in conjunction with the modern state. Zavaleta's 'Cuatro conceptos de democracia' [Four concepts of democracy] inspired the author's *La velocidad del pluralismo* [The velocity of pluralism] (2002) and *Política salvaje* [Savage politics] (2008).

This English translation is the work of Alison Spedding, edited by Anne Freedman and Sinclair Thomson. It slightly abridges the original Spanish text and seeks to streamline the exposition throughout. The author is very grateful for their efforts.

To conclude, Zavaleta's project need not be seen as only Bolivian or Latin American. It may serve others to think about history, politics, and knowledge on other continents, as well as to reflect on Latin America and Bolivia from a wider, deeper, and more complex conceptual horizon. Just as the author of *The Production of Local Knowledge* has elaborated his own conceptual strategy built upon ideas found in Zavaleta, others may find that engaging with Zavaleta and with this volume's exploration of his work will serve them in their own critical intellectual and political projects.

Introduction

I. What Are We Studying?

This book is a study of the works of a Bolivian intellectual, René Zavaleta, who lived from 1939 to 1984. He began to write at the end of the 1950s, during the period of revolutionary nationalism. From then on, he developed works that focused on politics and history, of Bolivia in particular and frequently of Latin America. His work of explanation of Bolivian history was accompanied by a theoretical analysis and an epistemological reflection on the conditions of possibility of knowledge in heterogeneous societies such as Bolivia and the margins of validity and necessity of general theories or models.

His work began with writings within the framework of nationalist discourse and later continued within a Marxist framework, which involved the production of a set of special categories for thinking politics and history in heterogeneous societies.

The development of his thought was closely linked to the principal social forces in the contemporary history of the country—the nationalist movement and the proletariat—and their forms of organization and political projects. He focused specifically on modern history, but as he did so he sought its causes further back in the past.

This book presents a reconstruction of his work as a whole, so as to analyse the maturity of that which is the focus of interest of my investigation: the production of local knowledge. By this I refer to two things: the specific knowledge of Bolivian society and the way in which this is produced, together with the production of theory carried out to make it broader and more pertinent.

The general idea that guides this book is that the production of local knowledge has developed by elaborating categories that can explain the autonomy of politics and the specific nature of histories, as moment, process and totality. This relates to theories of a more general nature, but with respect to which one cannot assume constant regularity or the capacity to subsume all aspects of politics and all historical facts.

The production of local knowledge can be analysed and explained by way of the study of the general ways of thinking about history and, above all, of the way in which history is explained. In the explanation of history, the study and conceptualization of politics is the backbone of the explanation of the motion and articulation of social processes and their forms of global and national synthesis or configuration.

Hence, this is a study of history and politics in the works of René Zavaleta that proposes to explicate a strategy and a product that I consider a vigorous self-reflective alternative mode of production of local knowledge. Implicit in this is the conviction that the study of politics and its autonomy requires a mode of revision of general theories and of relativizing them. It is the nexus or space where one can begin to articulate that which remains outside but is complementary to the general models.

In this the study of politics has an epistemological function, which is that of studying the limits of validity of general models of social theory. Upon experiencing these limits, one begins to generate an intellectual production within those margins so as to think their specificity, which in turn establishes the nexus or link that articulates a complementary system of categories. This occurs above all in forms of synthesis of historical configurations.

This book studies this problematic, which situates political theory in a broader context of belonging to a greater universe of conceptual labour, within which it receives conditions and support from other dimensions and other fields of intellectual production. Political theory is analysed as a specific analytical and theoretical space, in the context of a multidimensional intellectual process. At the same time, theory and historical explanations are analysed and studied as a process of development and as intellectual history. In synthesis, Zavaleta's work on politics and history is studied as a multidimensional intellectual process, as a process of development and as an intellectual history of the conditions and problematic of his time.

II. Why and to What End Are We Studying Zavaleta?

The value of a work with regard to the aim one has proposed, or for a discipline, is something that has to be demonstrated over the course of a book such as this one. In addition, a prior knowledge and evaluation directs the labour of analysis to one particular *oeuvre* and not another. I believe that the works of Zavaleta are those which have contributed most to the knowledge of Bolivian society and history.

In this sense, the point is not only to study what he wrote about Bolivia (this work of reconstruction is secondary here) but also and above all to study how he arrived at this analysis and the set of explanations that resulted, with the aim of seeing if some of the sharpest cognitive moments of the past, or of our intellectual history, may allow us to continue working on the elaboration of consistent explanations of other processes yet unknown and unexplained, and also of other contemporary processes that already exist.

We study Zavaleta's work as a project that aimed to elaborate knowledge of local or national history by way of the development of political theory, although the analysis is carried out on a multidisciplinary plane.

Zavaleta deals with the development of a theory concerning the autonomy and the complexity of politics, which serves to explain history, that is to say, the global articulation of social processes. Perhaps because he not only studies its autonomy but also its complexity, his work is not limited to political science but also constitutes a way to investigate and think through global configurations. Through a conceptualization of the specificity of politics, it is possible to think globally, because he also thinks that the specificity of politics is in one moment a process of articulation and in another one of synthesis.

A large part of Zavaleta's mature work was published outside Bolivia, during his long years of exiles, and in consequence is only partially known; although from the decade of the 1980s onwards it has begun to influence the principal researchers of the country.

The study and analytical reconstruction of his works as a whole allows us to present a window into this intellectual history that Zavaleta lived and in which he participated from the 1950s till the middle of the 1980s. He left us an intellectual patrimony of which this book is a preliminary map.

Another reason to study Zavaleta's work is it allows us to carry out a revision and analysis of revolutionary nationalist and Marxist thought, which are the two traditions of greatest influence in the modern political life of Bolivia, and also in the intellectual production of the twentieth century.

Because he took an active part in the production of both discourses, his intellectual history is an axis that allows and requires the reconstruction, at least partially, of the basic structures and intellectual spaces configured by revolutionary nationalism and Marxism in Bolivia. At the same time, this makes possible an analysis of the broader context of social and political thought in the country, and of the relation between these political discourses and the development of the social sciences.

We study Zavaleta because his works can be a good starting point to investigate, analyse and explain the state and development of social knowledge in Bolivia.

III. The Structure of This Work

1. This study is carried out in the form of an intellectual history, which is at the same time a narrative and analytical reconstruction of the routes of Zavaleta's thought, and an analysis of the structure of his ideas and the way in which they were produced. The different phases of development are delimited in each case or moment. Once we reach his mature period, we turn to an analysis organized by thematic fields or problematics.

We have a special interest in analysing how and why his thought changed, to what intellectual and historical challenges it responded. We do not only present what he thought or wrote in each phase of his intellectual production. This is an intellectual history that contains an analysis of the theoretical structures and the processes of development of his thought.

This task is carried out with recourse to various theoretical frameworks and disciplines, which I will outline below. But what I consider the principal mode of procedure or the nucleus around which I articulate the different tools and analytical practices is what I call the critical analysis or thought of a work from within the intellectual spaces that it configured or within which it was produced, on the basis of the routes it followed, with the intellectual elements it used and produced, in the context of the problematic it proposed.

With this I do not attempt to reproduce the strategy of empathy on an even higher level. It is an alternative way of working which consists in immersing oneself in his thinking, until one comes to belong to a universe of concepts and historical knowledge, and begins to think other things with those concepts. In no way does this mean wanting to think as if one were the author of the works in question. It refers to a way of thinking, not to placing oneself in the situation of another person.

Starting from the condition of interiority of a body of thought, a situation that is always partial and relative to the moment and form of insertion, we begin to develop a labour of re-exposition, which is at the same time the comprehension of that thought on the basis of what the analyst brings from outside. It becomes a sort of development of the thought through the reconstruction of its history, in the sense that the process of appropriating the thought can turn into a reflection on it, that is to say, a critical revision. The application from within of ideas that one brings from without may allow one to further elaborate elements implicit in the body of thought, even illuminating them with new light.

Access to the interiority of a body of work depends on the moment and the manner of insertion. The moment of Zavaleta's on the basis of which I have carried out my process of insertion and generated the strongest sense of interiority and belonging is that of his most mature and complex production, running from 1971 to 1984. Studying how this came to be has not, however, brought me to study his previous history in a teleological sense, that is, selecting the aspects and ideas that would appear to contain this theoretical, historical and political endpoint. I have tried to introduce myself in his thought at each moment, in each phase, and to relate it to its period in terms of its insertion in other intellectual and political processes, in the history of his society.

Where I have experienced a lesser level of interiority and belonging, the analytical apparatus that I have set up with conceptual elements that I have introduced from outside the reality that I am studying is more evident. This occurs in the first chapters on the nationalist period, in which I appear to reconstruct and analyse it from outside, with elements distinct from those that are the object of study. I have, nonetheless, practiced in principle this process of achieving interiority, although not necessarily identification, in this phase, as in the others.

As the interiority of the analyst with respect to Zavaleta's thought increasingly becomes an identification with or incorporation of those ideas and ways of thinking into the structure and life of his own thought, the external conceptual apparatus is transformed into an organic complement. One comes to carry out the analysis and the critique on the basis of the same elements contained in the object of analysis, as a principal strategy and starting point. Around that nucleus one begins to articulate other ideas and modes of analysis, so as to think its limits, so as to introduce reflexivity by the route of inter-theoretical contrast; or, at times, so as to make more explicit the virtues and forms of procedure.

In synthesis, this study does not aim to apply a uniform internalist strategy of analysis to all of Zavaleta's works, nor does it seek to apply a uniform strategy of analysis applied from without, as would be the case for example in using [Michel] Foucault or the theory of communicative action of [Jürgen] Habermas to revise Zavaleta's works. The aim is to analyse and reconstruct it from within, as nucleus and axis, around which the recourse to diverse disciplines and theories can be articulated.

This mode of working on the thought of Zavaleta from the inside means that at many points the author's material cannot be distinguished from my analytic intervention. There are parts where the task of reconstruction or synthetic presentation predominates without much analysis, and points at which the labour of critical analysis is concentrated. The former prepares the way for the latter and also complies with functions of narrative continuity in the articulation of the author's intellectual history.

It so happens that my intellectual formation has also strongly incorporated Zavaleta's thought, which has produced a strong identification and leads me to think in those terms. In many cases it would be artificial to apply more external elements in the analysis, when these were not also incorporated in my way of thinking. The weight of Zavaleta's thought in this study of his works reveals his presence in the structures and mode of thinking of the analyst.

I have thus chosen to move Zavaleta's ideas, critically, and to move with them, towards a new exposition, no longer centred on what he said about Bolivia and the history of other countries, but rather on the analytic exposition of the structure and composition of how he said this.

An analysis of this kind cannot, however, be separated from the content of the explanatory discourses. A mode of thinking is also its contents. The forms and means of working already contain a part of what can be said concerning the different processes that are analysed and the results of previous work of structuring thought.

To carry out this new exposition of Zavaleta's works, it is necessary to expound them from within, but the support of external analytical apparatuses is also necessary, so that it may be a reconstruction for the present. An up-to-date reconstruction allows one to have a critical consciousness of intellectual patrimony. A critical consciousness of the past and its incorporation in our present-day thought cannot come to be without the intervention of ideas of the present, in such a way that new blood can be injected into the productions of the past.

One might ask, how is it possible that a body of thought can analyse and criticize itself without being repetitive, and without going outside itself? This is achieved by inscribing oneself in the movement of thought. In practice, each author or thinker develops and produces his or her ideas by moving them, advancing in the directions they contain, contrasting them with others, creating a wider and more complex conceptual universe (something that usually occurs more in philosophy and social science) or creating one which is simpler but has greater explanatory capacity (something that is usually sought in physics via inter-theoretical reduction).

The analysis of a work also puts those ideas in motion, reactivating them, to extract some other results potentially contained in them, so as to think other historical configurations, or so as to think them with other ideas.

One way to move ideas and theories is to submit them to inter-theoretical contrasts, including ideas from other times, when we are dealing with an intellectual history. Another way to move ideas is to move with them, as one thinks other things, testing and consuming them in the elaboration of new explanations. In moving ideas by moving with them, one alternative is to rearticulate them among themselves, the other to rearticulate them with other theories. In the final chapter of this book I outline some possible parallel routes in relation to present-day currents of thought on the basis of the paths and spaces of Zavaleta's works.

The first thing I do in this book is move among Zavaleta's ideas, so as to get to know their quantity, the spaces they occupy, their texture, their shape, their relations, their power and their weaknesses. At first, one begins to move with other ideas (with external analytical models), as if in a foreign language, until one has learnt, adopted and begun to think with the ideas and the internal mode or language being investigated. But this apprenticeship does not lead to forgetting the other languages with which the journey began, nor those which we can continue to learn in order to continue moving with and among those ideas, from within and from without.

A study that chooses to analyse from within tends to be an exposition in several voices, or the movement of the interiorized ideas or thought and the movement of the other languages and theories that one also speaks in order to think critically about the object of study, which is also in part the object of appropriation, revision, reconstruction and reactivation.

Critique is thus polyphonic. It is learning and developing the languages of the works that are analysed, and it is the articulation of various other discourses that operate from outside, in the service of the analytical penetration that leads one to think from inside with a multiplicity of windows and antennae that communicate with the plural process of the world.

In this sense, this book attempts to avoid reducing itself to a sole analytical model applied to the different phases of Zavaleta's work and the different levels of analysis. It tries to enter into and analyse each moment and theme with a special articulation for each case. In each chapter there is a specific articulation of internal and external ideas and theories; but there is also a specific set of ideas that serve to carry out the articulation of the other chapters on different analytical moments in terms of an intellectual history. In what follows I present these guiding ideas. They do not, however, exhaust or express all the processes and procedures applied.

2. Here I put forward some problems that arise when one attempts to study a work that writes the history of a society and reflects theoretically on the epochal possibilities of thinking about it and coming to know it. I sketch some ways of carrying out the task of an analytical history of its problematic, with a particular interest in the relations between historiography and politics.

If one thinks that writing history means constructing a narrative out of various processes, the political or social historian articulates a set of explanations and interpretations that attributes a meaning and direction to the historical reality that is the object of study, on the basis of a selection of political concerns and theories to be used. On the other hand, one has an analysis of the structure and movement of that thought and of the effects and relations it establishes with its historical and intellectual contexts. The results of this analysis end up articulating yet another narrative, which is at one and the same time an intellectual history and an analysis of theory, or rather, it is a narrative in so far as, and in the moments in which, it articulates the different analytical elements, attributing movement and meaning to the body of thought.

Hayden White has suggested that historical writing can also be thought of as a narrative in which the plot of the history that is developed is given by the subjective construction of the person who writes it, in a similar way to a literary work.[1] The person who writes history selects the events that are articulated in his or her text, and also interprets and gives meaning to certain articulations in the process of events and structural configurations.

In this sense, writing history also becomes a kind of cultural production or intervention. It proposes to articulate the memory of a society, the memory of a lived time, of an era, of an event. It is a memory that posits models of explanation and interpretation. Writing history gives roots to contemporary processes by developing plausible arguments, which individuals and social groups then use to think historically, looking back and looking forward, about their present.

Writing history organizes events, processes, and the meaning that these had and can have for the individuals, groups and societies that hold them as vital referents. Writing history weaves together what individuals and groups lived within more or less local horizons of experience and interactions. Doing history thus also means connecting social and political spaces and times.

Another possibility of history is that of producing self-consciousness in a society. In this sense, writing history does not cease to be a constitutive and reconstitutive event, configuring, each time it is carried out and its results circulate, a shared subjectivity that recognizes itself in those texts and orientates itself to a greater or lesser degree by them.

A history as the formulation of a possibility of collective consciousness may contain, on the one hand, elements of a laborious search for knowledge which might mean the inclusion of pain and shame, that is, of a critical questioning of previous forms of consciousness or points of ignorance; on the other hand, it might also contain elements of justification, of concealment, of deceit, somewhat in the sense in which [Louis] Althusser formulated his idea of ideology, which is at the same time the recognition of existing relations and the ignorance or transfiguration of them.

The analysis of a historical discourse must, therefore, detect the rhetorical strategies that the historical text develops in order to expound both dimensions. In reference to the cognitive critical aspect, it must study the epistemological aspects of its production. The meanings proposed are objects of cultural and political interpretation.

The history of a body of work is not only a description of how a thinker changed in their production, what new themes they introduced and which were left aside. It must also consider how these works were produced. An intellectual history is therefore also an epistemological analysis of the process of production of the texts that are its object of study, which structure a narrative that articulates the results of a series of epistemological moments.

This movement of thought is also the object of interpretation on the part of the historian who might attribute determinate meanings to it. The analytical-epistemological dimension is at times accompanied, *a posteriori*, by a hermeneutical-interpretative phase, without this implying a determination or teleological presuppositions about the process or history of the works.

It is possible to think the meanings of a body of work above all from the perspective of its reception and reproduction, which should include the scholar's own intellectual history, written as a self-reflexive and critical intervention in the networks of circulation of meaning within a cultural horizon. When the author of a work writes about their epistemological consciousness, it becomes more necessary to situate that work historically, not only in its

---

1 Hayden White, *The Content of the Form: Narrative Discourse and Historical Representation* (Baltimore, MD: Johns Hopkins University Press, 1987).

textual surface but also in the structural production and configuration of its discourse.

In Zavaleta's case, we are dealing with a set of texts that presents a proposal of one or several historical memories, and of collective self-consciousness, but which also presents a self-consciousness of his work and a reflection on the conditions of possibility of the production of knowledge in societies like Bolivia. This becomes a sort of epistemological memory and, in that sense, a condition for later or other works within that intellectual horizon, above all if the work in question is that which most powerfully organizes and illuminates, for a time, that intellectual space.

Doing intellectual history, in this sense and in this case, also means thinking about the actual conditions for historical work and for political thought, in terms of unsolved problems, fertile intellectual recourses, mapping the conditions, programs and limits of an intellectual horizon. Doing intellectual history sheds light on why and how some of us think what we think about our society, above all recognizing those who articulated the basic narratives of the collective representations according to which we situate ourselves today in time, claiming some identities, recognizing some processes, and ignoring others.

For the work of intellectual history to be not merely a synoptic description of what was said or written but rather an analysis of its production, one must work on at least two analytical levels. One is that which is generally called epistemological, in which one works on the suppositions and cognitive principles and the programs of research[2] or strategies of production of knowledge together with their theoretical matrixes. Another level would be that which I will call rhetorical strategies.

Rhetoric is here understood as the analysis of the strategies of argumentation, in the sense in which the works of Chaim Perelman have proposed to understand this discipline in the present day, recuperating the way in which the philosophers of classical antiquity, particularly Aristotle, had proposed. All discourses unfold a rhetorical dimension in so far as they are emitted with the aim of persuading their public with respect to the relevance and the truth value of their enunciations and affirmations. Argumentative strategies may be understood as the ways of organizing arguments with the aim of persuading a particular audience. This implies that the articulation of discourses already takes into account the moment of reception, which is where or when it is hoped that they will be effective. Strategies of argumentation contain some assumptions or knowledge concerning the audience to which their narratives or arguments will be addressed. They have an inter-subjective intentionality. The consideration of the other in this communicative relation of historical and political writings, for example, has effects on the structure and style of the texts.

At this point I am interested in the relation between the rhetorical requirements of discourse with hermeneutic practice. In rhetoric, discourses are not thought of as being emitted in a vacuum but, rather, as precisely addressed to particular audiences; it could be said that they are emitted in a determinate form and for a determinate cultural horizon of understanding. I take the specific case of historical and political discourse to illustrate this relation.

A specific historical narrative is interested in articulating as process a series of events, to which it attributes causal relations and, thus, proposes an interpretation. In another parallel instance it may present a cultural interpretation of the meaning of the processes under consideration. In both cases, but especially in the interpretative moment, historiographic writing works with the presuppositions of the cultural horizon within and for which it is produced. It tends to take for granted a knowledge of beliefs, facts and values which are not explained in the text but rather act as referents of shared and assumed understanding on the part of the reader, the cultural community.

In the case in which historical-political texts, which propose to modify beliefs about the past and in this sense the political culture and forms of collective action, as is the case of the writings of political history of Bolivian revolutionary nationalism, it also becomes evident that the historical narrative takes into account a determinate set of beliefs that function as presuppositions, but this time as the object of critique, of historical and cultural revision. The aim is to change these beliefs or part of a culture through historical revision, presenting new information and above all reinterpretations, and therefore, new meanings and valuations. Taking a roundabout path through historical revision, it also carries out a cultural and political revision. The historical text, then, enters into a political dialogue with the tradition of its cultural horizon and with the audience that its rhetorical strategy anticipates. The writing of history thus becomes cultural critique in so far as it revises the foundations, suppositions and historical referents of collective beliefs about

---

2 In the sense of Imre Lakatos, *The Methodology of Scientific Research Programmes, Volume 1: Philosophical Papers* (John Worrall and Gregory Currie eds) (Cambridge: Cambridge University Press, 1978).

the past, which configure a cultural horizon; it may also be political critique in so far as it affects the relations of political power and its exercise.

An intellectual history of a body of work and its intellectual space also entails a history of this dialogue established with its cultural horizon, that is to say, of the rhetorical strategies that it articulated so as to inform, explain, criticize and interpret its past. The history of the dialogical relations between a work and its cultural horizon has implications for epistemological and not just rhetorical changes; at times the changes in the epistemological dimension and the theoretical strategies proceed from critical moments in the dialogical relations with/in the cultural horizon, moments in which it is not sufficient to modify the form of argument but it is also necessary to modify the production itself of historical knowledge. It is also fitting to think of rhetorical changes demanded by epistemological changes in the theoretical strategies. I analyse both of these dimensions in the development of Zavaleta's thought, as well as the articulation of rhetoric with theory and epistemology in the texts.

Up till now it seems that I am only concerned with how this text was produced and not what it was that it said, that is, with the content of the historical narrative and the knowledge that it made possible, not with the theory and the political analysis that these historical texts display. With regard to the content of the texts there are two levels of analysis. One is that of the historical knowledge that a work produced, that it studied and revised in relation to prior and subsequent historical work, so as to evaluate its contribution or its place in current historiographic knowledge. Since the aim is not to write another history that would be a summary of that which Zavaleta wrote, it is necessary for the analytical study to outline more general conceptions of historical processes and enter into greater detail in those cases in which the analysis of a conjuncture, event or structure in particular has opened up greater possibilities of understanding, or has modified the global conception, the rhetorical strategy or the program of investigation.

The other level is that of theory in the strict sense, that of the theory produced in these works, which is basically political theory. In this it seems to me to be necessary to analyse that conceptual production in the context of its theoretical framework, on the one hand, and on the other in relation to the intellectual horizon of the period and its society. For example: the theoretical framework of Zavaleta's major works is predominantly Marxist, therefore the specificity of his production is analysed on the basis of and within this framework, considering which conceptual tools he used, how he modified those which already existed and proposed others. On the other hand, it is fitting to analyse this production in relation to the political and theoretical debates of the period within the intellectual horizon of his society and within the broader horizon created above all in exile and in the knowledge and experience of other cultures.

I want to make one more point about the analysis of thought or political theory that is articulated with a historiographic work. If one writes an intellectual history of a body of work in which the concern for political theory and collective concepts in the processes studied is present, one may at the same time do a little history of the concepts of politics which have existed in the society whose history is treated, and of the political theory of that period. A theoretical-historical work allows this type of amplitude and may be the axis of a study and mapping of the intellectual horizon of an era with reference to its political thought and its historical self-consciousness. I do some of this here.

3. I will now propose some more specific hypotheses about the relation between narrative and analysis in working on intellectual history.

The first analytic moment is that in which one takes apart the object of study, which in this case is a body of work on history, theory and political analysis, and one specifies the elements and structures of that thought with recourse to theories and methodologies from various disciplines. After this comes the moment of articulating the results of several analytic moments, to which end one may also have recourse to several strategies. But at the same time, when one does the history of an intellectual corpus, one also ends up articulating a narrative of that process, or of several processes that justified the various analytical moments, and a narrative of the process of their articulation.

The hypothesis which I sustain here is that the way in which a work is taken apart or analysed will leave a strong mark on the narrative of its re-articulation and movement; that is to say, the form of analysis conditions the intellectual history that one constructs. More specifically, this means that the strategies with which one analyses, in each analytical moment, produce the events (denominating them thus in analogy with the elements of historio-graphic practice in general) that the intellectual history will relate. I say here that it produces them as elements of the narrative since the historical events are the writings of the author or authors studied. Here we are postulating, therefore, a powerful connection between theoretical analysis and intellectual history. The elements of the narrative in an intellectual history are theoretical objects, which are the processes of thought and its products, in their subjective and intersubjective dimensions.

I would also argue that the intellectual history which in one of its analytic moments studies argumentative or rhetorical strategies also has its own argumentative or rhetorical strategies for the presentation of its results with the intention of convincing readers of the relevance of its narratives of the processes of a body of work or the thought of an era and a society, together with the aim of attributing meaning to the history of these productions.

Histories are generally written with concerns and questions that correspond more to the time of the historian than to those of the time of the thinkers studied, but in order to understand and explain these works of the past it is also necessary to trace the questions of those thinkers and their time. Thus, one practices what [Hans-Georg] Gadamer called 'the fusion of horizons', the horizon of the writers and that of the historians, who also become cultural and political interpreters.

For example, when it is suggested that some elements of the thought of one or several authors are relevant for understanding and guiding contemporary action, the rhetorical strategy may consist in arguing that there are similarities in the structures of reality[3] of both times, which means that the questions and answers of the two periods can enter into dialogue, or that the questions that those thinkers in a past time asked themselves are repeated today, or that it is necessary to ask them again because the structure of reality suggests them once more, or because not much has changed and the problems that gave rise to them were not overcome or resolved.

The historian asks themself what is worth telling, explaining and analysing, and makes a selection, among other things, in accordance with the questions that they ask themself in their present. When the interest in certain questions and answers takes on a genetic dimension one may carry out historiographical or epistemological work; that is to say, one may do intellectual history so as to produce a kind of consciousness of the cognitive conditions of thought today in a particular society. My project shares this intention.

On occasion I refer to the ideas of Walter Benjamin,[4] tracing fragments of consciousness from the past. On the one hand, there are fragments that register moments at their climax and for that reason contain, in addition to the expression of their time, the illusion or fantasy of its superiority in relation to what came before and the feeling that the problems of the past had been solved. One can see from this perspective part of the historical and political

---

4 See Walter Benjamin, *Selected Writings*, 4 VOLS (Cambridge, MA: Harvard University Press, 2004–06).

literature produced by revolutionary nationalism on the 1952 revolution in Bolivia and the subsequent process. On the other hand, one can trace those fragments of consciousness, which became historical and political discourse, which in various moments contain and express the projects of social and political emancipation that were partially overcome or forgotten, but which, nevertheless, because they were not carried out, can convey latent elements susceptible to being revived.

In Zavaleta's works elements of both types can be found. Some of his texts, above all those which participate in the ideology of revolutionary nationalism, form part of those fragments of consciousness which at the same time as they criticize the past, present illusions about its forces in the present.

On the other hand, Zavaleta recuperates fragments of memory that contain elements of rebellion and projects of emancipation that were not carried out, although he does not refer to Benjamin's theory. He recovers these fragments to make history, offering a macrohistorical explanation, reuniting the discontinuities from the horizon of visibility of various historical times; he also recovers them in the service of cultural interpretation and political analysis.

In writing the history of a body of work, Benjamin's ideas are useful for understanding the kind of recuperation that the author does in writing history and political analysis, as well as for doing a critique of the moments in which the author participates in the illusions of their time.

Doing an analysis and history of a work that took part in the production of the illusions of a new era, a revolutionary moment that fostered the intellectual and political critique of the colonial past, allows one to acquire a little more critical consciousness of its illusory aspects, although some of this has already been achieved. One traces how in the same moment in which, for example, the process produces its greatest phantasms, it recovers some fragments of memory and emancipatory projects, including its own, but in the dynamic of its rise and rush to exercise of new powers, it buries and forgets part of its own emancipatory elements of discourse, and also its own illusions. Doing the history-analysis of a body of works like that of Zavaleta also allows one to have a fragmented history of some moments of production of the great illusions (prejudices, projects and dominating forms of consciousness) and

---

3 Chaïm Perelman and L. Olbrechts-Tyteca, *The New Rhetoric: A Treatise on Argumentation* (John Wilkinson and Purcell Weaver trans) (Notre Dame, Indiana: University of Notre Dame Press, 1969).

of the recovery of projects and memories of emancipation and cultural sovereignty.

In synthesis, I proceed in the following way, with particular variations in each analytical moment. The aim is, first, to establish the cognitive interests of each moment and its political interests and ends. I go on to reconstruct from within and without the explanatory strategy and the theoretical structure, which is complemented by a synthesis of the reconstruction's specific analyses. Its explanatory proposals and the way in which they were produced are contrasted with other alternatives or productions of the epoch. After that I articulate the narrative which unites significantly, although with certain discontinuity, the several analytical moments in terms of an intellectual history. In this I take note of new theoretical and explanatory facts, of the changes and the movement of this thought in the context of the social processes which it aims to analyse and explain.

IV. Objectives

This study attempts in the first place to elaborate a critical memory of one of the principal moments of modern political thought in Bolivia, and in this sense, to present its achievements in social science, political analysis and history.

One objective of this book is not only to analyse a body of work but also to insert itself in a tradition of Bolivian social thought, through an appropriation which in this case is the elaboration of its internal history.

This book also aims to expound how politics has been thought and analysed and how history has been written in Bolivia since the decade of the 1950s, and in particular to argue that in Zavaleta's works there is a consistent and complex alternative for the production of local knowledge. This involves a process of articulation of theoretical models that claim a degree of transhistorical validity with the specific articulation of each local history, for which a set of intermediate categories of synthesis has been produced, allowing us to think conceptually about the specificities of history and politics.

PART A

Nationalist Moments

CHAPTER ONE

From Telluric Culturalism to Revolutionary Nationalism

The age is a horizon of existence that provides the matrix for the processes that form the individual, as a specific configuration of a set of macrosocial processes that are articulated to varying extents as local societies, and as the global world or cultural horizon of the present. It is true that globalization is more or less intense from one society to another, and also that each society articulates its specific (and more or less heterogeneous) cultural horizon which it lives most intensely.

By horizon of existence in this case we mean the heterogeneous set, articulated or not, of the general conditions and possibilities of the existent and virtual forms of social life in a historical space, which generally today is organized and delimited at once as nation, state and country (of course, this list does not imply that these terms are synonyms).

Specifically, I would say that the horizon of existence is a notion that synthesizes the historical articulation between the (in the strict sense) material forms of organization and production of social life, and the forms and scope of the symbolic processes that express the forms of consciousness and attribution and production of meaning.

I will use this notion as a categorical backdrop that allows me to connect the analysis of René Zavaleta's works to historical processes that give meaning to them and at the same time allow one to explain some aspects of the production and development of his thought.

This study does not consist in a personal biography. I will not narrate the formation and the life of the author. The very brief references of this type serve only to relate his works to the context in which they were produced.

The object of this study is his intellectual production, in the context of the political and theoretical debates of the different moments in which it was carried out. I will privilege references to the historical background to which I will add a few notes referring to Zavaleta's political life. My primary concern here is the relation between national political life and intellectual production.

René Zavaleta was born on 3 June 1937 in the city of Oruro. At the time it was the city most connected to the principal mining centres of the department of which it is the capital, and also to the mining centres of the department of Potosí. At the same time, mining was the principal economic activity of the country, on the basis of which political power and government were organized and executed.

The years of Zavaleta's childhood and youth are those of the crisis of the state—of the era of domination by the mining and landlord oligarchy, and of the first nationalist experiences, which appear as brief and tragic interruptions in the governance of a political order which, up until 1952, was based on a strategy of a limited suffrage[1] that excluded all the indigenous communities and the majority of the working class, with criteria that only awarded citizenship to that fraction of the population that was literate and had an annual income not earned from domestic service.[2]

When the Chaco War (1932–35), which Bolivia lost to Paraguay, came to an end, a period of crisis in this mode of state domination began. On the one hand, coups by nationalist military officers who headed brief governments—David Toro Ruilova (1935–37), Germán Busch Becerra (1937–38), Gualberto Villaroel López (1943–46)—took measures that increased the collection of the surplus produced by the mining companies, and nationalized the oil industry. Precisely for this reason, those whose interests were affected organized their overthrow.

On the other hand, this was a period of growing conflicts with the mine workers' unions, the object of fierce repression and massacres[3] by the army at the orders of powerful mine owners. The 1940s also witnessed the rise of the Movimiento Nacional Revolucionario (Revolutionary Nationalist Movement, henceforth MNR), which would later reorganize the state after 1952, and of which René Zavaleta would be a member for a number of years, until 1970.

There is a nationalist period in Bolivia, and also for Zavaleta, which arose precisely in a period of development of the nationalist critique of the power

---

1 See Ángel Flisfisch, 'La polis censitaria. La política y el mercado' in Francisco Rojas Aravena (ed.), *Autoritarismo y alternativas populares en América Latina* (San José, Costa Rica: FLACSO, 1982), pp. 107–40.

2 See James Malloy, *Bolivia. La revolución inconclusa* (La Paz: Centro de Estudios de la Realidad Economica y Social, 1989).

3 See Agustín Barcelli, *Medio siglo de luchas sindicales en Bolivia* (La Paz: SPI, 1956).

of the mining oligarchy. This chapter aims to analyse Zavaleta's contribution to this discourse of revolutionary nationalism from the time when he was a rank-and-file militant of the party that declared itself the representative of that post-revolutionary ideology and program.

The aim of this part is to analyse the specific modality of Zavaleta's nationalist discourse together with its general framework and influences.

Telluric Culturalism

Zavaleta began to write for newspapers when he was very young; he worked as a journalist throughout his writing life, in different countries. Here I use a couple of articles published in newspapers in 1954 to give a brief sketch of his early thought, and to trace and point out the influences of other Bolivian intellectuals of that time.

In 1954, when he was almost 17, he published 'Los ciclos históricos y la aptitud creadora del individuo' [Historical cycles and the individual's creative capacity] and 'El porvenir de América Latina en la elaboración de una nueva humanidad' [The future of Latin America in the elaboration of a new humanity] in the La Paz press.[4] The level or conceptual horizon of this moment is that of culture, which appears as a sort of actor in history.

Zavaleta's concern is the relation between cultures, and the relation between history and the individual, all of this marked by certain intellectual influences that still held sway at that time. Let us examine this in detail.

In 'El porvenir de América Latina', following the idea that there are two Americas,[5] he writes: 'Only one is the true one, that of the character preserved by the race in the soul of its original man.' And: 'The indigenous soul is found in the heart of every American, because we believe that everything created by the action of the landscape and the emotional environment of this continent is Indian.'

This America of indigenous culture is opposed to a decadent Western culture. The decadence is supposedly due to an exhaustion of its creative force in general, to the fact that, in this specific context, the conqueror, despite

---

4 René Zavaleta, 'Los ciclos históricos y la aptitud creadora del individuo' (1954), *Presencia* (2 February 1957); 'El porvenir de América Latina y su papel en la elaboración de una nueva humanidad', *La Paz* (4 April 1954).

5 In Bolivia, the two Americas are not North versus South, or Anglo versus Latino, but, rather, creole or white settler America versus native or indigenous America. [Trans.]

being the dominator, passes through a process in which what is called the Spanish soul 'is slowly and eternally integrated into American indigeneity'.

In consequence, this is an America that, despite being politically defeated and economically exploited, has a cultural strength that not only resists the conquest but ends up transforming the conqueror's cultural elements in the ancestral and telluric historical cultural substrate.

The conquest repressed and halted the development of this cultural form. Once the West is in decline and its elements that arrived through conquest are reformed by the indigenous soul and the power of the landscape, it is this culture's time to unfold once more; only the oppressed can renew history. The idea of the oppressed expressed here is that of those who suffer 'the anguish and the thirst for humanity'; it is not an idea defined in socioeconomic terms or as political domination. Oppression is cultural, felt and perceived in cultural terms, as is the project of liberation.

Zavaleta establishes a distinction between cultural substrate and historical force. Once Europe loses its creativity and energy, it becomes a cultural substrate that now can only contribute its major achievements of the past, to nourish another historical force with the desire to create. America is this force.

There is an underlying concept here of history as a quasi-natural dynamic of cultures and civilizations that arise, develop and die, coexisting in conflict for a time and succeeding one after another. This idea, advanced by Spengler, circulated widely in Latin America in the first decades of the twentieth century and had influence in Bolivia.[6]

Another debate and dichotomy of the time to which Zavaleta returns is that of culture and civilization. Here it serves to complete the previous discussion of the relation between history and individual. With respect to this, Zavaleta writes:

> Every civilization—if by this one understands technical progress and in a certain way, material wellbeing—will have as a necessary consequence a culture. [. . .] Culture is the inclusion and integration of

---

6 Juan Albarracín Millán has carried out the broadest study of Bolivian social thought from the end of the nineteenth century until the 1960s. The collection of studies to which I refer are *Orígenes del pensamiento social contemporáneo en Bolivia* (La Paz: Empresa Editora 'Universo', 1976); *El gran debate. Positivismo e irracionalismo en el estudio de la sociedad boliviana* (La Paz: n. p., 1978); *Sociología indigenal y antropología telurista* (La Paz: Universo, 1982); *Geopolítica, populismo y teoría sociotriconopano-rámica* (La Paz: Universo, 1982).

spiritual and personal human values in historical processes so as to alter the natural change, the spontaneous novelty that is civilization.[7]

All these concepts have as an aim the fully realized man, since 'Societies are made so that man may carry out what is only potential and general in him, so that he attains fulfilment.'[8]

This kind of teleological optimism is nevertheless combined with the idea that those men who wish to overcome their actual condition of suffering live in a state of anxiety and anguish, directing their actions to the realization of justice.

The intellectual climate at this moment can be characterized as cultural telluric existentialism, derived from the combination of a conception of reality and history as a dynamic between entities called cultures, the priority given to the indigenous soul or culture, powerfully shaped by the land and the landscape, and finally, a feeling of anguish coupled with the need to develop the potential of the indigenous culture imagined as energy and primal force. Although these discourses are not clearly defined, I think that a trace of vitalism and existentialism appears in Zavaleta's youthful thought.

The defining feature of the brief writings mentioned here is their emphasis on the indigenous American soul and the potential energy and force of autochthonous culture. The main point of reference is the thought of Carlos Medinaceli, whom Zavaleta cites, explaining that his strategy consists in 'looking at the original potentials of our condition.'[9]

Maya Aguiluz, in her study of Medinaceli,[10] indicates that he thought that *mestizaje*[11] would produce the true national type, which would foment the unification of the ethnic heterogeneity that was the origin of the problems of national disorder. He wrote novels and critical cultural essays developing the idea of *mestizaje* as the matrix of the development of the nation that as yet did not exist.[12]

---

7 Zavaleta, 'Los ciclos históricos'.

8 Zavaleta, 'Los ciclos históricos'.

9 Zavaleta, 'El porvenir de América Latina'.

10 Maya Aguiluz, *Una lectura sociológica. El caso de un pensador boliviano. Carlos Medinaceli y su época* (México City: FCPyS-UNAM, 1991), pp. 25–6.

11 This term is derived from *mestizo*, literally 'half-breed' or 'of mixed blood', but it refers as much to cultural mixing (bilingualism in Spanish and native languages, syncretic religious practices, dishes that combine native American foodstuffs with products from other continents, etc.) as to being the descendant of mixed marriages. [Trans.]

These early essays by Zavaleta were published two years after the revolution of April 1952, which produced a general reorganization of the state and its relations with a civil society expanded by the revolutionary moment itself. Revolutionary nationalism is the predominant ideology in the phase of critique of the previous state and society and in the post-revolutionary period. These texts by Zavaleta are not conceived in terms of the nationalist discourse, despite having been written during its boom years, but neither do they go against it; rather, they exhibit influences that precede revolutionary nationalist discourse, but that were also a condition of its development, in particular in the work of Carlos Montenegro,[13] who was the first to present the framework of this ideology in a work of historical revision and interpretation.

Here it seems that Zavaleta was reproducing or expressing in his way the previous phases of the tendencies in Bolivian thought that aimed to find roots in local history and cultures. Several decades later, the strategy of turning one's gaze to the indigenous had passed from the general valuation and critique of cultures to the formulation of a political discourse that identified political subjects in those cultures who, on the one hand, exercised oppression and, on the other, would incarnate the struggle for emancipation and the fulfilment of those cultural potentials. It had turned into revolutionary nationalism.

This intellectual phase of Zavaleta's youth can be understood as an expression of the type of education he received, more universalistic and less politicized. Nevertheless, I think it is already imbued with a sensibility that recognizes what is national and American as the matrix of development of ideas, feelings, identifications and values.

Under Revolutionary Nationalism: Political Journalism

The next extant texts by Zavaleta are his journalistic writings for *Marcha* (1956–57) in Uruguay during his years as a law student in Montevideo, where he also wrote for the newspaper *La Mañana*, and his articles as one of the editors of the newspaper *La Nación* (1959–60), an official organ of the MNR.

All his writings of this period already express ideas developed within the political and ideological framework of revolutionary nationalism.

---

12 Medinaceli's writings include *La Chaskañawi* (novel, 1947), *Estudios críticos* (1938), *Educación del gusto estético* (1942), *El huayralevismo* (1972), and *La reivindicación de la cultura americana* (1974).

13 Carlos Montenegro, *Nacionalismo y coloniaje* (La Paz: Ediciones Auto-nomía, 1944). I will discuss this work later on in relation to revolutionary nationalist discourse.

His contact with national politics led him to specify, nationalize and politicize his previous pro-*mestizo* and indigenous culturalism.

I will discuss the texts of this period to show how Zavaleta incorporates the discourse of revolutionary nationalism and, finally, I will propose some hypotheses concerning the development of nationalism in Bolivia, as a step towards the consideration of Zavaleta's most mature and original texts.

With respect to intellectual sources, Zavaleta's internalization of revolutionary nationalism occurs through Augusto Céspedes and Carlos Montenegro. Here I speak of internalization in the sense of getting to know and beginning to belong to a current of thought, taking possession of a core of ideas and beginning to think within that horizon.

Augusto Céspedes is the author of *Sangre de mestizos* [Of mixed blood] (1962), tales of the Chaco War; *El dictador suicida. 40 años de historia de Bolivia* [The suicidal dictator: 40 years of Bolivian history] (1956); *El metal del diablo* [The devil's metal] (1945), a novel based on the life of the mining magnate Simón Patiño; *El presidente colgado* [The hung president] (1975), referring to Gualberto Villarroel; *Salamanca o el metafísico del fracaso* [Salamanca or the metaphysician of failure] (1973), referring to the president who lost the Chaco War. Carlos Montenegro wrote *Nacionalismo y coloniaje* [Nationalism and colonialism] (1944); *Frente al derecho del estado: El oro de la Standard Oil, El petróleo, sangre de Bolivia* [Standard Oil's gold versus the rights of the state: Oil, Bolivia's blood] (1938) and *Las inversiones extranjeras en América Latina* [Foreign investment in Latin America] (1962).

Augusto Céspedes is one of the people responsible for spreading the idea that the Chaco War (1932–35) was the principal landmark in the development of national consciousness. *Sangre de mestizos* is the book of that moment of encounters and divergences. Commenting on *El dictador suicida*, which relates the history of the rise of nationalism and the liberal power that it criticized, Zavaleta writes:

> When they departed from their cities and towns to go to war in the Chaco, although they apparently went to face an enemy, in fact they left to discover their own destiny and its diseases and myths as a nation. The catastrophe sowed in their souls not dissolution nor defeat but, rather, a fierce will to recover and affirm their own roots, because the task at hand was not solely to reform the existing structure but to make another, giving the country, for the first time, an existence, that is to say, independence.[14]

14 René Zavaleta, 'Augusto Céspedes y una historia chola', *Marcha* (7 December 1956).

Or, more concisely: 'The Chaco War signified Bolivia's return to itself.'[15]

The moment of the Chaco War is important for the nationalists because it was when the nation, until then solely a potential but not an existing political community, began to organize itself with more strength. From the Chaco comes an impulse to articulate the nation, from below to above, counterposed to the seigneurial republic which, rather, inhibited from above the process of national formation, since it was based on excluding the whole of the indigenous population and the greater part of the workers from citizenship and maintaining relations of servitude and tributary exploitation.

The historical narrative of nationalism privileges the development of national consciousness, but this is a development that, far from referring to general cultural ideals or to the dynamic of ideas and values worthwhile in themselves, is conceived as the result of lessons learned from frustrations, experiences such as the war lost by an inept and irresponsible command, the frauds of mining companies that exploited the resources of the country while paying almost nothing for them, of the inorganic nature of every collective enterprise, because political and economic power divided everything except its profits.

Nationalists such as Céspedes and Montenegro tell how the fragments of the potential nation begin to organize themselves and establish relations, to extend and replace the political leadership of the country, which they considered foreign or anti-national. The actors were primarily from the urban middle class, which had taken part in the war and organized the League of War Veterans, and from the miners' trade unions. But this is a long process.

Céspedes writes: 'It was not a consciousness that emerged from the Chaco but, rather, the disorder propitious for its incubation.'[16]

According to Zavaleta, Céspedes's work takes up and continues that of Montenegro, although he sees Céspedes as a combination of documentation and memory, personal memoirs that at the same time write the history of the country.

On the other hand, he writes: 'In Carlos Montenegro, there was for the first time a philosophy of Bolivian history.'[17]

---

15 Zavaleta, 'Cinco años de revolución en Bolivia', *Marcha* (26 April 1957).

16 Augusto Céspedes, *El dictador suicida. 40 años de historia de Bolivia* (Santiago de Chile: Editorial Universitaria, 1956), p. 145.

17 Zavaleta. 'Augusto Céspedes y una historia chola'.

It is worth reviewing here the conceptions of history of these two authors who are the most important of the first phase of revolutionary nationalism, so as to sketch the backdrop of the intellectual tradition in which Zavaleta's work of that period was produced.

Céspedes presents his conception of history in the following way:

Facts are the chromosomes of history, whether this is considered as a spiritual event or as engendered by the forms of production. To trace the profile of the facts, it is useful to consider history not as linear but, rather, in a cyclic, global movement, in such a way that, on slicing it along a plane, one reveals all the existential forms that correspond to the cycle. The judgements that emerge in the course of this narrative tend to be syntheses of several events which, occurring in different periods, integrate sequences that belong to the same mode and style.[18]

The principle of globality that should be the basis for the interpretation and explanation of the facts already implies the determination of an axis of rotation and the cutting plane (to use Céspedes's terms) that make possible the syntheses that are the other important aspect of this conception.

That axis that allows one to understand Bolivian history as a totality composed of past, present and future is the opposition between nation and anti-nation proposed by Montenegro. The facts acquire a profile insofar as they affirm or deny one of these two great tendencies in Bolivian history. On the one hand, there are the potentialities and forces of the nation; on the other, the practices and the subjects who perpetuate foreign domination or direct efforts and labour towards external ends.

This is, then, a historical totality already peopled with facts and meanings which are the condition and the means not only of the interpretation of new facts but also of their constitution. This is a synthetic history which articulates and propels the facts considered and selected towards a nucleus constituted by opposed historical forces and tendencies. These are the basic elements that condition the actions of individuals who are thus not only atoms of action but also the conditions of the activity of the historian who writes taking sides. This might mean silencing the struggles of the nation to articulate its sovereignty and make its independence real, that is, relating the facts in such a way that the historical meaning of the facts is lost, as Céspedes would say,

---

18 Céspedes, *El dictador suicida*, p. 49.

marking the general lines of surrender in the acts of coercion of the nation,[19] or relating the memory and consciousness, especially when this is collective, of facts that affirm the nation and its potentialities.

Montenegro, to whom Zavaleta attributes the first formulation of a philosophy of Bolivian history, postulates that his work

> offers an outline of the Bolivian past as a whole, giving this the continued life that is implied by the concept of the national as a historical energy that is affirmative and, for the same reason, creative and sustaining. [. . .] It is a work that, moreover, aims to have a meaning that is not only circumstantial but also future-oriented.[20]

It is, thus, a work that interprets the past as a global process, not as an end in itself but in order to project it into the future. To do this, it has to combat the mentality that makes it impossible to realize the nation.

In a more explicit and specific way, Montenegro's program is as follows: 'The vitalist demonstration of the past constitutes, as such, nothing less than the great bastion behind which the authentic destinies of Bolivia can dig in to counter-attack and drive off the invasion that, consciously or unconsciously, has facilitated the colonialist psychology that created the anti-Bolivian process.'[21]

In this program, a teleological ontology of the nation is presupposed. There is something in reality that can be distinguished as the nation and that has a destiny. This provides the criterion for writing history—one relates that which expresses the nation's vitality. This vitality refers to two aspects of the same process. It can refer to the powerful expression of certain social and cultural forces; but the vitality that Montenegro speaks of seems to refer to an incompletion of things, of processes due not to voluntary abandonment but because foreign and contrary forces impede them. The nation's vitality also comes from this unfinished condition, that is, it has not yet deployed itself, it does not know its own limits, or its realization. It only knows and lives the limits of its external negation.

Here there is what could be called a romantic conception of the nation or of the national. The nation itself is not imagined to be capable in itself of

---

19 Céspedes, *El dictador suicida*, p. 48.

20 Montenegro, *Nacionalismo y coloniaje*, p. 17.

21 Montenegro, *Nacionalismo y coloniaje*, p. 17.

engendering subjects and structures that constitute the conditions of its final impossibility. That which negates or denies must be something external.

This distinction seems to make sense given the fact of the Spanish conquest and the continuation of colonial structures through the republic. What sustains colonial domination from within is conceived of as an external force.

The idea of globality or the whole mentioned by Céspedes and Montenegro is converted into a duality, but it is the globality of this duality that gives it meaning. This romantic notion of the nation isolates the positive possibilities of the indigenous and its historical *mestizaje* (cultural mixture) as an essence of the national, and the aim is to promote it in a history that generally takes the wrong course, paraphrasing Marx, here with reference to colonialism.

In Montenegro, historical revisionism has a militant character. To speak of the past when events are articulated as processes of struggle has political connotations in the present in which one aims to make (write, relate) history.

This militant historical revisionism was carried out by Montenegro and Céspedes in the pages of the newspaper *La Calle* as of 1936, the year in which it was founded.

> *La Calle* affirmed its position as the backbone of the resistance that refused to surrender national resources to foreigners, revealing the other side of the policies consecrated by presidents, ministers, lawyers and intellectuals of the mining camp that the country had been reduced to. What's more, *La Calle* put Arguedas's version of history[22] into question and revised history from the point of view of the 'common' people [. . .] *La Calle*, with its eight pages, was capable of confronting the apparatus of the oligarchy for ten years and constituted the cradle of the national revolution.[23]

After the moment of the Chaco War that the nationalists considered to be the birth of a consciousness of the disarticulation and absence of government, the other principal arena of national consciousness was the press organized by independent intellectuals, most of them socialists. The press exposed and denounced the corruption of the state, the de-nationalization of its resources and its servile posture in relation to the mining companies.

---

22 The reference is to Alcides Arguedas, a conservative writer and historian of the early twentieth century, best known for his indigenist novel *Raza de bronce* [Race of bronze] and his book-length essay *Pueblo enfermo* [Sick people] which blames Bolivia's plight on racial degeneration due to the mixed blood of its inhabitants. [Trans.]

23 Augusto Céspedes, *El presidente colgado* (La Paz: Juventud, 1966), p. 39.

Benedict Anderson's idea that novels and newspapers were the means for representing the nation as an imagined community[24] seems appropriate here. The first sense that Anderson attributes to the imagined aspect of the national community refers to the fact that the direct encounter of all the members of the community is impossible. Bolivian nationalists thought that the Chaco War was a moment of catastrophic encounter of the principal forces that, united, would constitute a sovereign nation. On the basis of this encounter, there was a material and historical foundation for a stronger capacity to imagine the national community. The other sense of the imagined aspect refers to its political finality, that is, the fact of being an independent and sovereign state.

La Calle's activity chronicles how the state governed Bolivia through a constant denial of its potential sovereignty and by affirming the power of mining over the whole of the country and its political institutions. Counterposed to this is the ideal of independence and sovereignty.

Anderson writes that the community of readers forms in its visible invisibility the embryo of the nationally imagined community.[25] The political journalism of the Bolivian nationalists represents the nation that encountered itself in the Chaco.

That said, in the Bolivia of those days, the mining bourgeoisie and other groups that exercised economic power did not aspire to the construction of a nation-state. The great mining capitalists, above all, preferred to maintain a weak and repressive state, servile to their particular interests. The capitalism that reigned in the mines was not presented as a model for the rest of the country.

The nation and its sovereign state was a subaltern project. In fact, *La Calle* and similar publications had to work in between periods of closure, making use of other newspapers financed by the economic powers that backed a project opposed to their own.[26]

It is significant that Montenegro's *Nacionalismo y coloniaje* is a history of the country carried out through a history of journalism in the Republic and the independence movements.

---

24 Benedict Anderson, *Imagined Communities: Reflections on the Origin and Spread of Nationalism* (London: Verso, 1983), p. 25.

25 Anderson, *Imagined Communities*, p. 44.

26 A panorama of the official and the nationalist press can be found in *El presidente colgado* by Augusto Céspedes.

When the press becomes a business or is articulated with capitalism, the newspapers, instead of fulfilling a more or less public function of control by the government by generating public opinion, devote themselves to justifying and producing the discourse of the dominant groups in power. In the 1940s, it can be seen how the traditional organic intellectuals of the dominant mining and landlord bloc and the organic intellectuals of a bloc that did not yet exist but which was in gestation confront each other through the press. Their organic nature refers to a political project rather than to an existing bloc.

The MNR was the main protagonist in the political opposition, together with the miners' unions, in the most critical phase of the political old guard. It was also the reorganizer of the state after the political rupture of 1952, the moment at which the party and ideology of revolutionary nationalism become dominant.

Zavaleta himself, following these thinkers, synthesizes and characterizes this type of nationalism and its differences from European currents in an article written five years after the revolution:

> But the people, in turn, cannot realize their historic destiny if it is not through independence and autonomy, that is to say, realizing the nation (a potential notion). When the concepts of the nation and the people were identified, it was immediately found that the nation did not exist except as dependency and subjection and a nationalism of existence was formulated, instead of the expansionist nationalism that was then on the rise in Europe.[27]

This nationalism of existence can serve to link our discussion of Zavaleta's influences with a stage of his life during which he worked together with Céspedes on the newspaper *La Nación*, for which he wrote in 1959–60.

Montenegro died in 1953, not long after the April 1952 revolution. Céspedes was the editor of *La Nación* and Zavaleta's best friend at that time; apart from his journalistic activity, the books he wrote after the MNR's triumph were also on pre-1952 Bolivian history.[28]

The journalistic articles of those years deal with the political conjuncture in a fiercely polemical key. The principal topics addressed include criticism of trade unionism and the relations between the COB[29] and the government;

---

27 Zavaleta, 'Cinco años de revolución en Bolivia'.

28 *El presidente colgado* (1975) and *Salamanca o el metafísico del fracaso* (1973).

29 Central Obrero Boliviano (Bolivian Workers' Centre): the national organization which unites all workers' trade unions and represents their interests before the government. [Trans.]

the political right wing, above all in relation to regionalism in the east of the country; *caciquismo*[30] among the peasantry; topics of economic policy and US aid; the internal polemic of the MNR and leadership problems.

This set of topics displays the concern with defending the national revolution from external and internal threats, to the party itself and to the social bloc that is the foundation of the process.

Here, it could be said that Zavaleta continued to practise what he himself called nationalism of existence, in the sense that, despite being in government, there is a feeling that the revolution is in danger, that it has to be defended, that its existence is not assured unless one fights constantly for it. At the same time, there is an attempt to develop a nationalism of development, not of expansion, since the best way to defend the existence of something is to develop it.

Zavaleta's articles offer a good survey of the political problems of the period. I will make a very summary and selective presentation of them, with the aim of sketching the political context and the way in which the author espouses and participates in revolutionary nationalism.

In order to understand the references to particular aspects of the country's politics, it is useful to take into account the global political framework of Zavaleta's interpretation at that moment, provided by a brief journalistic essay on the middle class:

> Politically, nevertheless, societies—all societies—are divided into just two great classes: that of the exploited on the one hand and that of the exploiters. On the basis of this opposition, more immediate and functional than the new technical dissection, the Bolivian revolution was carried out.
>
> In the case of Bolivia, a semi-colonial and underdeveloped country, with an imperfect and diminished sovereignty, a country besieged and half existing due to the depersonalization imposed by the invasion that has lasted for four hundred years, this dichotomy is expressed in the national class struggle against imperialism, whose

---

30 The term is of Mexican origin. It refers to the syndrome of local political bosses who retain control over a province or region through networks of clients and the distribution of favors, often embezzling funds to this end and at times making use of violence to suppress their rivals. [Trans.]

political components are metropolitan interests and the demographic parts of Bolivian society that serve them and join with them, constituting themselves as the foreign classes of national politics.[31]

Although the existence of a broader class spectrum is recognized, politics polarizes the class structure. The historically exploited tend to unite and form alliances. This is the result of a political over-determination that finalizes and synthesizes the class divisions, which is otherwise only a technical division. The exploited are those identified with the nation.

'If nationality somehow exists, it is through the flesh, that which is active and everyday, that which is the people, *khesti*[32] and poor, the opposite in every sense of a myth.'[33]

On the other hand: 'By sociological determination, the Clique (the foreign classes)[34] have always formed a common front, an insoluble alliance. The oligarchy is one, although it may have several political parties.'[35]

After the 1952 revolution, the Clique (*rosca*) was articulated and acted politically through two main channels: the Falange Socialista Boliviano (FSB,

---

31 René Zavaleta, 'Ambivalencia de la clase media', *La Nación* (1 August 1959). An appendix with a list of newspaper articles, both those which have been quoted and those which not, organized by period and newspaper, can be found at the end of the book.

32 The linguistically correct orthography is *qhisti*, 'soot' or 'sooty', by extension 'blackened', in the Andean native language Aymara. This is a multiple metaphor for the dirt of poverty, kitchens literally blackened by soot due to cooking with firewood or dried animal dung (still the case in many rural areas in the twenty-first century), the grimy faces and hands of agricultural and mine laborers without access to water to wash with. It is also significant that the author took for granted that the middle and upper class public who bought and read newspapers would automatically understand this native expression, indicative of a level of bilingualism in native languages which, ironically, no longer exists despite the widespread political postures in favour of 'indigenous culture' which were in no way accepted by those classes in the 1950s. [Trans.]

33 René Zavaleta, 'Los muertos que no han vivido', *La Nación* (1959).

34 The Bolivian term *rosca* (originally meaning a small kernel) is here translated as oligarchic clique or Clique. It refers to the small nucleus of economic elites, especially mining magnates, and the coterie of lawyers, politicians, and men of influence who did their bidding. [Trans.]

35 René Zavaleta, 'Ante las elecciones, Falange prefiere el camino del golpe', *La Nación* (26 May 1959).

Bolivian Socialist Phalange)[36] and the Civic Committee of Santa Cruz.[37] Both are objects of analysis and criticism on Zavaleta's part. In the post-revolutionary period, the unity of the mining capitalist–landlord front was made visible by the FSB, the party that it presented for the elections of 1958. Before and after this date, this party privileged the coup as a means of political change. It became the party of the oligarchy defeated in 1952 and of the middle class that feared a popular uprising.

'In the case of Phalange supporters, the inclination towards the irrational and terrorism is the result of an inborn fear of the people, a real hatred of reality because it does not move in the same direction as oneself.'[38]

According to Zavaleta, the FSB was the product of a frustrated importation and transculturation, characterized by a fetishistic politics which tends towards myth[39] and is organized around the leader and terror.

The FSB was, in the post-revolutionary period, the party that the displaced oligarchy used to intervene in politics and attempt to break the new regime, at the same time as it was the medium through which opposition was expressed after 1952. It represented a minority in defeat but still active in a process that denied it socially and politically.

The Phalange failed in the elections, making evident its minority character, and it therefore opted for a coup, continuing its tradition until the death of its leader in 1959, precisely on the occasion of an attempted coup.[40]

---

36 A right-wing party modelled on the Phalange fascist party of Franco's Spain, supported above all by the displaced landlord class. [Trans.]

37 Santa Cruz is the capital of the largest department in the Eastern lowlands of the country. In the 1950s it was geographically isolated from the rest of the country and its sparsely populated landed estates were organized on the basis of paternalist relations rather than the strictly controlled labor tenancy systems of the Andes; the rural population did not participate in the rejection of landlords by the Andean peasantry and there was no mining proletariat to rebel against the great capitalists. The combination of these factors meant that the revolutionary reforms had to be imposed by force, with the help of Andean peasant militias, experienced as an invasion by the local upper class which was organized in the Civic Committee. [Trans.]

38 René Zavaleta, 'Falange o la caída de un estilo político' *La Nación* (29 April 1959).

39 'The myth which is the abstract prolongation of the fetish' (Zavaleta, 'Falange o la caída').

40 The official version is that [Phalange leader Oscar] Unzaga de la Vega committed suicide upon hearing that the coup had failed; some members of the opposition claimed that he had been murdered by government agents. Zavaleta's chronicle of these events

After the failure of its policy of manoeuvers, it passed to the tactic that Zavaleta called the retreat to politically lateral institutions. Regarding an occasion when the Santa Cruz Civic Committee carried out an armed assault on regional public institutions, he wrote: 'The manoeuvers are part of the Clique's retreat to politically lateral institutions—universities, civic committees and others—after its repeated electoral failures, its defeat by arms, its frustrated attempts to compromise the members of the institutions of national defence.'[41]

After failing on the level of national government, the right wing tried to break up the new state by invalidating its sovereignty at a regional level. Zavaleta's articles on this subject combine analysis and political critique, that is, he attempts a sociological explanation of the reasons for and the nature of this type of phenomena, as well as a reply to those political forces that were their protagonists.

They combine political analysis with political struggle. In order for the analysis to be effective, there is a certain distance that avoids reducing the explanation of the facts to making evident the intentions of the actors. But it is not an impartial distance; it is a distance that allows the facts to be related to the totality of the process. As his predecessors would have said, it is a partisan distance.

These are texts that are addressed to those whom revolutionary nationalist discourse considered in that moment to be the nation or its potentially sympathetic public, which had to be constantly interpellated so as to maintain and continue the constitution of the national actor, showing it where, with whom and how the enemy and the reaction was operating.

It is a journalism that reports the movements in society, analyses and takes positions. At the same time, these texts are addressed to those criticized. One senses that the author is not transmitting the government's official opinion on the events discussed but, rather, his personal analysis and opinion, although it is that of someone who belongs to and thinks from within an ideology and political movement.

Trade unionism and the relations between the COB and the government are another topic of constant debate. Towards the end of the 1950s, the relations in the left wing of the MNR itself—basically, union leaders and their

---

can be found in: 'El sangriento domingo onomástico. Tema para la calumnia y el absurdo', *La Nación* (1959).

41 René Zavaleta, 'La subversión armada de la rosca cruceña, un atentado contra la unidad nacional', *La Nación* (27 May 1959).

grass roots—were problematic. At the same time, within the COB there was intense activity on the part of other left-wing forces which disputed the leadership of the workers' movement, especially the Trotskyist Partido Obrero Revolutionario (POR, Revolutionary Workers' Party), which authored the Pulacayo Thesis, the official document of the Federación Sindical de Traba-jadores Mineros de Bolivia (FSTMB, Bolivian Mine Workers' Union Federa-tion), which was also the core of the COB.

At the end of the 1950s, what Zavaleta called the 'PORist assault'[42] took place, consisting in a series of movements through which the POR attempted to displace the MNR in union leaderships and influence the direction of the workers' movement with its programme.

The root problem consisted in the separation of the workers' movement or the COB from the MNR. According to Zavaleta, this was a false separation; since the COB and the MNR basically contained the same social group, there was no sense in separating them. He considers the proletariat as the leading class in the alliance around the MNR[43] and establishes a distinction between the leading class and the executive of the national revolution, which would be the party, the MNR. In this sense, when the influence of the POR and the communists was growing within the COB, Zavaleta thought that this occurred in a class that was mature but lacked leadership, and this was due to the party having distanced itself from its base in the mining proletariat.[44]

His writings in these years are a constant polemic against the salary-based unionism promoted by the POR and the policy of separation in search of class autonomy. The critique is directed at POR policies, as well as at the policies of the so-called left wing of the MNR, basically composed of union leaders and Lechín,[45] who was both leader of the COB and a member of the MNR leadership. It is a criticism of the external opposition from the left, and the internal opposition expressed by Lechín and his followers, but also of the party itself for having moved away from the workers.

Here I would like to refer to an aspect of the criticism of the left that is significant in a way that will later find its historical explanation, with

---

42 René Zavaleta, *El assalto porista. El trotskismo y el despotismo de las aclamaciones en los sindicatos mineros de Bolivia* (La Paz: n. p., 1959).

43 René Zavaleta, 'Funambulesca teoría expónese en nombre del sindicalismo', *La Nación* (1959).

44 Zavaleta, *El asalto porista*, pp. 6–7.

45 Juan Lechín Oquendo, life-long leader of the national miners' union and for many years important collaborator and holder of government posts under the MNR. [Trans.]

sociological and psychological dimensions. Firstly, regarding what he calls the schizophrenic aims of the PORist left and the Phalangist right, he writes:

> The imperative to be, common to all men, acts by diversion, through the desire to transfer what is in the self to the exterior world and, in the service of that compensatory will (reality is for them a vacuum which has to be filled by the self) makes use of the circumstances provided by reality's faults.[46]

He continues:

> The hard left is always the result of an alienation proper to the middle class which, due to the possibilities of its ambivalence (it is a class of dreamers that invades others), can only achieve itself historically by embracing the material presence of the proletariat (something that does not occur with the POR, which embraces proletarianism, an idea, not a class).[47]

For Zavaleta, the primary reality was the alliance or bloc around the MNR in its flesh and blood and its undifferentiated politics, and the fault was the distancing of the party or its leadership from the leading class (which leads because it is the active social class of the revolutionary process).

The POR, with an increasing base of middle-class members, would have taken advantage of this fault to attempt to carry out its schizophrenic project of a second revolution separating the workers from the rest of the nation. It tried to realize a particular (although not individual) ideological self, over and above the national self, exploiting its weaknesses.

In this, Zavaleta did not see signs of a development towards the autonomy of the working class that could be taking place beneath or through the policies of the left-wing parties within the COB. I think this is due to a more general feature which characterizes the whole of his thought in this period, and which consists in thinking *on the basis of the party*, not on the basis of class. He believes that he thinks on the basis of the nation, which contains the class and the party. The class and the party, however, although united in politics, remain components potentially differentiable by their specific histories. The nationalists did not use the notion of alliance for nothing.

Still, the point of alliance is the party. In other words, Zavaleta thinks on the basis of the political expression of the alliance around the MNR, not on

---

46 Zavaleta, *El asalto porista*, p. 9.
47 Zavaleta, *El asalto porista*, p. 12.

the basis of some point at the class level of its components. He thinks on the basis of the predominant political synthesis of the period. This is why his concern is centred on how the various individual and collective actors, and the various dimensions of the reality of the country, contribute or not to that political synthesis that is the *national revolution*, as general process and program of the age, and to the MNR government as its specific leadership.

The breadth of diagnosis within this framework is due to his notion that the problems and obstacles come not only from outside the movement, here in the broadest sense of the nation, but also from within: namely, the growing distance between the proletariat and the nationalist party, which is an internal obstacle. I have already mentioned what he thought about the right wing and the old oligarchy, which are external to the movement but internal to the country.

There are two more aspects worth noting in order to broaden the panorama of his vision of the moment. One of them is the 'boss system' (*caciquismo*), developed primarily in the peasant sector. *Caciquismo* consists in the organization of local and micro-regional powers on the part of union leaders who, counting on rank-and-file militias, negotiated their support for politicians in the governing party in exchange for support for their almost sovereign local power.

This negotiation or political exchange[48] is not generally carried out with the government as a whole but with leaders or politicians of factions of the MNR, who made use of this in their own internal struggles. Zavaleta's articles document these internal battles, although he writes 'the great majority of the MNR base does not have factions.'[49]

The articles in *La Nación* also point out that there are politicians in the MNR who promote their personal and factional interests and power, reducing the unity of the nation-state through *caciquismo*. This is an internal obstacle or fault, which in the conjuncture he considered could be combated through the rural property tax, a united system of land tax replacing the various existing forms of taxation. This, in political terms (which is what matters at this point), implied that the tax paid would include the union dues which would

---

48 See Gian Enrico Rusconi, 'Intercambio político' in *Problemas de teoría política* (Mexico City: Instituto de Investigaciones Sociales, UNAM, 1985).

49 René Zavaleta, 'La estructura democrática del MNR no admite imposición de fórmulas', *La Nación* (23 August 1959).

be collected by the state and then redistributed to the unions.[50] The union dues were 5 per cent of the tax.[51]

According to Zavaleta, the political benefit of this would be that the local bosses would not be able to pocket the dues;[52] that is to say, it would weaken the *cacique* system and fortify the nation-state.

Finally, there is the problem of economic policy and US aid. A concern that Zavaleta echoed in some of his articles was the need for capital to invest in development. After the nationalization of the mines, the government began to foment investment by foreign capital. A measure in this direction was the Petroleum Code. There was a hope that the arrival of capital by this route would make it possible to develop industry upon converting the currency obtained from exports into organic development of the economy.[53]

I will leave this point aside to turn to another aspect that allows me to point out some contradictions in Zavaleta's position in this conjuncture: the question of US aid. The president and the government expressed a favourable attitude in relation to this from the moment immediately following the 1952 uprising.

---

50 The 'unions' here referred to are the *sindicatos agrarios* or agrarian (peasant) unions. In fact, they are local peasant community organizations which include all heads of household who hold land in the community. They take charge of local infrastructure such as roads and schools, maintained by communal labor, solve disputes over land and interpersonal conflicts (theft, fights, family problems, etc.) and represent the community before government instances. Unlike the workers' or trade unions (*sindicatos*) which gave them their name, they do not intervene in questions of hiring, firing or payment of agricultural laborers (which in any case are not a significant group in many rural areas, and were less so in the 1950s). Costs incurred by the leadership are covered by a monthly subscription (*cuota sindical*) paid by all members and administered at the discretion of the leadership. Zavaleta's idea was to remove the control of these funds from local leaders and thus limit their capacity to recruit clients by giving funds to their supporters. [Trans.]

51 René Zavaleta, 'Opónense al predial rústico dirigentes mal informados y explotadores bien informados', *La Nación* (27 February 1963).

52 René Zavaleta, 'Caciques enriquecidos adoptan para el campesinado una tesis rosquera', *La Nación* (27 January 1963).

53 René Zavaleta, 'La explotación del petróleo', *La Nación* (11 January 1957); 'Campaña sin sentido favorecida por equivocados y extremistas', *La Nación* (20 August 1959).

In some of Zavaleta's articles, one finds echoes of the official vision of the executive and the party, that is, that this was friendly assistance in development,[54] although he did not express this very strongly. There was a moment when Zavaleta expressed his criticism of the results and allocation of the so-called aid.

We can sum up the situation as follows. Yankee aid, taking advantage of its indispensable nature, fortifies an oligarchic minority which, indirectly, comes to sustain the patently anti-popular counter-revolution. In compliance with the theory of importing private initiatives into Bolivia, it refuses to stimulate nationalized entities and the plans for the central economic structure of the country, perpetuating the crisis and impeding the possibility of creating our own wealth. It becomes a constant devaluation of the national upon creating a power parallel to the state, independent of it, and by using foreign rather than domestic technicians.[55]

This criticism of US intervention, while the government became more and more dependent on and solicitous of the same, means that an organ of the press such as *La Nación*, considered to represent the official point of view, had a degree of autonomy, although its writers were party members. In particular in the articles by Zavaleta and Céspedes, it criticized the opposition and also presented internal criticism within the limits allowed by its membership.

This may also be a sign of a certain heterogeneity within the MNR, which was expressed in various ways: left-wing trade unionism, this type of political journalism, the caciques, the pro-US tendency, among others; it is also a sign that, in order to stay in power, this freedom had to be allowed, despite the risk of weakening the organization.

Returning to the previous topic, it could be said that for a time Zavaleta did not establish an organic link between the policy of legal encouragement of foreign investment and what he called Yankee aid that, in the passage above, now appears as a neocolonial investment program on the part of a type of civilization which implies the development of the economy and culture of the imperialist metropolis and not that of the nation and its sovereign state.

---

54 René Zavaleta, 'Imposibilidades de alto nivel', *La Nación* (25 May 1958).

55 René Zavaleta, 'Dogmas y paradojas que anulan a la ayuda norteamericana', *La Nación* (15 November 1959).

Up to a point, the articles of this period, in their interstices, display the contradictions between his participation in the defence of government policies (via the official press) that were thought to be leading the national revolution but were largely dependent on North American intervention, and the anti-imperialist ideology of that current of revolutionary nationalism that Zavaleta and Céspedes represented at the time.

In his comments and analyses of the problems of the late 50s, above all those that had to do with the distance between the party and the workers, internal divisions in the party and the general direction of the process, Zavaleta clung to the formula of 'all power to the leader'.[56] This expressed a political mentality that viewed the problems and weaknesses of the revolutionary process from the position of the party considering itself the synthesis of the national movement, and at the same time trusting its unity and political continuity to the figure of its leader. The centrality of the leader served to reduce complexity and to concentrate policy.

This may be overly schematic, but it merely serves to show that there were problems of political capacity to resolve political complexity created by the growing disarticulation between the MNR and the COB, and the contradictions between economic policy and ideology. The strategy of concentrating on the leader indicates that there were no collective actors or forces that could solve them; in fact, they tended to do quite the opposite.

In this first chapter, my aim has been to sketch the political and intellectual context in which Zavaleta formed his ideas and entered national politics.

In the second chapter, I will focus on Zavaleta's thought so as to analyse and characterize its specificity.

In the third chapter, I return to consider the more general context of revolutionary nationalism as a whole, outlining its phases and changes.

---

56 Expressed collectively in 'Elijamos un presidente y no un prisionero. Militantes del MNR exigen todo el poder para el jefe del partido', *La Nación* (22 April 1959).

CHAPTER TWO

Interpretation and Constitution of the National Being

The relation with meaning is always a dialogue. The act of understanding is already a dialogue. [. . .] With explanation there is only
one consciousness, one subject; with comprehension there are two
consciousnesses and two subjects. There can be no dialogic relation
with an object, and therefore explanation has no dialogic aspects [. . .]
Understanding is always dialogic to some degree. [. . .] The text is
not a thing, and therefore the second consciousness, the consciousness of the perceiver, can in no way be eliminated or neutralized.

—Mikhail M. Bakhtin[1]

This chapter focuses on Zavaleta's thought in its nationalist period, on a small
group of texts from the 1960s which I have selected as representative of his
revolutionary nationalism in its most developed form. For the time being, I
will leave aside the question of influences and privilege what is specific to
Zavaleta.

Luis H. Antezana[2] and Fernando Mayorga Ugarte[3] have opened up and
developed a field of analysis of the discourse of revolutionary nationalism
which is today the basis and core of the scholarship on the topic. Antezana
understands revolutionary nationalism as an episteme, and Ugarte has studied its capacity of interpellation and constitution of actors/subjects. Here I
aim to work in a different way, which I consider does not controvert but rather
complements their work, which is moreover a condition of my own.

In 1961, Zavaleta obtained a bachelor's degree in juridical, political and
social sciences from the Universidad Mayor de San Andrés (UMSA) in La

---

1 Mikhail M. Bakhtin, *Speech Genre and Other Late Essays* (V. W. McGee trans., C.
Emerson and M. Holquist eds) (Austin: University of Texas Press, 1994), pp. 105–111.

2 Luis H. Antezana, 'Sistema y procesos ideológicos en Bolivia (1935–1979)' in René
Zavaleta (ed.), *Bolivia hoy* (México City: Siglo XXI, 1983), pp. 60–84.

3 José Fernando Mayorga Ugarte, *El discurso del nacionalismo revolucionario* (Bolivia:
CIDRE, 1985).

Paz, completing the studies which he had begun in Montevideo. In 1964, he earned a law degree.

At the end of the 1950s, Zavaleta was a cultural attaché in the Bolivian embassy in Uruguay (1958–60). At the beginning of the 1960s, he was first secretary in the Bolivian embassy in Chile (1960–62); he was also a member of parliament (1962–63) and Minister for Mines and Petroleum (1964). The texts which I consider here were written during those years.

I propose to analyse here the rhetorical strategy and the notions of history and politics which will serve an axes for the analytical reconstruction of Zavaleta's discourse.

I will work primarily with three texts: *Estado nacional o pueblo de pastores: El imperialismo y el desarrollo fisiocrático* [Nation-State or a people of shepherds: imperialism and physiocratic development] (1963); *La revolución boliviana y la cuestión del poder* [The Bolivian Revolution and the question of power] (1964); and *La formación de la conciencia nacional* [The formation of national consciousness] (1967). I will also refer to some shorter texts from this period.

The Ontology of Nationalist Historical Revisionism

Mikhail M. Bakhtin's ideas, cited at the beginning of this chapter, serve to support my contention that in Zavaleta's texts it is impossible to eliminate the consciousness that reads them—they are written taking that other consciousness into account, and they are intended to constitute, develop and extend it.

This is a series of interpretative texts on Bolivian history in which the guiding thread is the process of the formation of national consciousness, which is precisely the title of the essay which synthesizes Zavaleta's thought during this period.

The text *La formación de la conciencia nacional* includes entire sections of essays which were included in his previous books, but in a new narrative configuration. These early essays were written in a climate of fierce debate and political struggle, when the MNR was still in government and Zavaleta was first a member of parliament and later a minister. Zavaleta finished writing *La formación* in Montevideo, by then as an exile, after the fall of the MNR in 1964; perhaps for this reason a more reflective tone replaces the more polemical style of the days of direct confrontation and politico-intellectual struggle. The earlier writings were basically intended to intervene in events of public debate.

Zavaleta writes, in the introduction to *La formación*: 'In these lines I have tried to briefly enumerate the ways in which Bolivians, over the last thirty years, have aimed to achieve an identity for themselves and for the country.' And also: 'History is the only thing which defines us, in so far as Man, although he is always an animal in flight, can achieve roots, a face and a time, that is, an identification.'[4]

The aim is, then, to work on an interpretation of a national identity which is not conceived as a substance or an atemporal cultural identity but, rather, precisely through lived social and cultural practices of what he calls the factual nation, or the body from which the national self [or ego] is constructed.[5] He does not assume the existence of a national culture or essence which the Bolivians incarnate or express at each conjuncture. This is a history which is open, although not unconditioned. In general, it can be said that this historical opening is due above all to politics, and the set of political and cultural conditions can be synthesized or are synthesized in the notion of a semi-colony.

First of all, it is worth reviewing the concept of politics:

[P]olitics is, in effect, destiny,[6] the forward-looking definition of the fate of the polis or city, an entity of common life whose version in our time is the nation, or more properly the nation-state [. . .] Politics is the air we all breathe, given that it refers to the fate of everyone's lives.[7]

Here, Zavaleta identifies the mode of formation of collective identities of our time, which is the national, something that is configured by politics. Identity is related to a deliberately chosen destiny, to autonomy and sovereignty. He establishes another relation between the processes of formation of individual and collective identities:

---

4 René Zavaleta, *La formación de la conciencia nacional* (Cochabamba: Los Amigos del Libro, 1990), p. 22.

5 We translate here and elsewhere in this chapter as 'self' Zavaleta's term *yo*; 'ego' would be an alternative rendering.

6 *Destino* in the original; the physical place at which one aims to arrive at the end of a journey, but also 'fate' or 'destiny' in a mystical sense, the result of a moral judgement and a moral objective, as in the phrase 'Heaven's my destination'. [Trans.]

7 René Zavaleta, *La revolución boliviana y la cuestión del poder* (La Paz: Dirección Nacional de Informaciones, 1964), p. 7.

Men[8] follow the fate of the place in which they live and it is useless to flee it. One cannot hope to fully realize oneself in a nation that has failed. We knew that each man is, to a certain extent, the same size as his country and that the nation is an element of the self, that the individual self cannot be fulfilled except through the national self.[9]

This does not only refer to the historical and social conditions of the formation of individual subjectivity but also to the political dimension of this constitutive relation. Politics is to determine oneself, but one can only determine a self together with other people. This is not only a relation that is socially and historically conditioned but also a deliberate self-constitution. Here, history is condition and decision, since 'to be is not only to resist, but rather it is also necessary to determine oneself.'[10]

Strictly speaking, the historical conditions of social life are also given by politics: 'Men exist as history when they organize themselves politically with historical objectives.'[11]

Politics is that teleological temporal dimension of human association.

This way of presenting politics as a synthetic or decisive dimension in the configuration of the destiny of individuals and collectivities, as a dimension of choice and the constitution of autonomy, serves to introduce the nationalist critique of the semi-colonial condition that Zavaleta ascribes to

---

8 It should be recalled that Zavaleta wrote long before the social sciences accepted concepts of gender as part of their theoretical apparatus. In those days, 'man' or 'men' was widely considered an acceptable description for 'the human race', 'people in general', 'all human beings' and so on; not even women writers found this objectionable or observed the implicit exclusion which has been emphasized by feminist intellectuals in the late twentieth century (and a few forerunners, such as Virgina Woolf who wrote 'Women have no country' on the basis of declarations such as Zavaleta's where 'men' are the subjects of the 'nation'). [Trans.]

9 *Suerte* in the original: 'luck', which at times refers to arbitrary chance (as in 'luck of the draw') but the teleological tone of Zavaleta's arguments suggests that this is a 'luck' which expresses the moral quality of the actions which gave rise to the more or less 'lucky' result expressed as 'fate'. [Trans.]

10 Zavaleta, *Formación*, p. 67. The same text appears in 'La revolución boliviana y el doble poder', *Marcha* (20 July 1962).

11 Zavaleta, *Formación*, p. 29. *Elegirse* in the original has this double meaning of 'choose' (among alternatives in general) and 'elect' (by voting in an election, naming a political representative). [Trans.]

Bolivia. This is the condition under which Bolivians pose their problems of identity and existence.

The semi-colonial condition is that in which one ceases to be autonomous and, in consequence, 'the historical evolution of the country and the national body has to endure an exogenous, unequal, jolting growth, introduced from outside, which is difficult to get used to, within which they have to act defensively because the historical initiative does not belong to them.'[12]

In this sense, it can be understood that the semi-colonial condition is a condition of partial de-politicization, which here would mean the negation or absence of endogenous or self-referential practices of collective decision. Historicization and politicization seem to run parallel to processes of formation of national identities. History, which is the direction taken by the will of the polis, is also the struggle against that which denies it. Zavaleta writes: 'In broad terms, the history of the country is the theatre in which the invaders and the national being contradict each other, often with violence.'[13]

The Rhetorical Strategy of the National Self and the Specific Negation of Local Pragmatism

In what follows, I return to the point we have reached in our reconstruction to advance an interpretative hypothesis. This hypothesis approaches an articulation of what I will call rhetorical strategy, interpretative strategy and the ontology of history.

In these texts, Zavaleta seeks to produce consciousness while interpellating or developing the national consciousness. His voice, an individual self, is constituted as the national self constitutes itself. In this sense, it is a consciousness that speaks to the factual nation with the aim of producing a relation between the consciousness of this semi-colonial reality and the political tasks of the moment and of the age.

The rhetorical dimension of a discourse is that which organizes or structures it in order to persuade. The aim is to produce a credible discourse, by way of its reference to reality. Chaim Perelman uses the notion of the structure of reality[14] to define the way in which a discourse or argument accounts for its referents and presents itself as truth. I will use this terminology and also that of ontology when speaking in more general terms.

---

12 Zavaleta, *Formación*, p. 29.

13 Zavaleta, *Formación*, p. 28.

14 Perelman and Olbrecht-Tyteca, *The New Rhetoric*.

Zavaleta's rhetorical strategy consists in elaborating a polarized historical ontology that has as its extremes the nation and the anti-nation, which would be the most general structure of reality, with the aim of convincing his audience to recognize itself as part of the nation and that this choice is a matter of life or death.

'The crossroads that our generation faces is, therefore, a choice between being a semi-colony forever, a republic of shepherds, and the nation-state made real and lord of itself.'[15] And: 'What is at stake here is the existence of the nation itself, its historical existence and not only the characteristics or attributes of that existence.'[16]

The general structure of this reality is characterized as a semi-colonial condition in which, nevertheless, two courses of social and individual action are possible. This is a polarized and simplified ontology, which is, however, open in the sense of allowing for self-determination, despite this context of conditioning factors that deny national autonomy. At the same time, it should be noted that this opening, this possibility of vital decision, assumes a specific form: that of the nation-state. Differences can be developed, but within the form of the nation-state. There is also an ontology of interdependent development between the individual and his or her nation, by way of this relation between the individual self and the national self.

A life that also aspires minimally to be conscious of itself desires to differentiate itself and does not accept itself if it is not free. The individual self, in effect, is incomplete and restless, frustrated and imprisoned when it is not made real in the national self. The organic need for a self extends to the equally ontological and innate need of a self as a people and thus proposes the historical construction of a type, of a tempo of one's own, which is the origin of all cultures. The struggle for individual personality is carried out amid the assault from without, but the national self is also constantly invaded. The individual self fails where the national self is not made real.[17]

This firm imbrication or relation between the individual and national selves is also a rhetorical mechanism or strategy which is also a form of political interpellation. As it continues the development of the national consciousness in its interpretations of history and its ontological structure, it demands the politicization of those selves.

15 René Zavaleta, *Estado nacional o pueblo de pastores* (La Paz: E. Burillo, 1956).

16 Zavaleta, *Revolución boliviana*, p. 9.

17 Zavaleta, *Formación*, p. 56.

There is an interdependence in the elaboration or unfolding of an ontology based on the rhetorical necessities of the discourse and that which is based on the conception of history and politics, or, in other words, there is an articulation of two processes of ontological generation. In this way, the ontology sketched in rhetoric seeks to complete the historical ontology. Interpretation entails thinking this synchrony of discursive-ontological levels.

A process of politicization of the discourse and the conception of historical reality is given through this rhetorical strategy and this polarized ontology, which can be thought of in terms of Carl Schmitt's conception of politicization, as the friend–enemy distinction. I am not suggesting that Zavaleta was influenced by Schmitt, but merely that he may be useful here for a better explanation of the polarized and politicized character of the underlying rhetoric and ontology of Zavaleta's historical interpretation.

The common ground between Zavaleta's and Schmitt's ideas is the polarized nature of political reality. For example, in the last passage Zavaleta writes that one's own personality is developed under assault from outside. The enemy is basically external and has internal agents, which, in the Bolivian political language of the time, were 'the Clique' (*rosca*). The difference is that the notion of national self is not identical with that of friend. The national self is not a group of friends; it is an identity, not a flexible and changing alignment of political forces.

Zavaleta conceives the friend–enemy distinction primarily at the interstate or international level, which, according to Carl Schmitt, is the way in which this distinction existed until the nineteenth century, before competitive liberal politics internalized it within the nation-state as the new space of political struggle.[18] Zavaleta argues[19] that in semi-colonial countries, this internalization of the friend–enemy distinction has not occurred, precisely because they have not achieved a nation-state, and that it is impeded by the consolidated nation-states which have become imperialists.

For Zavaleta, 'The fundamental characteristic of the nation-state is, in effect, what in political law is called sovereignty, which is an essential element of the state.' And: 'The formidable obstacle that impedes the realization of sovereignty on the part of the Bolivian state is, without a doubt, that which has been called [...] the mining superstate. This mining superstate became

---

18 Carl Schmitt, *The Concept of the Political* (George Schwab trans.) (Chicago: University of Chicago Press, 1996).

19 Zavaleta, *Estado nacional*, pp. 9–10.

part of imperialism through a well-known process by which native oligarchies join forces with international oppression.'[20]

For Schmitt, sovereignty or the sovereign is that which determines the friend–enemy distinction. Sovereignty is precisely that which, according to Zavaleta, does not exist in the semi-colonial condition. In this sense, the development of a national identity or self and its materialization as a state is a politicization that distinguishes the enemy on the basis of subordination and the act of denial which one wishes to be free of.

I will continue to discuss the politicization of Zavaleta's historical interpretation moving to a more Hegelian framework, which is explicit. With regard to the Bolivian conception of universality and specificity, he writes:

> To affirm one's nation, to make it exist, it is necessary to deny the highest phase of the oppressing nation that does not allow it to affirm itself, that is, which denies it. One must deny a denial and thus one's situation is delimited, specific, determined and defensive, which is entirely the opposite of the standpoint of universal thought. This is more defence than thought, and the latter exists to defend itself; it is armed thought. It does not have to comprehend and, in order to affirm and affirm itself, it must deny.[21]

This denial is specific, it affirms its own tempo; at the same time, it participates in or is oriented towards a general condition of the age, which is the nation state. The specific denial is a partisan and local mode of thinking. It is neither humanist nor universal. It is nationalist and existential in the sense of not being a programme aimed at making real anything beyond what is potentially contained in the factual nation, and it is bellicose.

This is the foundation of Zavaleta's nationalism. First, I will discuss the passage from the factual nation to the nation for itself, and then the role of consciousness in this passage and, hence, how he conceives revolutionary nationalism.

The factual nation is expressed in various ways:

'The factual nation, that is, the undeniable flesh-and-blood nation, which at times is passive but always present and which exists without a doubt.'[22]

---

20 Zavaleta, *Estado nacional*, pp. 9–10.

21 Zavaleta, *Formación*, p. 85.

22 Zavaleta, *Formación*, p. 65.

'The factual nation, which persevered in an introverted resistance, which insisted on itself in a petrified patience.'[23]

And hence arises its dialectical negation:

It is the transition from the factual nation to the nation for itself and from the resistant country to the historical country in a process by which, after having resisted the denial of the nation, the classes that contain it deny the denial of the nation and attempt to realize a nation-state, substituting the partial state forms created by the foreign classes.[24]

The form of the Hegelian dialectic and the difference from the same should be noted. Here, the factual nation assumes the place of the nation in itself, but unlike Hegel, who thinks of the moment of the thing in itself as something which must be overcome dialectically (that is, partially denied, conserved, and finally, containing the self-reflexive novelty), Zavaleta thinks of an factual nation that, in a way more reminiscent of Spinoza, persists in a way of being, and which, in its moment of denial, will not principally deny itself but that which comes from outside. This is mainly due to the way in which contradiction is conceived, which in this case is external to the nation, although internal to the country. The specificity of the negation of Hegelian negation is that it comes from within; it is a labour of the self, in the sense of overcoming oneself.

Now, it could be said that if the frame of reference of the reality under consideration is the world-system, as Zavaleta claims in expounding his polarized ontology of the historical reality of the age, the pole of the oppressed nation is differentiated from the imperialist pole that denies the potential autonomy of the other; but this is not a dialectical contradiction in the strong Hegelian sense.

The denial (or negation) of negation of which Zavaleta speaks gives rise to a more metaphorical concept of confrontation, politically articulated by revolutionary nationalism, between two historical bodies in relation of ontological exteriority, although they belong to the same historical moment. This becomes clearer when he says that the denial of denial would not take part in an overcoming that entails another superior modality of unity of opposites but, rather, consists in tearing oneself away or moving away from an autonomy that forgets integration for a while, until it has developed sovereignty.

---

23 Zavaleta, *Formación*, p. 66.
24 Zavaleta, *Formación*, p. 67.

Now, a thought that conceives the negation of negation is a thought that refuses to be universal or universalizable; it is *for itself*, almost in the broad sense of the term, a turning inside that at the same time has to objectify itself as a state, which for a moment excludes all others. It sets up a polarized ontology of historical reality and takes a position at one of its poles, where its existence and freedom depend on the development of a national form of collective identity. It is a thought that chooses one of the poles of its ontology in order to develop its being. It is a partisan thought in this sense of thinking of reality as a conflict and of its own development as part of that conflict, and in another sense that I will explain in the discussion of revolutionary nationalism, which is how he identifies this thought of conflictive constitution of the national self.

'Nationalism links the middle strata with the proletariat, but not as a broad pact, as a vast brotherhood, but rather as a conspiracy and if this had been so general ultimately it would not have been politics but rather pedagogy.' Or, more briefly: '[T]he conspiratorial agreement that, from the beginning, is revolutionary nationalism.'[25]

Revolutionary nationalism is, thus, an ideology and politics that are not general, because the first articulates a part of the society and not the whole of it, and because it is a discourse of specific denial which cannot be universalized. Finally, it is not general because it is a conspiracy, not a dialogue. This way of conceiving itself as a conspiratorial politics has to do with the non-existence of a political community with public rights in the pre-revolutionary country, and in consequence, the political constitution of those who were excluded passes through or is converted into a plot against the old political order.

This way of thinking of revolutionary nationalism also explains the representative nature of such a discourse and politics. Revolutionary nationalism is not yet the general consciousness of the nation. A more developed part exists politically and in this sense represents the other part. This is a sort of local illuminism, of individuals more enlightened than others and as such more representative; yet it does not advance any universal idea of political order and reason but, rather, a will to local state sovereignty, to which the form of the political regime is secondary. Politically, it is a kind of vanguardism in the sense in that a small group of men represent the nation and do politics, publicly when they can and privately in order to subvert the political order and thus, perhaps, make the nation public.

---

25 Zavaleta, *Formación*, p. 103.

But the statist orientation of this revolutionary nationalism paved the way for the nation to go from a marginal or underground existence in the semi-colony to a representation monopolized by the nationalist state, with little public space for plural and autonomous political life, in the post-revolutionary period. This public space was possible thanks to the workers' movement; the party (MNR) took another path.

The locus of enunciation of this discourse should be taken into account. The writings of Zavaleta under consideration are from the early 1960s. The revolution was in 1952, and he writes these texts as a congressman representing the MNR from 1962 and as Minister of Mines in 1964; that is to say, they are produced from one position or another within the state, although they express personal views.

Now, this characterization of revolutionary nationalism as a conspiracy refers above all to the revolutionary past; it no longer serves to characterize revolutionary nationalism when its party is in government and has reorganized the state. He does not have a satisfactory definition for this new phase.

Here I will go on to note some problems that Zavaleta encounters in that period, but it should first be noted that this inadequacy reveals a common mechanism of revolutionary nationalism, which consists in seeking to legitimate itself by identifying itself with reference to the past, to the glorious moment of the revolution, to a political and temporal moment in which all the conquests of this process would be included and for which revolutionary nationalism and the MNR claim to be principally responsible. On the basis of this moment, it continues to reproduce its political identity as representative of the nation. The criticisms or references to actions or moments outside this nucleus are delegitimized, treated as secondary, lacking in importance. Thus, revolutionary nationalism delimits the discursive space of political struggle after 1952.

Zavaleta, nevertheless, identifies a field of divergences, contradictions and struggles within revolutionary nationalism and the state, expressed through the conflict between the project in favour of heavy industry in opposition to what he calls physiocratic development, which translates politically into the dilemma between remaining a republic of shepherds or constructing a nation-state. The conflict is internalized after 1952. It now takes place between representatives of both tendencies within the party. The alternatives are the following:

'What will increasingly determine the political forces of the country, between nationalism and liberation and submission [to imperialism], is the problem of the country's march towards heavy industry.'[26]

'In my opinion, Bolivia, as primarily a mining country, should first develop the industrialization of its mines before dispersing its resources in the development of its periphery.'[27]

Physiocratic development is directed towards the development of agriculture and secondary branches of industry with the idea of diversifying the structure of the economy, with the result of perpetuating the predominant export-based and primary character of its productive activity.

In these writings from 1963 and 1964 there is, on the one hand, a characterization of revolutionary nationalism still marked by the way in which it was conceived before 1952, and on the other, a discourse on the debate within the MNR on the routes for achieving national sovereignty. Despite being enunciated from the position of a member of parliament and minister, it can be noted that they express, in a combative style, a point of view that does not appear to be the predominant one.

Thus, the nation's own existence and autonomy is not something that must be affirmed and made real denying the external enemy but, rather, it is necessary to determine the form of development of sovereignty within the nation and its leading groups, in a moment in which, after exercising political power for a decade, the critical side of revolutionary nationalism feels that the existence of the nation is in danger because it has not decided the policies nor developed the conditions for the exercise of sovereignty. This is not a mere legal question but also, and fundamentally, a question of the forces and material conditions of sovereignty which in this case demands, according to Zavaleta, heavy industry.

From 1952 to 1964, which is the period during which the MNR was in government, there were debates on economic and political strategy, most fiercely between the workers' movement and the government but also between the physiocratic policies (to use Zavaleta's terms) predominant in the post-revolutionary governments and the pro-industry nationalists who were in general closer to the workers' movement, and formed something like the left wing of revolutionary nationalism.

---

26 Zavaleta, *Estado nacional*, p. 22.
27 Zavaleta, *Estado nacional*, p. 19.

This is a process in which the nation for itself is problematic, and something that the critical sector considers not to have become a material reality. Perhaps in taking into consideration another dimension of revolutionary nationalism, it may be seen that some of the conditions for this failure are present in the same characteristics which, according to the nationalists, explain or make possible its success. Zavaleta himself writes of the MNR: 'From the beginning it aspires to practise and in fact does practise a kind of national pragmatism that turns out to be singularly rich and active because, thanks to the sui generis factors that constitute it, it acquires a rapid capacity to integrate itself with historical events and take them over.' And:

> From the beginning, the MNR demands autonomy for its ideological and practical development, which, not based on universal ideological suppositions, continually prefers methodical inference and theoretical induction. It resolves to present a historical proposal and, in consequence, renounces the conversion to a universal philosophy. But since the facts themselves cannot be conceived without giving them a more general frame of reference, revolutionary nationalism is obliged to perform a continual ideological synthesis, which no doubt would have concluded in an abundant and erratic speculative elaboration—in the manner of APRA[28]—if it had not been supported by a class content that corresponded to the most active sectors of the national classes.[29]

And finally:

> [T]he national classes are not united by an ideological pact but rather by common action, by praxis, by the tactical flexibility indispensable to create and maintain the alliance, by doctrinal induction—which begins with concrete facts in order to synthesize them in the doctrine as such—to form an ideological repertory that determines its own limits.[30]

---

28 Populist political party founded in Peru by Víctor Raúl Haya de la Torre in the 1920s. For most of its existence, it was illegal and obliged to act clandestinely. When it was finally voted into government in the 1980s, it had lost all ideological consistency and merely implemented opportunist versions of the dominant neoliberal ideology. [Trans.]

29 Zavaleta, *Formación*, p. 98.

30 Zavaleta, *Formación*, p. 99.

This pragmatism and tactical flexibility, which is presented here as a virtue, may also be part of the explanation of the MNR's accommodation to the physiocratic model which, according to the same nationalism, is criticized as growth that does not liberate. That is to say, it is a pragmatism that does not only work for the politics that first criticizes oligarchic political power and later articulates a social base for the reorganization of the state and the economy, to articulate programmatic ideas, but also works in order not to put into practice a programme of sovereignty and nationalization for civil society, and to thus maintain itself in the government of that society.

It is pragmatic for the articulation of a part of civil society, to represent and mediate it, and to bear the standard of a programme that synthesizes its demands and aspirations, presenting itself as the representative of the nation's programme; it is also pragmatic insofar as it does not implement the most complete and hard-line version and justifies itself through two moments, one located in the past and one in the future.

In the past, it refers back to 1952, when the fundamental task was accomplished, justifying the path of a gradual development that goes from the secondary to the primary, which is the task for the future, via the gradualist conception or strategy that considers that it has to begin with developing the agrarian sector as a base for later industrial development.

This rhetoric of local pragmatism, anti-universalism and tactical flexibility, which resulted from the alliance of forces and gives rise to political and doctrinal syncretism, which is how Zavaleta characterizes revolutionary nationalism, is the discursive space within which the programmatic synthesis of the most radical moment of the Bolivian revolution, with its strong proletarian presence and socialist ideological elements, is produced, and also the space within which the physiocratic discourse is articulated. I use Zavaleta's terms to show that the conflict arises within a single discursive universe; and, on the other hand, that Zavaleta's characterization of revolutionary nationalism serves to also include what it criticizes.

I now want to discuss the assumptions of this rhetorical strategy concerning the audience it addresses. One of the concerns of rhetorical analysis, according to Perelman, is the consideration of the other, or the audience, in the selection and elaboration of the arguments that might best achieve the aim of persuasion. Zavaleta writes: 'The MNR is the party of the *cholos*[31] and

---

31 Historically, the term *cholo* referred to someone of Indian origin who no longer lived in a rural indigenous community or dressed in Indian fashion and had plebeian class

the psychological characteristics that inform the tempo of MNR militants are the result of this.' And: 'Mobs fought the guerrilla wars of independence; the mob is the natural way in which our people fight their wars, and if the MNR triumphed over the oligarchy it was because it is, in effect, a mob, in the best sense of the Latin American tradition.'[32]

Cholos are, culturally and ethnically, mestizos, but above all they are those mestizos who construct their identity predominantly with cultural elements of local origin. Zavaleta says explicitly that MNR members are *cholos*, and it is implicit that the majority of the factual nation is too. In this sense, nationalist rhetoric, including Zavaleta's, assumes that its audience's cultural composition is similar to that of the authors of the discourse. It is a discourse between equals. The only difference would be the self-perception of the nationalists as consciousness for itself and as the politically organized expression of a cultural mass that is homogeneous in its condition of historically mixed descent. It should be noted, then, that this highest point of consciousness for itself lacks characteristics of purism and teleological linearity in the development of a predetermined national entity and is, rather, an open, pragmatic and tactically flexible synthesis.

In this sense it can be said that there are no significant differences, if there are any differences at all, between the discourse articulated to constitute themselves as political subjects that circulates horizontally among MNR members and the discourse addressed to the rest of the nation. Class differences within the nation are rhetorically secondary.

Now, I am interested in relating this *cholo* identity that Zavaleta proclaims for the MNR to the national pragmatism and the syncretic character that he attributes to revolutionary nationalism. There is a connection between being *mestizos/cholos* and political pragmatism and doctrinal syncretism. It would seem that the *cholos* who have cultural ties at once to ancestral cultures and in the most modern urban society do not have a cultural code with respect to which they must maintain orthodoxy, and so their culture can and must be pragmatic and syncretic; at the same time, it must also be local and national, precisely in order to affirm an identity, a territory and a state that

---

standing, generally an urban artisan or petty trader. By the twentieth century, this came to include mine and factory workers, that is, the proletariat. It has connotations of vulgarity and is often used as an insult. Zavaleta's use of it here involves a defiant recuperation and defence of a stigmatized identity attributed to subordinate and oppressed social groups. [Trans.]

32 Zavaleta, *Revolución boliviana*, pp. 19, 20.

correspond to them. The revolutionary nationalist project is not to make real or carry on, now in freedom, with the old cultures of the area; rather, it is a mestizo project, elaborated by and for mestizos.

The Bolivian nation is thought around this idea of a nation of *cholos*. The old oligarchy of landlords and mine owners neither dared nor wished to think of the idea of a Bolivian nation. On the other hand, neither did the indigenous cultures, given that they were already nations and Bolivia was for them a form of domination and exclusion. The Bolivian nation is basically a *cholo* idea, but it is an idea that begins to germinate in a moment of encounter with the other inhabitants of the country, in the Chaco War which made them equals at the same time as it made them feel they were not integrated. The trenches brought together middle classes, proletarians, Indians and soldiers. In the Chaco, the combatants understood that they were the germ of a nation that had to be converted into a nation-state.[33]

In the nationalist narrative, this is a landmark in the development of national consciousness, and it interprets post factum the historical events between this war and the revolution as the first steps towards the collapse of the semi-colonial order, and as a sovereign affirmation of the Bolivian nation.

The *cholos* know that Bolivia is not homogeneous, indeed that the process of cultural-racial mixture is not, but they try to forget this or put it aside, so as to produce a discourse of unity and, thus, produce the Bolivian nation in their image. Revolutionary nationalist rhetoric in Zavaleta's version insists on the similarity of the MNR to the rest of the Bolivian nation; this is why he identifies the political form and struggle of the MNR with the guerrilla tradition of the so-called Bolivian people. With the idea of the MNR as a *cholo* party, he identifies or makes culturally equal the authors of nationalist discourse with the audience that receives it. Through the idea of the mob, he identifies these same speakers and their audience in the moment of political mobilization and struggle.

The nationalists of the MNR were a group of conspirators who could also be a mob or form part of one, since they were *cholos*; but this was, once more, a discursive possibility both before and during 1952. The MNR does not have a similarly convincing discourse on its identity for its period in government. The references to the past are not adequate for contemporary practices.

I want to return now to the epigraph from Bakhtin. Zavaleta's texts are directed to two types of consciousness or audience: on the one hand, members of the factual nation or of the nation for itself, and on the other, their enemies.

---

33 Zavaleta, *Revolución boliviana*, p. 44.

The rhetorical strategy developed for the first group supposes that he is speaking to equals with a shared cultural framework. This is an almost horizontal discourse. It is a kind of dialogue with these equals, in which he warns them of the present dangers for the sovereign realization of that national community, centred on the debate over the model and method of development, a choice in which the fate of the nation is at stake.

At the same time, he interprets the history and meaning of events that constitute the process of development of national consciousness. It is a kind of interpretative memory, one that does not serve to recognize a cultural tradition in the past but, rather, to affirm the constitution of a politicized identity in the present conjuncture. It is also as if he were speaking to another who is, at the same time, himself.

He speaks to his fellows to affirm and develop a national self, which, as he conceives it, is also the condition of realization of the individual self. One may think that when one speaks to others in order to reaffirm oneself, this is a monologue, although it may involve a community. But it seems to me that in this case there is a kind of dialogue, that, while the rhetorical strategy and the ontology of this discourse proposes a homology between the identity of the producer and that of the receiver, they are texts that are motivated by the recognition of the existence of differences that threaten their collective destiny and, therefore, make it necessary to determine a specific path for that community of men who can only define and redefine themselves in history. In this sense, they are arguments within a community of equals who, nevertheless, do not agree on how they should develop and direct themselves. It is therefore necessary to establish a dialogue within the community to which a common identity is attributed. Of course, each time that a real dialogue is established, that identity is revised or brought into play, so that it can be reaffirmed, developed or modified.

The notions of negative and positive otherness are useful here. The negative otherness of the nation refers to the receptor assumed in the rhetorical strategy under discussion. Zavaleta's texts refer to a negation of the nation by imperialism, by the Clique, finally by the set of practices and agents that perpetuate the semi-colonial condition. Zavaleta's texts are conceived as part of a negation of negation, or as negation of the negative otherness of the nation. This is otherness in two senses: as an externality and a force that denies autonomous development, and in the sense of alienation from oneself.

Zavaleta writes:

[T]o say that the man of the semi-colony is a parody of himself and owner of nothing is no more than a mockery that expresses the truth. In effect, he is a being who has not identified himself and one could well write at the same time that he is an incomplete being [. . .] an exile in his own home.[34]

The nation has a negative otherness within itself, which is that moment of alienation, of incompleteness.

In contrast, it can be said that the positive otherness of the nation is that which is not yet, or its possibility of emancipation, which is contained in its actual being, in the struggle between its denial and the affirmation or development of a freely chosen possibility.

I say *otherness* because the exercise of sovereignty which negates the negation, a project not yet made reality, is a qualitative change, an Other that has overcome itself; it is a desired other self. As long as it is not made real, it continues to be a positive other because it guides the forces of autonomous self-development.

Zavaleta's discourse assumes that negative otherness as one of its recipients, precisely in order to deny and confront it through the affirmation of a possibility of its own national identity, an affirmation that has to be at the same time a development. In this sense, it contains the relation with its positive otherness.

It seems to me that Zavaleta's discourse or texts of this period develop a set of dialogical relations in three directions: first, a debate and dialogue within a collective self to determine a particular form of development; second, and as a precondition for the first, a conception of positive otherness, which functions as a regulative idea both on the symbolic level of projection and on the pragmatic-political level; and third, the critique of negative otherness, including both external domination and the alienation of the nation.

Thus, the ontological polarity of the rhetorical strategy can be extended, without denying it. In any case, this is a dynamic ontology, which does not present a static image of the reality it thinks, since this is a discourse that does not only explain and interpret its social reality but also constitutes it. This ontological dynamism is accompanied by a politicization of the discourse that makes it possible, since as Zavaleta himself says, politics is the forward-looking definition of the polis.[35]

---

34 Zavaleta, *Formación*, p. 21.

35 Zavaleta, *Revolución boliviana*, p. 7.

I discovered, retrospectively, that this interpretation of Zavaleta's discourse is congruent with the way in which Paolo Valesio and Kenneth Burke characterize rhetoric. For Valesio, the whole universe of language is the object of rhetoric and that rhetoric is the key to ontology because it constitutes the principal instrument for showing that ontology is an ideological construction.[36] Burke writes: 'Rhetoric deals with the possibilities of classification in its partisan aspects.'[37]

The object of this chapter was to show that Zavaleta's writings develop an ideologically constructed ontology through a partisan rhetoric that is at once an interpretation and a construction-development of the national self.

Methodological Considerations on Nationalist Historical Revisionism and Social Science

In the discussion of nationalist discourse, one can make another point with respect to the importance of this kind of intellectual work in the production of social knowledge in Bolivia. In this country, the production of social knowledge in the decades before the 1952 revolution, and in those that followed it, has not been presented as a development of social science but, rather, as the development of national consciousness, implying that the production of knowledge has basically been presented as historical knowledge, in relations where ideology and politics are strongly present. I will briefly advance an argument for the importance of the work of these authors, and in particular Zavaleta's, in terms of social knowledge in Bolivia.

The first hypothesis is that social knowledge in Bolivia, in that period, is carried out as historical revisionism, precisely by that group of nationalist authors among which the work of Montenegro, Céspedes and Zavaleta stands out. These authors were historicists; they conceived reality as history and, therefore, their thought was focused on historical knowledge. The task they proposed was to revise the history written from a seigneurial point of view by members of the oligarchy, in which the real, flesh-and-blood nation is absent. The presence and the action of that nation appears in the new history, which foregrounds the meaning and the value of the struggles of resistance against colonial power and in the republican period against oligarchic power,

---

36 Paolo Valesio, *Ascoltare il silenzio. La retorica come teoria* (Bologna: Il Mulino, 1986), p. 146.

37 Kenneth Burke, *A Rhetoric of Motives* (Berkeley: University of California Press, 1969), p. 22.

and after that the struggles to organize among mine workers, artisans and others, for the democratization and nationalization of the country. This is a collective task, and a political task, since the aim of historical revisionism is to put an end to alienation.

In *El desarrollo de la conciencia nacional* [The development of national consciousness], Zavaleta writes that to be alienated is to give oneself up to facts that do not belong to one's own reality and that Bolivians had been in a situation of alienation in which they had not been able to constitute their identity, in part because the exclusionary seigneurial ideology had provided exogenous points of reference for thinking about their own reality, and produced a discourse that denied the national. There were theories about the geographical absurdity of Bolivia, about Bolivia as a sick people. In revising history, the nationalists provided the facts that were absent in the seigneurial version, those which make possible the construction of a self-referential identity.

At the same time as historical revisionism provides knowledge in the sense of recognizing facts previously denied, now incorporated in a new historical narrative with a popular subject, it also serves as the condition of possibility of the political and cultural task of the constitution of a national identity, which is a process of de-alienation. The subject is that which they begin to call the nation, the protagonist of these struggles.

This task of historical revisionism, which could be called the production of social knowledge of an age, is constructed ideologically. Some of the elements with which social and historical knowledge is produced are of an ideological character. In the case of nationalist revisionism, this refers to the overarching historical ontological duality of nation and anti-nation, which is the criterion of selection and interpretation of the facts that are incorporated into the new historical narrative.

The regulative idea of the nation, on the one hand, is a political objective to be constructed and made real; on the other, it is a referent for the construction of individual and collective identities. Finally, as a condition, it is the body of the practical subject of this life project. This idea serves to dismantle the existing seigneurial history; that is, the ideology of the nation serves to produce new knowledge about the past, not only in the sense of information but also in the sense of constructing political and cultural products.

To backtrack a little, it could be said that the political objective of the nation-state is sovereignty. A nation in those conditions is what motivates the historical revision that will produce new knowledge. In brief, there are political motivations that induce the revision of existing beliefs and the production of a new narrative of social processes or the history of the country.

Given the form in which the nationalist historians conceived reality, this historical revision ended up being also a redefinition of being or of reality in local conditions. This ontological conception of history or realist historical ontology is the basis on which history is revised and has a collective subject: the nation. This allows one to say that a predominant feature of this historical revisionism is a kind of methodological collectivism.

Individual actions and motivations are explained and interpreted in relation to the movement of macro-subjects, in particular the nation, of which they feel themselves to be an integral and constitutive part, in an active sense. This does not mean that the historical narrative is reduced to the movement of these macro-subjects which are the foundation and the interpretative framework of individual actions and events.

In fact, the histories written by Montenegro, Céspedes and Zavaleta are rich in the narration of particular events in which they also recognize individual responsibility. A conception of history as thus constituted by these macro-subjects does not deny the dynamic of individualities, but the macro is the key to interpret them.

This responds to what Zavaleta as well as the other authors called at some point the popular need for heroes. National liberation struggles need heroes to remind them of the struggles of resistance, to symbolize the moments when the nation mobilized to resist or to advance in the conquest of its freedom.

A hasty and superficial reading of these authors might lead to the conclusion that they do not take social structures into account and they explain histories on the basis of individuals' intentions. Individuals stand out in all the books they produced, but a consideration of the organizing framework of their historical revision as a whole brings into sight that structure which has been called dual ontology, the presence of macro-subjects that configure reality. In more contemporary terms, this might be called methodological collectivism.

I now want to propose a broader hypothesis. I think this historical revisionism of the revolutionary nationalists makes possible the development of the social sciences in the following decades.

The first moment of the history under analysis here is that of a kind of politics of non-recognition of social equality, or the seigneurial ideology that thinks of hierarchical difference as natural. There is a passage from this first moment of non-recognition and of natural difference to the moment of the project of nationalist equality, which is proposed on the basis of an assumption of homogeneity. The third moment is that which could be called free pluralist recognition of differences, which is a phase that we have only recently entered in social sciences and research in Bolivia, in the last few decades.

Nationalist revisionism substitutes, as a conception of society, equality for that of hierarchical natural difference; but this is not so much the universalist equality of the Enlightenment as equality as members of the nation. The conception of our historical reality as configured by two opposed parts, the nation and the anti-nation, which are not equal, implies an idea of the equality of the members of the nation. This also responds to the political need to constitute a collective identity, and to constitute the nation as a political subject.

The problem of unity predominates over the rest and, as a result, here the idea of the community and the homogeneity of the nation predominates over the need to recognize and explain the differences among the collectivities that compose it.

In terms of problems of knowledge, the passage is from the politics of non-recognition of seigneurial ideology to the politics of recognition of cultural, political, historical and local— not universal—equality among the members of the nation, of the subject that is to be constituted. History is revised looking backward, not to recognize the various differences denied by seigneurial history but to recognize a unity constructed in the moment when that history is rewritten. That is, the unity of events or of the subjects of struggle was probably not something given at the time when they occurred, but is constructed in this rewriting or new narrative of our history, which, in this way, is also a redefinition of the reality or the social being of the country.

This homogenizing hypothesis of nationalist historical revisionism consists in recognizing facts denied by the dominant history and, as a result, producing a new knowledge of our history which is at the same time new knowledge about our historical being in the present or for the present.

This can be seen from the distance of years. It is a hypothesis that also conceals the knowledge of the differentiation and complexity of what they called the nation. My interpretation is as follows: it is this homogenizing hypothesis of the nation in the historical revisionism of the revolutionary nationalists that allows them to produce new historical knowledge about the past and also about the present that they were living. Without that moment, without that work carried out by historical revisionism through the hypothesis of homogeneity, it might not have been possible today to propose the problems of knowledge of Bolivian diversity. The recognition and, above all, the construction of the common identity of the Bolivian nation is the first step and also the condition of possibility necessary to be able to propose, later, a knowledge of the diversity that it contains, in terms of history, culture and political life.

We can push this point further. The recognition of the equality of persons in political and social reality creates conditions for the development of knowledge and above all, for self-knowledge.

The recognition of the equality of persons has been accompanied in Bolivia by a nationalization of power, to put it in Zavaleta's terms. This is produced by the revolution.

CHAPTER THREE

Moments of Nationalism

Political-Ideological Phases of Nationalism:
Departure, Manoeuvre, Arrival

I will now refer to a stage in which a current of revolutionary nationalism goes on, in the 1960s, to carry out a political critique of national reality as governed by the MNR beginning in 1952 and, as of 1964, by a military dictatorship strongly supported by the US.

It turns out to be significant that the most lucid analysis and sharpest critique of the period come from the ranks of nationalism itself, from a current represented by Sergio Almaraz and René Zavaleta as its intellectual wing. I will consider this phase in the context of those which preceded it in terms of a process of change and continuity. To this end, I use the framework provided by Partha Chatterjee's theory of the phases of nationalism.[1]

My intention is not to prove the correctness of this theory by applying it to Bolivia, but to use it as a basis on which to introduce variations that respond to the Bolivian process. Chatterjee proposes a general theory on nationalism for processes that arise in colonial societies and their subsequent processes of independence. I aim to test this theoretical scheme, and modify or supplement it where Bolivian history suggests other conditions.

Chatterjee's theory consists in the following. Three political-ideological moments can be distinguished in nationalist discourse: the moment of departure; of manoeuvre; and of arrival.

The moment of departure consists in the encounter between national consciousness and the framework of knowledge created by post-Enlightenment rationalist thought, which gives rise to a cultural differentiation between East and West.[2]

---

1 Partha Chatterjee, *Nationalist Thought and the Colonial World: A Derivative Discourse* (Minneapolis: University of Minnesota Press, 1993).

2 Chatterjee, *Nationalist Thought*, p. 50.

The second moment, that of manoeuvre, consists in a combination of a war of movement and a war of position. The aim is to affirm and consolidate the nation, denying what is modern or Western, which means a preparation for an expanded development of capitalist production but through a discourse that is articulated to an anti-capitalist, above all anti-imperialist, ideology. As Chatterjee says: 'The development of the thesis by the incorporation of a part of the antithesis.'[3]

Finally, the last moment, that of arrival, is a discourse of order, concerning the rational organization of power. It is a discourse that amends previous divergences and contradictions at the same time as it incorporates in one body of discourse all the aspects and phases of its history of formation. At this moment, it becomes a passive revolution.[4] For Chatterjee, passive revolution is the generic form of transition of colonial countries in their processes of political independence and of modernization in the capitalist sense.

In the first moment, that of departure, the central point is the relation to Western thought. It is true that the idea of the nation and the project of a sovereign nation-state come from Europe, given that they all arise and take root mostly in intermediate groups who participate in some way in capitalist economic relations, or are linked to global commerce and markets and the urban centres that they foster.

The benchmark of individual and collective realization thus proceeds from what is considered to be the complete modern ideal or optimum, although with local roots, since the principal matrix of formation of these individuals is some combination of the predominant Western culture and local elements.

The principal objectives of Bolivian nationalist discourse, above all that studied here, are independence and autonomy for its own development, for which one must procure the structuration of a unitary, sovereign nation-state. Sovereignty implies political independence in the selection and direction of the economic model, and, above all and in the first instance, sovereignty over natural resources and the most general conditions of production.

---

3 Chatterjee, *Nationalist Thought*, p. 51.

4 Chatterjee, *Nationalist Thought*, p. 51. Passive revolution, a Gramscian concept, implies a process of successive and partial reforms by which there is a passage from one kind of society to another without loss of power on the part of the previous dominant bloc. It is a process of reform and transition directed from above, by the state, in which the dominant bloc itself is transformed.

In a first stage of nationalist thought, the aim is to differentiate Western culture from one's own, in Chatterjee's sense, the production of a consciousness of a valuable and vital difference. This might be in terms of race, or in terms of ancestral cultural roots; most often, it is on the basis of *mestizaje*, the particular result of the blending that the conquest produced in racial and cultural terms.

In this sense there is a line that runs from Tamayo,[5] who argues in terms of race, to Medinaceli, who centres his argument concerning the possibility of the development of the nation on American cultural-racial mixture. There is a first phase in which the national problem is considered, in the first decades of the twentieth century, in terms of race and culture.

With Montenegro and Céspedes, nationalism becomes a basically political discourse whose objectives and articulating axes are real political independence or sovereignty as a nation-state. Race and culture, as atemporal essence, are not the nucleus of articulation of the nation in that period; rather, it is the political history of popular struggles for freedom, first from the Spanish yoke and then from the oligarchic and at times despotic domination and government that continued under the republic.

In this sense, notions and values such as collective freedom, sovereignty, political dignity and the direction of the country's economy become the nucleus of nationalist discourse. It is a nucleus that is political and historical in character, no longer racial and cultural. What worries these nationalists is economic exploitation, the sacking of the country by what they called the Clique [*rosca*], which includes natives and foreigners on the one hand, and the condition of servitude and political abuse of the popular sectors, flesh of the nation on the other.

In this generation of nationalism, it can be said that the ideal of sovereignty basically proceeds, as Chatterjee says, from post-Enlightenment thought. It is an imported ideal, but the aim is to make it real on the basis of the Bolivian people and not the power elites who generally maintained themselves by denying the political condition of citizenship to the mass of Indians and workers.

In the first chapter, we saw how, in his youth, Zavaleta shared the first culturalist mode of conceiving the period with the affirmation of an autochthonous identity and destiny. In a second moment, we saw how Zavaleta shares the historical and political conception and formulation of nationalism in the style of Montenegro and Céspedes.

---

5 Franz Tamayo, *Creación de la pedagogía nacional* (La Paz: Puerta del Sol, 1981).

Now is the time to consider how on the basis of this ideological matrix formulated in those more political terms, a version with a more economic axis is developed. There is a nationalist discourse whose principal concern is economic development, the modernization of the Bolivian economy and the extension of capitalism to the whole of the country, substituting the mining-enclave economy of the bourgeoisie as it existed before 1952. Its project is the creation of a national bourgeoisie to substitute the mining bourgeoisie, which was anti-national.

The first and principal document that expresses this is the *Manifiesto a los electores de Ayopaya* [Manifesto to the voters of Ayopaya], from 1946, written by Walter Guevara Arce, who, together with the party leader, Víctor Paz Estenssoro, was a principal representative of this version. In this conception, the middle class becomes the political nucleus of the nation, conceived as the leaders and moderators of the process of capitalist reform and the germ of a new bourgeoisie.

The politics of passive revolution are articulated or given on the basis of this nationalist discourse of economic reform, but in a very peculiar situation. It is the case of a passive revolution by the dominant group of the MNR in government, in the context of a process originating in a popular uprising followed by broad mobilization that had the potential to develop greater radicalization and autonomy with respect to the government.

This is not a kind of passive revolution that might have evaded from the outset the insurrection and the revolutionary moment of substitution of classes and power relations. There is a political subject that substitutes the old dominant class and aims to take its place as a new and modern bourgeoisie, but in the end a bourgeoisie just the same. In this sense, it is concerned with controlling the process and the energy of the populace, aiming to implement gradual and no-longer-radical reforms. And so as to avoid problems with the North Americans who are now their allies, they choose what Zavaleta calls physiocratic development.

The nationalist discourse of gradual reform and bourgeois modernization contains what Chatterjee calls the development of the thesis by introducing part of the antithesis. Before 1952, the discourse of revolutionary nationalism was anti-imperialist in its enunciation. Afterwards, the predominant sector of the MNR abandoned this and substituted a language of alliance with foreign capital, since the imperialism identified with the Clique had been overcome.

It is symptomatic that Carlos Montenegro's last book, *Las inversiones extranjeras en América Latina* [Foreign investment in Latin America], should not have been published in Bolivia until 1984, after its first edition in Argentina in 1962, almost 10 years after its author's death in 1953.[6] In this text he maintains that:

> [T]he political character of foreign investment allows one to understand that money from abroad is not, as is supposed, an invariable and deliberate agent of progress and civilization, wherever it goes. It can, on the contrary, constitute an effective medium—deplorable proofs are witness to it—of impoverishment and decadence, and an internal source of threats to the security, power, independence and peace of the peoples.[7]

After 1952, anti-imperialist discourse persists in the workers' wing of the MNR while it fades and disappears among the party leadership. It will re-emerge in the ranks of revolutionary nationalism in the moment of its political crisis, and in the phase of strong US presence which will be the subject of this part of the present book.

First, however, I am interested in continuing to develop some thoughts on the moment of arrival of nationalist discourse. One of the characteristics indicated by Chatterjee is the articulation of the discourse, now the expression of the state, with all the previous moments of its history but as a discourse of a new order.

The dominant nationalists remind their audience of the negative realities that the revolution is supposed to have overcome, at the same time as privileging as the task of the present precisely the construction of the new state order. They have recourse to the struggles of the past according to the necessities of the new political state.

In some cases, aspects of its history are included in order to neutralize and eventually eliminate and forget them. This is the case of political and economic anti-imperialism. To make use of a previous distinction, it can be said that when revolutionary nationalism is emitted from the party and above all from the state, it eliminates and neutralizes the anti-imperialism of the last, which still persists when it is emitted from its social bases.

---

6 Juan Albarracín Millán writes in his Introduction to the book: 'The book, which would have had significant potential before April 1952, later became an obstacle to the plans of international cooperation and aid' (p. 8).

7 Carlos Montenegro, *Las inversiones extranjeras en América Latina* (Buenos Aires: Coyoacán, 1962), p. 13.

The party, after 1952, basically becomes the party of order, precisely that which it is itself re-organizing as an amplifying reform of capitalism in Bolivia. It is at this moment that the economic version of nationalism becomes the official discourse and is the basic ideology of the passive revolution phase of the regime.

In the several periods discussed so far, with the exception of the first two articles mentioned, Zavaleta participates strongly in the ideal of the nation-state and its economic and political sovereignty. His political horizon is modern and Western, although this does not deny local history; the aim is to realize the second on the basis of the first.

He shares the idea that the sovereignty of the nation-state will be achieved through the development of heavy industry in the country, although he does not share the idea of creating a new bourgeoisie even as a transitory phase. One deduces from his polemical writing on the topic that he rather imagines a sort of state capitalism without a bourgeoisie, which avoids the appearance of a new class with private monopolies of the means of production, thus making possible a not-too-distant transition to socialism, once favourable conditions have been created through industrialization and the development of the productive forces and the internal market that they would generate.

It should be recalled, however, that in the years of his articles in *La Nación*, he was in favour of the arrival of private foreign capital in order to foment development in the country, which suffered a deficit or scarcity of resources for investment. This vision of his youthful and primary adhesion to the MNR is displaced later on by the last conception I have expounded.

I recall these moments here in order to link them to Chatterjee's hypothesis. The young Zavaleta, as a typical nationalist of the period (although in the tradition of Montenegro and Céspedes), shared the ideals of modernization and national sovereignty of Western origin. He also participates in the phase of the arrival of revolutionary nationalism when it is a discourse of the new political order. As a journalist of *La Nación*, he supports the official government line, which he himself will later call physiocratic or secondary, when he represents a different position, neglected and defeated within the government, which is that in favour of heavy industry.

Nationalism's Farewell: Requiem and Fall

Until now I have tried to exploit Chatterjee's scheme which I have found very useful to examine phases of nationalism. On the basis of the history of nationalism in Bolivia, I consider that one has to think of a fourth moment in order to account for the specificity of Bolivia.

This is the moment of the separation of one current of revolutionary nationalism which is not that of the majority but is the most consistent, and which makes a political, ideological and historical critique of the implementations of nationalism and its party in the exercise of state power. It consists in demonstrating how, historically, the practices, programs and results of the government that proclaims itself nationalist implement weakly, or work against, what the doctrine, ideology or discourse enunciates as its political and economic aims.

Following Chatterjee's model—departure-manoeuvre-arrival—this fourth moment (which is not general but only partial) could be called the moment of farewell. It is a discourse of deception, although its critique is lucid and self-conscious; it is a moment of crisis. This current, which diverges from the trunk that continues to be a discourse of order, is generally that of those whose roots are in revolutionary nationalism in the tradition of Montenegro.

The outstanding expressions of this moment are Sergio Almaraz's *Réquiem para una república* [Requiem for a republic] (1969) and René Zavaleta's *La caída del MNR* [The downfall of the MNR] (1970). These titles are already symptomatic of this critical nationalist consciousness concerning the destination of the process.

Something is dying; nevertheless, these writings are not laments but analyses of the causes of the defeat and collapse, in the very entrails of the forces that constitute the new Bolivian reality, and of US intervention.

These works have individual and collective antecedents. Almaraz had carried out significant work, first in defence of sovereign national control of petroleum, presenting its history from the first decades of the twentieth century and the formation of monopolies at a world level, the context for his political and technical analysis of the oil industry before and after 1952.[8]

Afterwards, in the 1960s, he writes *El poder y la caída* [Power and downfall], which is a study of the formation of power structures during the domination of the mining magnates in the first half of the twentieth century, and an analysis of how this power impeded the construction of a nation state; this

---

8 Sergio Almaraz, *Petróleo en Bolivia* (La Paz: Editorial Juventud, 1958).

in its first part. The second part is a narration of the internal failures in the installation of foundries under the MNR government. It is narrated on the basis of his personal participation, combined with an analysis of the forces that boycotted or supported the project. It already announces how, within the very leadership of the national revolution, some of the causes of the frustrations of the strategy of independence and economic development were engendered.

Sergio Almaraz was a militant of the Partido de la Izquierda Revolucionaria (Revolutionary Left Party, PIR) from the 1940s until 1950, when he took part in the foundation of the Partido Comunista de Bolivia (PCB, Bolivian Communist Party). In 1955, he resigned from the PCB. In the 1960s, he began to collaborate with the MNR government in the Labour Ministry and on occasion in the Ministry of Mines, when Zavaleta was minister.[9]

In January 1964, not long before the military coup of that same year, a group of the MNR published *Un llamamiento para la constitución del frente de liberación nacional* [A summons to the constitution of the National Liberation Front], which called for the formation of movement within the party with the aim of defending the revolution and returning to a nationalist ideology.[10] In it, they characterize the process as follows: 'The measures imposed by the national revolution have been deformed by the undermining work of imperialism and the fifth column of its national servants who have embedded themselves in the popular front.'[11]

The principal enemy is still imperialism whose interests are antithetical to those of semi-colonial countries. Bolivia is characterized as still being a colonial factory.[12] That is the condition that they propose to overcome by defending the nationalization of the mines and the installation of foundries. The key political point is, above all, a call to return to policies based on the workers' struggle, since 'there can be no revolution without a workers' movement'.[13]

The imminent problem is the fracture of the party: '[D]ivisionism threatens to leave the party without a working-class base, threatening the force that until today has upheld the National Revolution. In these conditions, and

---

9 References taken from the biography of Sergio Almaraz included in CISO, *El pensamiento de Sergio Almaraz* (La Paz: Centro de Investigación de Sociología, 1993).

10 MNR, *Un llamamiento para la constitución del frente de liberación nacional* (La Paz, January 1964), p. 4.

11 MNR, *Un llamamiento*, p. 3.

12 MNR, *Un llamamiento*, p. 15.

13 MNR, *Un llamamiento*, p. 19.

having procured that the working-class faction join the opposition, the conditions would have been given for the fall of the regime.'[14]

With regard to the workers' movement, which was key to the duration of the MNR government, there is an awareness of the political implications of rupture with the party. On the other hand, with regard to the army which was already about to stage a coup, there is only a brief and general allusion to anti-national groups trying to betray their role and confront their own people.

Zavaleta's copy of this document includes notes that suggest his disagreement on various points and, above all, at the end, where he expresses doubts about the document's signatories, with the exception of Ñuflo Chávez, in a list among which Zavaleta's own name appears. I have not mentioned this document in order to attribute authorship to him but, rather, as an indication of movements within the MNR.

In November 1964, the army carried out a military coup that put an end to 12 years of government by the MNR.

Zavaleta goes into exile in Uruguay, during which time he writes for *Marcha* in Montevideo and *El Día* in Mexico. I will consider his characterization of the dictatorship and continental politics in a series of articles from these years. There are three centres of his analysis: the characterization of dictatorship; the imperialist plan; and the workers' resistance.

> The two faces of the military dictatorship in Bolivia are, in effect, a rigorous alignment with US foreign policy [...] and, in economic matters, the total de-nationalization of state entities created by the Revolution, the methodical handover of all reserves and the general Americanization of the national wealth of the mines, the only sector capable of generating internal reserves and creating a national capitalism.

> Economic de-nationalization, the systematic practice of espionage, submission in foreign policy and the fabrication of false elections with false candidates, with the expected vetoes, exclusions and interdictions are, without a doubt, characteristic of a common caricature conceived by the Americans for all the countries that fell under their control after the series of military coups of 1964.[15]

---

14 MNR, *Un llamamiento*, p. 21.

15 René Zavaleta, 'Las muertes de abril', *El Día* (25 June 1966). He completes this characterization in 'Muerte de los mineros de Catavi', *El Día* (8 October 1965); 'El derrocamiento de Paz', *Marcha* (29 January 1965); 'Los fracasos del terror', *Marcha* (28 May 1965); 'Barrientos. Realmente parece un norteamericano', *El Día* (15 January 1966); 'Las dos caras de la violencia más brutal', *El Día* (25 September 1965).

On the other hand, there is a diagnosis of the origins of the collapse within the tendencies of the Bolivian process itself. One of these is the MNR's pragmatism which would have been the source of the weaknesses of its economic policy. Zavaleta attributes this to the leadership of Paz Estenssoro, but Siles and Lechín, the other leaders of the MNR, would share responsibility for it: '[T]hey all seem to be perfect parts of an insomniac mosaic; it is a picture where no questions are asked of the Revolution and one gives in to enterprising ideas.'[16]

He also considers that the salary-based policies of the trade unions had gone backwards rather than advance upon the state. As a whole, all this led to the dispersion of power that made a national plan for industrialization and the creation of an internal market impossible. Thus, a national plan is substituted by the imperialist plan.[17]

Almaraz remains in the country and organizes the journal *Praxis*, the principal organ of the left at that time. He also directs the magazine *Clarín* which was more journalistic.

In 1967, Zavaleta and Almaraz can be found organizing what was called the Coordinadora de Resistencia Nacionalista (Organization for Nationalist Resistance) which publishes a document[18] from which I take three significant points for commentary.

The characterization made is that of an occupied country, a situation resulting from a US plan that has orchestrated a wave of coups d'état across the continent. On Bolivia, they write: 'It is a plan aimed at the direct occupation of the strategic sectors of our economy, the destruction or immobilization of the strategic sectors of the social composition of the country and, in sum, the eventual, gradual and systematic de-nationalization of the whole of Bolivia.'[19]

Two strategic subjects in the country are distinguished: the military and the mine workers.

'The US plan of occupation continues inside the army itself, which today is an occupied army as Bolivia is an invaded country.'[20]

---

16 René Zavaleta, 'Los orígenes del derrumbe', *Marcha* (22 January 1965).

17 Zavaleta, 'Los orígenes del derrumbe'.

18 Coordinadora de Resistencia Nacionalista (CRN), *El nacionalismo revolucionario contra la ocupación norteamericana*, La Paz (September 1967).

19 CRN, *El nacionalismo*, p. 5.

20 CRN, *El nacionalismo*, p. 11.

'The miners' unions are the only brake on this imperialist plan, which already controls the key political institutions of the country. […] The miners become, in a way, the natural defenders of economic sovereignty.'[21]

'Violent repression was unleashed on them during the years of the dictatorship and government of Barrientos.'

The final diagnosis:

'[F]acing the new reality, the program of 1952 itself has become inoffensive and the result is a political vacuum.'[22]

The political vacuum consists in the absence of a national articulation between the government and the social base that sustain it.

Almaraz develops this notion in *Réquiem para una república*, and it can serve as an introduction to an analysis and characterization of this nationalism in its final moment.

In a historical vision that articulates the pre- and post-revolutionary past, Almaraz writes:

[T]he traditional masters, great mine owners and landlords liquidated in 1952, left a vacuum of power that the political leaders and the Bolivian elite, not yet mentally and spiritually liberated from half a century of servitude, tried to fill by entering into the service of a new power. Trying to seek a new master is not a question of politics; it is the first psychological movement of an unsettled freedman.[23]

The creation of the economic basis for internal development did not occur because they did not have a perspective of their own. In the last instance, the non-realization of the industrialization of the country is due to this ideological weakness. This, in turn, is explained precisely by the ways in which the mining and landlord oligarchies exercised power.

For Almaraz, the vacuum is made evident when the government loses its popular character and develops a bureaucracy with a developmentalist mentality that adopts and receives US direction and its vision of how countries like Bolivia ought to develop.[24] The best expression of this bureaucracy is the army.

---

21 CRN, *El nacionalismo*, p. 9.

22 CRN, *El nacionalismo*, p. 15.

23 Sergio Almaraz, *Bolivia. Réquiem para una república* (La Paz: Biblioteca de Marcha, 1969), p. 29.

24 Almaraz, *Bolivia*, p. 101.

Almaraz's conception of a power vacuum is basically articulated around the analysis of the leadership elites and their capacity or incapacity to articulate a power structure that would include, although in a subordinated manner, the different classes, thus directed in an economic and state project. This is a more general bias in Almaraz's method of historical analysis, which privileges the study of the dominant pole of the economic and political power structure in explaining the history of the country. *El poder y la caída* is a study of the power of the mining oligarchy or 'old clique'; *Réquiem para una república* looks at what he calls the 'new clique' which is formed after the revolution.

In this sense, it is symptomatic that Almaraz did not write about the workers' movement; even the chapter titled 'Los cementerios mineros' [The miners' graveyards] is no more than an unequalled description of their exiled condition, but precisely about their living conditions and exploitation, not the constitution of the proletarian subject in the mines.

Unlike Almaraz, Zavaleta's writings make evident a progressively more pronounced tendency to study the workers' side of history and to explain it predominantly from this perspective, without neglecting the other.

In *La caída del MNR*,[25] Zavaleta locates the analysis of the power vacuum within a broader conception:

> The events of historical change occur either because politics accumulates or because politics is emptied. In the first case, it is the discontent of desperately starving masses or a shift in the consumption of previously tranquil groups, when politics, which is society in movement, sums up and synthesizes the contradictions.

> Then, the veil falls away and power is violently displaced. Emptiness, in contrast, is the lack of initiative of the masses; for some reason the contradictions do not summon everyone's participation; the classes have retreated. The state is left as no more than an empty shell.[26]

---

25 *La caída del MNR* [The downfall of the MNR], a lengthy manuscript essay which he finished writing in Oxford in March 1970. A short part of this text had previously appeared anonymously as 'Las últimas 24 horas del gobierno de Paz Estenssoro' [The last 24 hours of Paz Estenssoro's government] in *Clarín* 10 (53) (March 1968). The work was published for the first time at the end of 1995 in the collection of his complete works by Los Amigo del Libro. The page citations correspond to the manuscript.

26 Zavaleta, *La caída del MNR*, p. 173.

The rupture of 1952 was caused by accumulation. Emptiness is the result of the decomposition and disarticulation of that revolutionary synthesis of 1952. For Zavaleta, the void left by the working class is filled by the army, and that of the revolution as a whole is taken over by imperialism.[27]

'What is being lived through is a process of loss of form, of power fatigue.'[28]

The time of small things, as Almaraz said.

The situation to which this notion of political vacuum refers is not that of the absence of the exercise of power. In general, it refers to an inorganic relation between state and society, the absence of hegemony in Gramsci's sense. For Almaraz, in reference to post-revolutionary history, the vacuum is because a new elite with its own perspective did not develop. For Zavaleta, above all, it is because the working class did not advance to take control of the state. Both of them point to one of the poles of the composition of the national movement. The conditions of the crisis and downfall would be given by a conjunction of both aspects, which Zavaleta sums up as follows: '[T]his intermediate form, which was like the synthesis of two immature classes (the petty bourgeoisie and the proletariat), produced as a result the "third force", that is to say, the fascistoid tendency, directly introduced by imperialism, ben-efitting from the uncertainty generated by the local classes.'[29]

This brief review of the notion of emptiness will now allow me to present a typology of the nationalism of this phase.

The critique of pre-1952 nationalism centres on the pole of the anti-nation; and when it speaks of the pole of the nation, it tends to do so in a way that presents it as a politically homogeneous bloc. When it relates the history of the nation, it narrates its struggles, resistance, sacrifice; and when it narrates its defeats, they are basically explained by the strength of its enemies. At that political moment, this means a nationalist discourse that aims to articulate the high points of its history of struggle and construct a collective subject that, with political and historical consciousness of the most general contradictions, is mobilized so that that national body should have its sovereign state.

In this fourth moment of nationalism at the end of the 1960s, represented by Almaraz and Zavaleta, the gaze turns to the being itself of the national subject. It becomes a self-analysis. Just as before it was necessary to analyse

---

27 Zavaleta, *La caída del MNR*, p. 42.

28 Zavaleta, *La caída del MNR*, pp. 15, 35.

29 Zavaleta, *La caída del MNR*, p. 65.

the weaknesses of the anti-national oligarchy in order to defeat it, now it begins to analyse its own weaknesses to explain its downfall—the weaknesses in the conjuncture, in the political project, and their historical origins. This is, however, the analysis of internal conditions, since US intervention is the external determination that precipitates it all.

The political vacuum means that the nation did not achieve self-government and sovereignty. In consequence, other particular and external powers exercise their domination: the army and US imperialism. This phase of nationalism, as well as of self-analysis, also has an element of deception and bitterness, which appears in Almaraz.

In this nationalism of defeat two routes can be differentiated, which can be summed up by the names of the works that express them: one is nationalism as *requiem*, developed by Almaraz; and the other is nationalism as *downfall*, developed by Zavaleta.

The first is more an existentialist analysis and consciousness of the process; the second is more a social and historical analysis and, therefore, will become a bridge for the transition to a political and epistemological horizon that will subsume the national issue. The first is a pessimistic diagnosis; the second is not—it involves a consciousness of and in defeat, but it gestures toward a new dawn of the development of working-class autonomy and its irradiation.

I will briefly document these two modalities of the end of revolutionary nationalism.

'The government of the National Revolutionary Movement, before its downfall, lived the time of little things. A spiritual dictatorship enswathed it all.'[30]

'The revolution went on shrinking until it found the size indicated by the Americans, one revealed in turn in the country's own poverty.'[31]

'The Bolivian revolution shrank and along with it its men, its projects, its hopes.'[32]

'A double alienation arises: one material, with the loss of huge natural resources, and the other subjective, eliminating the possibility of the autonomous development of the state.'[33]

The conclusion is:

---

30 Almaraz, *Bolivia*, p. 15.

31 Almaraz, *Bolivia*, p. 16.

32 Almaraz, *Bolivia*, p. 17.

33 Almaraz, *Bolivia*, p. 135.

'A country that has come to such an extreme of depravity does not deserve to exist.'[34]

Here we are at the moment contrary to the development of national consciousness as a collective process. There is a disaggregation or decomposition not only of political leadership but also of the social subjectivity that allows the recognition of exploitation and of sovereign rights to the country's resources.

Almaraz has an interesting analysis of how US intervention becomes a permanent mediation between Bolivians, a decisive presence from local and specific levels such as plans for electrification, schools and so on, to the state's global economic policy. This external mediation between members of the nation generates a lack of communication and, in consequence, the dissolution of the nation, which in the end is the active shared subjectivity of a social body with a memory and projects.

This nationalist discourse narrates the decomposition of the nation, unlike the previous versions which narrated its development. It continues to be nationalism because it is a defence of what is decomposing from within and is disarticulated from without; it is a desperate call to once more nationalize resources and politics. Almaraz's last appeal in this sense was in 1968, in an intervention in a public debate on natural gas in which he participated together with Céspedes and Zavaleta and where he proposed the slogan: 'Nationalize our own government'.[35] This was when Barrientos was still in government, and they were imprisoned as a result.

The *Réquiem* of 1969 is an analysis more bereft of hope. There are no slogans or political lines. It emphasizes the seriousness of the evils it describes. The argument is about the depth of the alienation of the country and the dissolution of the nation. It could be said that it perhaps seeks the force of a requiem, so that the gravity of the announcement of this death awakens a collective consciousness and incites it to suspend those mediations and recover its historical memory so as to provide its own political leadership.

It is an existentialist thought: whoever does not possess their own proper meaning and direction does not deserve to live, or, to put it another way, is already dying.

---

34 Almaraz, *Bolivia*, p. 131.

35 Sergio Almaraz Paz, 'Lo básico. No perder el gas y ganar el mercado argentino para YPFB' in Julio Rojas Arajo (ed.), *Foro nacional sobre el petroleo y gas* (Cochabamba: Editorial Universitaria, 1968), pp 83–111; here, p. 111.

Once the nation no longer has a political project and its external negation has intervened in its internal communication, the defeated nationalist writes: '[W]e only know that this is an annihilated country.'[36]

At this point in history, the only alternative for existence would be on the far side of the previous destruction of the system;[37] in any case, it would be another country, another nation, another process. It would have to be another birth. I deduce this from 'Los cementerios mineros'; it is not explicit.

Réquiem was published posthumously (for the first time in 1969 by the UMSA). Almaraz died in 1968. In 1970, Zavaleta writes in the prologue to an Uruguayan edition: 'His desperation led him to ask for no more than a defence but we now know that that is not sufficient.'[38]

Zavaleta recognizes that it was Almaraz who awoke a consciousness of the need for the defence of oil and other natural resources. Almaraz's nationalism was basically focused on the nationalization of natural resources as the basis of any development to be called one's own, although it was he himself who formulated as a condition for that the nationalization of one's own government, that is, of politics. It could be said that Almaraz's is a defence precisely because it was a nationalism of natural resources which are not subjects of political action. If all that is to be done is the defence of natural resources, it will always be another subject which constitutes itself in order to alienate or defend them in relation to a political community.

It is Zavaleta who develops this idea of subjectivity. Zavaleta's nationalism tends to be more an analysis and constitution of political subjects. This was already noted with respect to *El desarrollo de la conciencia nacional* [The development of national consciousness], and I now return to this in the moment of 'the downfall'.

Zavaleta establishes a relation between politics and historical clarity, in which it is conceived that things happen clearly when politics is more intense, when there is history and not a mere administration of institutions. History is, thus, dynamism, change: '[T]he incorporation of the acts of men in the destiny of the historical progression.'[39]

---

36 Almaraz, *Bolivia*, p. 63.

37 Almaraz, *Bolivia*, p. 63.

38 René Zavaleta, 'Recordación y apología de Sergio Almaraz', Prologue to Almaraz, *Bolivia. Réquiem para una república*, p. 30.

39 Zavaleta, *La caída del MNR*, p. 4.

It is the movement that makes knowledge possible, and the more intense this movement is, the broader the horizon of visibility of society.

Zavaleta inscribes his reflections in a conception that is broader and more articulated than its predecessors:

> If we understand that society is the subject in a state of inertia, that politics is society in movement, that ideology is the form in which society thinks itself, and that history is the relation between politics and ideology, that is, society through politics and ideology, then we will see that it is not enough to know politics in general or ideology itself but rather the society to which they refer, the point where they are fused together.[40]

Politics is society in movement. There was a time when this movement went in the direction of the political constitution of the sovereign nation. But the movement can have many directions, including the opposite, its decomposition. If politics is also the shaping of society towards the future,[41] it is fitting to think here that, when self-definition can no longer be practiced, it is because the point has been reached where the movement of that society is no longer based on the exercise of its political sovereignty; that it has decomposed to such a point that its leadership comes from outside and it moves for others and in self-defence.

When a society moves for others, it begins to fail to recognize itself. Defensive movements permit knowledge of weaknesses which previously might have seemed to be strengths but are not sufficient for self-knowledge. In this line of reasoning, it can be said that one cannot know without having some level of self-government.

This is what the Bolivian process had lost. Zavaleta writes that the MNR had lost respect for its revolution, the peak political moment that gave the Bolivians unity and strength. When this becomes the object of negotiation and pacts between interest groups, the result is division.[42]

This loss of respect for one's own political achievements implies an ideological devaluation and deterioration. The party of the revolution thinks that it is no longer worth fighting for. The subjects of the process come to merely seek personal advantages from. It is what Almaraz calls the time of small things.

---

40 Zavaleta, *La caída del MNR*, p. 7.

41 Zavaleta, *Estado nacional*.

42 Zavaleta, *La caída del MNR*, p. 121.

If the revolution is no longer valued by its own leadership, then, the life of Bolivians is no longer worth anything either. And this is so for the Americans as well as in the self-perception of the defeated nationalists.

Unity is an indicator of high collective valuation just as division is an indicator of the de-valuation of the global process. What does this society think of itself in its moment of unity which is also that of political intensity? That it is possible, that it can be sovereign as a country, that individual freedom for all is also possible. This is the ideology of the moment of unity of the national movement.

In division and separation, the discourse of the self-image of society begins to come from outside, and to be received by some sectors as apprentices of the new modernization prescribed by the US in its cheap and downgraded version for poor countries.

That is, a divided society does not think much of itself because it is disarticulated and, therefore, it does not know itself because its parts do not communicate with one another. If there was a previous moment of unity and self-government, then division is accompanied by alienation, as Almaraz pointed out.

The movement of a society is not homogeneous; there is a sector that, instead of following the general tendency of the MNR, exploited the state of isolation and solitude to develop its autonomy and through it a new perspective for the country. In the majority of the country, separation and division produced alienation; in the workers' movement, they led to the development of self-government, this time centred on itself, no longer within the front of the nationalist movement.

At the end of the 1950s and in the early 1960s, Zavaleta criticized the movements within the workers' movement that fomented its separation and autonomy with respect to the MNR, even labelling them anti-national. The idea of unity as a condition for political development led him to make such judgements. If the MNR contained the workers' movement, there was no sense in duplicating its political existence, which only produced a loss. The idea here is that the MNR contained and synthesized the nation.

For a time, the MNR had been the medium of communication between classes, above all, for the working class which, left to itself, would have remained in solitude. The MNR itself later began to isolate it and break off its communication, a process that continued with the military dictatorship; but as Zavaleta says: 'In the end, a mass horizon still encompassed the political memory of all.'[43]

Two expressions and developments of this are, on the one hand, the defensive nationalism of Almaraz and his comrades, and on the other, the development of workers' autonomy.

At the end of the 1960s, when Zavaleta became convinced that the MNR could no longer reconstruct the conditions of unity of the nation and reconstitute itself as a space of communication and articulation, he began to value more and more this development of political and ideological autonomy within the workers' movement. I believe that this specificity of Bolivian history and the way in which Zavaleta follows it and takes a position on its trajectory explains the transition to Marxism as a central theoretical strategy organizing his thought.[44] The history of the country and of the workers' movement are fundamentally what explain Zavaleta's intellectual trajectory.

In *La caída del MNR*, Zavaleta proposes that history, as narration, is like a second life of the events, and that the events are not complete or do not cease to take place until men interpret them.[45] This essay is an interpretation of the coup of November 1964, which combines a narration of the events from within with an analysis with a degree of critical distance.

In 1964, Zavaleta was Minister of Mines. In that capacity, he was at the centre of the events of the coup, and well positioned to give an account of the events. But he is not only interested in bearing witness to the downfall; he is also interested in analysing or explaining its causes, its origins.

The coup was planned by the US, but the origins of the downfall are internal. This is a feature of Zavaleta's work over several of its stages—the analysis of internal processes is privileged as the basis for explanations that also take into account external intervention.

The 1964 coup is the clearest and most intense situation of open and extensive US intervention, but even so the explanation does not make this into an axis of explanation and much less into a sufficient cause. The gaze turns to internal causes: 'We cannot escape the logical necessity of warning that the origins of the collapse are already present in the same early days of coming to power, in 1952.'[46]

---

43 Zavaleta, *La caída del MNR*, p. 160.

44 This will be the subject of the next chapter.

45 Zavaleta, *La caída del MNR*, p. 138.

46 Zavaleta, *La caída del MNR*, p. 45.

Zavaleta's interpretation, as a second life of the events, is a history that turns back to its origins to explain its destination on the basis of the composition of the events in their moment of initial condensation and the way in which this then is disarticulated, producing its vulnerability. History, as social process, completes the programme contained in its origins, and that history, as narration, first of all completes the events with a reflexive interpretation of those same origins. When social history is intense, that is to say, when the movement of society is swift, the development of the events gives more clarity to the vision or consciousness of their origins and thus makes possible a more self-referential explanation.

If Zavaleta thinks that history is society through politics and ideology and, at the same time, that politics is society in movement, and ideology is how society thinks of itself in movement, *La caída del MNR* is a history of the movement of disarticulation and exhaustion of the revolutionary process, written from the ideology of the national revolution.

With Zavaleta and Almaraz, the thought of revolutionary nationalism reaches a degree of distance with respect to its own events or processes that allows it to become reflexive. This will be translated into a substitution of the nation—anti-nation duality which had served as the organizing principle of nationalist historical thought and on the basis of which the causes of national ills were attributed to the practices of the anti-nation or foreigners, by the idea of internal complexity and analysis of endogenous movement.

Finally, I will turn to some changes in Zavaleta's rhetorical strategy at this moment of the downfall of nationalism.

The first difference consists in that he now articulates a discourse that no longer has as a basic end the constitution of the national being and the choice of strategies for its development but, rather, reflection. The rhetorical mode passes from one of constitution to one of reflection. It is symptomatic of the downfall.

In a moment of reflection in a conjuncture like this one, the writer of the historical-political text does not privilege persuasion of the public but seeks to explain to himself and to those who are committed to the process. When this achieves coherence and credibility, it can become an explanation for the rest.

Another change that underlies the rhetorical shifts is the conception of the structure of reality to which I have already referred: the definitive abandonment of the polar ontology of nation versus anti-nation or anti-fatherland, in favour of an idea of social complexity that internalizes the negating principles and becomes a matrix of historical explanation that is both unified and heterogeneous.

The movement of national society contains both its possibilities and its impossibilities. International politics intensify them but do not create them. It could almost be said that a nationalization is carried out in the conception of the structure of reality. The nation as society is the unity of historical conception, instead of the duality nation—anti-nation.

The moment of the downfall is one of reflection on oneself as a political process; it is a dialogue with the origins and the history of its development, in which the ideal of a sovereign society nevertheless continues to be present as a referential horizon on the basis of which the present is criticized. Projects and political events are contrasted, and the explanation of their lack of correspondence with their own history is sought.

Looking Within

These works by Almaraz and Zavaleta are both products of an inward gaze, written from within the revolution; but there are differences in how they look within that are reflected in the conclusions they reach. I am interested in distinguishing these two modes of looking within concerned with understanding why the revolution failed.

Almaraz directs his attention, on the one hand, to the elites both before and after 1952, and to natural resources. His *Réquiem*, which is not only for nationalism but also for the country as a whole, refers to the fact that in Bolivian history the elites, both the mining oligarchy before 1952 and the new state bureaucracy configured by the MNR, fail to produce a national power structure for the country. A consequence of all this is that natural resources are once more alienated by the same state bureaucracy that takes over the leadership of the nationalizing revolution.

In Zavaleta's work, the inward gaze is orientated differently, as nationalist historical revisionism. It is directed towards that macro-subject, the nation, and aims to understand the causes of the dissolution of this subject. In thinking heterogeneity, it thinks the problems, weaknesses and possibilities of the nation as subject.

In Almaraz's text there is an emphasis on how American presence ends up shattering the revolution in the country as well as the capacity to autonomously articulate political objectives.

Zavaleta studies how, within the same subject that they had previously conceived of as a nation, there is a process of disintegration and division creates the conditions for the growing power of the US to determine internal policies. Zavaleta sees two causes at the same time: the heterogeneity within the nation as subject; and the division produced within it, which consists in the separation between the workers' movement and the nationalist party that sparked the revolutionary moment. He ultimately ascribes the ability of the working class to develop self-knowledge and ideological and political autonomy in that split.

Both Almaraz and Zavaleta decide to look within the revolution. Almaraz describes the internal dissolution as a product of American intervention, which can do what it does as a result of the ideological and political weakness of the country's leadership. The significant difference in Zavaleta's work is his conception of the composition of the nation in terms of subjects. Because of this focus on an active element—on subjects—his internal gaze is more radical, and his evaluation more hopeful.

CHAPTER FOUR

Local History and International Projects:
A Politico-Intellectual Transition

The end of the 1960s and the beginning of the 1970s was a time of critique of the authoritarian and militaristic outcome of the process of 1952. On the one hand, and first of all, there is the challenge posed by Che [Guevara]'s guerrilla forces to the dictatorship and to the state in Bolivia, and then the Bonapartist rupture of that state power with the [General Alfredo] Ovando government. Zavaleta wrote about both of these processes between 1969 and 1971.[1] Here I want to briefly consider the significance of these writings as a reflection on the process and its prior interpretations, and as preparation for the elaboration of a new strategy for an understanding and explanation of history.

In these years, Bolivia experiences the history of its continent via the presence of Che and the guerrilla strategy, as well as through US intervention; at the same time, it lives a sort of return to its recent history through the nationalization of the oil industry carried out by Ovando's government.

However, there is a significant difference: both events occur without the active participation of the Bolivian masses. Che's guerrilla force, given the short time it had to organize itself, did not connect with the popular movement in the country. It seemed that it arrived to construct the political conditions of struggle and revolution starting from zero, as if US intervention had done away with the workers' movement. It arrived and took up the burden of the continental revolutionary struggle but without articulating it on the local and national levels. This is the central point of Zavaleta's analysis.

On the other hand, the nationalization of the oil industry is carried out by a Bonapartist regime that likewise lacks a foundation in the mobilization

---

1 René Zavaleta, 'Reflexiones sobre abril', *El Diario* (11 April 1971), which also appeared in *Marcha* (23 April 1971), as 'Bolivia: desde el Chaco a la patria nueva'; 'El Che en el Churo', dated 8 October 1969 in Oxford and published in *Marcha* (10 October 1969); 'Ovando el bonapartista', *Letras Bolivianas* 9 (June 1970): 14–25; 'Los crímenes de Ovando', *Marcha* (2 April 1971); 'El peor enemigo de la Gulf' in *Marcha* (9 January 1970).

and participation of the Bolivian masses. Ovando, the Bonapartist,[2] operates from a state that had already expelled the masses from government through the MNR administrations and the military dictatorship, and that at the moment of nationalization summons what popular support it had from outside and as a momentary, partial, and, in this conjuncture, inorganic memento of the experiences of 1952; this time it is not the subject of initiative and political autonomy.

But my interest here is not in recapitulating Zavaleta's analyses of this period but in reflecting on its meaning in terms of intellectual history.

This conjuncture of the late 1960s and the early 1970s is at the same time that of the political crisis of revolutionary nationalism and of the dictatorial form that the state organized by the MNR adopted. Zavaleta conceives his task as learning from a distance in time, but not in history; from a moment that remains at the core of modern Bolivian society.

> We must learn everything in the great book of April,[3] in its lost pages. Everything that we are living today has its roots in the events of those days; everything is in that mirror of flames for us to see what has to be done and also what we must not do, because the project of the future is made out of fragments of the past.[4]

The first thing to be noted in this conception of history is the idea that there are powerful moments that configure the horizon and characteristics of a society for a long time afterwards. There are moments of density and intensity that, so to speak, organize the program of what might be the *longue durée*[5] of a society insofar as they create new structures of thought and social organization. It is a historical matrix of determinations, in the sense that each event is fundamentally determined by that central moment and, secondarily, by those other, more immediate processes that precede its occurrence and which, nevertheless, appear to be its direct causes.

Zavaleta emphasizes learning from the facts rather than explaining them. The aim is to learn from the great events of one's own history, events that contain the expression and unfolding of the possibilities and limitations of a

---

2 This is the title of one of Zavaleta's essays.

3 Referring to 9 April 1952, date of the uprising that brought the MNR into government, as a metonym for the revolutionary process that followed it. [Trans.]

4 Zavaleta, 'Reflexiones sobre abril'.

5 See Fernand Braudel, *La historia y las ciencias sociales* (Madrid: Alianza Editorial, 1968[1958]).

society, events that contain the epics and the tragedies of a history. Zavaleta writes: 'April is like an island that comes into sight. In reality, it is a submerged mountain. We only see its summit, but what is important is the existence of a mountain as a totality.'[6] And: 'April was the heroic event of the process of insurrection of the classes of the democratic-bourgeois alliance.'[7]

To learn from the April revolution implies thinking and rethinking, time and again, new experiences and new facts in relation to that event. It does not mean deriving explanations or meaning from the event, but referring reflections on other events to that exemplary moment, and thus correcting and completing our understanding of the facts of political and social life.

This conjuncture of the late 1960s is a moment in which the national project of 1952 is in pieces. This means that its components are disarticulated; Barrientos' government and the Americans made sure of this.

I say that the project is in pieces in the sense of disarticulation, in keeping with Zavaleta's view that the new project is made out of the fragments of the past, that is to say, the project for the future is a new articulation of the unrealized moments of the past, within another horizon of a global program for society.

In the two experiences that Zavaleta analyses, he is concerned with thinking of the events in relation to the projects to which history has given rise, above all that of April 1952.

In 'El Che en el Churo' [Che in El Churo], Zavaleta writes: 'The basic disconnection of the guerrilla force from the peasants and miners, which is merely the prolongation of its political solitude, is the result of its disdain for the past.'[8]

The disconnection of the guerrillas is double: political, in the present, in relation to the local workers' movement; and historical, in relation to the projects and subjects that had agitated for change in the region where the guerrilla forces were located and in the country.

The guerrillas' project was based on a superficial understanding of recent Bolivian history and of the process of the national revolution. It assumed that in Bolivia there were rebellious masses and a dictatorship firmly supported by the North Americans, but it ignored the key fact of the workers' organization and the centrality of the proletariat already established, with prior

---

6 Zavaleta, 'Reflexiones sobre abril'.

7 Zavaleta, 'Reflexiones sobre abril'.

8 Zavaleta, 'El Che en el Churo'.

experience in armed struggle and insurrection. It was another project without local masses, which did have a history and a triumphant one, but a different history.

Nevertheless, it is by circumventing this other history and its political project that part of Bolivian society, the intellectuals and the middle classes, enter into relation with the workers' movement and socialist politics of the country after 1952.

In his assessment of the conjuncture, Zavaleta highlights as the principal merit of Che's guerrilla force having put an end to the separation, ideological above all, between the workers' movement and the middle classes. This project imported from abroad, after its defeat, enabled these sectors to attempt new internal articulations which gelled around the Popular Assembly a few years later, in 1971.[9]

Middle-class participation in the guerrilla insurrection proves the interest of this sector in a leftist project, and that they were not only supporters of the conservative reaction carried out by the military dictatorship and its anti-worker project. If it is the case that the guerrilla forces, bearers of a project alien to the national history, were able to connect the middle classes with the workers' movement, in the post-1952 period, this also means, I believe, that those middle classes were experiencing a certain distancing from and rejection of the post-revolutionary project in general and some of its facets in particular. One of them has to do with social subjecthood. In Bolivia, the guerrilla movement basically recruits individuals from intermediate sectors that, at that time, lacked a project of their own in a country where, on the one hand, there was a class-based workers' movement that had its program and its leaders, and on the other, part of those middle classes participated in the MNR's project of becoming a new bourgeoisie or its political and state bureaucracy.

Zavaleta's reflections on Che's guerrilla movement in Bolivia and its consequences constitute a political and historical analysis of the disarticulations between forces, projects and history in that conjuncture of the political crisis of the 1952 state in its dictatorial phase, within the larger context of Latin American politics.

From Zavaleta's analysis of the April revolution, Che and Bonapartism, we can construct a kind of inventory or summary model of his mode of inquiry in that brief period, comprising the following elements:

---

9 This is the object of the analysis in his book *El poder dual. Problemas de la teoría del Estado en América Latina* (Mexico City: Siglo XXI, 1974).

Thinking the political present in relation to local-national history and the structures it has produced, but thinking on the basis of the political and social subjects and their projects. The aim is to make the present intelligible through an analysis of the projections that collective subjects and a few relevant or representative individuals make through practice, taking into account the historical process that organizes and delimits the conditions of possibility of their realization. Some projects fail or never take off because they ignore the part of the past that is in fact their condition of possibility but becomes their condition of impossibility when it is unrecognized. Other minor projects (as in the case of Che's guerrilla movement) rather appear as the result of historical failures produced by major projects in national history, such as Ovando's Bonapartism, as a result of the crisis of the state of 1952, both in its dimension of dependent bourgeois reformism and in that of Barrientos' authoritarian reordering under US direction.

There is a selective use of history, privileging the moments in which the subjects and projects that mark a whole era have been constituted and that they have lived through. This is not a history of data and processes petrified in the documented concatenation of proven facts but, rather, a living history in which it is most important to consider political and historical projects and the constitution of their practices, their origins, present relevance and force, in relation to the history and structures that they aim to transform, reform or maintain.

In thinking the projects and subjects of the present, Zavaleta refers to a primordial historical moment so as to evaluate whether the tempo and the actions of existing forces have exhausted or overcome, continue or transform, the moment and the content of their origin, and in what measure or with what intensity, with what limitations and prospects.

In this conjuncture of the end of the 1960s, Zavaleta basically evaluates political projects from a party position; but the aim is not to evaluate the others in relation to his own so as to prove that it is superior and more adequate. It is an evaluation of political projects in relation to history and its structures, in relation to knowledge.

Here there is (as was proposed in reference to *La caída del MNR* [The downfall of the MNR]) an evaluation of political projects that is at the same time a historical revision; that is to say, the evaluation of political projects is a task that must be carried out and begun as a cognitive investigation. The aim is not a mere calculation and balance of forces; it is also a historical reflection. The failures have to be explained on the basis of the processes of their past and not by mere individual ineptitudes and incapacities, possibilities and desires. The novelty they may contain must also be considered.

The writings of those years can be more generally characterized as combining elements of sociological and historical analysis, which is what gives them a measure of distance and analytical depth, together with a partisan and ideologically interested evaluation of the revolutionary projects and of the fate and possibilities of the national revolution.

It is an interest in the political dimension of the project that demands a socio-historical analysis. In order to position oneself politically, one must know and understand history and think the conjuncture historically, which means thinking of oneself as a product of that history, and as a more or less responsible part of it.

In these writings, there is a more or less balanced combination of these two components—socio-historical analysis and politico-ideological assessment-analysis, in which the politico-ideological interest that governs the cognitional element predominates, although the resulting analysis is mainly historical and sociological.

If one considers that the intellectual process includes not only the arguments set out in what is written but also the motivations for researching and articulating them, it can be thought that politics is what demands the development of historical and social knowledge, even if the result is that the latter permit one to think more broadly about politics and with the strength and profundity that only reflexivity can provide.

In Zavaleta's first nationalist writings, the political and ideological component predominates, above all, in the comprehension and explanation of history and society. His later works are characterized by the predominance of this second component. The writings of the years under consideration are an intermediate combination, in transition from the first type of composition to the second, with the general characteristics already indicated.

Theories such as that of social classes and of Bonapartism, for example, which serve functions of narrative and analytical support and structure, nevertheless appear subsumed by the historical reflection. This is a historical and political reflection that makes use of theories, but the weight and extension of history is such that it overwhelms these theories until they end up as narrative props which articulate and organize his thought on Bolivian political history.

If for a moment one turns one's attention to the rhetorical dimension of these writings, it can be noted that a privileged audience is the Bolivian left, above all the nationalist left and the left that developed in response to the experience of Che's guerrilla movement.

In these writings, Zavaleta emphasizes the errors and insufficiencies of the Bolivian left, not with the aim of external criticism but, rather, in order to learn from history, above all from the great book of April, as he puts it. On the one hand, it is an exercise in self-criticism, pointing out to the nationalist left which aspects of its program and which forms of political practice have already been shown by Bolivian history to be insufficient and out of date. One must learn from history in order to advance.

On the other hand, he points out to the left that developed out of the experience of Che's guerrilla movement the price one pays for forgetting history; he does not condemn the movement but defends it in order to reduce the distances between the heroic politics of the moment and the country's tradition of struggle.

These writings do not seek to choose between the guerrilla strategy on the one hand and the national tradition of popular uprisings and the organized workers' movement on the other as the axis and nucleus of the national revolutionary movement. Rather, they seem to argue for the possibility or necessity of uniting or combining both experiences or histories, for which it is necessary to criticize the weaknesses of both. One is criticized under the light of the other, and vice versa.

Although the guerrilla movement arrived quite ignorant of local history and the political and strategic nuclei that this had already established, Zavaleta's analysis does not dismiss the pertinence and necessity of revising and criticizing local history and the recent past, on the basis of this guerrilla experience, which, being in part an initiative alien to its process, perhaps for that very reason provides a critical distance, in this case both for political action and for political reflection. Moreover, it is itself already local history, given that Bolivia is the territory where it unfolds.

Zavaleta thinks in terms of a strong interrelation between history and politics. The relation between history and politics, which in my view deserves to be emphasized in this period, is as follows.

I will begin with history. Zavaleta's writings in these years deal with recent political history; now, the aim is not the simple narration of events but an analysis that tries to explain recent political history in light of its more remote past. In this first function, which is that of historical analysis for the purpose of explaining the present, that same past becomes an object of critique by the very present that it conditions and explains.

Zavaleta writes history and political analysis as a mode of learning from history itself, here understood as a global social process. In this sense, his history texts are a reflection on the present and the past, on the tendencies and political possibilities for the future, and not a mere narration of events.

The idea can be deduced from his work that if men do not live their history as a mere sequence of events but also as reflection and projection, then the history and political analysis that is written about them should also contain this dimension with a higher level of reflection and learning.

The historian and political analyst works and writes, first of all, in order to learn, and only thus is it possible and pertinent to socialize and communicate this history-analysis to the community with which one wishes to share the comprehension of those social and historical processes.

Zavaleta's learning process is a rewriting of history or of the past, and not its repetition. The past is a source of learning, of knowledge, of projects, of consciousness, of traditions, but it is also an object of transformation. The present, which needs to think the past in order to generate its explanatory and reflexive historical consciousness, modifies it; that is to say, one learns by recognizing the past but also by transforming it at the same time.

This means that the learning process has at least two aspects. On the one hand, the learning process appears as reflexive consciousness after the fact, but one can also think of it as preparation for new practices and events. One does not learn from history in order to repeat the past but in order not to make the same mistakes again, as a preparation for the production of the new, to open up the future, which is the domain of politics, not in order to fulfil its predestination.

The analysis of the present, and learning from the past through its analysis, entails the organization of the past in terms of present historical thought; Zavaleta thinks that there are privileged referents for analysis and for the learning process. This is implied in his idea that we 'should all learn it from the great book of April, from its lost pages [. . .] in that mirror of flames'.[10]

Politics is the practice through which Zavaleta approaches history. He thinks of history analytically and reflexively in terms of politics, and it is on that basis that both the narration and the analysis of general process are formulated. The consideration of social, economic and ideological structures, for example those of the social classes, is organized by political analysis,

---

10 Zavaleta, 'Reflexiones sobre abril'.

although at the same time they are the conditions of possibility of historical depth in thinking politics.

The analysis of structures and the use of social theory to think them allows one to write the political history of the country. The consideration of structures is what permits an intelligible articulation, whether symbolic or causal, of events and processes.

The other organizing agent of history is politics itself, in the sense in which for Zavaleta it is through political action that men strive to produce their destiny, that is to say, to direct or coordinate all their movements in a determinate temporal and social course; it is in the pursuit of a project, of destiny, in struggles for power, in which events and processes tend to coalesce.

Politics needs to know the past and learn from it because it is conditioned by it. History is the productive form of this relationship.

Politics can change history when it knows it, or knows its neuralgic moments, such as, for example, the great book of April. It can also change it without knowing much about it, as happens with Che's guerrilla movement, but in this case, men have less control over their destiny.

Finally, I will make some remarks on certain rhetorical aspects of these works by Zavaleta.

Two things interest me in his discursive construction of historical reality. First, Zavaleta's analyses have spurred the construction of a more complex reality among Bolivian intellectuals. It is no longer a historical reality that answers to the will of *caudillos*,[11] nor one organized by the nation–anti-nation dichotomy; it is a society governed by a multiplicity of processes, subjects and projects that make up a complexity which, in this conjuncture, generates a crisis due to their lack of confluence or their conflictive disarticulation. The state of 1952 does not govern its society organically. The workers' movement

---

11 This term runs through all the republican and dictatorial history of Latin America and is still current today, but has no real equivalent in English. It refers to a leader who is (usually) both founder and life-long leader of a party or faction and, eventually, a head of state, who is both charismatic and a demagogue and inspires heartfelt and emotional loyalty in his followers. At root, it does not matter if he achieves power via the ballot box, in an armed revolution at the head of the masses or by a military coup. The party or organization he heads depends on his symbolic figure to such a degree that it rarely survives his death or retirement. In Anglo-Saxon politics, the greater institutional rigidity and the downplay of emotion in public performance impede the development of real *caudillo* figures, although John F. Kennedy was probably close to being one. [Trans.]

has been separated from the state program, which is now alien to this society and is more organic to the US; the guerrilla movement confronts the militarized state but is not connected to the workers' movement and its history.

This is a discourse that, at the same time as it constructs the complexity of Bolivian society, as it thinks its history, is a political narration of its conflictive disarticulation, a reflexive discourse on crisis, which is the second point I want to mention.

I call it a reflexive discourse because it does not narrate the impossibility, decadence and end of things but, rather, calls upon us to understand through history, and thinks the reality of the crisis of political power and of the revolutionary projects historically at the same time as it constructs the crisis that thus acquires a dimension of historical and political reflexivity.

PART B

The Workers' Movement, History and Social Science

CHAPTER FIVE

The Workers' Movement and Social Science

The Historical Conditions of the Possibility of Self-Knowledge

At the beginning of the 1970s, Zavaleta undergoes a shift in theoretical strategy towards that which characterizes all of his later work and becomes the basis of his historical and political thought.

The purpose of this chapter and of this second part of the book is to sketch the outlines of this change, and then to analyse Zavaleta's mode of historical analysis and his conceptions of history and politics.

At the end of 1972, Zavaleta finishes *El poder dual. Problemas de la teoría del Estado en América Latina* [Dual power: problems of state theory in Latin America], in which he studies the duality of powers in Bolivia and Chile. This is an analysis carried out in Marxist terms, beginning with a detailed critical revision of Trotsky and Lenin, and continuing with a detailed discussion of the conceptions of dual power upheld by the political subjects of Bolivian and Chilean history. Zavaleta reads these two discourses against the global historical process.

I am not interested in reconstructing the debate on dual power but, rather, in the first place, in accounting for a change in Zavaleta's way of thinking of history in general and Bolivian history in particular from the perspective of the problem of knowledge.

I will use the notion of theoretical strategy to approach these questions. I understand theoretical strategy as an articulation of an open conception of reality (or ontology) with a theory of the processes of production of knowledge of that reality, converted into a programme of research and intellectual production that can expand or correct the possibilities that unfold.

A theoretical strategy includes a conceptual system, that is, structures that operate as means of thinking,[1] as well as ideas concerning the articulation of

---

1 In the general sense of Althusser. See Louis Althusser, 'Philosophy as a Revolutionary Weapon' (1968); available at: https://bit.ly/2xYJCuN (last accessed on 12 December 2019).

the elements it uses and produces along with ideas about the modes of validating its results.

Not all production is the result of a theoretical strategy, at least in the sense expounded here. But I think Zavaleta does work with a theoretical matrix which is applied rigorously and creatively to do historical and political analysis, and to develop more theory.

Previous works of his[2] had already opened the way for a thinking that, in the 1970s, acquires a Marxist language and structure. I can summarize the change in relation to his mode of historical thought with reference to the nationalist strategy as follows, before going on to advance my hypothesis.

As his nationalist thought matures, Zavaleta moves more and more towards a consideration of the structures that history has produced in order to explain the course it takes. It should be emphasized that these are structures produced by a history made by subjects, and not by a history that takes its course within structures whose origin and duration are independent of the events and practices that fill those spaces, without incorporating the effects of their social and political movement. History makes structures, as a mode of persistence in time, but at the same time as a way in which men's practices mark and direct their time, at least in part.

Bolivian nationalism, which was historicist, operated on the basis of the simplification of historical entities at the same time as it carried out their idealization. It made the idea of the nation, for example, into a principle that could be detected in the actions of various subjects and in various moments in which their relation of political contradiction with their negation constituted them as part of this history of emergence. The nation was a historical entity and an idea at the same time, and it was as an idea that the nation could be found at times in the actions of some and at times in the actions of others.

Zavaleta substitutes for this type of conception one of the centrality and primacy of the workers' movement as the nucleus that makes critical knowledge of this society possible. He integrates a thinking on the basis of a specific subject and its history with a more general theoretical strategy for the modern era, namely, Marxism.

The nationalism that was a historical discourse, although it was reductive as well as idealizing, connected revisionism and historical critique with a political project; it was already a discourse developed on the basis of the history of political subjects.

---

2 'El Che en el Churo' and *La caída del MNR*, above all.

Zavaleta articulates his thought on the basis of the history of a more specific subject, which was contained within the nation and was its social nucleus in 1952, with an explanatory theory. This is the axis: the workers' movement plus social science, with the aim of understanding history.

The political project is not eliminated, but it is relegated to a secondary place in the historical analysis. It could be said that it intervenes before and after. Before, it appears as motivation for studying the causes of the failures and limitations as well as the future possibilities of nationalist thought. After, it appears in order to judge and reflect on the past and think the possibilities of the project in the time to come. Obviously, the historical narrative does not express this division, but the mode of elaboration of his analysis of history does.

Here I am talking about a tendency, however; the transition is carried out in a text that is basically a political discussion of tactics and strategy on the basis of a historical and political analysis of two experiences that at the time seemed to open up the possibility of a transition to socialism, but ended in defeat: the Popular Assembly of 1971 in Bolivia and the government of Popular Unity (Unidad Popular, [UP]) under [Salvador] Allende in Chile.

The consistency of the political project also changes. In *El poder dual*, Zavaleta has in mind a workers' revolution in which the construction of the nation is subsumed under the socialist project.

These considerations serve as an introduction to my discussion of Zavaleta's later work, centred in this chapter on history and political analysis.

In the prologue to *El poder dual*, Zavaleta writes:

[O]nly the global analysis of society allows us to penetrate the conjuncture of its appearance. It is knowledge that an individual cannot obtain as individual, a knowledge that does not belong to the classes in general but specifically to the only class that has, in this structure, the capacity to become a universal class, and not even to that class in the abstract but, rather, to the class that lives for itself (that is, when it is and at the same time knows what it is), that is to say, when it becomes a party and, even as such, only insofar as it has within itself the structured will to power and domination. That is what state theory is for.[3]

---

3 Zavaleta, *El poder dual*, pp. 5–6.

And also: '[T]he form of modern society requires that men exist only within social classes; individuals are no more than the mode in which classes exist through them.'[4]

Zavaleta's programme consists in the global analysis of society via its nucleus, which is the class structure, and in particular from the position of the class that can be most universal in terms of knowledge and power.

> In Marxism we attend to reality, that is to say, the objective world, the social classes and their material existence, the scale of their development and the moment of their development.[5]
>
> [...]
>
> One does not adequately attend to reality except when one transforms it. There is no other way to know it. [...] Reality produces consciousness in men when its internal will desires that men should turn towards it and change it.[6]

It can be thought on the basis of this last passage that if one comes to know by transforming reality, on the one hand, nationalist consciousness at that time no longer permitted transformation and therefore it did not serve to know but rather to ignore. In this sense, a theoretical change was necessary in order to know; there had to be a transformation in the matrix of thought. On the other hand, Zavaleta is also saying that historical change or the process of reality changes men's consciousness, thus producing one of the conditions of its transformation.

Thus, Zavaleta explains that history is what changes, produces and develops its own consciousness and the mode of thinking its reality. The theoretical change or the assumption of Marxism as epistemological and theoretical core, according to Zavaleta, is therefore an adjustment or movement to put oneself in alignment with the development of the class struggle and the political history of the country, following the crisis of nationalism as subsumption of the working class in the programme of capitalist reform, and puts forward the possibility and necessity of the development of the workers' autonomy, not only for the class but also for the country.

Throughout the 1970s, Zavaleta writes several essays in which he develops his conception of the possibilities and the privileged mode of knowledge

---

4 Zavaleta, *El poder dual*, p. 5.

5 Zavaleta, *El poder dual*, p. 7.

6 Zavaleta, *El poder dual*, p. 7.

in this period in Latin America and in Bolivia in particular, as well as its problems. So as to avoid repetition, I will not proceed with a chronological analysis of the texts, but organize my analysis around a series of themes.

First, I analyse his conception of knowledge, and then, but closely linked to the first topic, I focus on the relation between history—the workers' movement—and social science. I then focus on political theory and the theory of the state in particular, and finally, I outline the changes in Zavaleta's way of thinking about the state and its history.

In a way that is unique in the Bolivian intellectual sphere, Zavaleta develops in what I will call his second intellectual moment, that of social science, a reflection on the theoretical and historical conditions of possibility of scientific knowledge in a backward society. He does this through an analysis of the relation between, on the one hand, the development of the productive forces and the relations of production, and on the other, the capacity for self-knowledge of a society, which is the Marxist project:

> The problem that concerns us is the question of the possibilities of knowledge of a backward society, that is to say, the relation that exists between the level of development of the productive forces and their repercussions (considering the relations of production as the movement of the productive forces and the political superstructure as the final result of the movement of the mode of production) and the capacity for self-knowledge of a society.[7]

This question about the historical conditions of the possibility of self-knowledge of modern society in general and our own society in particular had not been asked in Bolivia before, and I think Zavaleta's response to it gives greater solidity to his later theoretical work and to our reading of his preceding work, since he reflects self-consciously on the theoretical instruments he himself produced and used to elaborate explanations of historical processes in relation to the historical-social configuration that makes them possible.

How does he think the possibility of self-knowledge of society? At the root is the Marxist idea of reality as a totality of totalities in a process of totalization by the sum of social practices. The constitution of a science of society is made possible by the level of unification or totalization of the world carried out by capitalism: 'Society cannot really be known except when it has been totalized, that is to say, when nothing happens in it any longer with autonomy,

---

7 René Zavaleta, 'Clase y conocimiento', *Historia y Sociedad* 7 (1975): 3.

when everything occurs with reference to the rest, when, in sum, everyone produces for everybody.'[8]

The configuration of the structures and processes of society given by capitalism constitutes a horizon of visibility common to all, but whose maximal or optimal exploitation depends on the place that the knowing subject occupies in the whole of the social relations of production.

For Zavaleta: 'Marxism is no more than the scientific use of the horizon of visibility given by the capitalist mode of production.'[9]

Society is not made explicit for everyone nor from any position, but only from a certain point of view which, in capitalist societies (which are also the first in which social science is possible), corresponds to the proletariat.

This way of presenting the problem is closely linked to that of [György] Lukacs, in its tendency to identify the consciousness of the proletariat with social science, and in the methodological use of the idea of totality.[10]

This idea that Zavaleta sketches following Lukacs supposes that the working class is the subject of social science, which as I see it limits its explanatory potential. This identification follows from locating the exploitation of the horizon of cognitive possibility at the level of the relations of production, since at this level it is necessarily the class that becomes the subject of social science.

With reference to Zavaleta's proposal, one has to ask two questions: If a society's self-knowledge depends on the degree of totalization achieved by capitalism, in what measure are societies such as the Bolivian, where capitalism is underdeveloped, knowable? And, if Marxism is the scientific use of the cognitive horizon made possible by capitalist totalization, is this theoretical strategy pertinent to explain our heterogeneous and backward societies?

---

8 Zavaleta, 'Clase y conocimiento': 4.

9 Zavaleta, 'Clase y conocimiento': 4.

10 György Lukacs writes: 'It was necessary for the proletariat to be born for social reality to become fully conscious. The reason for this is that the discovery of the class-outlook of the proletariat provided a vantage point from which to survey the whole of society [. . .] Thus the unity of theory and practice is only the reverse side of the social and historical position of the proletariat. From its point of view self-knowledge coincides with knowledge of the whole so that the proletariat is at one and the same time the subject and object of its own knowledge.' See *History and Class Consciousness: Studies in Marxist Dialectics* (Rodney Livingstone trans.) (Cambridge, MA: MIT Press, 1971), pp. 19–20.

Zavaleta thinks that the key to self-knowledge in a backward or *motley* society,[11] as he calls it, is the development of the working class within these societies; the development of its consciousness and the diffusion of this consciousness to other sectors of society, and the process of its political organization: 'The proletariat cannot know itself without knowing society as a whole and, therefore, invading the upper classes, the groups that strictly speaking are not classes, that is to say, without the diffusion of its own consciousness.'[12]

It can be said that self-knowledge depends on the development of knowledge by the workers' movement and on its class accumulation in which the acquisition of Marxism as a scientific instrument is an important moment. It is through the development of this subject, the workers' movement, that Marxism becomes, for Zavaleta, an adequate theoretical strategy, one that is superior to others, for the production of our national consciousness and of scientific knowledge of these realities.

The existence of a powerful workers' movement in Bolivia allows one to ask profound questions of a social reality that demands not only explanations and theories but also real transformations. The existential density of this subject supplements, in part, the deficiency of capitalist totalization through the work of organizing this society.

The structural obstacle to knowledge is posited in the following way:

The systematic obstacle for a backward society is rooted in an essential moment: its own sum of determinations makes it incapable of looking at itself; its own evasions and cognitive fragmentations are a prolongation here of the ignorance of those determinations; compensations are the beginning and the end of all its forms of consciousness; and in general, it can be said that it is a society that lacks the capacity for self-knowledge, that lacks even the poorest store of information that could describe it. With relation to its own theoretical vision, this society becomes a noumenon.[13]

---

11 Zavaleta refers idiosyncratically to a 'motley' society (*sociedad abigarrada*) as one characterized by a disjointed heterogeneity. The term does not mean simply plurality or diversity, as in a multicultural discourse, but rather indicates a lack of social articulation in a territory marked by multiple modes of production and historical temporalities.

12 Zavaleta, 'Clase y conocimiento': 11.

13 René Zavaleta, 'Movimiento obrero y ciencia social. La revolución democrática de 1952 en Bolivia y las tendencias sociológicas emergentes', *Historia y Soceidad* 2(3) (1974): 3–35; here, p. 3.

In this type of structural and historical configurations, one cannot achieve the articulation of subject–object whose action can produce reflexive knowledge: '[I]t is not possible to elaborate the concrete-representation abstract-thought-concrete continuum that Marx defined as his sociological method.'[14]

The intellectual work carried out outside this basic articulation is therefore better prepared to ignore and distort than to know; that is, it arises as ideology that narrates and irreflexively sanctions its reality.

All this means that, in Zavaleta's Marxism, there is no epistemological reduction to the relation between class structure and social science. The essential mediation that makes the productivity of this relation possible in the modern world is precisely the subject and its history.

Zavaleta's is a Marxism of subjects within the basic and traditional theoretical structure of Marxism as a theory of the structures of history; but precisely for this reason it is also a theory of the practices of subjects determined by structures which at the same time they organize and reproduce.

The subject–object relation that comes from Hegel[15] is posited in Marxism in such a way that the object is totality, but not of the spirit or single substance that is only diversified in the reality of the time of its development but, rather, the totality of social relations which includes cultural structures and configurations and the objects that these produce. This implies that the knowing subject, which is at the same time the object of knowledge, assumes this totality as the horizon of inquiry and causality of something more particular, such as the existence of a class subject. The subject in this formulation is not the totality but a part of it that occupies a privileged position for cognitive reflexivity.

In this Marxist formulation, the object is the social totality but the subject is not. It is a particular entity that can and must diffuse its consciousness which has a general cognitive value, but which does not validate its intellectual production in intersubjective processes.

This is perhaps the root of the claims to truth and non-dialogical scientificity that some currents within Marxism have developed; that is to say, in

---

14 Zavaleta, 'Movimiento obrero y ciencia social': 3.

15 See G. W. F. Hegel, *Phenomenology of Spirit* (Peter Fuss and John Dobbins trans.) (Notre Dame, IN: University of Notre Dame Press, 2019); *The Science of Logic* (George di Giovanni trans.) (Cambridge: Cambridge University Press, 2015); and Ernst Bloch, *Sujeto-objeto* (Mexico City: Fondo de Cultura Económica, 1985).

the limitation of the epistemological application of the idea of totality to the side of the subject in the subject–object relation.

A more radical application of the epistemological principle of totality within this same conceptual structure would be to expand the principle of totality on the side of the subject, not postulating that anyone and everyone is capable of the same knowledge but, rather, extending the concept of the process of knowledge while maintaining the basic idea of the class nucleus expressed as the workers' movement as a starting point, to a dialogic process with other subjects and ways of thinking. This is one of the routes or modes in which Habermas has proposed the reconstruction of historical materialism.[16]

In these writings of the 1970s, Zavaleta formulates a version of the knowledge-class-totality relation informed by Lukacs' forceful intervention in Marxist theory, that is, the idea that the working class, due to its structural location and its history, is capable of knowing the social totality. This implies that the working class formulates its intellection of totality and then diffuses it to the other subaltern groups and, in the best of cases, to the whole of society.

In his writing on Bolivia, it can also be seen how Zavaleta studies and narrates the diffusion of workers' consciousness to the popular sectors of the country and even beyond the social horizon that tends to organize around the workers' movement.

This theoretical conception is a strong influence here, but it is a history that is explained and validated by it only for a time. Zavaleta himself would discuss the historical and theoretical limitations of this kind of conception when, around 1980, he began to reflect on the crisis of the state and the emergence of the Bolivian masses at the end of the 1970s.[17] Here he reflects not only on the diffusion of the workers' consciousness but also on how the other movements and subjects of Bolivian civil society extend and modify the workers' consciousness and its social movement not by negating its centrality but by reinforcing it through critique and giving it new forms through representations and actions; that is to say, he begins to think how the social totality acts on the workers' consciousness, modifying it, questioning it, correcting

16 Jürgen Habermas, 'Towards a Reconstruction of Historical Materialism' (Robert Strauss trans.), *Theory and Society* 2(3) (Autumn 1975): 287–300; and *Theory of Communicative Action*, 2 VOLS (Thomas A. McCarthy trans.) (Boston, MA: Beacon Press, 1984 and 1987).

17 See 'Las masas en noviembre' in Zavaleta (ed.), *Bolivia hoy* and 'Forma clase y forma multitud en el proletariado minero en Bolivia' (1983) in René Zavaleta, *La autodeterminación de las masas* (Bogota: CLACSO/Siglo del Hombre Editores, 2009), pp. 263–88.

it, extending it. Here he introduces the notion of intersubjectivity, which implies the introduction of a dialogic principle in the limited Marxist conception of knowledge and totality, which extends the application of the epistemological principle of totality on the side of the subject in the subject–object relation.

This broadening of Zavaleta's thought and of Marxism, therefore, is possible because of the conditions provided by the history of Bolivia itself and by its workers' movement. It is not a change or development that can be explained by a merely theoretical impetus.

In later chapters, I will analyse this process and the historical events that produced it in detail. At this point, I only want to outline the scope of development of Zavaleta's thought with respect to this problematic of knowledge, class and totality. We first have to analyse more extensively the structure and deployment of his initial formulation, which is similar to Lukacs's, which, in different variants, characterizes most of twentieth-century Marxism.

Crisis and Knowledge

Zavaleta's most important texts on Bolivian history focus on moments of crisis, because 'the principal sociological contribution of the Bolivian workers' movement is the study of the general national crisis as a method of knowledge of a backward social formation.'[18]

Although some Bolivian intellectuals were already familiar with Marxism, according to him what was lacking was that Bolivian history itself should require it: 'It was the movement of the socio-economic formation that demanded the use of a method that was not consciously assumed by anyone.'[19]

A method characterized by the analysis of concrete situations[20] but conceiving them as a synthesis of the social totality has a greater capacity for cognitive penetration, pertinence and foundation, above all in societies which have not been homogenized by capitalism, although they have been penetrated and transformed by it.

In the societies that Zavaleta calls backward, with reference to the degree of capitalist development and not as a general judgement of the civilization,

---

18 Zavaleta, 'Movimiento obrero y ciencia social': 4.

19 Zavaleta, 'Movimiento obrero y ciencia social': 4.

20 Zavaleta, 'Movimiento obrero y ciencia social': 4.

the processes underway are not revealed under normal conditions, precisely because of the disarticulations that characterize them.

> Crisis is at one and the same time fragmentation and universality. Inert or receptive classes break away from authoritarian unity, society sinks to the limit in its relations of production, which are presented in their atrocious nakedness following the collapse of the superstructure and, therefore, the crisis reaches the totality of the subjects of its sphere, that is, the whole political and actual reach of society and not only those groups included according to the indicators, undeniably volatile, that are commonly used to measure participation.[21]

In periods of calm there are greater limits to knowledge in this type of society; crisis is movement in these societies.[22] The class is the subject capable of knowledge in such moments. And knowledge is produced in relation to power: 'Knowledge will be subsequent to the objective perspective of power. And since power is, in the last instance, the unity of objective possibility and the subjective consciousness of that perspective, for that reason the crisis becomes a school.'[23]

The structural position of the working class is not a sufficient condition to know or exploit the horizon of visibility given by capitalist societies. There must be a break with the ideological subordination to the powers of capital, that is to say, when the possibility of overcoming the dominant type of social and political organization can be envisioned, its structures can also be better explained. The development of the subject, in this case a collective one, is a condition of knowledge and of its deepening: 'The subject must exist before its power.'[24]

If the class subject has developed the consciousness of the possibility of its own power, this is because it has developed practices that allow it to think about, first of all, its autonomy, and then its political project and leadership; this in turn produces a crisis in its society.

The event of a subordinate class developing the possibility of its own power causes a crisis insofar as it breaks with the condition of regularity and calm which, among other things, is due to the subordination of the subalterns,

---

21 Zavaleta, 'Movimiento obrero y ciencia social': 4.

22 Zavaleta, 'Movimiento obrero y ciencia social': 5.

23 Zavaleta, 'Movimiento obrero y ciencia social': 5.

24 Zavaleta, *El poder dual*, p. 71.

exploited and dominated by the political and material power of the dominant class and bloc. It tends to become a separatist class, as Zavaleta puts it, although it does so on the basis of the mode of production and type of society.

The development of this possibility modifies the articulations between base and superstructure that produced the continuity and certainty of domination. The following idea of Zavaleta's should also be understood as an epistemological principle: '[I]t is the objective rhythm of the class struggle that defines the type of relation between the economic base and the political superstructure in a given concrete situation.'[25]

This can mean at least two things. One: when in the field of class struggle a powerful subject has developed consciousness of its power, which can only occur through class struggle, it can establish a relation between base and superstructure that allows the social totality to be understood and explained. This implies the second aspect that I want to emphasize on the basis of the foregoing passage: developments in the superstructure are what make cognitive penetration possible and reveal the structure which, nevertheless, is the matrix of the process as a whole.

Crisis can be understood as the movement of society because it is the moment when the articulations between structure and superstructure change, corresponding to changes in the relations between social classes. Crisis is a kind of opening for knowledge. Under normal conditions of bourgeois domination, society is closed to thinking critically about certain questions, and the subalterns consume and believe the discourse or ideology of the leaders. A crisis breaks the predominance of a belief system which, recognizing and reproducing that reality, also produces ignorance of other processes that cause social divisions;[26] a crisis makes an extension of knowledge possible.

This implies that the crises of which Zavaleta speaks are crises produced by the development of alternative and autonomous class capacities. A crisis without the development of subjects does not produce knowledge. Strictly speaking, Zavaleta is talking about crisis within societies that are more or less modern or penetrated by capitalism, although they may be backward, and of a general crisis, not only at the economic level.

The crises that Zavaleta analyses, more specifically, are moments in which the working class moves away from the state and towards other subaltern

---

25 Zavaleta, *El poder dual*, p. 46.

26 See Louis Althusser, *On the Reproduction of Capitalism: Ideology and Ideological State Apparatuses* (Etienne Balibar pref.; Jacques Bidet intro.; G. M. Goshgarian trans.) (London: Verso, 2014 [1971]).

groups, or, rather, draws them into its movement towards autonomy, insofar as it diffuses the consciousness of its own and alternate possibilities.

In this sense, the crisis is also a movement of society; the social classes move, change positions, expand, retreat, are re-articulated with other subjects. Here, movement does not mean progress or development but articulation and re-articulation of the constitutive dimensions of a society. All this is implied by the idea of crisis as a moment of knowledge.

In *El poder dual*, Zavaleta studies two moments of crisis (1952 and 1970–71) in which the workers' participation is decisive, and in which political participation has connotations of the exercise and rehearsal of its own power.

In 1952, after having made possible the defeat of the army, the trade unions were a local power and political authority while or until a new state was organized. The working class organized and exercised an armed social power, which thus became a form of political power; but, since it had not yet developed centrality and autonomy on the basis of its own project, it became mediated and subaltern in relation to the party of capitalist reform, the MNR.

In 1970, the working class organized and tried out the Popular Assembly, a sort of class parliament, based on the COB, as a germ of dual power. Zavaleta does not choose 1952 (the revolution) and 1970–71 (the Popular Assembly) as focal points of his analysis of Bolivian history solely because they are crises, but because they are crises in which the conjuncture can be epistemically productive because there is a subject that creates epistemological and historical conditions as it develops a will to power. This implies a departure from the dominant ideology as a product of questioning the state and advances in understanding and directing the local world.

Here we are talking about political processes that are conditions of possibility for the production of knowledge; a certain degree of political autonomy makes knowledge possible. Political crises can produce epistemological openings, where there is a departure from the dominant ideology.

Now, all the potentialities for knowledge are not exploited or developed in the moment of the crisis itself. Crises create programmes and objects of research that only a longer and more reflexive time can carry out and analyse, to the extent that new events and political and intellectual processes illuminate or clarify the horizon of visibility that is articulated in the crisis as a programme and object of research and action. Things not known in the crisis may still become known because of it, later or in another crisis.

Crises as moments of fragmentation and universality are moments of synthesis and fluid complexity. Those who participate more fully in the crisis, ideologically or socially and politically, are perhaps better able to capture, understand and reflect on the changes taking place and the past itself. According to Zavaleta, crisis is a form of totalization in fluidity. Perhaps for that reason, those who move more and connect with others can see and know more.

One of the dimensions of fragmentation is ideological separation, producing the independence of consciousness, giving birth to one's own possibilities. It is the moment between the heteronomous certainty of the subaltern and the development of a certainty based only on the capacity developed and foreseen by oneself and one's relations. In this sense, crisis and ideological separation create, in the first place, uncertainty concerning the future in the global horizon of the society and also concerning the beliefs held about reality, about its present and its past. This gives rise, in part, to the receptivity[27] to adopt and develop new beliefs. The class that has in part produced the crisis due to its ideological separation, which ends by becoming political because it was also politically produced, is better situated to provide a new intellectual and moral horizon. For some, fragmentation is also liberation.

Crises are always ideological crises,[28] and, if this is so, they are preceded and produced by a period of dilapidation and critique of the dominant ideology or the set of beliefs, and by the development of new ideas and their dissemination to different social groups.

In the crisis that leads to the revolution of 1952, the proletariat participates in the more general national movement of critique of the ideology of the dominant oligarchy at the same time as it develops its class identity and consciousness. In this period, separation is easier, in part, because state political power is predominantly exclusive and repressive, and only partially and intermittently integrating.

In the next phase of crisis, the working class is now the principal subject responsible for critique and ideological substitution.

---

27 Zavaleta, 'Movimiento obrero y ciencia social': 5. Zavaleta's term *disponibilidad* normally means 'availability', however we follow Anne Freeland's use of 'receptivity' in her translation of Zavaleta's *Towards a History of the National-Popular in Bolivia, 1879–1980* (London: Seagull Books, 2018); see pp. 284–285. As Freeland notes, 'receptivity' should not be taken to mean passivity, and Zavaleta's usage conveys an active sense of openness or willingness. [Trans.]

28 See Jürgen Habermas, *Legitimitaion Crisis* (Thomas A. McCarthy trans.) (Boston, MA: Beacon Press, 1975).

A crisis is a moment that can produce knowledge only if someone is subjectively prepared to exploit it. This preparation consists in the ideological separation of the working class from the dominant state ideology.

Ideological separation, which is a political-intellectual process, thus becomes an epistemological condition for cognitive development. This implies a strong and constant relation between politics and knowledge, in which collective movements and relations of force in society create conditions of possibility for or obstacles to social knowledge.

In this sense I want to analyse Zavaleta's conceptions of ideology and science, horizon of visibility, class and subject of knowledge. What does Zavaleta understand social science to be? In 'Las formaciones aparentes en Marx' [Apparent formations in Marx], he offers something like a definition: 'It is the demystification of ideology, even changing it from a veil over reality to a message of social profundity, which we can call, at least in part, social science.'[29] It should be added that he understands ideology as: '[W]hat a society thinks of itself.'[30]

Here there is a juxtaposition of two notions of ideology, one sociological and the other epistemological,[31] and it is important to distinguish between them as we try to analyse problems of knowledge in a conception that does not separate them from political and social processes.

Ideology, or what a society thinks of itself, is a predominantly sociological notion. In this sense, ideology is impossible to overcome since societies will never cease to think of themselves. What can be said here with respect to the type of societies Zavaleta has in mind and with relation to the problem of knowledge is that the processes of totalization that occur with all their incompleteness and disarticulation in heterogeneous (backward) societies lead the majority to recognize reality via the ideas of the dominant class whose class interests do not lead them to open knowledge but, rather, to obscure many contexts and social processes.

The other notion, that of ideology as a veil over reality, is an epistemological notion. It refers to the level of knowledge or reflection on reality, but it is a product of the other, sociological, notion of ideology which originates

---

29 René Zavaleta, 'Las formaciones aparentes en Marx', *Historia y Sociedad* 18 (1978): 3–25, here, p. 4.

30 Zavaleta, 'Las formaciones aparentes en Marx': 11.

31 Carlos Pereyra suggests this distinction in *Configuraciones. Teoría e historia* (Mexico: Edicol, 1979).

in Marx's analysis of capitalist society; inherent to its configuration is a set of processes of transfiguration and concealment through which things or realities appear in men's consciousness in an inverted form. The organization of capitalism makes relations of exploitation appear as just payment for the elements of the process, capital and labour. Relations of domination appear as relations of equality and freedom via the juridical ideology that accompanies the configuration of politics as a monopoly and the concentration of force as the state.[32]

Ideology as concealment and transfiguration of reality is an ontological feature of capitalist societies. Social science develops as critique of ideology, in the epistemological sense, but, in order to carry this out, it must explain the social matrix of distortion and the concealment it produces. In order to develop, capitalism has disorganized the preceding communitarian forms and their knowledge and systems of beliefs together with their matrices of social organization. It has atomized and produced the free, commodifiable individual. According to Zavaleta: '[W]hen one is isolated, one tends to receive the official, ideological and authoritarian explanation as the only real or possible explanation of the world.'[33]

Not only has capitalism produced, via what Marx called primitive accumulation, the free man capable of being converted into a worker, but also the individual incapable of thinking for himself or with his community. It has produced his social solitude, his cognitive incapability.

Now, this occurs in the beginning, and it is a situation that is modified in the measure in which this type of society and its mode of production promote the formation of the collective worker, of the class, which is the condition of possibility of the critique of ideology.

> Consciousness corresponds to being and therefore an individual consciousness can do nothing where being has already become collective. The destruction of individual being is the condition for the appearance of the general horizon of visibility and, in consequence, the science produced on the basis of the exploitation of this horizon of visibility is also the only salvation for men in their new being, which is their collective being.[34]

---

32 See Karl Marx, *The German Ideology*; *Critique of Hegel's Philosophy of Right*; *The Communist Manifesto*; and *Capital*, 2 VOLS. All available at: www.marxists.org (last accessed on 13 May 2020).

33 Zavaleta, 'Clase y conocimiento': 6.

34 Zavaleta, 'Clase y conocimiento': 6.

This means that social science is possible when the class structure of the capitalist mode of production matures, not only as a scheme of positions and divisions but also as movement and struggle, since this does not only refer to recognition in a class structure but also to separation with respect to the ideology of this type of society, which only occurs as a history of collective organization and politics.

Another component in this conception of social science is that of the objects of knowledge. The configuration of capitalist society produces cognitive objects differentiated according to the social classes that it produces. The structural organization of the relations of production and the political history of the classes determine the horizon of visibility of a society and class interests condition the capacity for cognitive exploitation of such a horizon. Zavaleta sums this up in the following way:

> It is not the case that the mode of production itself provides one horizon of visibility to one of the classes and a completely different one to another, but only that one of the constitutive classes is able to exploit the horizon of visibility, which is shared by the whole of society, that is to say, the difference is located not in the horizon but, rather, in the capacity to exploit it. The class interests of the proletariat induce it to knowledge; the class interests of the bourgeoisie induce it to ignore, to obscure. The compulsion proper to the dominant class impedes its theoretical exploitation of the horizon of visibility, which is nevertheless objectively available in that society.[35]

The horizon of visibility is constituted by the social and intellectual conditions of the possibility of knowledge; at the same time, it implies certain temporal limits. The horizon of visibility is configured by the articulation of social totality; it is the scope of analysis and reflection given or developed by the movement of totality in each historical period.

The differentiation of societies also gives rise to the unequal exploitation of this horizon; it produces subjects with different capacities for knowledge. What differentiates their capacity is the interest in knowledge, but this is caused by the structure of the relations of production to which their identity and social life is tied.

So far, Zavaleta's concept of knowledge or social science has two components: the idea of the horizon of visibility; and the idea of a privileged subject of knowledge or social science. The theory that results from the scientific

---

35 Zavaleta, 'Clase y conocimiento': 6.

practice of this subject in the horizon of visibility of modernity is Marxism. The idea of the horizon of visibility contains the epistemological principle of totality, which is what links the two elements, once the subject in question practices the unity of subject–object in economic and intellectual production:

> It is from this, from the horizon of visibility given by the total worker and by the logic of the factory, that is to say, the combination of the collective subject and the transformation of matter, which is for the first time conscious (we are not talking about unconscious sociability or unconscious transformation), that secular rationalization of the universe, that is, anthropocentrism, is made flesh.[36]

In all these texts, Zavaleta speaks of the constitution of these processes in general; later, when we focus on the Bolivian workers' movement, it will be necessary to analyse how this anthropocentrism is expressed in the Bolivian proletariat, together with the practice of other non-capitalist local cultural traditions which have not undergone the rationalization of the Western core which, nevertheless, originates this type of conception of social knowledge and of societies in history.

Another component of the notion of social science in Zavaleta is the formulation of this as a message of social depth. Since this is an almost metaphorical definition, it requires interpretation.

First, the notion of social depth. It seems that this is not something internal and hidden but, rather, the articulated complexity of the totality of social relations, and it means that a historical event or any aspect of reality is immersed in a process that does not arise out of nothing, that has a distant origin, and an accumulation of determinations and conditions of possibility, and also forms part of a system open to understanding. This social depth is the history of societies that articulates in the determinations of the present their processes of formation and development as a horizon of possibilities and also of alternatives.

If this is framed as a message, it is because social reality is understood to be the source of the substance and conditions of knowledge, which include the formation of the subject that will make this intelligible, communicable. But it also suggests that the objects and events will explain themselves and that their truth will become apparent to an attentive, unprejudiced and alert subject. That is to say, it suggests a notion of knowledge in which the real

---

36 René Zavaleta, 'Antropocentrismo en la formación de la ideología socialista', *Dialéctica* 8(13) (1983): 61–74; here, p. 65.

object or referent is the most active element, rather than the knowing subject. It seems that this definition of social science as a message of social depth does not establish a distinction between subject and object in which the object emits the message and the subject receives it passively as a reflection but, rather, the message is already a product of the unity of subject and object in which the subject has produced other theoretical objects[37] to explain what its reality has made knowable. Thus, social science is what history produces as unity of subject and object in each moment of modernity.

There is an epochal node that becomes the core of social science because it encapsulates the condition of possibility of knowledge conceptually. According to Zavaleta, this is the law of value: '[N]ow it is the law of value which makes a society knowable and calculable.' 'The starting point is the advent of the free man as universal condition, that is, the emergence of the masses of individuals. It is on the basis of such a status, that of human equality, that a society arises which is for the first time knowable.'[38]

All this is a journey through Marx as a form of internalization and as a foundation for Zavaleta's own work. If he were limited to repeating Marx, the review of these exegetical reflections on social science would be of little value, but this summary is necessary because Zavaleta takes the theory of value as the cornerstone or principal starting point that organizes his whole pro-gramme of research, reflection and production concerning the history of societies that he will call motley, that is, those societies which are backward with respect to capitalist homogenization and regularity but which are already unequally and partially penetrated and articulated by the world system and, in consequence, heterogeneous and crisscrossed by different modes of production, temporalities and cultures. What is significant is that he uses this intellectual matrix of thought that came out of another history to think of societies, in particular that of Bolivia, that cannot readily be studied under the modality of subsumption to the model. He uses it as a matrix of production of explanations and ideas adequate to the specificity of these local histories and their relations.

It is a project that does not modify the law of value but, rather, broadens its horizon and capacity to be used to think of complex realities that do not respond in their totality and totalization to capitalist processes.

In *El poder dual*, Zavaleta grounds his work in this theory and clearly maintains its centrality. My hypothesis is that, from here on, all his works are

---

37 See Althusser, 'Philosophy as a Revolutionary Weapon'.

38 René Zavaleta, 'El antropocentrismo en la formación': 6, 70.

produced as the unfolding of a theoretical strategy and a programme of research whose core is the theory of value. In this sense, it can be said that his work expresses an orthodox Marxism, which is not in this context a pejorative term but simply means production based on or starting from a core of theoretic-intellectual identity.

This is present even in the last texts in which he analyses Bolivian history in the nineteenth and twentieth centuries within a horizon broader than that of social class, but based on it.

Most of the categories at work in 'Las masas en noviembre' [The masses in November] (1983), 'La fuerza de la masa: Forma clase y forma multitud' [The force of the mass: class form and multitude form] (1983) and *Lo nacional-popular en Bolivia* (1986) [*Towards a History of the National-Popular in Bolivia*, 2018] already appear in *El poder dual* and 'Movimiento obrero y ciencia social. La revolución democrática de 1952 en Bolivia y las tendencias sociales emergentes' [The workers' movement and social science: the Democratic Revolution of 1952 in Bolivia and emergent social tendencies] in their theoretical formulation and as a proposal. I refer to notions such as crisis as method, receptivity, accumulation within the class, motley society, the primacy of local history over world history, and others, which I will consider where they are pertinent.

I return now, after this brief justification, to some aspects of the law of value in Zavaleta's thought, still with respect to general problems of knowledge in our type of society.

What Zavaleta says is that social knowledge is something that can be produced once the traditional forms of community, and, therefore, collective consciousness, have been destroyed or disorganized, or at least debilitated, since market relations, for example of reproduction and consumption, have not been generalized in our societies, and above all once a new kind of modern collectivity has been constituted on the basis of individuals of a social class and their movement.

The fact that the global norm is no longer the traditional community leads to the desacralization and secularization of social life and makes it possible to think of it critically. The fragmentation that is the production of free individuals for capitalist commodification, although partial, and the insertion in productive and social processes in which subordination, exploitation and domination are experienced as a constant condition, disposes men to resistance, critique and, finally, secular knowledge of their situation.

Now, knowledge of one's own situation requires a broader knowledge of national history and the world; politics, as a system of relations with others and as collective organization that puts these relations into practice, allows one to create the conditions for knowledge of one's own class position.

The law of value speaks of the abstract equalization of men, but as a product of historical processes. It can be said that the law of value, with respect to conditions of social knowledge, parallels Hobbes' anthropology which posited a condition of general equality of individuals as a condition for knowledge.[39] The law of value explains this as a product of the formation and development of capitalism, not as a permanent or original human and social condition. The idea of equality as a condition of social knowledge circulates in the theories of modern thinkers; Marxism is distinct, then, because after repeating this idea, it goes on to argue that although this is the general condition or horizon of visibility, not everyone's knowledge is the same. This difference is due to the fact that Marxism brings together the idea of equalization of men with that of class organization of society, the conception of divisions or strong contradictions in its interior, in contrast to the majority of the other individualist anthropologies of knowledge which ultimately conceive modern capitalist society as composed of individuals whose differences are due to the rewards for their different merits and work.

The law of value as the core of social science means that societies begin to become knowable when there is no general consensus concerning the criteria of recognition of a society; in a kind of critical and complex situation in which society is divided and organized in such a way that the situation of the dominated no longer guarantees the acceptance and internalization of the dominant ideology, and there is an opening to the possibility of critical thought on the basis of independence which began as fragmentation and atomization or social solitude and moral-intellectual abandonment, produced by the process of primitive accumulation.

Thus, social science becomes possible with critique. It appears as critical knowledge, not as a consensual view of the world but as cognitive dissonance[40] with respect to the dominant ideology, although as part of the process of overcoming it within the working class, as the rational reconstruction of

---

39 Thomas Hobbes, *Leviathan* (1651); and Luiz Eduardo Soares, *A invencao do sujeito universal. Hobbes e a política como experiência dramática do sentido* (Campinas: Editora da Unicamp, 1995).

40 Leon Festinger, *A Theory of Cognitive Dissonance* (Stanford, CA: Stanford University Press, 1957).

the consciousness of life within a society that is not only increasingly differentiated but also socially divided and without a shared material and intellectual horizon.

Another implication of the law of value as the core of social science is that knowledge is produced from a situation of alienation and not as part of a process of actions that will negate part of this social being. Social science, thus, does not emerge as an 'objective' or de-subjectified discourse on historical reality but, rather, as the discourse of a new social intersubjectivity which is initially produced by capitalist development, that is, by the collective or socialized worker, and thence in the history of the organization and struggles of this collective subject, the workers' movement and its margins of irradiation.

In this sense, the Marxist notion of science, and in particular that which Zavaleta argues for, has Hegelian roots. Knowledge and its development are given by the work of the slave on the world and on himself, a process of self-negation and self-overcoming.

The law of value encapsulates the abstract equalization of men by the historical process of capitalism; Marxism is the cognitive utilization of the horizon of this new intersubjectivity, and at the same time a project of real equality between men.

In this conception of social science, Marxism converts the anthropocentrism that characterizes the formation of the modern world[41] into the centrality of the proletariat on the epistemological level. This is the condensation of anthropocentrism in a social class. Anthropocentrism corresponds to the idea of a horizon of visibility common to the era and to the whole of society, and the centrality of the proletariat to the idea that it works and transforms the world and thus its own self; it can know better, as with the slave as thought by Hegel.

The passage from anthropocentrism to the centrality of the proletariat on the epistemological level awards such privilege to the class subject that it generates at the same time problems of verification and corroboration. The idea of the centrality of a subject that does not consider the continuation of the process of knowledge beyond this privileged core of intellectual production implies that the task of verification and corroboration, in the end, of critical revision, becomes internal to the subject, in this case internal to the class.

Since no one else can exploit this horizon more broadly, the critiques and contributions of other subjects can only have a secondary character. Thus, all

---

41 See Zavaleta, 'El antropocentrismo en la formación de la ideología socialista'.

these processes of debate of the knowledge produced have to take place basically within the workers' movement. Pluralism within this movement, which is already broad and cultivates debate or intersubjective dialogue internally, therefore becomes epistemologically necessary. It does not yet contain a theory of debate, dialogue and intertheoretical work, although in practice many Marxists who uphold this conception of science have established strong and productive inter-theoretical relations in their intellectual work.

Zavaleta's work proposes thinking on the basis of this theoretic strategy formulated in terms of the centrality of the proletariat and the law of value. It contains tensions resulting from the problems and limits I have indicated, but also attempts to overcome them, first in his analysis of the limits of the scope of validity of the regulative models articulated around the law of value, and then with the problem of the expansion of the notion of class centrality above all in the analysis of Bolivian history. Here I will only mention the problems that must be studied.

A key idea in the relation between science and the degree of cognitive exploitation of the horizon of visibility is that of accumulation within the class. The structural specification of the working class's capacity for knowledge is not enough, since if one stops there this becomes an argument that assumes a class consciousness that does not yet necessarily exist. For this reason, the idea of class movement is important, which necessarily implies the consideration of its history and its collective and political practices. Knowledge can be produced from the history of the subject, not from its position, which is a starting point or condition of possibility. Given that it is reflection and conceptual production and not a snapshot image, it can only be produced in movement. There is no production of knowledge without history, that is, knowledge is produced in the process through which the subject is constituted.

Together with the idea of movement is that of interiority: 'Without accumulation within the class, the acquisition of the scientific instrument (Marxism) is impossible, and for that reason, the internal development of this class is also the key to the knowledge of a motley formation.'[42]

The internal development of the class implies various things: self-development; internalization of elements of information and knowledge; the circulation of experience of individuals and class collectivities; the achievement of autonomy and the constitution of identities; integration. All this is, at the same time, expansion and reflection. The idea of accumulation within

---

42 Zavaleta, 'Clase y conocimiento': 8.

the class implies learning, lived and experienced as self-development, and perhaps most importantly, the socialization of experiences, knowledge, aspirations and organizational capacities in a significant sector of the class. That is to say, it does not refer to a level of development of the leadership but, rather, to that of the social base that has incorporated its history in a reflexive manner and as a political practice. The accumulation within the class also involves experiences of defeat, failure and internal conflicts.

This is how the condition of possibility of the productive insertion (in cognitive form) of Marxism and, thus, of knowledge of society, is conceived, in terms of the concrete history of a class and society.

The notion of accumulation within the class appears in Zavaleta at the beginning of the 1970s in the group of essays I am discussing, beginning with *El poder dual*. It is the category that corresponds on the level of theory to the process of autonomy in the development of the Bolivian workers' movement. It is obviously not a synonym of this last idea, but it expresses its latest developments.

I also think that this idea of accumulation within the class tends to substitute the idea of development of national consciousness as the regulative concept and axis of historical analysis, which was a way of synthesizing the study and evaluation of the historical process.

To present history as the history of the development of national consciousness is to analyse and understand it basically through the conversion of historical processes into ideological products. Nationalist historiography of consciousness is thus the history of a mentality in local time and space; for some, it is also the history of a subject in a process of self-recognition and constitution.

The displacement of the idea of the development of national consciousness by that of accumulation within the class, more generally, implies a passage from the notion of nation to that of class as the axis of historical analysis, and in particular a double process which is what I am interested in pointing out: a passage from interpretation to explanation as the predominant modality, accompanied by a change in the weight and articulation of the ends of the historical analysis, that is to say, between ideological-political constitution and critical cognitive penetration of historical processes.

Nationalist historiography basically aims to interpret historical events within the frame of a local teleology awoken by anticolonial and anti-oligarchical struggles. The causality of events is generally ascribed to the intentionality of the dominant and dominated macro subjects. In addition, it is interpreted with a more or less explicit political intent: to criticize politically the antinational oligarchy, and to promote the development of national being and consciousness.

The intentions of these entities—the nation, imperialism, the oligarchy, the people—are found at the poles of the causal chain; and between these intentions and the meanings of historical events certain structures, material forces and individual and collective actions appear as mediators. One way to characterize nationalist interpretative historiography is as a sort of subjective circle mediated by social structures and actions.

In short: the objective is the interpretation of historical events, that is, an intersubjective conception of intersubjectivity. Causality is attributed to the intentionality of macrohistorical entities, another subjectivity. Thus, it can be considered a kind of teleological hermeneutic, as a result of the conception of history that frames the interpretation. The consideration of social structures and historical actions serves to mediate between intention and historical meaning.

This is a general tradition in which Zavaleta also participated. It is this way of thinking history that is modified by the practice of Marxism and the displacement towards the axis of class. In the traditional formulation of Marxism, the basic objective of science is to explain and not to interpret. Explanation consists in accounting for historical events and processes as results caused by the movement of economic and social structures and actions or practices, which can be understood as producing those structures at the same time as they are determined by them. Intentionality is not the key or the causal nucleus but is also explained by the dynamic of these structures. Historical processes and events do not express the intention of any of these subjects but are complex and overdetermined results of various causal processes structurally determined and mediated.

Interpretation can better be articulated by a political thought concerned with the production of meaning, for which it provides the understanding of a historical tradition. When the aim is to produce intelligibility through causal explanation and not the significance of the events, recourse to social science as causal explanation seems a preferable alternative.

I think Zavaleta's movement towards Marxism and his intellectual production from that framework has to do with his strong preoccupation with explaining the causes of the frustration and disarticulation of the revolutionary process and the nationalist project in Bolivia. Rather than thinking of the historical meaning, the aim is to study the causes so as to construct a less a voluntaristic meaning.

His writings of the 1970s as a whole, but in particular 'Movimiento obrero y ciencia social', 'El proletariado minero en Bolivia' [The mining proletariat in Bolivia] and *El poder dual*, express this preoccupation and in them historical-political interpretation is displaced by social science (as causal explanation). This did not imply the abandonment of a concern with political strategy but, rather, its revision on the basis of this passage through the study of structural causes.

The writings of this period are concerned above all with understanding the crisis of the state of 1952, that is, the passage to dictatorship in 1964 which did away with the civilian government of the MNR. This task displaces the production of meaning. Zavaleta tries to analyse the limits of the revolutionary process of 1952, and to this end the principal mode of organization of this kind of work is based on an analysis of the history of social classes. It is an analysis focused on class, but on the historical processes of the formation of social classes and their conflicts, that is, on the political life of social classes, rather than on the economic structure. Zavaleta works with a class-based analysis, but basically on the political-ideological level—on the class struggle. The level of subjects and politics is privileged in the explanation of history.

There is a continuity here with respect to Zavaleta's previous works; there is a change on the level of the guiding conceptual framework, from the nation to the class, without abandoning the former but assuming that the latter is a primary nucleus for social explanation, based on which the understanding of the nation has to be reformulated. This dimension will be reworked on the basis of Gramsci (I will come back to this later).

This chapter deals with the appearance and development of the centrality of the proletariat on the epistemological and historical level in Bolivia. It is this historical centrality that makes possible its centrality in the production of knowledge. This relation has consequences for the way in which the history of the country is written or made and also for class identity.

First, for Zavaleta the central process of modern Bolivian history is the process of the formation of the Bolivian working class. On the basis of the history of the development and political life of this subject, one can articulate a narrative of other aspects of Bolivian history.

This historical and epistemological centrality exists insofar as the workers' movement expresses the nation better than the state, above all after 1964. The workers' movement might have incorporated the wider horizon of visibility in the country to make it known; however, it ultimately was not able to do so with the conditions of possibility and limitations proper to its time.

In general, it can be said that these depended on the level of political-cultural organization of civil society that the workers' movement managed to achieve, in terms of communication and collective action.

Zavaleta introduces this dimension of knowledge in his conception and evaluation of the Bolivian workers' movement. In Bolivian historiography, there was already an evaluation of the importance of the workers' movement[43] in the struggles against the mining oligarchy and its participation in the revolution and reorganization of Bolivian society, but Zavaleta is alone in linking the development of this movement with the possibility of self-knowledge of our society and with the depth and amplitude it can reach.

The workers' movement is no longer thought solely as a political subject but also as the condition of historical and social knowledge. In more general terms, this means that the configuration of the political life of a country strongly conditions the possibilities of self-knowledge of the same. Knowledge generally has to do with intersubjective dialogue and social communication. What the Bolivian workers' movement could have done was to establish relations of communication and coordination with various organizations of civil society, and also with these in relation to the state, above all in the absence of dictatorship.

Knowledge and dialogue imply encounters and this is what the workers' movement promote, more than the state.

The notion of accumulation within the class responds, at this moment, to the need to connect the general idea of exploitation of the modern horizon of visibility by the working class whose result is Marxism with the Bolivian historical process, and the mode of application of this conception not in economic terms of structures and relations of production but, rather, in terms of subjects and the ideological-political dimension of the social classes.

Thus far I have analysed Zavaleta's argument in a quite general way. In a second section of this second part, I sketch the structure of an analysis put into practice to reconsider the revolution and Bolivian history after this theoretical displacement in these writings of the 1970s.

Zavaleta's work on these topics is motivated by an attempt to understand the causes of failure. He seems to feel the need to have recourse to social science

---

43 In particular, the 4 volumes of Guillermo Lora, *Historia del movimiento obrero* (Cochabamba: Los Amigos del Libro, 1967) and the rest of his works.

and produce a set of categories able to explain Bolivian history. The tension between localism and generality or universality appears, something which the nationalists denied. General theories and their pertinence for thinking the country imply the recognition of a significant degree of general, even universal validity.

Zavaleta's transitional writings express this tension between localism and universalism or the need for general theories. For example, in 'Movimiento obrero y ciencia social', written under a strictly Marxist theoretical strategy, in defining science this tension appears between the general and the importance of not reducing what is local and concrete to its subsumption under general theories so that local features are only secondary narrative elements:

> [W]hat we call sociological science is no more than an elaboration of a scientific level, insofar as we have been provided with one, of inclinations or impulses or arrangements which are already present in the movement of flesh and blood social forces. We do sociology from the position of a class, a country, a concrete situation. It is evident that the same must be represented and that a *concretum* has to become a categorical *concretum*, in thought, to be known, and that nothing can be explained in the last instance without its universality.[44]

The emphasis is on the concrete. Science is done from particular situations; but these can only be explained from a position of universality, that is to say, by some type of general theory.

Zavaleta's work is a good example of a transition in social thought in Bolivia—one from a nationalist thought that basically developed as historical revisionism to the social sciences. The necessity and pertinence of general theories, the acceptance of a significant degree of universal validity, appear in this transition. This is what is implicit in the passage from nationalist historical revisionism to contemporary social science which, in the Bolivian case and in the period under analysis, took place through Marxism.

Marxism introduces the pretension to science in modern Bolivian social thought. In general, most of what has been produced as social knowledge in Bolivia is history—social history; there is no systematic sociology or political science. This process by which the pretension to social knowledge as science is introduced also introduces it into the field of history. The aim is to do social science in dialogue with history and as history. This also responds to the fact that social reality is thought as historical reality. Insofar as Zavaleta comes

---

44 Zavaleta, 'Movimiento obrero y ciencia social': 17.

from a nationalist framework, he puts strong emphasis on what is local and concrete, and therefore, doing social science basically means doing concrete history, but now making use of elements of general theory.

This is a theoretical problem that Zavaleta himself considers in 'Las formaciones aparentes en Marx': What are the limits or scope of validity of general categorical systems? From the start, Marxism itself recognizes that the character of its critical theory is that of an epochal theory which corresponds to the time of capitalist modernity.

In terms of problems of knowledge and also of ideology, nationalist historical revisionism believed that to produce knowledge, which in its terms meant producing national consciousness, it was sufficient to revise the seigneurial version of history and rewrite it including the presence of the nation.

Later, Zavaleta comes to think that this is not enough. It is a task already carried out and the matter is more complex in various ways, of which at least two must be pointed out here. The first has to do with a problem to which he referred as a vestige at the margins of self-knowledge. The other is the problem of ideology in capitalist societies. The first refers to the problem of the relation between totalization and knowledge. The horizon of visibility exploited by Marxism is articulated on the basis of the generalization of abstract equality between men in politics and economics, on the basis of the equalization of their labour time as conceived by the law of value. The law of value is the core of the knowability or of social science in this type of society. As a result, a society in which the substance of the law of value has not been generalized, or that which has not been totalized in this dynamic, is not knowable.

This is not a problem of concealment of the facts on the part of history and seigneurial ideology. It is a much more complex problem that responds to processes caused by colonialism, in which different types of societies and relations of production generate highly heterogeneous or, as he would come to call them, motley societies.

CHAPTER SIX

Histories and Interpretations of 1952

The nationalists revised Bolivian history as written by the oligarchy as part of the articulation of a political subject. In the 1970s, Zavaleta revised nationalist history itself in order to understand and overcome the crisis of the nationalist project.

Zavaleta moves from a way of seeing history on the basis of the reality and virtuality of the nation to what he calls the class's exploitation of the horizon of visibility provided by the scope of capitalist modernity. This chapter aims to sketch synthetically and analytically the consequences of this change in Zavaleta's way of thinking, writing and revising Bolivian history, in particular the 1952 revolution, and to compare his scheme with other histories and interpretations of this historical moment.

Two texts that best represent these new works of Zavaleta's can serve as focal points for this study. One is 'Movimiento obrero y ciencia social. La revolución democrática de 1952 en Bolivia y las tendencias sociales emergentes' [The workers' movement and social science: the Democratic Revolution of 1952 in Bolivia and emergent social tendencies],[1] which focuses on political analysis and periodization of the revolution; another text is *50 años de historia* [Fifty years of history][2] which is at the same time a continuation and revision of *El desarrollo de la conciencia nacional* [The development of national consciousness], in which we see the effects of these methodological and theoretical changes in a study of a longer historical time span.

---

1 This essay was prepared in the Centro de Estudios Latinoamericanos (Latin American Studies Centre) in the Universidad Nacional Autónoma de México (UNAM) and presented in the 11th Latin American Congress of Sociology in Costa Rica in 1974. An amplified and revised version was published in the *Revista Mexicana de Sociología* as 'El proletariado minero en Bolivia'.

2 This essay was part of one of the books co-edited by Siglo XXI and UNAM: *América Latina: Historia de medio siglo*, and is now published independently as part of the complete works of Zavaleta.

History: Science and Memory

The interpretation and explanation of history has two concerns and tasks: science and memory. The articulation of these elements enables the production of local history with more universal tools of analysis and conceptualization. Zavaleta puts forward these two dimensions thus:

> Historians see countries from the perspective of the present, and this is not necessarily an error because things become known in their outcome; but each country, on the other hand, sees itself with the eyes of memory. That the country as such should stall its knowledge at one moment in its past or should mystify it is not fundamentally important because what matters here is what it believes itself to be.[3]

> [W]hat we call sociological science is no more than an elaboration of a scientific level, in so far as we have been provided with inclinations or impulses or arrangements which are already present in the movement of flesh and blood social forces. We do sociology from the position of a class, a country, a concrete situation. It is evident that the same must be represented and that a *concretum* has to become a categorical *concretum*, in thought, to be known, and that nothing can be explained in the last instance without its universality.[4]

This means that in doing history one works with representations and interpretations of the time lived and transmitted, and with categories with a certain level or load of generalization, which is what allows the historical narrative to reach a certain level of analysis, which as such implies some distance with respect to the memory and consciousness of the subjects of the process.

The nationalist historiography, which was also historical revisionism, aimed to articulate the country's memory, to convert it into political consciousness. Zavaleta's new work continues to work with memory, but it now also carries out a critique of the ideology which it contains, which here means petrifications and mystifications.

Thus, a revision of what Bolivians believed about the revolution in the time of its crisis serves as a critique of the revolution itself via the production of knowledge of the limitations and tendencies of the subjects who carried it out.

This critical revision of memory is done from the point of view of the working class, but only on the basis of processing this memory within the

3 René Zavaleta, *50 años de historia* (Cochabamba: Los Amigos del Libro, 1992), p. 20.
4 Zavaleta, 'Movimiento obrero y ciencia social': 17.

class, that is to say, via a process of assimilation-participation, which can then become critique, which would at the same time be self-criticism and self-knowledge, and, in consequence, partial self-negation. This is the Hegelian process of self-consciousness-negation-overcoming.

This articulation of science and historical memory processed via accumulation within the class is what allows the introduction of sociological science, as Zavaleta says, to avoid a highly structuralist and abstract vision of Bolivian history as a substitution for social beliefs, and introduces the analysis of economic, social and mental structures in the study of history, thus surpassing the historical narrative primarily, and at times exclusively, carried out on the basis of the intentions and actions of the most prominent individuals.

I can begin with the question of how history is thought and articulated from the epistemological centrality of the class. Here I refer to historiographic work, and not to social processes in time. In the first place, this implies thinking history on the basis of a subject as its backbone, and, in consequence, already implies politics and beliefs or ideology.

Doing history on the basis of this epistemological centrality does not mean doing economic history, which is an analytical distinction necessary at some point, but becomes a blinding reduction if it aims to be the history of the general process or a synonym of class history.

Periodization

One of the principal implications of this interweaving of economic structures, politics and ideology in the making of history on the basis of the idea of class centrality is that the criteria for periodizing history, which is a way to mark and narrate social changes over time, are a combination of economic, ideological and political factors. This is what appears in the works of Zavaleta that I am analysing here, in particular in 'Movimiento obrero y ciencia social'.

I argue that Zavaleta carries out the narration and periodization of the 1952 revolution in the following way: The linking of history and social analysis begins with a moment of crisis and change of direction in its social processes, be this a foundation, a re-foundation or a wide-reaching reform; a revolution, for example, or what he called a constitutive moment.

On the basis of this moment, a study, analysis and characterization of the structural processes prior to it and the changes that follow it is developed, in particular the political history of the subjects who produce the crisis and how they produce it.

History is periodized not only on the basis of changes in economic and social structure that mark the longer historical cycles, but also on the basis of changes in the political subjects, which change the political composition of a society and in this way, the change in the relation of forces can be used as a criterion to explain changes in the nature of the political regime and the character or political-social content of the state.

The class structure serves as a framework for a more complex and dynamic analysis of the history of the constitution, development and struggle of political subjects, who do not live and act purely on the level of disembodied intentions but rather within the historical context in which their structural relations are embedded.

In analysing what Zavaleta calls 'the democratic revolution of 1952 and the emergent sociological tendencies', he uses this criterion of the transformation of political subjects and their relations of force in order to establish a periodization scheme and give an account of the reconstruction of the state and social reform after 1952. I will briefly reconstruct the way in which Zavaleta proceeds.

He first establishes as a starting point the singularity of the historical matrix of the period that he is analysing, in this case what he calls the matrix of 1952, which is the moment of general crisis surrounding the popular uprising.[5] In the moment of crisis the social classes are reconstituted, which implies changes on the level of the relations of production, and what he calls a moment of general receptivity is produced, as an effect of the destruction of the ideological apparatus of the previous state, a task carried out by revolutionary nationalism during the previous decades.

This historical matrix is a moment of flux, of substitution of ideologies, beliefs and power relations; in this sense it is a matrix of new dominant tendencies. After having identified the matrix, he differentiates the phases of political change in the revolutionary and post-revolutionary processes. The focus here is on the transformation of the general political composition of society.

Zavaleta distinguishes the following phases: (a) a phase of hegemony of the masses; (b) a semi-Bonapartist phase; (c) a military-peasant phase; (d) a military-bourgeois phase.

I will review the presentation of these phases with the basic end of expounding the way in which he explains the transitions from one phase to another, which is a political criterion of historical periodization.

---

5 Zavaleta, 'Movimiento obrero y ciencia social': 5.

The matrix is characterized by a crisis produced by what Zavaleta calls the general democratic movement, which includes the nationalist party (MNR), the workers' movement, the peasants and other popular sectors. In the first phase, he thinks that hegemony is exercised by the proletariat which appears as the leading class, basically for two reasons. First, because it carries out the nationalization of the mines and agrarian reform, and thus organizes the rest of the people. The other reason is that 'the repressive apparatus is the armed population'.[6]

But at the same time as Zavaleta expounds this dominance of the working class in the most intense moment of the revolution, he also notes that the proletariat is not only immersed in the general democratic movement forming an anti-oligarchic bloc, but this immersion also participates in the ideology of the nationalist party and ends up becoming subordinated. Here, the notion of hegemony does not have the content Gramsci gives it as unity of domination and intellectual and moral leadership, which Zavaleta will take up years later.

According to the way in which he himself marks the changes of phase in that moment that he calls one of hegemony, in 1974, the proletariat has partial moral and intellectual leadership, organizes the people, imposes nationalization, but ends up handing over the leadership of the State to the bourgeois nationalist party. It is dominant in the sense of the new monopoly of armed force after the moment of the uprising. It is a subject in arms, organized, nationalizing, but still incapable of the reorganization of the state on the basis of its own historical and political centrality.

This explains the passage to the second phase in which the phenomenon of mediation appears, through which the nationalist party becomes a new state bureaucracy, which at the same time now contains or includes workers' leaders and peasant bosses. It is the moment in which the state achieves relative autonomy due to the peculiar situation of flux of modes of production caused by the revolutionary process:

> The relative autonomy of the State emerges here as an occasional crossing or form of transit: a correlation of modes of production in flux and the same backward articulation of one mode of production with another offers an improper basis for the real practice of the theoretical illusion of the autonomy of the state.[7]

---

6 Zavaleta, 'Movimiento obrero y ciencia social': 10.

7 Zavaleta, 'Movimiento obrero y ciencia social': 10.

The degree and mode of relative autonomy is produced by the substitution and displacement of the landowning class and the capitalist mining oligarchy, and by the absence of a new bourgeoisie, which will only appear as a result of state capitalism, which will finance and subsidize it. In this moment and situation of flux, the middle class and the petty bourgeoisie in the MNR can temporarily come together to form a leadership representing the general interest as they are able to reorganize the state, since they shared a bureaucratic and modernizing vocation.

This degree of relative autonomy and level of Bonapartism articulated by the MNR is possible due to its ideological penetration and predominance in the workers' movement.

The third phase is characterized by the alliance of the state bureaucracy with US imperialism, which produces the rupture with the workers' movement, at the same time as it allies with conservative sectors benefited by the agrarian reform. This culminates in the displacement of the civilian bureaucracy by the military, which establishes the military-peasant pact as the new internal axis of the state.

Finally, the military-bourgeois phase appears when the reconstituted bourgeoisie is allied with the military right; this is a dictatorship over the working class, as in the previous phase.[8]

In summarizing these phases I want to focus on the way in which Zavaleta explains political change and periodizes history on the basis of these criteria.

Political change is thought in terms of the changes in the composition and development of social and political subjects, or the appearance of new subjects, and in terms of the relation of forces that results from their unfolding in the same political space and time.

It is the general movement of society that allows the characterization of its various historical moments via certain political effects, in this case the various phases of a single state. That is, we proceed from the consideration of the movements of the various social subjects to the relation of forces, all this within the horizon of the historical matrix which is the principal source of meaning and also provides the structural organization.

The different moments or phases of a historical period are explained by the modes of articulation of effective power and by the agents of state leadership or its substitute:

---

8 Zavaleta, 'Movimiento obrero y ciencia social': 11.

When social phenomena occur through masses in movement, not only sharp ruptures but even subtle changes of emphasis can only occur through forcible measure or brusque impositions from the social site where effective power is located. In effect, one cannot conceive, for example, the substitution of phase a by phase b without the production of a sharp rupture or fragmentation, due to the displacement of the repressive apparatus of the people in arms by an organized army. There is a class change in the apparatus of the bourgeois state. The proletariat no longer heads the revolution; instead it is the bureaucracy which, defensively, acts as a group. It is a coup d'état against the proletariat.[9]

The distinction between dictatorship and democracy is secondary here with respect to the strongest criterion of the matrix which, being a complex, dense and multifaceted historical moment, nevertheless has as its core the class nature of the political power exercised by the state. This criterion, which is generally used in reference to the economic structure, is here, for Zavaleta, used in reference to the political presence of class subjects.

The argument is that the privileged mode of periodizing history is political; it is periodized according to the presence and political development of class subjects, and the results of their relations of force.

Now, political changes tend to occur at a faster pace than changes in the economic structure. With respect to this Zavaleta distinguishes two temporalities within the same historical process. One would be that of the capitalist process and the other, that of the bourgeois revolution.

The dispersion or annihilation or evaporation of the previous power bloc, which is something different from a mere displacement or extension, does not necessarily imply the substitution of the existing type of state. That is, the continuity of the same capitalist process can contain several bourgeois revolutions and not only one; a new bourgeois class destroys and substitutes another, thus complying with the requirement of a revolutionary character.[10]

Here, Zavaleta sustains an idea similar to that of Enrique Semo,[11] who proposes a cycle of bourgeois revolutions in the transition to capitalism and in

9 Zavaleta, 'Movimiento obrero y ciencia social': 11.

10 Zavaleta, 'Movimiento obrero y ciencia social': 5.

11 Enrique Semo, *Historia mexicana: Economía y lucha de clases* (Mexico City: Ediciones Era, 1978).

its development instead of a sole event on the political level. Zavaleta will later extend or complete this idea by incorporating Gramsci's idea of passive revolution.

What is here called capitalist process can be thought as a *longue durée* in the style of Braudel[12] and the revolutions as brief periods or conjunctures within this broader horizon; but it happens that for Zavaleta the revolutions are a matrix, which is the start of a long duration that is denser but shorter than that which characterizes the unfolding of capitalist civilization.

In terms of time, politics is shorter, but denser, in relation to the economy. This implies that various criteria which mark different levels and temporalities are used to periodize history. The work on 1952 considers the idea of the matrix, that of phases of change within the same type of state, and the historical backdrop of the capitalist process which precedes and indeed in part prepares the revolution.

The political weight of subjects is always considered as relational. For example, the Bonapartist phase which implies the predominance of the political bureaucracy of the MNR is not only explained by the capacity of the subject which defines the moment, but also by the system of relations with the workers and their level of development, in this case, the level of maturity of the working class which, at this moment, does not imply political-ideological autonomy and becomes dependence and subordination. In the case of the bourgeoisie, it is precisely its absence, the disorganization of that previously existent and the beginning of the organization of another.

The degree of political-ideological autonomy of the working class, on the one hand, and the development of a new bourgeoisie, on the other, are criteria which serve to mark changes of phase when they achieve significant advances in development and above all, when they achieve articulations with other social classes and groups, that is to say, rearticulations of the blocs that exercise effective social power and of their social bases. This, the rearticulations of the blocs of social and political power that respond to developments of the social classes and their system of relations, is the criterion of political periodization of Bolivian history.

The ideological dimension, and within it that of the political project, is central to the development of the subjects; whoever lacks a project tends to depend on others or be subordinated. Now, a political project which becomes social power is the product of the constitution of a collective subject, that is, of

---

12 Braudel, *La historia y las ciencias sociales.*

collective action organized and articulated by a class, which is interiorized in the life of a collectivity, which is also identified with and developed around it.

In 1952, the workers' movement possessed the contents of a programme for a new state but not the capacity to be the new governing subject, nor did it have a general institutional programme for a new state. The MNR had all this, although with a more modest and dependent programme; it also had ideological and organizational penetration in the workers' movement. Its superiority in the moment of substitution and reorganization of the state comes from this articulation.

The political composition of these subjects and the composition of the relations between them marks the rhythm of history and the periodizations that we can make of it.

Comparing Histories

I will now go on to present Zavaleta's conception of Bolivian history on the basis of the 1952 revolution, and to carry out a brief comparison with some other histories of 1952, above all with reference to their methods, but also their idea of Bolivia and its past.

I will begin with the other histories or visions of 1952, commenting on four basic groups of works, typified in the following way: there is a group of histories done from revolutionary nationalism, generally written by MNR militants; there are other works done by Trotskyist Marxist writers; there are various histories of 1952 that are testimonies and personal narratives that, nevertheless, express what can be called in general a nationalist point of view; and finally, I will take into consideration as a point of comparison some analyses done from a position of reaction against the revolution or by its critics.

A common characteristic of the history books on the Bolivian revolution written by Bolivians in the two decades that followed it is precisely their partisan character. These are not academic investigations but rather political analysis and evaluation that frame a historical narrative, or vice versa, that is, a historical narrative articulated and accompanied by a political evaluation and critique, or historical or sociological texts that articulate the meaning of the process, that is, semanticized defences.

Let us begin with the Marxist Trotskyist authors. The principal among them is Guillermo Lora, who published *La revolución boliviana* [The Bolivian Revolution] in 1964, an extensive critical analysis of the process up to Barrientos's military coup more than a decade later. It is also an exposition of the position and opinion of the Partido Obrero Revolucionario (POR, Revolutionary Workers' Party), led by Lora, on the politics of the country and problems of revolutionary theory.

It is worth reviewing, even if briefly, Lora's work to consider precedents in class analysis of Bolivia in relation to Zavaleta's work on the 1952 revolution. I do this with the hypothesis that several conclusions that Zavaleta reached in the 1970s had already been put forward by Lora, due precisely to his theoretical matrix and his political-ideological position. I will focus first on pointing out the parallels and then the differences.

Lora's starting point is as follows: 'The theory of the revolution has to begin by typifying with total clarity the nature of the country, pointing out the mechanics of the social classes which arise from this reality.'[13]

At the same time, all of Lora's work focuses on the history of the workers' movement, on which he has published several volumes. He has converted it into the axis of political analysis due to its economic centrality:

The Bolivian proletariat has been able to turn itself into the political axis of the transformations we are living through because it was already the economic axis. This is not a problem of numbers but of the relations between social classes. [. . .] What is decisive is how it produces its social life, the place it occupies in the national process of production.[14]

Here, in Lora, class analysis is the starting point and the proletariat is central to Bolivian history, points also proposed by Zavaleta. In Lora's version these ideas are directly deduced from the ideas of the development of the productive forces and the economic structure, which makes Lora's discourse almost exclusively centered on social class, illuminating this core in a way but leaving other topics in the shadows.

While Zavaleta's work does propose the centrality of the proletariat, which he recognizes in our history, class analysis is an axis of articulation of other dimensions, such as the nation, and these other dimensions are not excluded or reduced to it. Even in the moment of greatest intensity of the notion of class composition in his thought (in *El poder dual. Problemas de la teoría del Estado en América Latina* [Dual power: problems of state theory in Latin America]), Zavaleta was never a reductionist; the centrality of class and

---

13 Guillermo Lora, *La revolución boliviana* (La Paz: Difusión, 1964), p. 41.

14 Lora, *La revolución boliviana*, p. 78.

the proletariat is a core of articulation and it is therefore the basis of explanation of a reality that is not reduced to that core.

For proletarian centrality to exist in history and politics the criterion of the development of the productive forces is not sufficient. The US is proof of this; political history and the development of the workers' movement as subject are also necessary.

Although Lora writes the history of the workers' movement, he gives more weight to the idea of the development of the productive forces and its expression in the political life of classes, on the one hand, and to a scheme of phases of development of the working class that passes from its structural location to the revolutionary political project, on the other, than to the recognition of its effective forms of being in each stage.

Lora views the Bolivian revolution exclusively from the perspective of class and the centrality of the proletariat, while Zavaleta presents the proletariat as a core or axis of a particular articulation of national history.

Lora anticipates all the analysis of political and union bureaucracy within the workers' movement, and with it the critique of the bureaucratization of the COB and its government shared with the MNR.

According to Lora, the problem is that the COB's leadership was organized from the top down, and as a result it was not directed by the rank-and-file representatives but rather by its old leaders, who also had strong links with the MNR, and so ended up functioning as 'government agents within the popular organizations'[15] and producing a sort of semi-governmental trade unionism.

In a wider context: 'the MNR faction in the COB led this organization to act as the far left of the democratic bloc.'[16]

The notion of the democratic bloc corresponds to the concept of revolutionary stages, in which democracy does not refer to forms of organization and exercise of political power but rather to the bourgeois reform of society, above all at the level of the economic structure. The mediation of the COB with the unions achieves the integration of the workers' movement in a project that is not its own but that of the bourgeois reform of capitalism, which at that time in Bolivia was the programme and direction of the petty bourgeoisie organized politically in the MNR.

---

15 Lora, *La revolución boliviana*, p. 313.
16 Lora, *La revolución boliviana*, p. 263.

According to Lora, this was due to the lack of organization of a revolutionary proletarian vanguard.

In his writings in the 1960s, Zavaleta saw the proletariat as totally pertinent to and a necessary part of the democratic movement in general, and regarded dissident or critical trade unionists as anti-national. I think this was because he thought the process from the point of view of the revolutionary petty bourgeoisie, which overvalued its own leadership in the process.

In so far as Zavaleta comes to know and recognize the greater importance of the workers' presence as the body and soul of the long-term revolutionary and national process, and also comes to know the limits of petty bourgeois leadership, he displaces the proletariat cognitively and politically, recognizing it as the core of the general democratic movement and not just an important component of it. In this displacement, which implies internalization, what was previously a positive general pertinence begins to be recognized as bureaucratic mediation within the workers' movement, which appears more strongly in what he calls the semi-Bonapartist phase, that is, in the moment of reorganization of the state after a phase of the physical-military predominance of the workers, which is that of the destruction of the previous political power.

In this Zavaleta continues a type of critical analysis already proposed by Lora and other Trotskyists, as an unfolding of Marxist thought that he begins to develop on the level of political theory.

Another shared topic is that of dual power. Lora considers that in the stage after the uprising the trade unions and the COB concentrated power and authority over the masses, acting as a power parallel to that of the government, and that this is the meaning of a duality of powers. In addition: 'the first MNR government was no more than a puppet in the hands of strong and powerful organizations.'[17]

In 'Movimiento obrero y ciencia social', Zavaleta thinks that there was a first stage which he calls proletarian hegemony, in agreement with Lora, but in his detailed analysis in El poder dual he concludes that this was no more than the seeds of dual power, since although the unions predominated this was not accompanied by their organization and conversion into an alternative state with its own project or under their leadership. Since most of the movement adopted the national project, it did not propose as a reality the idea of two states tussling for control and leadership of society.

---

17 Lora, La revolución boliviana, p. 154.

The complex and unequal relationship in which the workers' movement had material and military power and authority, but was ideologically and hence politically subordinated to the nationalist project, did not lead to the configuration of a situation of dual power, but rather to a reorganization of the state in which the tasks of the bourgeois revolution were carried out by different subjects, whose projects were differentiated but not to the point of being opposed as two forms of state contending for the direction of the process at that moment.

It should be noted here that a feature of Lora's mode of political analysis, very widespread among the Bolivian left, is to compare it to Russian revolutionary history.

Lora writes:

The 9th of April 1952 can be considered, apart from all the differences due to the circumstances, as the Bolivian February. The most notable analogy is that the workers make the revolution and power goes to the political party of another social class. The Bolivian petty bourgeoisie, up to a point, played the role of the liberal Russian bourgeoisie. Our 'October' took too long to arrive; this is the difference that leaps into view. What we thought of as a momentary lull of the movement has been excessively prolonged.[18]

The tendency is to characterize and periodize Bolivian history with reference to Russian history. This is a general tendency in the analysis and history of revolutions: those who do this generally take great revolutions as a reference both to judge the revolutionary character of a process and to periodize it. In the past, the French Revolution was the principal referent. I mention this so as to mark some differences between Lora and Zavaleta. The first tends to comparisons with the Russian model, while Zavaleta tends to an internal view of the specific development of the political subjects.

Zavaleta also makes a comparative analysis of political histories in *El poder dual*, considering for example the Russian Revolution, the 1952 Bolivian revolution and the Popular Assembly in 1971, and the epoch of Allende in Chile, not in order to find equivalents to the model referent, but rather to understand what is specific to each history.

Another historical-political analysis of the Bolivian revolution from a Marxist perspective is the book by Liborio Justo (alias Quebracho) *Bolivia. La revolución derrotada* [Bolivia: the defeated revolution], published in 1967.

---

18 Lora, *La revolución boliviana*, p. 305.

Justo's work goes back to the Inca empire and summarizes the forms of social organization and domination and the liberation struggles in this territory. Justo's work uses a framework of class analysis to characterize social and political structures, as well as historical changes. On this basis he develops a lengthy narrative of the events that make up the body of the historical process. This text does not theorize, as Lora and Zavaleta do, but rather presents a political class analysis of Bolivian history. Like the majority of Bolivian writings on our history and that of 1952, it shares the feature of being a partisan history.

For Justo, 1952 was the first proletarian revolution in Latin America because the proletariat had taken power in Bolivia: 'this same proletariat in arms created its own organ of power, organized in the Bolivian Workers' Centre (COB) the 17th of April 1952 [. . .]. All the revolutionary political tendencies were represented in it, on the basis of the most effective union democracy, and the same with the peasants.'[19]

This would have proposed a duality of powers which was resolved not in favor of the proletariat but rather of the MNR government when the COB named worker ministers in the so-called co-government.

In Justo's text, the analysis of the events that he narrates is a political critique that includes opinions on what should have been done in order to favor proletarian leadership in the process.

Justo's work has the following structure: roots, process, autopsy. The revolution becomes the point or moment of history on the basis of which historical events and meaning are revised and ordered. History is done to explain and justify the revolution, and also to criticize the contemporary tendencies that undid it.

History is done on the basis of a scheme of birth, growth and death, centred on what is considered the most important moment in terms of liberation. A history of this type largely adopts a kind of narrative that is a teleology after the facts, root and process, to then become a historical criticism that emits judgements with reference to the historical ideal of the liberating proletarian revolution.

This is a feature shared by Marxist Trotskyist and nationalist writers: they write interpretative histories with a narrative structure of teleology after the facts, although their referents and interpretations may differ, precisely, over the core or organizing historical finality of the history narrated.

---

19 Liborio Justo, *Bolivia. La revolución derrotada* (Cochabamba: Ediciones Ryr, 1967), p. 156.

Several works from the 1960s address the end of the revolution. *Bolivia. La revolución derrotada* is one of them, from the point of view of the proletarian revolution; *Réquiem para una república* [Requiem for a republic] by Sergio Almaraz is another, from the point of view of the nation-state and sovereignty over natural resources. Zavaleta's *La caída del MNR* [The downfall of the MNR], a lucid analysis of decomposition from within, is part of this corpus, but at the same time it stands out as a more future-oriented and hopeful text, since it imagines a transition from the exhausted horizon of exclusively bourgeois nationalism towards a workers' horizon. Thus it is only an analysis of the MNR and neither a requiem for the nation nor an autopsy of the revolution.

There is another book by Ernesto Ayala, *¿Qué es la revolución boliviana?* [What is the Bolivian Revolution?] which completes the range of these Marxist interpretations, and serves as a bridge to the consideration of nationalist historical narratives.

Ayala was part of what was known as Trotskyist entryism in the MNR, that is, joining the MNR with an ideological position that included at least the following precepts:

> [T]he so called democratic-bourgeois revolution is no more than the democratic-bourgeois phase of the socialist revolution, in that as it advances it puts on the agenda, more and more forcefully, properly socialist objectives.'[20]
>
> [...]
>
> The problem of class liberation is dialectically linked with the problem of national liberation.[21]

Social struggles, in consequence and necessarily, are multi-class blocs which tend to organize 'popular governments that represent all the classes that integrate the front of national revolution.'[22]

The idea is that these governments take measures such as the nationalization of natural resources, agrarian reform and universal suffrage, and as they advance, a duality of powers emerges, because in order to maintain itself the revolution must advance.

---

20 Ernesto Ayala, *¿Qué es la revolución boliviana?* (La Paz: Burillo, 1956), p. 16.

21 Ayala, *¿Qué es la revolución boliviana?*, p. 19.

22 Ayala, *¿Qué es la revolución boliviana?*, p. 21.

In this sense, nevertheless, the Bolivian revolution is not characterized as bourgeois, because there is no bourgeoisie to lead it; nor is it socialist, because that would require a high level of economic development, which Bolivia does not have.

'Thus, the Bolivian revolution, without being either bourgeois or socialist, partakes of both and has created a popular, nationalist and revolutionary state as the direct expression of the interests of workers, peasants and poor sectors of the middle class.'[23]

This characterization of the Bolivian revolution is based on the notion of unequal and combined development, and a particular conception of political processes in colonial and semi-colonial countries,[24] that is, countries that have not solved their national question. Hence, the principal problem they face is that of national liberation with multi-class fronts. This is accompanied by the following conviction formulated as the iron law of the revolution: 'The struggle for national liberation is inevitably transformed into the struggle for social liberation.'[25]

The possibility of this transformation is given precisely by the duality of powers, which is configured as an expression of the contradiction already contained in the subjects who participate in the process and carry out various successive and simultaneous tasks.

Ayala thinks that the contradiction between petty bourgeoisie and proletariat is present from the beginning. The first only has political objectives of regularizing political power under its direction, while the peasants and workers, on the other hand, have economic and social objectives such as nationalization, industrialization, agrarian reform. This is expressed in the existence of ideological factions within the nationalist political front, which are the consequence of that contradiction.

This leads Ayala to propose that the duality of powers appears within the executive power itself in the moment when the COB enters into co-government.

Zavaleta challenges this interpretation in *El poder dual*, arguing that if there are not two opposed states, there is no duality of powers. It is absurd to postulate that this occurs within the executive power itself.

---

23 Ayala, *¿Qué es la revolución boliviana?*, p. 45.

24 The first chapter of Ayala's book is titled 'Notes on the Character of the Revolution in Colonial and Semi-colonial Countries'.

25 Ayala, *¿Qué es la revolución boliviana?*, p. 51.

Ayala's is another partisan interpretation of the Bolivian revolution. He writes from a perspective that combines a conception of national and world history in times of colonialism and national liberation with a political strategy that corresponds to that vision of unequal and combined development in which the semi-colonial peoples tend to demand the struggle for national liberation, which, as it advances, becomes social liberation.

Ayala does not offer a history of the revolution but rather an explanation and interpretation that is in part a justification or argument for the multiclass alliances of the movement. He works on the basis of this scheme of unequal and combined development that is common to the Trotskyists, but he is also sensitive to the particularities of the Bolivian experience, and this is notable in his text. However, it can be said that the first tendency subsumes the second, propelled by a desire to speed up the process and to replicate world revolutionary history. This is expressed in the problem of the duality of powers. Taking into account the theory of unequal and combined development, on the one hand, and the organization of the COB, the workers' presence and power in 1952, on the other, he postulates a duality of powers, forgetting its central feature, the fact that it implies the belligerent co-existence of two alternative and mutually exclusive states and not the co-existence of two differentiated forces within one and the same state.

In *El poder dual*, Zavaleta criticizes Lora and Ayala for assuming what he considers only the seed of dual power to be its implementation. It is not possible without the ideological and political autonomy that could potentially configure a different state. The working class and the COB in 1952 still partook of the nationalist ideology and project, although another horizon was already developing within them.

Although these authors are the object of Zavaleta's political critique, I consider, nevertheless, that for having anticipated the Marxist and class treatment of the revolution, they are a precedent which is in part a condition of possibility of Zavaleta's work.

I formulate the following hypothesis about these relations and their tendency. After José Antonio Arze,[26] the Trotskyists were the practitioners of Marxism who formulated a class-based critique of Bolivian history. There is a tendency in Trotskyism to apply historical materialism rather than to

---

26 Arze was the only one in the first half of the twentieth century to develop in his own fashion general theory as Marxism, in particular 'Marxist Sociology' (*Sociología marxista*).

develop it theoretically. With the group of authors reviewed here, this mode of utilization of Marxism, that of the simple application of theory to history, reaches its limits. Zavaleta initiates a new phase in which, drawing on this tradition, he takes Marxism into the phase of theoretical production, so as to continue explaining and interpreting Bolivian history. This theoretical production is basically on the level of political theory.

Another group of histories and interpretations of the 1952 revolution was done by nationalists who took part in the political process and in the MNR. The majority of the writings of these nationalists recounts the struggles against the mining oligarchy, which they denounce as anti-national. Augusto Céspedes' books, *El presidente colgado* [The hung president] and *El dictador suicida*, deal with processes prior to 1952. *Historia del Movimiento Nacionalista Revolucionario* [A history of the Nationalist Revolutionary Movement] by Luís Peñaloza also narrates with passion and detail the struggle leading up to 1952. *El signo del estaño* [The sign of tin] by Ñuflo Chávez, vice president for the MNR from 1956 to 1960, is what its subtitle indicates, a 'trial of half a century of history', that of the domination of the mining oligarchy.

There seems to be a common tendency among individuals who participated in the post-revolutionary process and who write about the 1952 revolution and the events leading up to it. Up till then they do political history, then when they get to the time after the uprising, that of the organization of the new state, they turn to justifying this and the government as the expression of those struggles for national liberation in multi-class popular blocs.

Works that cover the time after the uprising tend to be more critical, both on the left (for example, Lora and Justo) and on the right (for example, Siles Salinas).

I will take Hugo Roberts' book[27] to illustrate this tendency and some characteristics of nationalist historical narrative and interpretation of 1952.

Hugo Roberts was at first a member of the FSB and then joined the MNR, believing that he would continue his nationalist struggle; he was a minister in the first MNR government and in 1953 he went into exile due to political disagreements that had to do with the subordination to US imperialism.

Firstly, *La revolución del 9 de abril* [The revolution of the 9th of April] is a richly detailed text about the conspiracy that prepared the coup, the tactics and the battle of April and the phases of the coup, preceded by some reflections on the rise of nationalism in Bolivia; it is also accompanied by a critical

---

27 Hugo Roberts Barragán, *La revolución del 9 de abril* (La Paz: n. p. 1971).

analysis and assessment of the post-1952 policies that frustrated nationalist aspirations and forces by submitting to US power.

A primary feature common to histories of 1952 written in Bolivia at the time is that they are personal narratives of the revolutionary experience, of which this book is a very good example. They tell what happened on the basis of the author's own participation, a narrative generally accompanied by judgements of situations and political decisions. They consider the protagonists' intentions, their loyalties, their betrayals, on the one hand, and on the other, their ideals: the nation, sovereignty, the fatherland. In Roberts' historical narrative there is an explicit duality on the basis of which history is thought: on one side are the people and on the other the political leaders, the elites:

> The people never join any party en masse. The groups of standard bearers are insignificant minorities in relation to the popular mass [...] The people are volatile and support whoever they like, through spontaneous sympathy or antipathy towards the opposing force, and this circumstantial support is habitually switched for indifference, contempt, or even hatred, upon the slightest shift of events.

> In all revolutions the people support the revolutionaries out of sympathy, as a reward for their courage and as a reaction to the repressive power of the government. Without calculating or conditions, they insist on a fierce struggle, spilling their blood in torrents, sacrificing their best sons, until they obtain a victory which does not belong to them and, after cheering the winner, go back home in search of calm. Out of ancestral ignorance of their rights and perhaps an instinct of collective preservation, they let the elites establish a government, which will impose order upon the convulsions of the nation, without having obtained any rights for themselves and much less for third parties who did not intervene in the fight.[28]

The historical narrative of the revolution turns on the actions of the elites who fight for national interests and those who betray them. The author does not go back to the causes or the reconstruction of a structural context. Notwithstanding, two underlying structures appear—the mining oligarchy and US imperialism—but both are conceived as intentional entities.

Roberts' work has the following structure: the rise of Bolivian nationalism, the conspiracy, the victory, the frustration, US aid.

---

28 Roberts Barragán, *La revolución del 9 de abril*, pp. 50–1.

It is somewhat similar to Justo's framework of emergence, rise and fall, but unlike Justo's historical narrative, which is organized around classes and social structures, Roberts' is based on individual actions by political elites on the one hand and ideals on the other.

Many histories of Bolivia have been written starting with the moment of victory, but many more begin with the moment of the fall, and thus constitute a reflection after the facts on its causes, as well as a narrative that organizes and selects the events that lead up to great moments such as a revolution. The great political moments of history determine the selection and organization of the events integrated into the histories written after them. Because moments of change are revelatory, they provide the characterization of the social structures existent until then and give meaning to the particular events and actions of each moment.

In Bolivia, the 1952 revolution is the political horizon that organizes the narration and interpretation of history; it is the core around which history is revised and written.

The political-cultural moment of the revolution also activates historical writing and interpretation. The intensification of historical time that is produced with a revolution is a powerful stimulus which activates intellectual and historiographic work. In other words, the intensification of historical time demands interpretation, reconstruction of the past, reflection, and also direction.

Zavaleta's idea is that the social and cognitive capacity to carry out these tasks is not always present, that it exists in accordance with the construction and development of the subjects and their location in the set of social processes. A mature class-based understanding of 1952, which is superior to others, cannot arise in 1952 itself but only once the proletariat has developed its ideological-political autonomy.

I consider that the strong point of Zavaleta's work and what sets it apart is precisely this type of relation proposed between cognitive capacities of historical explanation and comprehension and the development of social and political subjects and the forms of configuration of society over time, which give rise to what he called horizons of visibility.

In contrast with this more complex vision of things, books like Roberts' have, nevertheless, a wealth of details, data and experiences, which convey from the heart of the events their microcomposition and their relation in the conjuncture, to be read from a greater analytical distance.

Roberts' text is a mixture of testimony, political analysis, interpretation and political history. That was how things were done at the time. What varies is the degree to which these elements are present and their positions in the composition of each work.

It would be worthwhile here to briefly review the work produced as a political reaction to the 1952 revolution. For this I will consider two books, unequal in the richness of their analysis and which I in no way mean to equate with one another.

Jorge Siles Salinas' book, *La aventura y el orden. Reflexiones sobre la revolución boliviana* [Adventure and order: reflections on the Bolivian Revolution] (1956), is a good representative of the right-wing conservative reaction which at the time was channelled via the FSB. Siles was a member of the FSB; both he and his party were Hispanic Catholics, inspired by the Spanish Falange.

Siles' characterization of the Bolivian revolution brings together two components. On the one hand he finds that the revolution expresses and contains features and tendencies already recurrent in Bolivian history: the turbulence of the masses, disorganizing tyranny and utopian pretensions. These three historic currents, however, would not have had the strength they did at that moment without the agglutinating conjuncture provided by communism.[29] This is the other component of the Bolivian revolution that marks the predominant character of the MNR regime. A large part of the book denounces the Marxist elements in the discourse of MNR leaders and the measures they would take for communism.

The revolution and the MNR are presented as destroying a tradition whose essence is Catholic and Hispanic. Siles' book is also a critique of the liberal modernization attributed to growing individualism. He supports the nationalization of the mines but not in the way it was carried out; it should have been done via the distribution to a wide group of private national companies and not as state administration under union control.

Siles' critique of the Bolivian revolution focuses on what he considers to be pernicious tendencies in Bolivian history which lead to an incurable extremism. Their causes are the following: a lack of intellectual development which leads to the adoption of alien doctrines; the lack of cultural traditions of critique of new ideas; the spread of individualism which replaces reason

---

29 Jorge Siles Salinas, *La aventura y el orden. Reflexiones sobre la revolución boliviana* (Santiago de Chile: Bustos y Letelier, 1956), pp. 105–06.

with will; the exclusion of intermediate alternatives, admitting only heroic and final options; the predominance of young people in politics; poverty; and political romanticism, which exacerbates the tendency of leaders to adopt grandiose plans. These sociological-cultural tendencies are coupled to the denunciation of the MNR as communist, communism being the worst enemy of our Hispanic Catholic historical character.

It is in this last aspect that a large part of the interpretation of 1952 is forcefully revealed as mediated and directed by an ideological discursive structure widespread in the postwar period of the Cold War, but older than that, which comes from the years after the Bolshevik revolution and from Spanish history. This is where the sense of an attack on Catholicism originates.

Siles' interpretation is a case of a characterization on the basis of appearances taken in a fragmentary way and a reading on the basis of an ideology and experience dislocated from the country. The workers' presence and union organization, the presence of class in political discourse, are taken as an index of communism, while the reorganization and US presence in the country indicates an opposite process. Nor is there any evidence that 1952 was an attack on Catholicism. In fact, the state continued to recognize it as the official religion, although it began a transition in the direction of the modern separation of church and state.

The most interesting thing in Siles' book is not his interpretation of 1952 as such, since it is largely spent battling the phantom of communism perceived in the MNR, but his ideas about cultural and sociological tendencies in Bolivian history that lead it to live in anarchy.

Here, the paradox appears in characterizing Bolivian history by these tendencies to extremism and anarchy, while the essence of the national being is supposed to be the Catholic Hispanic tradition. The only way to reconcile both ideas is through a belief in the value of the governing elites, although upon assigning them value at the same time their political deficiencies are revealed. With respect to this, Siles writes: 'Nothing is so notorious, in the process of our history, as the absence of a governing class, endowed with responsibility, which could give the social life of our country a hierarchical form, a lasting order, in sum, a structure.'[30]

And: 'The truth is that Bolivia has always been a prisoner of anarchy, not due to the excessive power of its governing classes, but precisely on the contrary, due to the excessive weakness of the minorities who represented the nation.'[31]

---

30 Siles Salinas, *La aventura y el orden*, p. 107.

31 Siles Salinas, *La aventura y el orden*, p. 110.

Almaraz[32] also comes to the conclusion that the dominant class in Bolivia did not manage to organize a power structure, but he was referring to one which would articulate the nation in the sense of an economy that integrates the dominated into production and political and cultural participation, not to a structure with a hierarchical order.

It is notable that Siles and those he represented are interested in a hierarchical symbolic order, not in production. Almaraz demanded the construction of the nation.

In 1964, Marcelo Quiroga Santa Cruz published a little book, *La victoria de abril sobre la nación* [The April victory over the nation], which collected a series of essays with a common theme, published in the newspaper *El Diario* in March and April of 1960. Quiroga Santa Cruz's prose is much more captivating than Siles', and the collection of texts is richer in analysis and political thought. The two coincide in several aspects. The first has to do with the destruction and defeat of tradition, which for Quiroga Santa Cruz is: 'a social group and a set of ideals [. . .] comfortably installed in the greater part of our history.'[33]

'[T]radition should be understood as two political parties with identical doctrinal roots and a minority born from those parties and conserved, although in highly precarious conditions, despite their own efforts; minorities which, justly or unjustly, exercised the right of inheritance of whatever of our history had been incorporated into their national profile.'[34]

The revolution is seen or thought as an attack on and destruction of those minorities and also of the middle class, via the displacement of the political centre from the city to the countryside, which will result in the Indianization of politics. Quiroga considers that the ethnic residue has wounded national history due to a paralysis in time and space:

> Bolivia has been formed as a nation with complete exclusion of the autochthonous element. The spirit of its republican structure is frankly Europeanizing. In this sense, our republic, far from constituting a nation that emerges from the historic Indo-Hispanic synthesis, continues to be the primitive colonial nucleus extended at the

---

32 Sergio Almaraz Paz, *El poder y la caída. El estaño en la historia de Bolivia* (Cochabamba: Los Amigos del Libro, 1967).

33 Marcelo Quiroga Santa Cruz, *La victoria de abril sobre la nación* (La Paz: Burillo, 1964), p. 29.

34 Quiroga Santa Cruz, *La victoria de abril sobre la nación*, p. 38.

expense of a constant retreat (geographical and spiritual) from the Upper Peruvian[35] autochthones.[36]

The April revolution contained in part precisely the negation of this negation, the political incorporation and growing citizenship of Indians and peasants, indeed a process through which national identity would be more and more marked by their presence.

In another part of *La victoria de abril sobre la nación*, Quiroga affirms that the MNR government has substituted dialogue, which characterizes good politics, for the official monologue which evades debate. This remark of Quiroga's contains a paradox and an interesting critique, forcing the extension of its application.

He demands political dialogue, considering that this should take place between members of the minority and the middle class, not with the indigenous population who are not part of the Bolivian nation. He demands dialogue within the minority, which represents tradition, that is to say, dialogue among those who monopolize, not with the rest. On the other hand, the avoidance of dialogue as the normal way to do politics in the 1950s and 1960s is not exclusive to the MNR but also typical of the FSB and almost all the collective political subjects. There is a strong tendency to monologue in so far as revolutionary nationalism becomes the dominant discourse and is considered to be the only one adequate for the period and the country; but political dialogue was no more a virtue of the pre-1952 tradition or of the opposition. In any case, in the moments when a broad nationalist movement existed, this was a theatre or space of dialogue, but also of struggles, with various orientations.

Zavaleta immediately published a criticism of Quiroga[37] characterized as a representative of the defeated Clique (*rosca*). According to Zavaleta, this essay reflects the feeling that the defeat of the Clique is the fall or apocalypse of the entire nation, since they felt that they were its most pure incarnation. Quiroga's novel *Los deshabitados* [The uninhabited] is also characterized as

---

35 In the colonial period, 'Peru' referred to both what is now Peru and Bolivia, but the actual Bolivia was distinguished as 'Upper Peru' from 'Lower Peru' which is present-day Peru. [Trans.]

36 Quiroga Santa Cruz, *La victoria de abril sobre la nación*, pp. 48–9.

37 René Zavaleta, 'Joven deshabitado culpa al país por sus desgracias personales', *La Nación* (17 March 1960). The title reads 'Deserted Youth Blames the Country for His Personal Misfortunes'; 'deserted' (*deshabitado*) refers to Quiroga's novel *Los deshabitados*, published in 1957.

the literary version of the ideas expressed in *La victoria de abril sobre la nación*, the description of the society and of individuals who were members of the Clique or oligarchy.

In 1960, Zavaleta and Quiroga clashed intellectually and politically. Years later Quiroga was one of those responsible for the nationalization of oil in 1969; he went on to found the Partido Socialista (PS, Socialist Party) in the days of the Popular Assembly at the beginning of the 1970s, becoming the principal socialist leader in the country. Today, Zavaleta and Quiroga are considered the foremost contemporary socialist intellectuals in Bolivia.

The days of the Popular Assembly, the moment in which these two intellectuals coincide in workerist positions, was when the workers' movement was at the height of its autonomy in ideological and political terms, since it was proposing the possibility of dual power.

Around 1960, they both criticized from different positions the politics that favored the development of separatist class-based workers' parties. Zavaleta criticized it because he considered that the working class formed part of the nationalist bloc and was well established in the MNR and in any case, the political and organizational separation of the working class was a pointless duplication. At the end of *La victoria de abril sobre la nación*, Quiroga writes that the MNR only includes one class, the proletariat, but it is a party created by the state, giving rise to the paradox of a state institution that subjugates the class it claims to liberate.[38] He warns of the danger that this situation of a class-based party could become a class without a party, with the autonomization of the proletariat, that it could become a class which acts as a party. The problem with this tendency is that a class party provokes confrontations, unlike national political parties, which proposed to represent the nation. This constitution of a working-class party that Quiroga opposed at the time would later become a principal objective when he became the founder and leader of the Partido Socialista.

The fact that the two principal socialist and workerist intellectuals came from other contexts and political-cultural traditions, revolutionary nationalism in the case of Zavaleta and the enlightened seigneurial tradition in the case of Quiroga, is perhaps a significant index of the strength the workers' movement was acquiring in the life of the country at the end of the 1960s and beginning of the 1970s. It is the referent and condition of possibility of the principal intellectual transformations of the period in the country. One could

---

38 Quiroga Santa Cruz, *La victoria de abril sobre la nación*, p. 65.

put this idea the other way around: the most lucid of the nationalist left and the seigneurial critique of 1952 converge in workerist positions around 1970, because the presence and political and ideological autonomy of the working class was the principal event of those times. Zavaleta and Quiroga take up the moral and political heart of the historical moment and project it intellectually. They did not invent the workerist and socialist strategy, but it seems that in order to carry on living with vitality, they recognized where the endogenous potency of local events was and set to thinking them as historical revision and as political strategy.

To conclude, we can sum up the conceptions of politics with which these histories and interpretations of the Bolivian revolution are elaborated: On the one hand, there is a group of interpretations, those of Siles, Quiroga and Roberts, which contain or unfold an axiological-idealist conception of politics. Good politics is conceived as an activity carried out by an urban minority, representative of the nation as incarnation of tradition or essence of our national being, responsible for social and political order. Bad politics is identified with the anarchy produced by the extremist tendencies of the Bolivian people, the attack on and destruction of tradition, when politics is decentred from the minority towards the plebs.

Tradition is the principal or most profound category and politics is its servant in the hands of the representative minorities; it becomes dangerous when it loses this center.

On the other hand, there is the conception of politics linked to the Marxist conception of history as class struggle. Politics is thought as domination by a class or as practices of liberation from that domination. In its simplest versions the conception is dual—a political practice collaborates in maintaining and reproducing class domination or serves to question it and promote the power of another class.

The peculiarity of Zavaleta in the context and within the Marxist tradition practised in Bolivia consists in that he conceives politics as closely linked to the processes of development of social classes as political subjects with a life of their own and not only as expressions of structural determinations, which implies not conceiving of power as something already constituted, which the classes struggle to exercise.

Within Marxism there has always been a concern with the problem of the development of consciousness, which some proposed as the passage from the class in itself to the class for itself, generally within a teleological horizon. Without abandoning this horizon, Zavaleta thinks, in explaining these processes, of the development of the working class in a less schematic fashion, as he has to account for the ideological-political relation of this class with revolutionary nationalism and the MNR, as part of its specific development but within the configuration of broader political phenomena in which it took part, such as the political constitution of the people in 1952 and of the national-popular bloc that surpasses parties and unions because it contains them all, as condition of possibility and at the same time expression of their constitution and development.

Finally, I want to repeat that in these Marxist works of revision and explanation of Bolivian history organized around 1952, Zavaleta periodizes history on the basis of the political criteria of the development of the class subjects in so far as they are political subjects and on the basis of the shifting articulations of these subjects, which allow him to explain the phases of change in the political regime.

The political development of the social classes and of their articulations, which configure the social bases of the phases of the state, organizes the explanation of history; but it is in the history of the country that the explanation of the political development of the social classes is to be found.

CHAPTER SEVEN

The Development of Workers' Autonomy:
Autonomy in Politics and the Logic of Place

When he wrote *El poder dual. Problemas de la teoría del Estado en América Latina* [Dual power: problems of state theory in Latin America],[1] Zavaleta shifted towards a Marxist theoretical framework and programme of research, which we have already analysed with reference to his conception of social science and the problem of knowledge.

This chapter aims to review Zavaleta's reflections on the problem of power, on two levels: on the one hand, his general reflections on the state, the party, sovereignty and the problem of power from the perspective of the revolution; on the other, the experience of the Popular Assembly in Bolivia and the 1952 revolution.

In *El poder dual* more than in anything else he wrote, he debates questions of power theoretically and politically, both from the point of view of strategy and from that of tactics. *El poder dual* combines analysis as social science, as previously expounded, with a long series of political reflections from a partisan position. They cover two things at once. One is the Bolivian historical process, in particular the conjunctures that lead one to imagine the existence of a dual power, that is, the revolution of 1952 and the 1971 Popular Assembly; the other is Marxist political theory of the state and the revolution, in particular Leninist and Trotskyist theory, but also that of Marx as a backdrop, which is approached in a particular way via the theory of dual power.

What Zavaleta does is to use one to revise and think the other, that is, Bolivian history is used to revise and develop up to a point the theory of dual power. He also uses this revision of state theory and dual power, in particular the Leninist version, to explain, first, the political course of Bolivian history, and on that basis the obstacles, possibilities and impossibilities of the revolution in

---

1 He finished writing the first part in December 1972, and the second, on the Popular Assembly in Bolivia and Allende's government in Chile, in December 1973. The book was first published in 1974 in Mexico City by Siglo XXI. A second edition was published by Los Amigos del Libro in Cochabamba in 1988.

Bolivia, and then, in consequence, the tasks which the revolutionary subject has to assume with the aim of transforming this society.

In *El poder dual* Zavaleta is also a partisan thinker, in the sense that he is not only interested in studying Bolivian history and offering an exclusively historiographic version of this process, but also revises history, in particular these two key political conjunctures marked by a strong workers' presence and in which there is a possibility for the presence of workers' power to become an alternative political power and state, for a strategic evaluation of the destiny and political project of the working class and socialism.

What Zavaleta is interested in studying and explaining is why this was not possible and, in consequence, which tasks remain pending as a necessary development in the workers' movement so as to make the revolution possible in Bolivia. If *El poder dual* is the first text in which Zavaleta proposes to analyse Bolivian history on the basis of a research strategy strongly centered in social science, it is also the text with the heaviest load of political-strategic reflection, and ultimately, therefore, of partisan thought. The incorporation and assumption of social science as the basic mode of explanation of historical processes, and the assumption of a specific theoretical identity—Marxism— are not carried out via the negation of political subjectivity but in a way that contains it together with the theory. This is so because, among other things, Marxist theory proposes from the outset this strong interrelation between social science, the explanation of the tendencies and structures of social reality, and strategic political thought, that is, the projection of how human beings intervene on the basis of that knowledge and in those realities with political aims of social emancipation.

First, I summarize the structure of *El poder dual*, and then discuss a limited set of problems; above all, I synthesize Zavaleta's conclusions, on the basis of which I would like to offer some reflections on his thought.

In the first chapter, Zavaleta debates 'The general theory of the duality of powers', with a minute and erudite revision of the theories of dual power, in particular those of Lenin and Trotsky, in which Zavaleta inclines towards Lenin's vision. In the second and third chapters he analyses 'The duality of powers in Bolivia' and 'The question of the duality of powers in Chile', texts which he finished writing at the end of 1972. In the second part he includes a complementary chapter on Bolivia, 'Some leftist problems concerning the Torres government in Bolivia', and another on Chile, 'Notes on bourgeois democracy, the national crisis and the civil war in Chile'.

Zavaleta wrote *El poder dual* as a contribution to the organization of the consciousness of the Bolivian working class;[2] essentially, it ought to reflect on the problem of why, having been in a situation of political victory and close to attaining state power, it ended up recomposing itself in its condition of a subordinated class.

Two aspects of this question should be studied at once: the internal limitations of the class and the form in which political power is structured in the history of the country, which is a step forward as a condition of possibility of possessing more adequate political tactics.[3]

Zavaleta thought that the fact that the debate on the subjects of power and the state become more frequent and occur with greater intensity within a class is a sign that this class has become capable of reorganizing society and political power in its own image, or in accordance with its project for the state, which it has germinated in its history.

The political power of the dominant class ultimately unifies itself in the state. Political parties are the form of competition between its fractions. In contrast, the working class basically constructs its identity via the party. A good way to articulate the problematic of this chapter with the previous analyses is via the centrality of the proletariat.

Zavaleta has argued that Bolivian history has produced or developed what he calls proletarian centrality as a social reality. We have reviewed the implications of this with reference to his conception of social science and the mode of producing historical explanation. Here we will analyse some of its political dimensions. I have expounded how, in the development or history of Zavaleta's thought, his appropriation of Marxism was closely linked to the process by which the Bolivian working class developed autonomy, that is, their process of ideological and political separation with respect to the dominant ideology and thus, of progressively overcoming its incorporation in the state of 1952 as a subordinated class.

In *El poder dual* Zavaleta analyses the culminating moment or the strongest expression of this process of political autonomy, which is the constitution of the Popular Assembly in 1971.[4] This occurred during the Torres

---

2 Zavaleta, *El poder dual*, pp. 7–8.

3 Zavaleta, *El poder dual*, p. 12.

4 This was first proposed by the COB in May 1970. General Juan José Torres took power in October 1970, in an atmosphere of left-wing fervour favourable to proposals of co-government between the military, radical intellectuals and workers, which led to the

government, which took power through a counter-coup against the right wing of the army, made possible by the intervention and support of the workers.

According to Zavaleta, Torres set up a semi-Bonapartist government, composed in large part of left-wing nationalist intellectuals. During the first period of his government he negotiated the inclusion of the workers with the COB, but although the COB supported Torres' government, after a few months the workers decided to set up the Popular Assembly which was a sort of workers' parliament and an embryo of a dual power.

The Popular Assembly is a transposition of the COB on a more explicitly political level of organization and representation of the class and its margin of irradiation, which begins to prefigure the type of political power that could form an alternative government of the country. The Popular Assembly conjoins unions and parties, with unions predominating. In this sense, and also more generally, the Assembly constitutes a kind of soviet. In the first place it is a form of representation and organization of the class with political ends. It is a form of political participation and begins to prepare the forms and composition of its government.

The Popular Assembly begins to organize itself in an embryonic form parallel to the Torres government and to the army, which had not been modified or even touched. It begins with the tasks of organizing representation and deliberation. This led many left-wing currents in the country, in particular the Trotskyists and, more specifically, the POR, to think that a dual power had already been set up. Zavaleta's analysis questions this characterization, not with merely academic ends of determining whether or not this existed, but in order to determine the causes of the defeat of the workers' movement in that conjuncture, and also in the past, in the 1952 revolution.

His analysis is minute. I will summarize it briefly, since I am interested in recovering a limited set of ideas so as to present Zavaleta's political perspective on the conjuncture, in order to establish links with the past and the future, in terms of his intellectual development and the way in which theoretical and political reflection accompany or respond to the dynamic of the historical political process.

---

formation of the Popular Assembly in June 1971. Dominated by miners' delegates (132 out of a total of 223), it was in session only for 11 days, but its radical rhetoric terrified business and right-wing sectors, while it also refused to support the government. The outcome was a right-wing military coup in August 1971 and a return to dictatorship. [Trans.]

Zavaleta considers that the Popular Assembly did not manage to propose a dual power in Bolivia, but only the seed of dual power. It was a seed because the Popular Assembly configured a sort of soviet, which is a form of autonomous organization of the working class and its allies. It is a form of organization that aims to prefigure and develop a new state, or at least part of one, that which corresponds to the form of government of a new state, which is not an artificial institutional apparatus but one which emerges from the depths of the history of the Bolivian workers' movement, as Zavaleta says. It is a phase in the development of ideological-political autonomy and in the process of separation from the state of 1952.

According to Zavaleta, there are three principal aspects due to which the Popular Assembly did not end up configuring a dual power in the country. For a dual power to exist in the strict sense, there must be two states in confrontation. The Popular Assembly did not manage to constitute another power in the general sense, because it lacked its own apparatus of coercion, an armed wing or its own army, which was the main defect of the Popular Assembly, as shown by its negative experience in the clashes of August 1971, when the whole of the Bolivian governing class, the right wing and the army organized the overthrow of Torres and the military coup which also did away with the Popular Assembly.

This Assembly is formed and begins to organize itself within the existing Bolivian state, governed by Torres and supported by the workers. The workers' movement and its parties were taking advantage of the democratic context of tolerance and acceptance of workers' freedom in Torres' government so as to start to organize and prefigure their own form of government; but the Assembly was not an organ of power which could have developed the capacity to compete with or substitute the existing state. It was a parallel development, but within the existing state and in a political setting in which the army of the state of 1952, which over the last decades had also developed its bureaucracy and coercive capacity under the new conditions of US penetration in the country, had in no way been disorganized.

Nor had it achieved the maturity of two other components, of the highest importance according to Zavaleta. One of them is the political vanguard or the party form and, closely linked to this, the capacity of the class, above all via its party, to offer a new leadership or government for society. This goes with having obtained a majority in society. In the brief space in time during which the Assembly existed, and before that during Torres' entry into government, the workers' movement was trying first of all to recover some of its previous

achievements—shared administration of state enterprises and the nationalization or re-nationalization of some mining companies, and co-government.
These are things that the workers' movement had accomplished in 1952.

These two things, shared administration and co-government, and the fact
that in 1952 and after the victory the armed workers had a monopoly of physical force in a large part of the country, above all via the unions, also led the
Trotskyists in particular to put forward that in 1952 a dual power had also
existed.

I go back to 1952 to bring up other factors that limited the Popular
Assembly so as to bring the discussion to a theoretical-political level that will
allow me to locate Zavaleta within the currents of the Marxist tradition, and
to situate this moment of his thought within the development of his ideas.

Zavaleta considers that a duality of powers was not produced in 1952 for
two reasons: these were the absence of a proletarian party which could provide political direction to the class and its movement, and the fact of the ideological subordination of the workers' movement to bourgeois ideology in
its nationalist reformist mode, politically articulated by the MNR.

In 1952, the army and the previous political power or state were disorganized. Armed workers destroyed the old army and for a while predominated in terms of physical force in the country, but without autonomy and
certainly without achieving the ideological and political hegemony of the
working class. Most of the class subscribed to revolutionary nationalism and
took part in politics via the MNR.

The workers' movement operated as the most radical wing, both in terms
of nationalization and of democratization, of the national and nationalist ideology. When Zavaleta refers to the absence of a proletarian party, he does not
mean to say that there were no workers' or workerist parties. Before the organization of the class in unions, the Trotskyist POR had been active and the
PCB was founded at the beginning of the 1950s. Zavaleta refers to the non-
existence of a workers' party that was the principal form of class unity and its
action on the strategic political level as ideological leadership and with the
capacity to organize another state. There were workers' or workerist parties,
but they were not the principal centre of organization, self-understanding
and political strategy of the class. The form of class unity was the trade union.
The majority of the class was not organized around a party with an ideology
and a political project distinct from that of revolutionary nationalism, whose
party form was the MNR.

Without ideological autonomy and a party which organizes this autonomy as the germ of a new state, there can be no duality of powers. The fact of possessing material or even military power does not constitute duality if there is ideological subordination, since in that case there are not two opposing state projects but rather two versions of the same state, one more radical and the other more reformist and conservative.

In this sense, shared administration and co-government are the forms of inclusion of the working class in the 1952 state that carried out the bourgeois reform of the country's economy and politics. They are not forms of dual power. Of course, they are forms of inclusion that involve a certain degree of differentiation, which is why they are known as co-government and shared or co-administration. They express class and political differentiation, but they are not yet forms of autonomy and ideological-political separation which could be opposed to the official state as a real alternative, another state.

In so far as, over the following decades, the Bolivian working class had to organize against the state, which adopted a dictatorial form, that is, concentrated its form of domination in the army and forged an alliance with the most conservative sectors of society, it began to develop its ideological autonomy and to separate itself from the state of 1952.

The level of maturity of these processes is expressed in the organization of the Popular Assembly at the beginning of the 1970s. What Zavaleta calls accumulation within the class (which occurred in these decades of resistance to a state that was fiercely anti-worker), carried out basically through the trade union form, takes on a political form in this conjuncture. It becomes a soviet, a national assembly of workers' unions and left-wing parties. It is an assembly where the unions predominate and not the parties, which for Zavaleta is a sign that the political development of the class had not yet produced its strategic subject, its vanguard, the unified leadership that provides the rationalization of tactics at the level of the conjuncture and the state project in terms of historical destiny.

Zavaleta relates this to the Russian experience, which is the origin of the theory of dual power, beginning with Lenin, who thought that dual power was something particular to the Russian Revolution and not a general theory of the transition from one state to another, which was what Trotsky tried to make of it. In Russia, apart from constituting the soviets as an initiative of the masses, there was a vanguard party which was able to become the leadership of that extensive movement of self-organization of the masses. There is a subject with political initiative which, over and above the creativity and spontaneity of the mass movement, has the organizational and ideological capacity to propose and carry out the substitution of the existing state and, therefore, convert all that mobilization into not only the embryo but also an effective, mature dual power.

This is what did not happen in Bolivia. Zavaleta makes the comparison in *El poder dual*, although in a much more moderate way than is usual in the Bolivian left. He bases his discussion of dual power in an erudite revision of Lenin's and Trotsky's theories. The Russian experience and the theories of these political thinkers becomes a referent for the analysis of Bolivian history. Bolivian leftists, in particular the Trotskyists, tended to interpret Bolivian history according to the Russian revolutionary experience, trying to find equivalents; that is to say, in the modality of historical repetition, which supposes an underlying conception of regularities or laws of revolutionary process.

Trotsky did try to convert the Russian experience and the theory of dual power into an element of all revolutionary processes and, more generally, a way to account for the differentiation of the forms of power within a single state structure. He turned this theory into a general theory of revolution. Russian history would have revealed the laws of history corresponding to the moments of its political revolution. Trotsky incarnates what Gramsci called cosmopolitanism in theory and political thought.

This contrasts with what Zavaleta, also following Gramsci, characterizes as localism in political thought and in politics itself. Lenin thought that the duality of powers was a peculiarity of Russian history. His theory responds to the political movement of the Russian working class, of the Bolshevik party, which became its organized consciousness, and of the type of worker-peasant alliance that gave a majority to the party-class bloc in the experience of the soviets and, in consequence, allowed for the constitution of a duality of powers.

Zavaleta also uses the Russian revolutionary experience in his analysis, but not in order to find equivalents in the Bolivian process, as expression of the general laws of the revolution which found their clearest expression in Soviet history assumed as general point of reference, but rather to learn from this experience in a manner sensitive to what was peculiar in that history and is peculiar in Bolivian history.

Zavaleta analyses Bolivian history with reference to some more or less general theories, in this case above all Lenin, since he is critical of Trotsky. He also makes use of Soviet history. So far, these are widespread features among the Bolivian left. The difference is that Zavaleta does this recovering another peculiarity of Lenin, which he came to call locality or the logic of place. His vision is as follows:

> It is evident that in this case perhaps more than in any other we can see (something which is present, as well, in all his thinking) that Trotsky tended to perceive with more lucidity or transparency the unity of world history, which is after all the essential fact of our times, while Lenin or Stalin and Gramsci himself could understand more easily and exhaustively the difference or peculiarity of world history, an attitude without which a revolutionary movement cannot succeed now or ever. The logic of place, certainly, usually defeats the logic of the world.[5]

El poder dual is a highly Leninist book. Zavaleta does not use Lenin as representative of general theory and the Marxist truth of the twentieth century, but, rather, as a guide to think the peculiarities of the history of the Bolivian workers' movement, or what he calls the logic of place; since Lenin was the Marxist politician and theorist who thought with greater rigor and vitality the peculiarity of Russian history.

El poder dual is a Leninist book not in the sense that it aims to fit the events of Bolivian history into the explanation that Lenin elaborated for Russian history, but because in its search to understand and explain the logic of place, it takes as its guide someone who was able to account for the specificity of his local history and for that reason, also had the capacity to direct its political transformation.

Zavaleta does not conclude that a duality of powers was not produced in Bolivia in 1952 and 1971 was because there was not a repetition of the whole process of the Russian Revolution. Although the way in which Lenin theorized the Russian experience serves as the principal political and intellectual point of reference in his discussion of the Bolivian events, these ideas are used to account for Bolivian peculiarity. In sum, Zavaleta uses the theory of dual power that Lenin elaborated to account for the peculiarity of Russian history to attempt to account for the peculiarity of the Bolivian workers' movement, although in the shadow (or light) of Lenin.

This is an example of how the explanation of a historical specificity can, at times, make better use of a theory that served to account for another specificity than of theories at a more general level and with pretensions to more universal validity. Specific, local processes cannot always be defined with reference only

---

5 Zavaleta, *El poder dual*, p. 39.

to endogenous elements, but their definition may be helped by the mode in which it has been possible to think other specificities, which at the same time have been studied with some elements of more general theorization. Zavaleta's Leninist version gives a better account of the specificity of the history of the workers' movement in Bolivia than, for example, the POR's Trotskyist version.

Lenin's local or nationalist view is more useful to him than Trotsky's cosmopolitan vision. *El poder dual* is not a work whose objective is to expound a general theory of the duality of powers in order to comprehend and analyse Latin American states. It is a work that assesses previous theorizations of this type of reality, but whose end is to participate in the development of the theory of the state within Marxist theory on the basis of the analysis, explanation and discussion of the political problems faced by workers' and socialist movements in Bolivia and Chile. It takes elements of Marxist theory as a guide for the explication, above all, of the peculiarity of the Bolivian and Chilean experience. On this basis it contributes to the development of a Marxist theory of the state.

Many readers take it to be the other way around. *El poder dual* seems to be an orthodox Marxist text that applies general theories to frame national events, in a doctrinal and repetitive manner that lacks creativity or theoretical originality. I think that one reason for this impression, which in the end is superficial, is that Zavaleta still uses the traditional language common to Marxism in general to explain the peculiarity of Bolivian history. He had not yet developed a new language that would account for the diversity and complexity of local history or of societies like Bolivia, although new ideas begin to emerge here.

El poder dual is not just a work of formal application of Marxism or a demonstration of theoretical mastery via his commentary on two historical conjunctures in Bolivia and one in Chile. It is an appropriation that produces an explanation of the specificity of Latin American histories, although with a more strictly class-based discourse than his later works, something that limits its ability to account for the social totality.

In *El poder dual* the ideas with which Zavaleta would carry out his particular development of Marxism are present in embryonic form: accumulation within the class, the crisis as moment of totalization of society and, above all, the idea of the primacy of the logic of place, both for explanation and for political action, in particular for revolutionary strategy and action.

This is the general orientation and basic theoretical structure of what I have come to call the production of local knowledge on the basis of Marxism.

El poder dual is an appropriation of Marxism in the modality of a theory that serves to account for historical specificity or the logic of place on the basis of a framework that explains the central structures and tendencies of the modern world. For that same reason its use to account for the logic of place cannot be expressed by a group of universal laws of which our history is one more case but, rather, by converting it into a core around which to articulate the specific configuration of social totality as local history.

El poder dual is the expression of the logic of place within the horizon and the limits of a class-based account of history and society. From this core, going beyond it but never denying it (except in the Hegelian sense), Zavaleta elaborates the complexity of his later thought.

I return to the more political dimension to characterize Zavaleta's thought at this time. The basic axis that he discusses in *El poder dual* is the articulation of class-ideology-party-state, in particular for the working class.

It can be said that the consolidation of the link between the class and the party implies in some sense the existence of the state.[6] Zavaleta believed that without a proletarian party there was no possibility of a proletarian State.[7] He recognizes that it was Gramsci who insisted in this implication, since Gramsci thought that the constitution of a historic bloc on the basis of the working class ought to experience in its development and articulation the seed of a new state, and that the Communist Party in particular carried in its breast the form of the new state. Without this there is neither substantial political development nor the effective capacity to produce a revolution. However, Zavaleta recognizes this with certain reservations. He considers that the party cannot become a state:

> In reality, the party can never, strictly speaking, be a state. The idea of the state itself responds to the needs of class oppression; it is the result of a society divided into classes. The party, however, contains qualitatively only one class, which uses this instrument to destroy the domination exercised over it and to organize its own domination in society. That the party should be an indispensable element for the construction of the proletariat's organs of power and, in consequence, for the existence of a true duality of powers, does not convert it, for that sole reason, into a state in itself. But it is certain that in the party

---

6 Zavaleta, *El poder dual*, p. 30.

7 Zavaleta, *El poder dual*, p. 48.

the class learns and acquires all those elements with which it will construct its dictatorship.[8]

The constitution of the party is the condition of possibility of the organization of another state, but it is not in itself the organization of a new state, although it may be its embryo. It is above all the condition of the production of ideology and of political leadership. The dominant class in the state form organizes its sovereignty over the working class and society as a whole. In the measure in which the working class is able to construct its party it no longer recognizes this sovereignty in the state but rather prepares its own sovereignty.[9]

The organization and development of the proletarian party is, therefore, the form of ceasing to belong to and separating from the state. It is a way to break the sovereignty of the state or reduce its sphere of validity, and to prepare another sovereignty, which in principle must exist within the class and the party before it can expand to encompass society.

Zavaleta's discussion of class, party and state in *El poder dual* are informed by Lenin and Gramsci, with Lenin still predominating over Gramsci. When Zavaleta talks about working class hegemony in Bolivia, for example, in the first phase of the 1952 revolution, he uses this notion in Lenin's sense, as a synonym of worker predominance, and not as the articulation of domination and leadership or direction, which is the concept that Gramsci develops in his prison writings. As the years went by Zavaleta's thought, or his Marxism, would be more and more marked by the general conception of Gramsci's mature thought and the group of categories that it contributed to Marxist thought. Lenin would be left behind although never abandoned. In *El poder dual* Gramsci complements Lenin; later Lenin would at times complement Gramsci in Zavaleta's Marxism.

Zavaleta's argument in *El poder dual* is that the great failure in the history of the Bolivian workers' movement is in the construction of the proletarian party. In this he has a basically Leninist idea of the party. It should be recalled, however, that Gramsci was also a Leninist, in that he conceived of the party as vanguard. According to Zavaleta, the problem of the party is on the level of autonomy in politics, which is the moment of tactics.[10]

The party is the exercise of workers' freedom on the level of the super-structure. The exercise of this liberty implies the organization of a self-

---

8 Zavaleta, *El poder dual*, p. 33.

9 Zavaleta, *El poder dual*, p. 62.

10 Zavaleta, *El poder dual*, pp. 34–5.

referential class consciousness, although this limits social duality and the flexibility of the movement. Because of its level organization, the party has the capacity to respond to the correlation of forces with political initiative. The party is the form in which the working class develops political autonomy or takes part in the development of the general process of its society, which, under bourgeois domination, generally takes the form of representative democracy and bureaucracy.

The development of the proletarian party can reach such a degree of political autonomy that it becomes a condition of possibility for a change in the type of society; that is to say, when it no longer responds to the strongest determinations of the productive moment which generally lead to the reproduction of the mode of production and its type of society.

Political autonomy developed at the state pole can never go so far: it tends to be configured in the mode of general representation, that is to say, the sublimation of the concealment of the class character of the foundations of its power. Political autonomy in the state is developed via an ideological production that universalizes on the political level the predominance of the interests of the dominant class. In contrast, the development of political autonomy by the working class appears, in the way Zavaleta saw things in that conjuncture or that period, as the development of class autonomy, that is to say as the development of an openly class-based identity and party, although the proposed task is the construction of a social majority, generally via a worker-peasant axis.

Political autonomy thus has two general forms of development, which correspond to the two class poles of society. On one side, the state, which is the form of domination of one class, appears as a form of government in the general interest, that is to say, the autonomy of politics as a form of reproduction of the mode of production and the form of domination. On the other side, there is basically the proletarian party, which is a form of political autonomy through separation, reaching autonomy by the route of the suspension, partial at the moment and ultimately total, of subordinate membership within the state and, in consequence, of the reproduction of the mode of production. It is a strong form of political autonomy because it consists in a process that begins to negate the factors that reproduce the mode of production to which it belongs.

Both things occur at once. The working class exists within the capitalist mode of production, but in the measure in which it transforms its structural location, which is subordinate to capital, into a history of resistance, increasing its autonomy and separation in order to negate it, it develops political autonomy in another direction.

To conclude this part, it can be said that what Zavaleta proposes for the country at this point is the need to develop proletarian sovereignty through the construction of its party as axis and condition for the construction of national sovereignty.

This is the moment in which Zavaleta's political thought is most focused on class and on the centrality of the workers.

Through the experience of the Popular Assembly, the Bolivian working class comes to know what can be the skeleton of a future form of its power. *El poder dual*, as a contribution to the organization of working class consciousness in the country, is a reflection on the weaknesses and limitations that its movement has not yet overcome, for a new moment in the history of the country in which the working class might promote the possibility of a revolution, the suspension of state sovereignty and its substitution by its own sovereignty, on the basis of its own development or interior political accumulation, as a conquest of the new social majority.

This way of seeing things will be the condition of possibility of the later development of his work, and also a moment that he will propose to overcome in a conclusive manner.

PART C

Political Theory

CHAPTER EIGHT

The State

With Zavaleta, Bolivian Marxism passes from its phase of application to the history of the country to a phase of debate and theoretical production, in dialogue with other modes of thought in the contemporary social sciences, although he wrote his later works in other countries.

After the 1971 military coup, Zavaleta left for Chile, where he worked for a while. He was a consultant for the Oficina de Planificación de la Presidencia de la República (ODEPLAN, Planning Office of the Presidency of the Republic) between 1972 and 1973, and coordinator of the Centro de Estudios de la Realidad Nacional (CEREN, Centre for the Study of Chilean Society) of the Universidad Católica de Chile between 1971 and 1972.

After that he was based in Mexico, where he published most of the essays that I will discuss in my presentation of his thought on the state and his work in political science.

In Mexico, upon his arrival in 1973 he worked as chargé of social affairs for the Comisión Económica para América Latina y el Caribe (CEPAL, the United Nations Economic Commission for Latin America and the Caribbean) and as a consultant for UNESCO. Later his professional activities were primarily academic, and he worked at various universities, principally in the Facultad Latinoamericana de Ciencias Sociales (FLACSO, Latin American Social Science Faculty) from 1976 to 1980. He also worked as teacher and researcher at the Latin American Studies Centre of UNAM (1974–75), as a lecturer in the Postgraduate Division of the Economics Faculty of UNAM (1980–84) and as a tenured lecturer of the Social Relations Department of the Universidad Autónoma Metropolitana—Xochimilco (1980–84).

From 1971 to 1973 he was a member of the Movimiento de la Izquierda Revolutionaria (MIR, Revolutionary Left Movement) and from 1978 to 1984 he was a member of the Bolivian Communist Party. From 1971 to 1972 he edited *Vanguardia*, the MIR organ. During the 1970s he wrote columns for *Excelsior, Proceso, Plural, El Día* and *Cuadernos de Marcha*. I use this material to review his analysis of Latin American and Bolivian politics during the 1970s.

In this decade Mexico was a hub of intellectual work and encounters, due to the welcome this country extended to intellectuals and politicians from several Latin American countries that had suffered coups d'état. Mexico became a good place from whence to think about Latin America, and in particular about the countries Zavaleta knew from the inside.

The following five chapters are dedicated to Zavaleta's work on political theory: first, his ideas on the relationship between base and superstructure, and therefore, between the state, capitalism and ideology; a brief chapter on the national question; then his studies on forms of the state and politics in Latin America; a chapter on anti-imperialism and sovereignty; and finally, one on four concepts of democracy.

The intellectual and political context of Mexico and its academic networks, as well as the broader political context of the region, has significant bearing on each of these topics in Zavaleta's work from this period.

Model of Regularity and Historical Diversity

Zavaleta's broadest, most systematic and theoretical discussion of the state and ideology is to be found in an essay he published in 1978, 'Las formaciones aparentes en Marx' [Apparent formations in Marx]. This text will serve as a focal point around which concepts from other texts are organized in this chapter.

In 'Las formaciones aparentes en Marx', Zavaleta carries out his broadest theoretical discussion of central Marxist topics such as the relation between the productive forces and the relations of production, between base and superstructure and between production, state and ideology.

The value and interest of this work lies, first, in the reflection on the scope of validity and the limits of Marx's ideas. The idea is that the productivity and explanatory capacity of Marxist theory depend on a clear consciousness of the modes of analysis and thought through which it can produce sound explanations.

Zavaleta distinguishes two important ways in which Marx's ideas on history, its structure and the critique of capital can and should operate: as models of regularity and as a conception of societies in history.

It will be helpful to begin by outlining the parameters of Marxism in the field of social science in order to then situate it in its general context.

Zavaleta uses the classical Marxist distinction between base and super-structure as a starting point from which to develop a set of ideas that complicate the unidirectional relation of causality and relativize rigid distinctions.

The starting point is the notion of totality:

> The simultaneity of base and superstructure is the central fact of social knowledge (because in capitalism no part lacks integration with the other, just as individuals cannot exist on their own); in other words, society exists here as an organic totality. Its own reductive actions or particularizations are no more than quantitative shrinkages which are in their quality bearers of that totality.[1]

The idea of totality is both a regulatory idea and an ontological conception. The simultaneity of base and superstructure implies both, as does the notion that a particularity contains that totality. There is a relation here that is similar to the Hegelian conception of reality in which each moment contains or expresses the totality.

Now, this relation between particularity and totality does not always occur in the same way. Zavaleta's work is concerned with distinguishing the area in which one can think in terms of laws, which is the domain of social science.

When the idea of totality appears in a historicist mode, that is to say, as a process of totalization in specific historical processes, as a product of time that never ends, the other connotation of the idea of totality as simultaneity of base and superstructure appears more clearly as a regulative idea.

The type of totalization that makes social science historically possible is the capitalist mode of production. The substantial totalization in question is an abstraction: the expression of the different kinds of work and their results in terms of socially necessary labour time, as the social relation that unifies the world in a new way and allows the knowledge of societies to be quantified.

The totalization which is the basis of the possibility of social science is a great historical abstraction, which Marx summarizes in the theory of the law of value. The possibility of thinking models of regularity is given by the development and extension of certain relations of production that progressively homogenize and equalize human labour over and above its specific quality.

Zavaleta writes:

---

1 Zavaleta, 'Las formaciones aparentes en Marx': 5.

The model of regularity or mode of production reveals the unity of the history of the world, its present homogeneity, while the superstructures display its singularities, its diversity and incommensurability. The operation of such social phases is, however, the opposite when each formation is considered on the basis of its autochthonous movement or internality. Here, on the contrary, the economic base contains the elements of social heterogeneity while the superstructure displays the lines of unity.[2]

This type of distinction is not absolute, since Zavaleta considers that there are zones of regularity in the superstructure or moments in which it takes part in the model of regularity. The principal point of superposition or correspondence is that of the relation between the character of capitalism as a mode of production of juridically free men and the superstructure of a modern state, which produces and recognizes on the political level this condition of surplus value as an economic-social relation.

This participation of the superstructure in the model of regulatory does not apply to the periphery but to the centre, at the origin of the value—surplus value relation, which, as Marx indicated, consists in the creation of free men with respect to servitude and the possession of the means of life.

The relation between the representative democratic state and the capitalist mode of production is based on this co-participation of base and superstructure in the constitutive moment or relation of capitalism.

While both dimensions participate in the configuration of society that makes possible its self-knowledge as social science, Zavaleta follows Marx in considering that there is a core of society, in terms of the possibility of knowledge. This is the moment of production,[3] and this is the context of what are called social laws.[4]

Zavaleta does not centre his work on the analysis and theorization of the moment of production, but rather takes on the analysis of superstructures and history, as the lived time of simultaneity of these analytic distinctions. His work consists in studying how the law of value operates on the political and ideological level, the scope of its power of determination on these levels, and also how politics and ideology are present and operate in the articulation and operation of the law of value.

---

2 Zavaleta, 'Las formaciones aparentes en Marx': 12.

3 Zavaleta, 'Las formaciones aparentes en Marx': 12–13.

4 Zavaleta, 'Las formaciones aparentes en Marx': 11. This is a way of commenting on the way in which Lenin presents Marx's work.

An important implication for political theory proceeds from this idea of totality as the union of base and superstructure, which is as follows. While Zavaleta, following Marx, conceives of a core of society that corresponds to the practices and relations of production, explained by the model of regularity that is the theory of the capitalist mode of production, he also holds that these social relations produce as one of their results a group of apparent forms. On the level of the superstructure, they produce an ideology that partially conceals reality. It is typical that a society with capitalist relations should produce a transfiguration which appears in ideology as forms that generally enunciate equality, equity and justice between men.

In general, Zavaleta says that the superstructure is like the shell of a hidden social substance.[5] The union of base and superstructure in capitalist societies signifies the composition or articulation of an ideology that conceals the quality of its determinant causal base, and political power maintains this. It reproduces but also in part produces this ideology. In doing social science, then, while the core of society is constituted by the relations of production and the core of social science is the law of value, this cannot be targeted in a direct or immediate way but rather it is necessary to approach it via the critique of ideology and the critique of political power.

One of the implications of the principle of totality is the conception of a unified social science rather than a group of social sciences. In the same measure in which the explanation of the core of society emerges from the consideration of the political power that reproduces the ideology that has to be substituted in order to explain society, political theory acquires relevance.

The way in which Zavaleta thinks the problem of the state, above all in the essay 'Las formaciones aparentes en Marx', responds to this kind of analysis in terms of totality and a vision of the most general structures of a capitalist society.

Zavaleta's idea is that while the economic structure displays the elements of diversity, the state displays the elements of unity. The unity provided by the state is not the homogeneity produced by the relations of production expressed in the law of value, but a formal type of unity, above all juridical. It is a unity achieved through ideology. The power and form of the state are ideological; they cannot be reduced to the monopoly of force, which is its basic condition.

---

5 Zavaleta, 'Las formaciones aparentes en Marx': 11.

The other idea that accompanies this idea of the state as unity is that of the state as the synthesis of society. Zavaleta recalls that Lenin insisted on this, following Marx.[6]

In a more epistemological key, it can be said that these ideas do not mean that the theory of the state could become a complete model or a model of regularity that would explain social totality because the state is unity and synthesis; the synthesis referred to here is a specific synthesis articulated by each state and each society, that is, it is always a historical and local synthesis on the basis of which it is not possible to elaborate a model of regularity.

In fact, according to Zavaleta, it is not possible to elaborate a model of regularity for politics, not even for politics in capitalist societies. Zavaleta's idea is that the relevance of models of regularity corresponds to the modes of production, and only a part of politics can be thought in terms of correspondence with this core. The rest responds to what he calls the special accumulation of the superstructure in the vertebration of each local history.

Zavaleta, however, proposes to study the reach, in terms of determination, of the law of value in politics and ideology, which is a way to deploy on a general level the idea that superstructures are determined by their structural base. At the same time, Zavaleta's task is that of thinking the limits of this scheme of thinking reality. Both things are done at once. The idea is used, it is put into practice, and its limits are also theorized.

This implies that diversity is conceived on the basis of politics, as is history, in so far as history is diversity. Diversity is conceived on the basis of politics because this is the context in which the weight of the action and choices of subjects appear with more force. The dimension of freedom and variation in history is introduced via the consideration of subjects.

'The state form corresponds to the course of the superstructure that this formation brings from the past, that is, the way in which men's freedom intervenes in the determination of history.'[7]

Freedom is exercised within social totalities which organize strong structures of determination of their practices and actions. Freedom and the effects of its exercise are something that must also be explained firstly in terms of their conditions of possibility according to the type of development and configuration of the social totality, and thence as forms of variation, development, transformation and rebellion that reconfigure a social totality.

---

6 Zavaleta, 'Las formaciones aparentes en Marx': 22.

7 Zavaleta, 'Las formaciones aparentes en Marx': 6.

Politics is also the reproduction of social structures and, therefore, of forms of domination, which is usually the more everyday form of its exercise. This repetition is organized in the form of the state. Here it is necessary to emphasize that politics is not a synonym of the state. The state tends towards a monopoly of politics and achieves this in different degrees according to the type of relation between state and civil society and the system of mediations that connects them. Nor is the superstructure a synonym of the state, but something much broader, which includes politics as a set of practices not limited to the state, and also includes ideology. Zavaleta conceives it as the set of conscious and unconscious forms of extra-economic connection.[8]

The State as Synthesis, Unity, Mediation and Rationality

I will sum up the formulation of this problematic in schematic terms in order to then continue the analysis. There is a core of determination of society, which can also be thought of as an organizational principle, which is the moment of production; but at the same time social reality is conceived as a totality which is basically articulated by the superstructure. The state and ideology are fundamental in this. They are the principal forms of its realization.

Zavaleta recalls Lenin's idea of the state as the synthesis of society, and adds that this synthesis is carried out from a particular point of view, that of the dominant class; that is, it is a synthesis qualified by the dominant part of society.[9]

Zavaleta habitually says that the state is the form of domination of the dominant pole of society. The state is synthesis, firstly, because it responds to the process by which the society has produced the separation of politics as state, and it is so above all because it is the node in which society unifies the organization of culture and economic and social life.

In the measure in which the state is a synthesis from the point of view of the dominant class or in which this is predominant, it is a synthesis in which the ideology of that class also marks the quality, breadth and limits of that synthesis. It is a synthesis which reveals what predominates in a society and what it integrates of the dominated and subordinated, in the measure in which it tends to negate and conceal that which it excludes or has not managed to contain in a hegemonic way. The state is a synthesis, but also a modality of the apparent form.

---

8 Zavaleta, 'Las formaciones aparentes en Marx': 8.

9 René Zavaleta, 'El estado en América Latina', *Ensayos* 1 (1984): 59–78.

The mystified form necessarily responds to the capitalist mode of production. The 'apparent formation' of a society never coincides with what the society is: exploitation is masked as equality, class collectives figure as individuals, repression as ideology, value appears as price, the economic base as superstructure and surplus value as profit. Everything is travestied and disguised. This last point, however, the split between reality and appearance that corresponds to the duality surplus value—profit, is what is important. What then is this whole set of apparent formations? It is bourgeois ideology. This, in turn, is no more than the analysis of society from the point of view of profit.[10]

The state as synthesis of this whole reality is thus the principal apparent formation, although it is not the origin. The task of the state is to articulate this set of apparent formations that are generated in different moments and contexts of capitalist society. Its task is also the production of what Zavaleta calls the necessary ideology, which is the skeleton of the total ideology or universalization of the interests and conceptions of the dominant part of a society as a general conception of its world.[11]

This necessary ideology is the internal ideology of the dominant class,[12] the production of the conviction of its own domination, which then has to produce its discourse or external ideology in the process of conquest and integration of the dominated. The synthesis may have a different quality from that of the reality it synthesizes; moreover, the state tends to become mainly responsible for the dissemination of the necessary ideology and for its production when the class has not managed to previously diffuse it in society.

The modern state is in large part an ideological form, sustained by the materiality of the concentration of physical force. This state acts basically on the basis of ideology, and only resorts to force in its moments of crisis, or makes use of a physical violence as a tactic that is subordinate to the predominant and hegemonic exercise of ideology.

Explaining society by means of its synthesis in the state is a shortcut that requires explaining the origin of this form of state. Otherwise, it becomes one more repetition of the ideology produced to reproduce the same.

---

10 Zavaleta, 'Las formaciones aparentes en Marx': 18.

11 Zavaleta, 'Las formaciones aparentes en Marx': 19.

12 Zavaleta, 'Las formaciones aparentes en Marx': 24.

Zavaleta writes that ideology is at once identification and a proof of itself.[13] In ideology, men find the answers before the questions.[14] From the perspective of the problematic of the state, this means that with and in ideology an identification with the existing type of society and state is produced. The less persuasive the dominant class within civil society, the more this task is carried out by the state.

The fact that ideology provides answers rather than questions has to do with that basic function of the state which is reproduction and preservation. Ideology, above all that of the state, functions to impede the rise of new questions concerning what else could be done or in what other ways one could live. The ideology that circulates in the state and the dominant class is a discourse on what should be done within the existing order. It is a kind of intellectual ordering of well-defined answers concerning what has to be done in everyday life as things stand.

In order for the state's answers to pre-exist the questions that might arise within civil society, this state ideology has to correspond to the most advanced sectors of the dominant class.

According to Zavaleta, it is necessary to distinguish between the ideology that already circulates in society and that which the state produces in order to maintain its type of society. The state knows best what society needs to be reproduced and preserved:

> That is why the state always contains the objectives that arise from the most advanced sectors of the dominant class—because, precisely, it is concerned with the dominant class and not only with its own present advantage. Such is the nature of capitalist rationality, its reason or its necessary ideology, which corresponds to the next rotation of the productive forces, up to the point at which they obey the fundamental law of expanded reproduction. But this only means that the necessity of the mode of production is combined in a given way with its surplus ideology, that is, with the pre-capitalist ideological burden or that which corresponds to a previous phase of evolution of that same capitalism.[15]

---

11 Zavaleta, 'Las formaciones aparentes en Marx': 19.

13 Zavaleta, 'Las formaciones aparentes en Marx': 14.

14 Zavaleta, 'Las formaciones aparentes en Marx': 13.

15 Zavaleta, 'Las formaciones aparentes en Marx': 25.

For its reproduction a society does not need a static state but rather a highly dynamic one, able to ideologically synthesize the changes that come with the dynamic of the forces of production and, in consequence, produce the ideology necessary to prepare for expanded reproduction, which is its other fundamental task.

Capitalism is the existence of several capitals which compete among themselves to exploit the labour force and for markets for their commodities, through which they obtain their profits. Each capital has a kind of microeconomic rationality, but competition itself leads to expanded reproduction. The market in which they encounter each other does not become macroeconomic rationality by and of itself. The state is the level on which capitalism acquires this kind of rationality, at least in part.

The reproduction and preservation of capitalist society not only require a macroeconomic rationality which will always be partial in so far as microeconomic decisions will always be made according to particular interests. The preservation of the mode of production and its type of society requires a type of macro social and political rationality that, in the first place, unifies the dominant class around the reproduction of that type of society and in relation to the other classes, in particular in relation to the working class.

Here Zavaleta takes up a line of thought proposed by Engels and adopted by Marxists in the 1970s in order to develop a theory of the state in advanced capitalist societies, which consists in the idea of the total capitalist: 'The capitalist state is the form of unity of the bourgeois class; it can well be claimed that the state itself is a collective capitalist in its advanced moment, or at least that this is the superstructure most in accord with the increasingly collective character of the capitalist.'[16]

This idea is taken up, for example, by Nicos Poulantzas,[17] James O'Connor,[18] the Capital logic school, Claus Offe[19] and the majority of the Marxist works on state theory written in the 1970s and part of the 1980s.[20]

---

16 Zavaleta, 'Las formaciones aparentes en Marx': 21.

17 Nicos Poulantzas, *State, Power and Socialism* (Patrick Camiller trans.) (London: Verso Books, 1980).

18 James O'Connor, *The Fiscal Crisis of the State* (New York: St. Martin's Press, 1973).

19 Claus Offe, *The Contradictions of the Welfare State* (John Keane ed. and introd.) (Cambridge, MA: MIT Press, 1984).

20 See John Holloway and Sol Picciotto (eds.), *State and Capital: A Marxist Debate* (London: Edward Arnold, 1978).

The state thus becomes a mediator between fractions of the dominant class. It is a political unit produced at the state level via these mediations. This mediation is possible and more effective in so far as the state has generated its own subject, that is, its bureaucracy. This imposes rationality on the preparation for expanded reproduction in a general sense, and on its own mediation between the fractions.

The state is a system of mediations in several senses. It mediates between the dominant class and the rest of civil society. It is the form in which the dominant class appears before the rest of society not as a particular class but as the general power of society. The state is not only this major mediation, which is the principal apparent form produced by a capitalist society, but also the mediation between different sectors of civil society. Once the state is more developed, it is a set of mediations between the interests and subjects of state power and civil society, along with the other mediations. It no longer only organizes mediations between third parties but also organizes its own system of mediations between the state and civil society.[21] This is what Holloway and Offe call the state's own interests.

This is how Zavaleta conceives the specificity of the constitution of the state and the culmination of political autonomy:

> The particular form of the modern state apparatus, therefore, proceeds under capitalism from an organizational economic fact constituted by a body of state subjects endowed with what Gramsci called the 'spirit of the state': it is a conscious and professional evaluation of a calculable society. This is the subjectivity of the modern state, in such a way that the state is not a mere mirror image but a will within the result or image.

And responding to the question on the origin of the power of the bureaucracy:

> It is a result of the circulation of surplus value at the height of political autonomy. If the society is calculable and also knowable (even if only within the limits of bourgeois consciousness) its bureaucracy has, via the appropriation of surplus value, in the course of its circulation, an immense arsenal of means at its disposal which allow it to control society without denying its non-antagonistic inclinations by means of the organs of mediation [. . .]

---

21 In this sense, John Holloway's work agrees with Zavaleta. See, in particular, John Holloway, *Fundamentos teóricos para una crítica marxista de la administración pública* (Mexico City: INAP, 1982).

> Bureaucracy is the memory of the state and state reaction; it thus reorganizes its mediations, in accordance with the messages produced by the bureaucracy. But if the available surplus or the state's share of surplus value is reduced, (as we Latin Americans know all too well) it will have recourse to dictatorship.[22]

The level of development and the form of class division generated by the capitalist mode of production produces a great mediation between those social strata, the classes, via the separation of politics in the form of the state. It is a form of mediation that appears as a general political form conjoining two things: production and systematization of the elements of the ideology of equality between men, and the task of mediating to maintain the internal division between social classes. In this sense, the state is an apparent form. At the same time, it is the principal thing responsible for articulating and ideologically synthesizing the set of other apparent forms produced by this manner of organizing and reproducing social reality.

This is why the modern state is a highly ideological reality, since although it is founded on the concentration or monopoly of physical force as political power, the state is not reproduced, implanted, extended and above all internalized on the basis of the simple exercise of this force, but rather on the basis of the type of mediation it carries out between the forms of the social division into classes by means of the universalization of the general ideology.

This great mediation that is the state then becomes a group of mediations in various settings. First of all are the mediations within parts of the dominant class so as to construct its unity in the state itself; then there are the mediations between other sectors of civil society and, finally, a sign of the level of maturity of this whole process, the state organizes its own system of mediations between its own interests and the set of differences of civil society, including the sectors of the dominant class.

This occurs when the state has constructed its autonomy via the development of the bureaucracy and a spirit of the state that provides a rationality for the preparation for expanded reproduction and its necessary ideology. This state does not only have to mediate between the interests of social classes and other subordinate groups, but also has to mediate its own objective interests, both strategic and conjunctural, with social classes and other forms of economic, social and political interests and practices.

---

22 Zavaleta, 'Las formaciones aparentes en Marx', pp. 23–4.

The bureaucracy, which is the subject that organizes and maintains this set of mediations in various contexts and produces the strategic rationality of the state, exists and develops in so far as the surplus value that the state manages to collect from its society or from others is invested in the organization and development of its internal structures.

This becomes a circular process that feeds off itself in so far as the appropriation of surplus value, its retention and investment in the development of state bureaucracy, is converted into efficiency and rationality in the preparation for expanded reproduction, when it does not remain as a simple tribute or go to waste in ineffective sinecures but is invested in the development of the state—reproductive rationality, systems of mediations and ideological production that consolidates and extends the sphere of validity of the state.

The separation of the economy in a mode of production that internalizes the mechanisms of appropriation of the surplus and the separation of politics as a general form and type of mediation of the differences produced by historical time produces the primacy of ideology, because it is the principal means by which social totality is articulated and its new divisions are mediated: 'The hypertrophy of the repressive system is proof of the survival of precapitalist structural (state) forms or the decadence of the capitalist state forms. The primacy of ideology is, in contrast, characteristic of the modern superstructure that corresponds to the capitalist mode of production.'[23]

Separation and Development of the Autonomy of Politics

The autonomy of politics is a historical process in which several moments can be differentiated. The first is the foundational or genetic moment, which is that of separation, and which is what Marx called primitive accumulation. The condition of possibility of the autonomy of politics is the production of this state of separation on the level of the mode of production. Another component of this process is ideological production or the production of the primacy of ideology, in particular a general ideology of equality, which is the framework of the group of mediations. The other component is the conversion of surplus value, which circulates via the state bureaucracy and through the group of mediations that articulate state and society.

With this the autonomy of politics matures as a reality with a structure and state subjects who have their own interests and specificity in the context of the general process of expanded reproduction of capitalism.

---

23 Zavaleta, 'Las formaciones aparentes en Marx': 20.

This is one of the tendencies of the development of political autonomy, that which is located in the axis of the state, the separation of politics as the state. Once the transition from one mode of production to another has generated the separation of politics that tends towards the formation of a state, de-politicizing civil society, which corresponds to the foundational moment of capitalism, this same fact also creates the conditions in which, once interactions within civil society have produced a new set of forms of collective organization and public life, politics reappears within civil society but now marked by a quality of separation and autonomy.

In this context of the development of the autonomy of politics, there are also phases that generally begin with corporative forms, that is to say, the presentation and representation of particular identities and interests versus the rest of society and the state.

The political party form generally develops political autonomy within civil society, under the structural conditions of separation. The party form begins to produce the articulation of particular interests in a new general project or a politics or ideology capable of being universalized in its society.

The party form is the mode in which ideological and political formulation is separated from the direct and exclusive expression by social classes, fractions of classes and diverse corporative groups, on the level of the recognition of a more general thought about society and political projects for the whole of society and not only for parts of it, although it does this on the basis of the existence of practices, interests, aspirations and projects put forward by these parts.

In modern societies, within civil society the party form carries out this process of political autonomy while the bureaucracy does the same within the state, that is, they establish a strategic rationality through mediation between classes, partially but effectively overcoming particular interests and corporatism.

There is another dimension of political autonomy, beyond these processes, which consists in the organization of culture. This is the articulation of social totality beyond the expression and direct determination of the productive moment in the rest of social life, which is produced by the initiative of social and political subjects who carry out the task of organizing the culture, that is, of configuring the social whole that responds to a historical causal process. This is specific to each country in so far as its history contains different traditions, temporalities, economic forms, mentalities and political practices.

Political autonomy also corresponds to the ambit of the subjects' initiatives with reference to the mode of organization of the culture in its local histories. This implies the mode of organization of the state, the system of mediations and the type of ideological production that integrates all of these.

The different levels and forms of development of autonomy in politics have given rise to various interpretations within Marxism, which Zavaleta reinterprets in the following way. The works dedicated to the analysis of Marxist conceptions of the capitalist state have established a variety of explanations of its nature, in particular concerning its relations with the mode of production and what kind of determination exists with respect to this. Among these are the theory of state monopoly capitalism, the capital-logic school, the current generally known as structuralist and attributed to [Nicos] Poulantzas, and the Gramscian tradition; there is a neo-Ricardian school, and the more empiricist position of [Ralph] Miliband. This diverse spectrum is analysed in the works of Ernest Laclau, Bob Jessop and John Holloway.[24]

Zavaleta was particularly interested in commenting on what he called the instrumentalist and structuralist positions. According to him the question should be formulated in the following way: 'What has to be defined are the phases of lineal determination of the economic base over the superstructure and the moments (which are clear when they exist) of the primacy of politics. This is not a question of laws but of situations.'[25]

The aim is not to indicate who is generally correct, but rather, to which type of situation each conceptualization refers. For Zavaleta there are structuralist and instrumentalist situations, which respond to different historical configurations of the state.

The instrumentalist situation of the state has a theoretical correlate in the explanation put forward by Lenin, who is classed as an instrumentalist, which according to Zavaleta corresponds to the longer or shorter period of primitive

---

24 See Ernest Laclau, 'Teorias marxistas del estado. Debates y perspectivas' in Norbert Lechner (ed.), *Estado y política en América Latina* (Mexico: Siglo XXI, 1981), pp. 25–59; Bob Jessop, 'Recent Theories of the Capitalist State', *Cambridge Journal of Economics* 1(4) (December 1977): 353–73; John Holloway, 'Debates sobre el estado en Alemania occidental y en Gran Bretaña', *Críticas de la economía política* 16–17 (1980): 223–50; and the compilation by John Holloway and Sol Picciotto (eds.), *State and Capital: A Marxist Debate* (London: Edward Arnold, 1978).

25 Zavaleta, 'El estado en América Latina': 62.

accumulation and preparation for the subsumption of labour to capital, still incomplete and unfinished in Latin America.[26]

> In reality the instrumental form is a remnant of the primary moments of power. In any case, until the state is de-personalized, which only occurs when it attains relative autonomy, there is a long way to go. [...] The immediate occupation of the state by men who belong personally to a dominant class does not indicate an instrumentalist vision or interpretation of the state but rather an instrumental situation.[27]

The structuralist situation corresponds to the phase of organized capitalism, when a bureaucracy has developed which is the subject of strategic and administrative rationality of reproduction and mediation, and the form of domination incorporates the dominated in the movement and dynamic of conservation and development of this type of society:

> In the structuralists' analysis it does not matter who is the titular head of state power, since this power is an objective relation, that is, it includes not only the will of the dominant class but also some ground conquered by the subaltern sectors. It thus assumes the social struggle as a whole and not only its results. Underneath this what we can call reciprocity or complicity is at work. The conqueror contains the conquered, the oppressed has something in common with the oppressor. It is, in other terms, hegemony, or at least its reward.[28]

This type of situation has developed in some countries but not in others. In general, it corresponds to some countries where capitalism is deeply rooted and there is a significant degree of correspondence between civil society and the state. This occurs in particular in Europe, where societies have been governed by a social democratic consensus.

Zavaleta thinks that these different configurations of the capitalist state correspond to different forms and levels of development of capitalism and to the ways in which the superstructure tends to correspond with them. They are useful referents even for thinking realities where the same type of articulation has not occurred historically.

---

26 Zavaleta, 'El estado en América Latina': 65.

27 Zavaleta, 'El estado en América Latina': 65–6.

28 Zavaleta, 'El estado en América Latina': 63. This type of conception is best developed in Poulantzas' last book, *State, Power and Socialism*.

The point is not to choose one of these conceptions, but rather to identify the theory that is adequate for the type of reality one is explaining. In this sense, what are called instrumentalist conceptions can be useful to account for present aspects of a reality that contains them in various degrees in its composition.

In fact, Marxist state theory in the 1970s and 1980s develops and had to develop accounting for the most advanced situations, that is, where the autonomy of politics has reached a higher level and, in consequence, has organized a structural state with a great capacity for appropriation of surplus value and for investment in the development of its internal structures and its subject.

The study of the state in Latin American societies, just as the study of the level of the mode of production takes as a point of reference for its optimal development a formal and abstract model of regularity, cannot avoid taking into account the theory developed to explain the modalities of the states of societies that have achieved the highest level of capitalist development, where hegemony has been achieved; but in our societies this either does not exist at all or only exists in a very partial and intermittent way.

In this sense, the argument is not that instrumentalist theories are more adequate for Latin America and structuralist theories more adequate for European societies, but rather that one must think with both points of reference, and know how to recognize the instrumental aspects, dimensions and situations that still characterize part of the realities of the state in Latin American societies. The emphasis that Marx and Lenin placed on the state as an apparatus of political domination by the dominant class in the productive moment is foregrounded, not out of an allegiance to those ideas and those authors, but because Latin American realities largely correspond to this this model.

Latin American states are not purely instrumental, but rather have a composite form and are in that sense complex. In Latin America, there have been long and arduous processes of development of political autonomy linked to the construction of national states, and there is also a tradition of anti-imperialist struggles. This is a history with discontinuities, retreats and a generally incomplete character, due to the diversity of structures and historical temporalities that characterize the majority of Latin American societies. Politics is no longer thought of as a mere reflection or instrument of realities defined by the economic base, as a simple result of determinations by the mode of production. In this conception of reality as a totality with a nucleus of determination which predominates but is not sufficient to organize the whole of society, its specific historical and local articulation is carried out by politics and ideology.

An example of how this works is the relation that Zavaleta establishes between the state and the forces of production. In 'Las formaciones aparentes en Marx' and in other texts, he takes up an idea of Marx's from the *Grundrisse*. Marx thought that the principal productive force is the community form, that is, the type of relations that exist between men. The idea of productive forces is an analytic category and not an ontological one. In this sense, the state is also a force of production, which does not only mean that it organizes productive enterprises, but that its principal function is the global organization of society, embodying the totality and the ensuring the simple and expanded reproduction of capital.

This vision entails both the fundamental idea that the state organizes itself to reproduce the most general and fundamental conditions of the mode of production, that is, in the service of accumulation, and the idea that this is not possible via an instrumental and external action of politics on the economy. Rather this is something done through the mode of articulation of the social totality, the production of ideology, the organization of the culture and, in particular, through a state form that has the capacity to integrate the dominated in the general form of representation of these divided societies, in such a way as to obtain their consensus.

In order to carry out its task of reproducing the economic base, the state has to produce and articulate other realities which are not economic and allow it to reproduce and extend the forms of exploitation and domination.

The mode in which the state is organized affects the productivity of capital and, therefore, its individual profits. For example, the way in which the state organizes tax collection and the mode and rhythm in which it returns this income in the form of infrastructure or state spending extends the conditions of private accumulation, as state investment in infrastructure, energy, education and other areas obviously improves or worsens the cycles of reproduction of capital, that is, its productivity.

In this broader sense, the state, which is a form of organization of the community, is a force of production. One has to think at one and the same time of the development of political autonomy as a response to the determination of the productive moment, and of how the set of superstructures responds to the tasks that the structure of the mode of production poses for it, unfolding its creativity and specific capacity of social construction.

This differs from the way in which one of the principal contemporary Marxists, Gerald Cohen, has presented an analytic defence of Marx's theory of history. Cohen prefers to maintain a sharp distinction in which the productive forces are a context totally internal on the analytic level of the mode of production, in which, strictly speaking, the political dimension does not participate, and at the same time there is a clear difference between forces of production and relations of production, which is the analytical separation of the presence of politics and the state in the conception of forces of production.[29]

This is not the only view in the development of contemporary Marxist theory. Derek Sayer[30] has developed an argument similar to Zavaleta's, in which the relations of production, as an analytic moment, can in certain aspects or moments become forces of production. This follows Marx' idea that the form of the community, which is a general way to enunciate the problem, is also the principal productive force, and not just one among several forces of production.

Cohen's separation of the productive forces implies a more technological or technocentric vision of historical development, as the author himself recognizes.

The other perspective, developed by Zavaleta and Sayer, among others, considers that productive forces and relations of production are entirely specific analytical distinctions, such that at certain moments some social relations of production, in particular the form of a community, are also considered to be productive forces. This type of Marxist analysis posits a dynamic totality, which refers not only to historical reality but also to the system of conceptual categories. Once the categories, in this case forces and relations of production, have been defined, and these more complex levels of analysis have been articulated in accordance with composition of reality itself, the primary definitions have to be revised and completed, incorporating into the analytic scheme actions, conditions, determinations and variations that a more general and integral vision of each can produce.

This is a more complex and processual way to conceive and practice Marxism, which does not reduce each component of its general conceptual

29 Gerald Allan Cohen, *Karl Marx's Theory of History: A Defence* (Princeton, NJ: Princeton University Press, 2001[1978]).

30 Derek Sayer, *The Violence of Abstraction: The Analytical Foundation of Historical Materialism* (London: Basil Blackwell, 1987).

system to a kind of categorical hypostasis, but rather aims to account for the historical specificity and complexity of each society. It corresponds to Marx' brief methodological exposition of the practice of science in which, once it has established the analytical distinctions, it has to pass through a process of re-articulation of each of them within the totality. This re-articulation is not just grouping things together, but rather implies modifications on each level of analysis and in each category.

The Reform of Marxism

Finally, it is time to ask, what is of interest in Zavaleta's essays and theoretical production? What new ideas does it introduce?

Zavaleta's main contribution is his reflection on the theory of the state and its development from the perspective of social totality as a general explanatory strategy. I would summarize its relevance as follows.

Zavaleta begins by taking up the Marxist thesis that social reality is a totality or simultaneity of base and superstructure and proposes to work on the explanation of how this social totality is articulated, which is not a natural given but something that is historically constructed. He takes on this task via the development of a theory of the autonomy of politics, in the first place a reflection on the limits of the validity of what he calls models of regularity, that is, the theory of the core of society or the productive moment. This is accompanied by the proposition that this establishes the primary, inescapable and principal determination for the organization of the rest of society.

Zavaleta defends the Marxist theory that corresponds to the level of the model of regularity, not by extending it as a model of general explanation, but rather by delimiting its context of explanatory relevance, by creating a clearer consciousness of its limits.

The context of the model of regularity is the capitalist mode of production. Only part of some aspects of the superstructure correspond in a direct and necessary manner to the configuration of the elements of the model of regularity. This occurs in the measure in which the capitalist mode of production tends to homogenize the world, allowing a model of regularity to be elaborated and upheld on an intellectual level.

In contrast, in politics, ideology and culture, what we find in the history of societies is the emergence of a broad diversity, which cannot be contained, reduced or subsumed in the more general and common aspects of the model of regularity.

Zavaleta's work proposes that there can be no general theory of the capitalist state, except on the margins of the structural correspondence with the organizing principle of the mode of production. This generally has to do with the translation of the abstract equalization of human labour in terms of socially necessary labour time, which reappears as juridical equality at the level of the state, which, in turn, in its best but not necessary expression can be converted into representative democracy.

Nor does Zavaleta propose a dichotomy between a general theory of the economy and an explanation of politics and history that lacks any kind of general theory, but only offers a descriptive and phenomenological account of each social process and each local history. The resulting perspective is composite. One has to work on the basis of a core of general theory, the validity of which is historically contingent: it is possible only in the capitalist era, which can explain the configuration of the core of society. From this starting point one has to elaborate the historical framework and accumulation of each society and each period, in an almost artisanal fashion.

An example of this is the development of a theory of the autonomy of politics that is an explanation of how other human practices, ideology and politics organize and produce realities that ultimately constitute and integrate that which remains external to that core of society, which is the model of regularity. The theory of the autonomy of politics, in which Zavaleta's ideas about the state and ideological production are developed, is oriented towards the model of regularity. In this sense, it produces the supplement that articulates a theory of social totality and a historical-political explanation of that totality.

I say that it is oriented towards the model of regularity, but not in the sense of being a derivation of the logic of capital in the context of politics. This is not an attempt to derive regional theories on the basis of the model of regularity, extending it into other contexts. It aims to develop a set of concrete categories of thought that rationalize the explanation of those other moments of social life, which in general are less susceptible to integration into models of regularity within the scope of validity of the law of value.

There are various proliferating nuclei[31] originating from a fundamental centre around which they express their specific productivity in a complementary fashion. If social reality is conceived of as a totality composed in a

---

31 This is an idea of Alejo Carpentier which he uses to characterize the Baroque and which I recover with more amplitude to elaborate a characterization of Zavaleta's thought.

heterogeneous way in terms of historical and social substance, it no longer makes sense to posit a model of regularity that corresponds to only part of the totality, however central and important it may be, as the general form and model of explanation of the whole society and its history. It seems more adequate to work with a group of nuclei of theoretical production, each directed to the specificity of one moment within the diversity of social life, articulating them within a theoretical framework that accounts for the general configuration and contains at one and the same time the idea of unity and that of diversity or irreducible heterogeneity, as much in ontological terms as in terms of social explanation.

This is a sort of reform of the ideas generally held of Marxism. It rejects a simple and linear image and practice of Marxism as the recognition of the law of value as the scientific theory of the whole of social reality that can be generalized as a model of explanation for all aspects of social life via the derivation of subordinate regional theories. It produces a consciousness of its own limits as it produces theory about these other regions of reality. Although Zavaleta does not make this point explicitly, his work constitutes a practice of Marxism as a group of nuclei of theoretical production that are not circumscribed by that which corresponds to the moment of production.

This more complex and diversified practice of Marxism will produce a more consistent and richer explanation of Bolivian history.

Marxism is a general theory, but relative to time. Marx developed his basic theory, in particular in *Capital*, as a theory of the capitalist mode of production, valid for the temporal and social contexts of this type of structure. Only some of the ideas produced for this historical time can be used to think societies prior to it or other societies in general. These are the most formal elements, such as the categories of productive forces, relations of production, and mode of production.

Zavaleta's work, in particular 'Las formaciones aparentes en Marx', in my view, contributes to a clearer consciousness of the relativity of Marxist theory on several levels, in relation to time and social contexts. It is a relativism that does not deny the validity and need for general theories, but raises the question of the limits within which a general theory is possible. For Zavaleta, Marxism provides this genetic explanation and critique of the organizational principle that predominates in contemporary history, to go on to explain the existence of Bolivia and Latin America. In Bolivia, local history has posited the centrality of the proletariat as the basic historical condition for the relevance of an explanatory practice founded on a Marxist strategy and theoretical framework.

In an attempt to emphasize the limits of general theory for the analysis of the state and politics, Zavaleta writes: 'In the last instance the theory of the state, if it is anything, is the theory of each state. What matters, therefore, is the course of events in the edification of each state.'[32]

Here he seems to me to pass over or fail to recognize the other aspect of his own work, which always implies a certain level of generalization, without which he could not account for the state in terms of genesis, process, structure and totality. General theory is necessary in order to explain local histories in these terms, but it is also necessary to be conscious of the limits or scope of relevance of each general theory. This is what Zavaleta aims to do in the essays discussed in this chapter.

---

32 Zavaleta, 'El estado en América Latina': 67.

CHAPTER NINE

The National Question

From Separation to Real Subsumption and Moral and Intellectual Reform

The nation and the construction of the nation-state were a central concern in Zavaleta's youth, in his years of militancy in revolutionary nationalism and in the work he did as part of what I have called nationalist historical revisionism. The national question never ceased to concern him, but the way in which he conceived it changed substantially.

In his early work, he posed the problem assuming a factual nation and its presence in the struggles of Bolivian history. He proposed the development of a national consciousness as part of the process and the project by which this nation could come to construct its nation-state. History intervened to develop something that was already given in a more natural way.

In the 1970s and 1980s, Zavaleta went on to consider the national question in a more complex way. First, he came to conceive it as a completely historical question. From a conception centred on a factual subject and the development of a national consciousness, he went on to conceive it as articulated around social macro-processes linked to the principal tendencies of a whole new historical time, that of the implantation and development of capitalism and the configuration of a world-system.

From thinking the nation in itself, closed off to thinking from outside and also trying to overcome an internally produced alienation, Zavaleta comes to a consideration of the national in terms of how it occurs on a global level and on the basis of elements of a general theory that corresponds to that historical time and type of society.

Zavaleta considers the national question in relation to the development of capitalism, although not exclusively. In his nationalist period, he had thought that the nation-state was the form in which peoples in modern times tried to organize their sovereignty in the context of the world system. This was based in a conception of politics as form of organization of sovereignty of a society that already contained a nation de facto. This does not include a consideration of economic and social structures.

Within the Marxist tradition there was once a tendency to pose the national question on the basis of a logic of the accumulation and reproduction of capital, concluding with an almost exclusively economic explanation, with roots in some of Marx's own writings. The principal axis of this explanation was around the idea of the development and articulation of the internal market, that is, the space in which a group of capitals organize the markets that realize the surplus value they generate, and the delimitation of the space within which their expanded reproduction tends to occur. In this sense, the nation-state fulfilled the task of organizing the political sovereignty that corresponded to the scale of expansion of the internal market, attempting to create loyalty and a sense of belonging among the individuals who worked and consumed in those markets and lived in those territories where the state arises as the general form of reproduction of capital not only in the interior but also in the international context.

This explanation operates on the level of circulation and reproduction and not on that of production. It is basically derived from an economistic explanation. It does not address the question of political autonomy.

Zavaleta corrects and extends this point of view with the analysis of the nation developed by Gramsci; that is, considering political autonomy, its constructive capacity, as the organization of culture. This is a notion of social totality that implies the integration of various levels of analysis instead of a reduction to the economic logic.

Zavaleta works on the national question on the basis of an articulation of Marx and Gramsci. He reconstructs an axis that goes from the constitutive moment of the capitalist state or the production of the state of separation to the real subsumption and the moral and intellectual reform that accompanies it, a perspective completed with a consideration of the construction of historical blocs and hegemony.

Zavaleta thinks that the conversion of societies into nations basically has to do with the growth of social equality; that is, with the production of a certain homogeneity of social substance and the sense of belonging to something in common. This implies that he considers the national question to be closely linked to the growth of democracy in society and politics.

This idea of the growth of democracy, which Zavaleta takes from Weber, refers to processes of increasing equality and social and economic integration that are generated by the modernization of the economy as it is reorganized according to the criteria of formal rationality and capitalism. The production of the state of separation due to primitive accumulation leads to the foundation of the state within which processes of political democratization must be anal-ysed. This marks a significant difference with the more usual way of thinking about this within Marxism.

The key point that links the analysis of macro processes of transformation of socioeconomic structures with the organization of culture and the state is the idea of real subsumption elaborated by Marx to account for the phase in which capitalism is not only a substitution of the juridical and social relations of production, but also modifies the prior forms and implants a new mode of transformation of nature, of the organization of work and the rule of capital.

Zavaleta connects the idea of real subsumption in a peculiar way with Gramsci's moral and intellectual reform. He thus establishes a link between dif-ferent moments of social totality. He sums up the origin of these articulations:

> A typical constitutive moment is without doubt that of primitive accumulation. We must distinguish at least three stages within this. First, the mass production of detached men, that is, of juridically equal individuals, a negative moment—one of estrangement—of accumulation that supposes vacuity or a state of receptivity. Then, the hour of formal subsumption, which is the real subordination of labour to capital. Here is where interpellation can be produced, that is, the suppression of vacuity in a way or from a certain point of view. In third place, real subsumption, that is the application of conscious-ness and the force of the masses, and other higher qualitative forces, to the two previous factors, capital as effective command and free men in the form of masses.[1]

In the state of separation men tend to become equal. This equality tends to occur under new conditions and forms of unity. The processes of primitive accumulation destroy and disorganize the previously existing forms of com-munity and, therefore, the forms of collective identity, upon disorganizing their material social referents, that is, their communities.

Zavaleta thinks of the processes of becoming a nation as basically the form of unification under the new conditions created by primitive accumu-lation that capitalism implants; that is, on the basis of social atomization and the destruction of the forms of collective identification. The state of separation is the principal modern form of reconstitution of social totality, of the new forms of social life and political unity and government.

---

1 Zavaleta, 'El estado en América Latina': 68.

I want to support this with a series of passages from Zavaleta:

[W]here the state of separation independence has not been produced, the community or collective ground is also false, that is, mechanical and not organic as it must be in the national reconstruction of capitalism.

[...]

By nation, therefore, in principle and in general, we mean the collective self or socialized substance that is the result of the most basic premises of capitalism. It is, therefore, a self made up of the imaginary confluence of men in a state of detachment—alienated men. The relation between one and the other, the national self and the revocation of the prior communal identity or of a mechanical and inorganic solidarity, is not merely circumstantial, but entails a necessary causality; if the latter does not occur, the former cannot exist [...][2]

The state of separation produces a situation in which what Zavaleta calls an ideological void occurs, which permits the substitution of beliefs.

It produces the creation of the nation, that is, the substitution of a local character by a national character, and this is the true constitutive moment.[3]

The strongest points of national creation are equality and real subsumption accompanied by intellectual reform. The creation of the nation produces something new, both in terms of social substance and identity, and in terms of the political construction and organization of culture. It means that on the level of the productive moment there is a process of increasing equality among men, which is also the production of a new reality in this nucleus.

The construction of the nation-state is the culmination on the political level of the organization of power and the direction of a social reality basically composed of the population that persists under capitalist transformation. It produces on the political and ideological level a superstructure more adequate

---

2 Zavaleta, *Towards a History of the National-Popular in Bolivia*, pp. 168, 170.

3 René Zavaleta, 'Notas sobre la cuestión nacional en América Latina' in *Teoría y política en América Latina*, p. 285. This essay was also published in the journal *Homines* (January–July 1982), and has its precedent in 'La cuestión nacional' in *Revista de Antropología Americana* 4 (December 1981). The text quoted here is published in 'Notas sobre la cuestión nacional en América Latina' in Marcos Palacios (ed.), *La unidad nacional en América Latina. Del regionalismo a la nacionalidad* (Mexico: El Colegio de México, 1983), pp 87–98.

to the type of social structure and the development of the forces of production that characterize the dynamic of capitalism, but in such a way that this political construction is made with recourse in part to pre-existing elements, above all cultural and linguistic.

The nation and the nation-state appear as a particularity in the world context that tends to homogeneity in the measure in which the capitalist mode of production predominates and expands. The construction of the nation-state tends to require pre-capitalist cultural elements in order to produce the differentiation of its identity in the context of structural homogenization on the world level.

The ideological elements and forms that accompany it can be and usually are older traditions. Pre-capitalist diversity is used to produce a degree of differentiation among nation-states on the political and ideological level in a world which tends towards homogeneity.

The national question is a problem of unity on the political and ideological level. One cannot construct a strong and effective state identity if the socioeconomic bases that sustain it do not exist. If men have not achieved equality in the state of separation in the whole of society, the unity that can be discursively formulated and the type of political institutions that are produced and organized at the level of the state and official ideology as expression of the unity of the nation and the equality and membership of all its inhabitants is artificial, merely apparent.

Apparent State and Nation-State

One of Zavaleta's contributions to the study of societies like the Bolivian is the idea of the apparent state. The apparent state corresponds to a situation in which the state of separation has not been produced in the whole of the territory and the population among which this political form pretends to be valid; that is to say, it is inorganic with relation to a significant part of its society.

That the state of separation should not have arisen in the whole of society signifies, on the one hand, that this society is less homogeneous. There is greater social diversity in a strong sense.[4] Various types of society are present.

---

4 Opposed to 'diversity' in a weak sense, which would be the current 'politically correct' use of this term to refer to the exhibition of groups which mix skin colour, sexual options, religious practices, fashion choices, musical preferences, etc. while sharing, underneath this apparent diversity, submission to the same rules of social conduct, laws and economic conditions. [Trans.]

On the socioeconomic level this means that several modes of production exist, and, therefore, several forms of social differentiation; that is, of class structures. On the political and cultural level, it means that local forms of authority exist, which reduce the validity of the state form. It also means that other world views continue to exist as organizers of social life in local and regional contexts. All this does not create the conditions for national unity but, rather, for the disjointed co-existence of this diversity which is only apparently unified and represented by the state.

The state is presented as the unity of that which is not really unified, basically because it has not achieved equality. In this sense it is an apparent unity or a false nation. Zavaleta defines the situation of the apparent state thus:

> We have, in the first place, the situation in which formal or ornamental elements of the modern state exist but not the foundations of its substantive existence. This occurred with all the Latin American countries at the moment of independence. It is an apparent state because the cartographic dimensions do not correspond to the effective space of the state, nor does its demographic volume correspond to its enforceable legitimacy.[5]

> False detachment between state and society as occurs in the apparent state where what is nominally a state is really a faction; in reality the germ of the state is still submerged in civil society.[6]

This implies that instrumental situations are more frequent in the apparent state. The presence of the interests of the dominant class is more evident and direct. The existence of an apparent state is an index of the failure of nationalization, that is, of the production of sentiments and the materialization of belonging to a nation-state.

In the measure in which there are not only other forms of production but also local structures of authority and other world views differing from the rationalization that the state offers as the general consciousness and direction of its society, this state is experienced as apparent because it has not managed to integrate all this diversity in a new unity, more powerful than the old loyalties and, in consequence, substitute them at least in terms of primacy.

---

5 Zavaleta, *Towards a History of the National-Popular in Bolivia*, p. 216.

6 René Zavaleta, 'Cuatro conceptos de democracia', *Dialéctica* 7(12) (1982): 11–30; here, p. 28.

An apparent state is, therefore, an incomplete or partial state. It is broken in various ways, at various times and in various places. It cannot construct an optimal correspondence with civil society. It is neither homogeneous nor unified and exists only in some islands of society; it corresponds to a dominant part that has not managed to unify the social diversity that, nonetheless, coexists subordinated to it.

The processes of national creation are processes of development or construction of optimal relations between the state and civil society:

> The nation-state is what occurs when civil society has become a nation and has a sole political power; that is to say, the nation-state is something like the culmination of the nation. [...] In any case, it is certain that the concomitance of a state standing over a civil society made nation constitutes the optimum of the capitalist mode of production and completes the cycle of totalizations that goes from the constitution of collective classes to the socialization of production.[7]

Zavaleta considers the nation to be a force of production, taking up Marx's idea expounded in the *Grundrisse* that the principal force of production is the form of the community. The nation is a form of community that prepares and organizes the conditions for the development of capitalist productive forces: 'The nation, in so far as it implies a certain degree of homogeneity among certain decisive elements that concur in the productive regime, is in itself a productive force or, if you like, the indicator of the level of correspondence between the productive mode and the collectivity in which this occurs.'[8]

The nation is the type of intersubjectivity created by the processes of equalization induced by the capitalist mode of production. The nation is the type of community that substitutes those which primitive accumulation has destroyed. Unlike these, it is no longer merely local, but rather constructs a broader context, whose principal referents are the internal market and the horizon of sovereignty in political power organized on the basis of the state of separation. It is the space in which the new unity of the diverse and atomized is constructed in the constitutive moment: 'The nation can be understood as the construction of a collective ego, that is to say, the complex construction of a certain degree of centralization and homogeneity around the internal market.'[9]

---

7 Zavaleta, 'La cuestión nacional en América Latina', p. 282.

8 Zavaleta, 'La cuestión nacional en América Latina', p. 282.

9 Zavaleta, 'La cuestión nacional en América Latina', p. 281.

The nation thus implies a process of homogenization that operates basically on the level of the transformation of the mode of production and the construction of a collective identity. Here we enter the terrain of autonomy in politics. While according to the foregoing argument the nation is considered to be a productive force, as something that capitalism requires, this is something that may or may not happen and that occurs to various degrees. This brings us to the question of the deliberate processes of construction of men or of societies.

There are two levels of analysis of the national question. The first and most fundamental that of the mode of production and the type of human collectivity that this produces. This is what generates the elemental determinants from which the form of that community or collectivity completes its development on the ideological and political level.

In these texts and in all his later works Zavaleta thinks the national question on the basis of the law of value, that is, the type of equality, however abstract this may be, that is produced among men once their previous communitarian forms have been destroyed. He does not reduce the analysis of the national question to the law of value, which is a very strong tendency in Marx, but rather complements his analysis with the dimension of autonomy in politics, that is, the productivity of politics, incorporating the theory provided by Gramsci so as to think the nation as a political construction and as the organization of culture.

First, Zavaleta supplements Marx's more economic analysis with Gramsci's more developed theory of the superstructure, thus correcting the economistic biases of Marx's conception of the nation. Secondly, since he does so on the basis of the law of value, building on something that, although implicit, was not developed (and in part was forgotten) in Gramsci's analysis of the national question.

In Gramsci, this analysis is centred around the problem of the organization of culture, as a way to think the construction of hegemony, the union of base and superstructure in specific situations on the basis of the historical bloc that the dominant class produces in so far as it integrates the subalterns via consensus.

While for Gramsci these large-scale political constructions, which he calls historical blocs, are formed around a fundamental class, that is, a class that occupies a pole in the mode of production, the law of value is not present here with the force that it has in Zavaleta's thought. For Zavaleta the conditions of possibility of the construction of hegemony and its limitations are given in particular by the process of real subsumption, which is when the change in the relations of production ultimately transforms the labour process through the introduction of technology and mass production, which produces a concentration of historical time and, in consequence, the substitution of one worldview by another.

Gramsci privileged the ideological and political dimension in the process of national formation. Zavaleta argues that this cannot occur in a voluntarist way or unlinked to the conditions of possibility given by the homogenization produced in the base by real subsumption. He achieves a more balanced conception of the relations of production and the development of the productive forces and of culture and politics, integrating ideas provided by Marx and Gramsci, respectively.

In Zavaleta's more theoretical discussions of the national question, as in 'Notas sobre la cuestión nacional en América Latina' [Notes on the national question in Latin America], Marx's perspective appears more strongly, but the national question is not only treated on the level of the organization of the internal market, although this is an indisputable axis, but also from the perspective of the construction of social optima, that is, the correspondence between the type of state that is constructed and the configuration of civil society (the development of the forces of production).

In other works where he analyses specific historical processes, without abandoning a conception of the configuration of the superstructures on the basis of the conditions of possibility of a new national unity explained by the law of value, such as *Lo nacional-popular en Bolivia* and 'El estado en América Latina', Gramsci's basic categories feature more prominently until they acquire the same weight as those of Marx.

A good way to situate Zavaleta's thought on the national question is to describe it as an analysis on the level of the relation between the state and civil society in each local history, how the unity of base and superstructure arises, and within what limits, in each society and historical period. The topic is basically how societies are unified in modernity. The lack of unification in the economy is expressed by the existence of various modes of production and, in consequence, substantial inequality among the collectivities that live in a society or country that is supposedly a nation.

The lack of a national politics and ideology gives rise to a type of intersubjectivity that does not produce a feeling of identification and belonging to the same political and social unit among the whole population. Generally, this is permeated by conceptions of natural inequality among men. This is clear in Bolivian history, in what Zavaleta calls the seigneurial paradox: the recomposition of a dominant caste over several periods of its history and economic and political development, on the basis of the reproduction and reinforcement of a seigneurial ideology that excludes indigenous elements from the national culture and the social and political body of the Bolivian state.

Here, the persistence of the seigneurial ideology indicates that the nation has not completed its formation. As long as the aristocracy remains dominant, the nation is not the primordial form of social organization.

While Zavaleta thinks that intersubjectivity can precede its premises or material conditions, this pre-existence cannot persist for long since it is only a way to prepare for the advent of those changes in the social reality that sustain the new beliefs that arise within society. A nation-state cannot exist without social democratization.

Let us take the example of Bolivian history. In the decades prior to the 1952 revolution, between the Chaco War and the uprising of 9 April, a nationalist intersubjectivity emerges in Bolivia that precedes the constitution of a national state, in a period in which the material organization of society and the dominant mentality were seigneurial and oligarchic. This intersubjectivity prepared the conditions for the 1952 revolution, which in turn initiated, although partially, some processes of social democratization linked to capitalist expansion, including the agrarian reform and the nationalization of the mines. There is also a parallel process of political democratization in the recognition of universal citizenship for Bolivians and the installation of mechanisms of representative democracy, although with relatively less weight than other forms of mediation and organization of power articulated around the party-unions-state axis.

The year 1952 is a moment of nationalization not only because the mines were nationalized, but also because on the macro social level there is a set of processes favouring equality, obviously as a tendency and not a result. A more egalitarian form of unity is reconstructed.

While in 1952 the greatest processes of nationalization in the history of the country occurred, these were still insufficient for the consolidation of the nation-state in Bolivia.

On the one hand, the expansion of capitalism in the country was still very limited. The phase of real subsumption was even less advanced. There is another dimension of the construction of the nation that I want to mention in relation to the history of Bolivia, which has to do with the problem of sovereignty which, according to Zavaleta, is a requisite for the nation-state.

While, on the one hand, the 1952 revolution began to spread capitalism in the country and in that sense fomented some processes of social democratization, a line of development which would extend little by little into the country's contemporary history, the political history of this process of nationalization is more irregular.

An extensive and organic process of nationalization that achieves the articulation of political sovereignty as a nation-state generally comes about via the construction of a historical bloc. This gives consistency to the relation between the state and civil society, allowing this unit to exercise sovereignty externally as a nation-state and is not limited to the mere exercise of sovereignty over its own society, something which more often occurs when it has only managed to construct an apparent state. Although the latter appears as the unity of society, this is only in so far as it manages to rule over the social diversity that has not been really unified on the level of basic social relations.

The short period during which the Bolivian state exercised external national sovereignty is the period in which there was a strong relation with a significant part of its civil society, in particular with the workers' movement. Once the state began to reorganize in such a way that the workers were distanced from state power, in a process in which the MNR bureaucracy sought to monopolize political power, against the competing power of the COB and the workers, substituting that connection with an alliance with the US, the sovereignty of the nation-state began to shrink, and was dealt a final blow with the Barrientos coup in 1964.

National sovereignty exists and is exercised when there is an organic connection and correspondence between the state and civil society. It tends to weaken and disappear when the relations between state and civil society decompose and state politics become more a question of domination and less one of integration of the demands and movements of its civil society.

The nation is not a reality that exists independently of its political history. If the state that governs, dominates and directs a society does not fulfil the tasks of producing the feeling of belonging to that political unit, along with other processes of social equalization, nationalization fails, in two senses. It occurs more slowly or, if the nation had already achieved moments of correspondence between state and civil society, it begins to disintegrate.

An optimum in the construction of this relation generally allows the exercise of external and internal sovereignty. The state has national validity within its society and also has validity and identity in the world of nation-states. In so far as the existing state is more an apparent one with a history in which instrumental situations predominate, it has less validity within its society and as a result has less value externally and for other states.

An apparent state is one in which a significant part of its society does not feel that it belongs to it except by force of circumstance, not as a political community with a shared conception of the world and of the direction of its history. It is a state in which part of society exercises sovereignty over the rest, generally accompanied by its alliance with external powers. Part of its validity comes from outside. In consequence, in part of its territory it exercises a sovereignty that is not its own. It is not the sovereignty of the nation nor of the apparent state, but that of imperialist powers or of other nation-states in the fragmented territory of a country that is only apparently unified.

The exercise of national sovereignty is thus not a question of courage, resolution and will, although these are also necessary in countries like ours, but, rather, a process of construction of organic correspondences between the state and civil society. Strictly speaking, it is exercised by constructing what Gramsci called hegemony, a unity of intellectual and moral direction and of political and economic domination.

The making of the great modern nations is a process of construction of hegemony. This process, on the political-cultural level, has been more extensive when the homogenization of the economic base has been greater, due to the installation and development of capitalism in its phase of real subsumption.

Latin American societies in general have lived partial, unfinished and discontinuous processes both of nationalization and of the construction of hegemony. In fact, many Latin American societies continue to be characterized by significant social diversity and are only apparently unified by their respective states which, in consequence, are only partially national.

The weakness of national construction in these societies is thus due to the difficulties and limitations that they have experienced in the processes of social democratization through the homogenization of society by capitalist modernity, and the partial construction of historical blocs that has occurred in some conjunctures or periods of Latin American history—those in which the state has come closest to civil society. These are the conjunctures in which Latin American states have been nearest to existing as nation-states. In these nationalist and populist experiences they have exercised greater local sovereignty when the state has managed to respond more to the processes of social integration and political unification of the classes within the country over and above the processes of class alliance on the international level.

National sovereignty is the best index of the process of construction of the nation having achieved the reform of the state. It implies a strong unity of economics and politics, which depends on the advance of social and political democracy, that is, on increasing social and economic equality and greater representation, participation and freedom in politics.

The nation is the paradigmatic form of construction of community in the history of modern societies. It is the hegemonic form of the relation between the state and civil society where the state of separation has arisen.

Nationalizations

Here we have to introduce some subtleties in this apparent generalization of a progressive conception of the processes of nationalization, that is, of the formation of nation-states. In a very short, untitled manuscript, Zavaleta presents a series of succinct and critical theses on other dimensions of the process of nationalization that are as important as those presented up till now. I will call this text 'Nacionalizaciones' and will refer to it in concluding this chapter.

The first point is the relation between capitalism and nationalization, seen from another angle:

> 'Capitalism is also a despotic form of nationalization. It is based on the disappearance of the peasantry and its roots are the destruction of village culture. [. . .] The question of the disappearance of the peasantry proposes precisely the question of a non-popular creation of the nation. In other terms, the divorce between what is national and what is popular, which is perhaps the tragedy of this era in Latin America.[10]

This happens because the introduction of capitalism, which occurs via what Marx called primitive accumulation, is a violent way of producing the state of separation. It implies producing men dispossessed of the means of production and also men stripped of community, split off from their forms of social reproduction. In this sense the processes of nation formation in capitalist societies in general are processes of social reconstruction that operate on the basis or condition of the destruction of previous forms of sociability. They are an act of ideological, political and economic substitution.

---

10 René Zavaleta, 'Nacionalizaciones', manuscript.

Disorganizing the previous forms of community disorganizes the historical material referent for the reproduction of local cultures. The processes of nationalization that arise from the introduction of capitalism substitute the local cultures, which are disorganized to the core.

Hegemony as a form of production of consensus is also constructed on this basis, that is, out of the destruction of the previous culture. It is a form of reorganization of cultural fragments of those disorganized communities, in the production of the ideology of the global society which in this way acquires a national character.

In Zavaleta's terms, hegemonic construction is an organization of national culture that pieces together fragments of village cultures in a manner that subordinates them to the state ideology and politics that unify and reproduce the rule of capital.

In this manuscript Zavaleta distinguishes three situations of nation formation: '(1) Countries that have completed their nationalization. (2) Countries in an intermediate process. (3) Countries in an early stage of nationalization.'[11]

This is applied to the history of Latin American countries in the following way. The first is the case of what Zavaleta calls the 'false nationalization of countries with an alluvial formation', Argentina being the most representative case. These countries end up containing a population that suffered the loss of peasant status in another space and, in consequence, this de-peasantization does not accompany the process of nation formation. It is the case of countries that receive a large number of immigrants. De-peasantization or the abandonment of local culture is not accompanied by its substitution by a national culture. These countries are more capitalist than others on the continent, but at the same time their process of nation formation is more superficial or, as Zavaleta calls it, false. The loss of peasant status and the creation of the nation do not occur in the same space.

The second case, countries in an intermediate stage of nation formation, is characterized as follows: 'There are many types of marginal groups but they are all sectors that have ceased to be peasants but are still in a situation of ideological vacancy. Here we have men who are detached in that they are juridically free and not attached to the land as their means of production.'[12]

These countries have already undergone a significant process of de-peasantization but not of nation formation in the sense of the reconstruction

---

11 Zavaleta, 'Nacionalizaciones'.
12 Zavaleta, 'Nacionalizaciones'.

of ideological and political unity. Nor has there been economic integration in the sense of converting these ex-peasants into an industrial proletariat. Thus, the result is widespread marginalization.

In the third case, the early stage of nation formation, what happens is as follows: 'The constitution of what is popular resists the bourgeois form of nationalization, which up to a point is via marginalization; in consequence, the masses resist by shielding themselves in their traditional forms of life and culture.'[13]

This is the case of what Zavaleta calls motley societies, in particular that of Bolivia. In this manuscript Zavaleta presents a summary of national projects in Bolivia:

> In the concrete case of Bolivia it cannot be said that the national project is necessarily also popular. There is a first hegemonic national experience, which is that of the COB, but it is a completely embryonic project. Then there is the revolutionary nationalist project, which resembles the populist forms of assimilation, a Westernizing and unifying project. Finally, there is the oligarchic seigneurial project, which aspires to the suppression and reconstruction of the popular project in the service of its own hegemonic imposition.[14]

In Bolivia, as a country of the third type, the process of de-peasantization is limited. Initially it generally occurred through the transformation of a part of the rural population into the mining proletariat, and later through migration to the cities. Where this process of de-peasantization is incomplete, traditional forms of life and culture and local structures of authority persist.

The Westernizing and unifying nationalist project attempted to generalize what corresponded to that de-peasantized core for the rest of the country, with a strong seigneurial component. The project was and is extremely limited because the conditions for its reception do not exist in the economic base or the social history of the country, since it was not able to replace the existing ideology or politics, which had not been disorganized or fully destroyed.

In consequence, this project of nation formation contains a smaller and largely ununified population. Hence, in Bolivia, the connection between the nation and the people does not come from the bourgeois national project but rather from the workers' movement and the COB and its sphere of influence.

---

13 Zavaleta, 'Nacionalizaciones'.

14 Zavaleta, 'Nacionalizaciones'.

In this case there is what Zavaleta calls an intersubjectivity that precedes its material conditions. The national-popular is articulated within civil society around the COB and the workers' movement, ideologically and politically, in advance of the effective constitution of a nationalized social body, that is, one which is more unified in economics and culture.

This connection of the national-popular with the workers' movement is a process that, after 1952, is carried out in opposition to the state. In that sense it participates in the constitution of a historical bloc, which entails a certain homogenization, and at the same time it contains diversity, underrepresented but still integrated, under working-class hegemony.

This social diversity is what capitalism has not de-peasantized in Bolivia and what begins to be articulated by the working class. It is very difficult for this to become a nation via bourgeois projects. Nationalization via capitalist development in Bolivia becomes more difficult and would have to adopt more authoritarian methods. On the other hand, after the abandonment of the 1952 revolution's phase of general nationalization, the dominant bloc in Bolivia did not try again to put forward a hegemonic project of nationalization. Instead, after the exhaustion of the military dictatorships, what re-emerges is what in this manuscript Zavaleta calls the oligarchic-seigneurial project, which is what we are living at present.[15] It is a project that aims to be hegemonic in the sense of producing consensus on a neoliberal reform of society, but accompanied by a broad process of de-nationalization of the economy, of the state and also of its citizens.

---

15 This book was first published in 2002; the 'present' referred to is thus the late 1990s and the beginning of the 2000s, when Bolivia was governed by coalitions of centre-right parties entirely committed to the so-called Washington consensus of 'neoliberal' reforms and with close links to transnational capital and international financial bodies such as the IMF and the World Bank. The leading figures in these governments were members of the upper class, entrepreneurs and technocrats, who had often spent more years of their lives in the USA than they had in Bolivia. This is the context Tapia is describing in this paragraph. After the change of government in 2005, when Evo Morales' party MAS replaced what are now known as 'traditional' or 'neoliberal' parties, the context changed and gave rise to a novel project of a 'plurinational state', including the re-nationalization (in the conventional sense of the term in English) of hydrocarbons and other natural resources, although various commentators have questioned whether this inventive discourse really signifies a fundamental change in the economic matrix which is still based in the extraction and export of raw materials. [Trans.]

The actual dominant political bloc is trying to disorganize the working-class pole of alternative hegemonic articulation; that is, to disorganize the part of civil society that does not correspond to it. In so far as it does not substitute that political construction with processes of social democratization that could create the basis for a hegemonic construction and bourgeois nationalization, the result is a makeover of the apparent unification or apparent state, which is the traditional form of domination in Bolivia.

What is certain is that the Bolivian state now possesses a more abundant ideological production. This is a process of reinforcement and renovation of what Marx and Zavaleta call the apparent forms, but without an endogenous development of capitalism, and without nationalization. It is closely linked to the trans-nationalization and de-nationalization of the Bolivian economy and what Zavaleta called the passage from state forms of imperialism to the Bolivian state. It is linked to a change in juridical property relations and in the forms of appropriation. It is an ideological renovation that presents as modernization what is really the disorganization of what little national sovereignty there was.

CHAPTER TEN

Forms of Politics and the State in Latin America

At the end of the 1960s and the beginning of the 1970s, several Latin American societies went through processes of anti-imperialist mobilization, and also of the democratization of their societies, together with economic and social reforms in a redistributive direction. Shortly afterwards, most of those societies began to experience the authoritarian reaction of their most conservative sectors, in combination with US intervention.

Zavaleta was in Bolivia in 1971, at the time of the organization of the Popular Assembly, dismantled with the overthrow of General Torres' government by the coup d'état that led to the establishment of the [Hugo] Banzer dictatorship. After that, he once again left for Chile, where he stayed during Allende's Popular Unity government, until another military coup made him abandon that country for Mexico.

The 1970s were a long decade of exile. It is during these years that Zavaleta writes most about Latin America, perhaps in part as a result of his forced relocation to various Latin American countries. During this decade he produced several studies on politics and the state in Latin America, some for international organizations,[1] but for the most part works published as articles, mainly in Mexican newspapers, in particular *El Excelsior* and the magazine *Proceso*. He was also a regular contributor to the journal *Cuadernos de Marcha*, published in Mexico after its editors fled another military dictatorship in Uruguay.

Many of these articles are in fact short essays. Others are detailed analyses of the conjuncture in the countries of the Southern Cone.[2] These are centred

---

1 This is the case of the following studies: *The Agrarian Problem and the Formation of the State: The Cases of Mexico, Argentina and Bolivia* (published in the series 'Le problème agraire en Amérique Latine' of the Latin American Research Workshop, February 1977); *Unified Approach to Development Analysis and Planning. Case study: Chile* (United Nations Research Institute for Social Development, June 1972).

2 This term refers to the southern tip of South America and includes Chile, Argentina, Paraguay and Uruguay. [Trans.]

on the problem of the military dictatorships. He analyses the crisis of some of the previous forms of state and political organization, in particular populism and Bonapartism.

In this chapter, I use this material to discuss Zavaleta's work on the state and politics in 1970s Latin America. I begin with Bonapartism, followed by populism, and end with the problem of dictatorships and fascism in Latin America.

Bonapartism: Incapacities of Self-Representation and Autonomy in Politics

Zavaleta's first texts on Bonapartism concern the Ovando government in Bolivia,[3] but the most abundant material on this topic is in manuscripts that he never came to publish. He titled one of them 'Formas de operación del estado en América Latina (bonapartismo, populismo y autoritarismo)' [Forms of operation of the state in Latin America (Bonapartism, populism and authoritarianism)]; the other was left untitled and I will refer to it as 'Bonapartismo y nacionalismo'. It centres on the analysis of Perón in Argentina and Getúlio Vargas in Brazil. Fragments of the first text were included in various essays he published in the late 1970s. I will not fully reconstruct his analysis of these phenomena here, but only try very briefly to review the theoretical core of his characterization and conceptualization of them.

The principal reference points of Zavaleta's analysis are those of Marx on the relative autonomy of the state under Louis Bonaparte in his classic 'The Eighteenth Brumaire' and Gramsci's analysis of the same type of phenomenon, which he called Caesarism. Zavaleta relates Bonapartism to the phenomenon of populism in Latin America.

Here is his summary formulation of the importance of this problematic: 'The most powerful contribution of the model, it seems to us, is the elaboration of the theory of the relative autonomy of the state in its relation with the masses not capable of self-representation.'[4]

He understands 'relative autonomy' as follows:

The relative autonomy of the state refers to the separation between state power or class nature and the state apparatus or factual administration.

---

3 See Zavaleta, 'Ovando el bonapartista'.

4 René Zavaleta, 'Formas de operación del estado en América Latina', Unpublished manuscript (c. 1970s), p. 9.

This is the condition of modern hegemony or legitimacy; due to this partition in two or apparent formation, the modern state can serve the strategic interests of the bourgeoisie as a group even as it denies the concrete interests of the bourgeoisie. This is what gives it its final and non-instrumental character.[5]

On the one hand, this refers to the formation of both civilian and military bureaucracies that substitute for the dominant class as subjects of the exercise of sovereignty within the society or by the state in relation to society. On the other, it refers to the existence of classes that have not yet developed their capacity for self-representation in the new space of separation of politics and capitalist reorganization of the social matrix.

The development of autonomy by the state means that its function of representation and organization is extended, that is to say, it is no longer seen as the explicit and direct representative of the dominant class but, rather, as representative of the majority in society or, in the best of cases, of everyone. This is a characteristic of modern politics. Capitalist society produces its general representative in the state, but as this state develops it must also contain the representation of particular groups. It needs a space for the representation of internal difference, which at the same time becomes mediation. To this end, the state organizes a system of mediations of a more corporative type, and, in general, a regime of representative democracy.

This does not always occur; it is a product of political construction, which is linked to the capacity of each society to produce, retain or capture surplus value from its society or from others. Depending on the degree to which hegemony has been constructed in the society, the representation of difference does not contradict but, rather, complements the more global function of representation by the state.

The state is more successful in its domination when representation, in the most general sense, is in its hands, that is, when individuals and social classes have not configured in parallel other modes of self-representation. The state is a political form that corresponds to societies divided into classes. Bonapartism is a type of regime that also appears in certain conjunctures of these class societies. It has to do with the level of development of the class struggle.

Social classes, according to Zavaleta's proposal, are not the simple result of a structural location with respect to the poles of the mode of production,

---

5 Zavaleta, 'Formas de operación', p. 10.

but also emerge from their history of constitution as social and political subjects. A social class is always its structural location plus its history. In this process of constitution, self-representation is achieved when it has advanced in the process and has to do with the capacity for unity or unification as well as ideological and political autonomy or independence.

Bonapartism can be characterized according to this framework. The conditions for its emergence are a dominant class that faces problems of unification among its parts, which are divided and in conflict, and are therefore unable to present their class interests as the general interest of society at the level of the state. A significant level of unity within the dominant class is necessary for this type of ideological production or apparent formation to be possible. If this class is fragmented and divided, there are weaker conditions for the production of the illusion of general interest, and the marks of the particular interests of one part tend to appear in the exercise and configuration of state power. Hence, the state finds itself in a more instrumental situation.

On the other hand, Bonapartism is possible when the subordinate classes, in particular the workers and the peasants, have not achieved the corporative and political unification and organization that allows them to represent themselves in the new theatre of the separation and autonomy of politics. Since they have a limited capacity for self-representation, they tend to find their representation in the state. For this to be convincing it is also necessary that the state should have produced a certain level of development of relative autonomy.

In general, Bonapartism exists when the principal social classes of a society face problems of unification. It is more frequent in phases of political immaturity of social classes, and in periods of transition to or early phases of development of capitalist society.

It is a form of development of relative autonomy of the state where the bourgeoisie (or another dominant class) is not capable of developing the superstructural level of the state that is required for the tasks of industrialization and capitalist development, as in the case of Argentina.

In some other cases, such as Bolivia, it is a manner of compensating for a bourgeoisie that does not yet exist, although the state directs a process of capitalist development that has as one of its ends the production of a national bourgeoisie.

In Latin America, Bonapartism has been linked to phases of modernization of the state, to attempts to develop in state politics a degree of correspondence with the type of economic and social development taking place in their societies, in which the bourgeoisie lacks the political maturity to carry out the required tasks of hegemonic construction.

It is a partial solution to the retardation of the superstructure with respect to the dynamic of socioeconomic processes. For Zavaleta, 'Bonapartism generally fulfils the task of modernizing society as a whole and in consequence benefits the most modern or modernizable sectors, and in this sense ends up being general or universal but it begins from a starting point perfectly delimited from the class's point of view.'[6]

In general, Bonapartism in Latin America has been a political formation that attempted to obtain a compromise between classes in order to implant and develop capitalism as a mode of modernization and of the construction of conditions of possibility for economic sovereignty. In this sense Bonapartism aspired to be a political formation over and above social classes:[7]

> The idea of drowning class struggle in the superior apparatus of the state, of suppressing the contradictions by mounting their crest, of eluding all power by becoming a superior power, is always present in all Bonapartist formulations. The goal of Bonapartism, which is to obtain pure state power, should not, however, be confused with a loss of consciousness of what the flesh-and-blood classes are. Bonapartists aspire to a position above all classes but they do not aspire to put an end to them; on the contrary, the continual exploitation of class tension was necessary to Perón, at least for his rise to power.[8]

Bonapartist discourse usually recognizes the existence of social classes, but at the same time denies that this differentiation ought to become class struggle. On the basis of this recognition and denial it constructs the possibility of a compromise between classes which means the acceptance of a functional and social division of labour. This possibility becomes convincing when the state subject is presented as equidistant from those social classes, which does not imply that it is disconnected from them; a certain degree of relation is necessary for this mediation to be possible.

Bonapartism has had greater consistency and capacity to develop relative autonomy of the state and some other social and economic reforms when it

---

6 René Zavaleta, 'Bonapartismo y nacionalismo', Unpublished manuscript (c. 1970s), pp. 21–2.

7 Zavaleta, 'Bonapartismo, p. 1.

8 Zavaleta, 'Bonapartismo, p. 7.

had a certain type of presence and significant links with, on the one hand, the workers and, on the other hand, with the bourgeoisie.

The general mediator, in this case Bonapartism, cannot be external to what it mediates, if this mediation is to be convincing and effective, at least on the ideological level. It appears as a solution to the lack of unity in the dominant class in situations when there is already some degree of movement among the subaltern classes. When there is no restlessness within civil society the state does not generally need relative autonomy. The dominant class can maintain the state in a more instrumental situation as long as the type of organization and politicization within civil society does not require mechanisms of general representation for the reproduction and legitimacy of its political power.

It is worth considering the question of mobilization of the masses in this type of political process, and to look at the links and differences between Bonapartism and populism, situations that at times appear together in the histories of Latin American states.

As a starting point, here are two passages from Zavaleta, one on their links and common features and another on their differences:

> In fact, if the basic implication of populism is the subsumption of the class in the idea of the popular as masses, there is no doubt that it is not incompatible with Bonapartism. Bonapartism also aspires to a final recognition of the classes given by their identity with the state, from which its inevitable corporatist nature can be deduced; the corporations must be recognized by the state.

> Nevertheless, there is a subliminal feature of the most characteristic populist expressions, let us say Zapatismo[9] or the MNR in Bolivia in 1952; here, the masses are constituted on the margins and even in opposition to the state. They take the initiative and in many cases surpass and disrupt the state framework. This is a significant difference from Bonapartism that, by its nature, assigns the fundamental initiative to the concentrated culmination of power. In Bonapartism, the masses are at the mercy of power; in populism power is at the mercy of the masses.[10]

---

9 Referring to the movement headed by Emilio Zapata in the Mexican Revolution at the beginning of the twentieth century, and not that which took the same name, headed by Subcommandante Marcos, in Chiapas at the end of the same century. [Trans.]

10 Zavaleta, 'Formas de operación', pp. 15–16.

What leads a Bonapartist regime to exhibit populist features is basically the level and type of mobilization and organizations existent before the establishment of the regime, in particular within the working class. If there is a pre-existing organization, above all in the new industrial proletariat, the constitution of a Bonapartist regime no longer operates in a context of general dispersion but, rather, in that of a certain level of articulation of interests. In this sense it functions and appears as a form of balance among social classes, and not as a general representative in a highly atomized space. In this situation the power of one class is symbolically and really mobilized to moderate another, above all the power of the organized working class, to develop relative autonomy within the state, that is to say, the general and strategic promotion of the interests of a capitalist society, including the denial of the interests of particular groups and of particular capitalists. This is the case in Argentina and Brazil.

In so far as the working class lacks autonomy but is organized, its presence can be used to impose the general rationality of the development of its type of society on particular fractions of the bourgeoisie. Bonapartism is possible as long as the dominant class is not unified and as long as the working class, although organized, has not yet developed ideological and political autonomy.

This development of autonomy is a longer process, unfinished in Argentina and Brazil, and in consequence these regimes lasted longer there, while in Bolivia they were brief, because the separation of the working class occurred earlier.

A regime is more Bonapartist when it is the state that organizes the new masses. This is the case above all in Brazil, where the trade unions were basically organized by the state and existed within and as a part of it. The organization of the class is a state initiative. In this case, according to Zavaleta, the masses are at the mercy of power.

In the cases of Argentina and Bolivia there were pre-existent working-class organizations, with different degrees of development and autonomy, but they were not mature in either case before the populist experiences. Both in the case of the MNR after 1952 and that of Perón in Argentina, the presence of these masses determined the fate of the type of power they exercised. The working class was organized outside the state. Its subordination and integration was above all of an ideological type. This integration was much stronger in the Argentine case where, according to Zavaleta, the working class thought of itself as bourgeois; it belonged totally to the project of capitalist modernization in the country, with no other horizon beyond that. The Bolivian working class, in contrast, was in an intermediate situation where it belonged to and acted politically within the MNR via revolutionary nationalism, and at the same time was in the process of configuring its own ideological project.

Populism: Substitution of the People and Nationalization through Passive Revolution

Populism has served the modernization of some Latin American states, in a double sense: in integrating vast sectors of workers and other subalterns in the political context of the state via subordinated forms of participation, and with respect to the development of relative autonomy.

I will base my comments on the following passage from Zavaleta:

In Bolivia, revolutionary nationalism was the name taken by populism and populism expresses the idea that the classes within revolutionary nationalism are equal in power and rights. This could only result in a flagrant and extensive triumph of petty bourgeois notions of power, of the country and in general of all the problems.[11]

This is accompanied by the substitution of the notion of class struggle by that of unification in the category of the people. Populism served the tasks of construction of the relative autonomy of the state in Latin America because it is one of the modalities that, in our political histories, construct an ideology and a convincing discourse concerning general representation in the state.

When certain political forces not yet part of the government, and more so when they have become state subjects, manage to propose that the state represent the people who are organized in a manner subordinate to the state, or else recognize previous forms of organization, and the whole of the people are opposed as a unit to the oligarchies, the discourse of the state as representative of the whole of society is much more convincing than before. This ideology is a key component in the development of relative autonomy and favours the development of rational bureaucracies.

Populism, obviously, is not a form of individualized incorporation of ex-peasants in the new political and economic structures of capitalism; but it is a form of integration in the reforms. In societies where individualist atomization is not the dominant feature and, therefore, the basis of a more strictly liberal formulation of the ideology of the state as general representative,

---

11 Zavaleta, *El poder dual*, p. 224.

populism appears as a collective form of integration. When the masses lack capacity for self-representation or ideological autonomy because they are still new to capitalism, this type of incorporation reinforces the production of the state as general representative and thus its relative autonomy.

Here, the state, upon becoming the general representative, does not do so by distancing itself from the parts of society but, rather—although it may seem paradoxical—by integrating them. This integration produces relative autonomy in so far as the classes and subaltern sectors that are integrated lack ideological autonomy, being masses in a situation that Zavaleta called ideological vacancy, losing or already having lost their cultural structure due to de-peasantization. In so far as they have not constructed a new identity they are susceptible to receiving the discourse of the state as general representative. This reception becomes an effective interpellation when it is accompanied by some sort of integration in political life and in the processes of economic structuration and redistribution.

It can be said that some populist movements carry out a process of nation formation via the integration of workers and marginal groups into the market and politics, but in the modality of a passive revolution, that is, a process of reform and modernization of the dominant class and the state that incorporates large groups of workers in a subordinate manner.

Argentine history clearly illustrates the relation between redistribution and integration. Society disposed of a larger surplus or redistributed the surplus more widely in this process of integrating the working class into the processes unleashed by industrialization. Hence it achieved a greater integration of the working class. It is in this sense that Zavaleta said that the Argentine working class was a bourgeois class; mentally and ideologically, it belonged totally to that type of society.

All working classes are internal to the capitalist mode of production, and only some of them develop a degree of ideological and political separation in the course of their histories. The key of populism, in Zavaleta's perspective, is to achieve this subordinate integration of the working class, the peasants and others, in a process that produces the feeling and situation of belonging and at the same time avoids the development of autonomy and separation of these classes, that is, the development of the political contradiction inherent in the structure of the capitalist mode of production.

Zavaleta is critical of populism because of the way in which he conceives the development of class autonomy and the centrality of the proletariat. The working class is populist when it feels itself to be part of an undifferentiated people or of general popular democratic movements, as happened in 1952 in Bolivia; that is, when it does not assume the alternative leadership of a popular bloc that is no longer undifferentiated but, rather, organized around the centrality of the proletariat.

In this sense, populism is an index of the underdevelopment of the class and of the workers' movement. Populism is a possible strategy for Bonapartist or semi-Bonapartist bureaucracies so long as the working class has not developed political autonomy, and the dominant class has not achieved unity and expressed this in the state. Populism is a phenomenon that can appear in the phase of construction of relative autonomy of the state, but it is much more difficult for it to be a normal mode of exercise of political and ideological mediation when relative autonomy has been achieved and there is a unified dominant class with the capacity to intervene in a hegemonic manner in its civil society.

The latter situation is one that, under their new conditions, Latin American bourgeoisies have only been able to achieve in a partial manner, although this is increasingly widespread. As long as there is no complete integration and no development of proletarian centrality, populism and Bonapartism persist as possibilities in the political horizon of our societies.

With this, Zavaleta wants to dispel romantic conceptions of the people, one of the most sophisticated of which is that of Laclau, the principal theoretical innovator in the analysis of this type of phenomenon. For Laclau, the contradiction between the people and the power bloc is the general form of contradiction on the level of the socioeconomic formation, in contrast to the class contradiction that corresponds to the abstract level of the mode of production.[12] This ignores the fact that in many populist regimes the recomposition of the power bloc occurs precisely via a mediated incorporation of the people whose organization has been recognized by the state or which has been organized by it in a functional and subordinate manner.

Laclau's conceptualization, since it is elaborated on the level of discourse, seems to generalize the periods of struggle that precede the reform of the state, that is to say, prior to the entry of populist forces into government; in this period, on the level of discourse they effectively derive their force from an opposition between the people and the oligarchy. But characterization of populism accounts for only one phase of the process and is limited to the discursive level.

---

12 Ernesto Laclau, *Politics and Ideology in Marxist Theory: Capitalism–Fascism–Populism* (London: Verso, 1979).

Although Zavaleta does not develop his analysis of populism, he appears to consider it from a more general perspective, that of its development in the process of capitalist modernization as a whole, and in particular that of the state.

This implies that, where the idea of the people has been politically constructed, which is how Laclau thinks of it, this does not form an irreducible pole permanently opposed to the power bloc, but can rather form part of the reconstitution of that bloc with a reconfiguration of the relations of force between fractions of the dominant class, and its partial dislodgement by modernizing bureaucracies which fortify the state by developing its autonomy. The people are not always opposed to the power bloc, but can form part of its reconstitution, in so far as the state, having developed its relative autonomy, makes its function of class domination less explicit.

Zavaleta criticizes the romantic conception of the people present in Laclau and many others who have written on Latin America. The people can be reactionary. There are reactionary reconstructions of the popular world view[13] and situations and processes where the people form part of the process of constitution of the bloc in power and of the state itself. On the other hand, there are situations where the state is more progressive than its society.

Finally, a note on the articulation of popular participation can serve as a link to the discussion of dictatorships and fascism. Bonapartism is a politics that tries to represent the subaltern classes and thus substitute for their political participation. It aims to sustain and develop the relative autonomy of the state without mobilizing or integrating the participation of the masses. This is its strength and its weakness. It exists because it is a substitute representative of masses incapable of representing themselves, but its weakness lies in its failure to promote their participation. It expresses moments of catastrophic equilibrium that are resolved by the recomposition of the dominant class.

With respect to the Ovando government[14] in Bolivia, which is the first one he analyses as a Bonapartist regime, he establishes that it was already a

---

13 Zavaleta, 'Formas de operación', p. 16.

14 General Alfredo Ovando Candia governed Bolivia from 1969 to 1970. His most important action was to nationalize the Gulf Oil company's operations in Bolivia. Unlike the previous Barrientos military government in which he had taken part, which had close links with the USA, he initiated relations with the USSR and the Soviet Bloc. He was replaced in power by the even more leftist General Torres. [Trans.]

defensive Bonapartism[15] because it was established to put a brake on the previous movement of the masses. This explains why it was a Bonapartism more based on the nationalization, or renationalization, of petroleum, than on the integration of the working class in the state, which was difficult to do in a subordinate manner because the class had achieved a significant level of maturity, although it had not completed the development of its political and ideological autonomy. Ovando's government assumed the representation of the nation and manoeuvred between two classes in an intermediate situation of development, both spectators rather than participants in its policies. The outcome of this situation is the Torres government, which, according to Zavaleta, was a standoff between the army and the working class.

He sums it up thus:

> It must be said both of Torres and Ovando that they were an attempt on the part of the army to find a Bonapartist exit from the class struggle (because that is Bonapartism, peace vertically imposed on the principal classes in conflict, on the basis of a displaced representation of classes that cannot express themselves), an attempt that failed due to the structural conditions of the country, which were those of an advanced class struggle. On failing to achieve peace between the classes (Bonapartism), the aim is the political destruction of the working class (which is fascism).[16]

With this summary of Bonapartism[17] in Zavaleta's own words, I want to turn to the discussion of military dictatorships and fascism in Latin American politics.

---

15 In a short two-page-long manuscript in which Zavaleta compares the governments of Velasco Alvarado in Peru and Ovando in Bolivia at the end of the 1960s.

16 Zavaleta, *El poder dual*, p. 111.

17 In those years, especially 1975, Zavaleta talked about Bonapartism and fascism in various articles analysing the political conjuncture in Latin America. Among them are the following published in *El Excelsior*: 'Los idus de marzo. El golpe en la Argentina' (23 March 1976); 'La zona conflictiva. Balanza de una intriga' (16 December 1975); 'Perón y López Rega. Desventura de una mediación' (17 July 1975); 'Peruanizar al Perú. De Mariátegui a Morales' (1 June 1976); 'Dilemas argentinas. El tiempo no se detiene' (18 November 1975). See the bibliography for a list of the articles from this period in newspapers and other media.

Dictatorship and Fascism: Project, Mass Movements and Power Structure

In his analysis of the dictatorships Zavaleta distinguishes two phases:

1. The phase of the dissolution of the representative populist movements that took place between 1963 and 1965.
2. The phase of constitution of the authoritarian regimes of the 1970s in the Southern Cone.

The first phase is characterized by a series of coups d'état that begins in the Dominican Republic, continues in Ecuador, Brazil and Bolivia and then in Argentina, following a common model induced by imperialist policies. Zavaleta centres on the second phase, elaborating two levels of analysis. One can be called an analysis of the internal articulation between the state and civil society, in which Zavaleta proposes in turn to distinguish three levels, with reference to the debate on fascism: 'a. fascism as project or social proposal; b. fascism as a mass movement; and c. fascism as a power structure.'[18]

The other dimension under consideration is the US political model that the coups and subsequent military dictatorships aimed to impose.

Zavaleta notes, first, that the dictatorships established in Latin America in the 1970s, did indeed have a fascist project of authoritarian remodelling of the society. Banzer[19] had one in Bolivia, Pinochet had a more powerful one in Chile, and so did the Argentine and Uruguayan military.

The discourse of the military that takes charge of this reorganization of the state is more or less explicitly fascist. So are their projects of political and social reordering. The fascist component in Latin American politics in that period is given by the military and the conservative bourgeois bloc. These forces worked together with the US project for the political reordering of the region.

Zavaleta characterizes the US model as follows:

---

18 Zavaleta, 'Formas de operación', p. 26; 'Fascismo, dictadura y coyuntura de disolución', *Revista Mexicana de Sociología* 12(1) (1979): 75–85; here, p. 83.

19 Hugo Banzer Suárez governed Bolivia as a military dictator from 1971 to 1978. His government was characterized by the repression of students and intellectuals, the torture, exile and at times assassination of political opponents, and support for big business, favoured by the boom in raw material prices in that decade. Outside the scope of this book is his reinvention as a democratic politician after 1985 which eventually led to his second presidency from 1997 to 2001. [Trans.]

a. In the verticalist reorganization of society, the aim is to replace forms of organization and natural groups (produced by the natural movement of society) with corporative forms. [. . .] The reconstruction of social anarchy in terms of 'governability' [. . .]

b. The economic strategy is based on the dogma of the world system in the sense that nothing outside its sphere of operation or power is acknowledged. [. . .] In consequence the trans-nationalization of production is distanced in a schizophrenic manner from national logic.

c. The so-called doctrine of national security, which is the politico-military side of the theory of the ungovernability of democracy, is the explicit official ideology. There is a logical schism in this: the solution to dependency is the definitive institutionalization of dependency.

d. The model proposes the generalization of terror as a movement of ideological reconstitution, that is, the function of repression is not directed towards an identifiable subject of resistance but, rather, serves to reconstruct of the sphere of reference. This is what is called the erection of a negative hegemony.[20]

According to Zavaleta, the fascist project failed because it did not manage to constitute a mass fascist movement and, in consequence, neither did it manage to configure itself as a power structure. Its failure in these latter aspects has much to do with the type of US intervention. To clarify this, Zavaleta reviews the prior history of fascism, in particular that of Germany, where two important components appear. The fascist world is configured on the basis of a mass movement, above all petty bourgeois, around a project of an authoritarian remodelling of society. It appears in a situation of crisis where the workers' movement has managed to put the state in a partial crisis but has not yet managed to offer a global alternative for the rest of society. This situation generates uncertainty, produces an inclination towards authoritarianism in intermediate sectors of society and, ultimately, mobilization for the establishment of a fascist regime on a general level.

This all happened in Germany in particular in response to the problem of the national question. The fascism that was imposed as a general reordering of society combined a movement by which monopoly capital restructured the

---

20 René Zavaleta, 'Problemas de la determinación dependiente y la forma primordial' in Susana Bruna et al., *América Latina. Desarrollo y perspectivas democráticas* (San José de Costa Rica: FLACSO, 1982), pp. 55–83; here, pp. 63–4.

power bloc, a late introduction into the world economic and political system, and the consolidation and fortification of the nation-state. He mentions this briefly as a comparative reference point to underline the causes of the failure of the fascist project in Latin America.

In the Latin American dictatorships, the project of those who exercise state power in the authoritarian mode established by the coups is out of phase with the movements of their respective societies. A principal cause of this is that the fascist project does not respond to a process of national historical causation.[21] It is, rather, implementation of a political model that the US had designed for the region by the national armies, which had been trained in subordination over several decades.

In so far as the fascist project of the Latin American dictatorships was directed towards implementing the trans-nationalization of their economies, therefore further weakening the socioeconomic structures that had allowed for some level of national sovereignty, they blocked the development of a mass movement around the national question, which is generally the basis of a reactionary mass movement.

Without a national question, there is a very narrow margin in which to form a social bloc that would allow the fascist project to find forms of correspondence within civil society for its model of vertical and authoritarian reordering.

This implies that the constitution of a type of state does not only depend on the will of the governing groups, but also on the type of relations that they manage to forge with their respective civil societies. In this case there is a fascist project that has access to the exercise of state sovereignty over its society, but there is no fascist mass movement; in consequence, there is no organization of a fascist power structure as a form of social totalization. This can also be seen in analysing the relation between the armed forces and the state from the perspective of their articulation with civil society.

For Marxists, the state is basically a form of domination, and thus always contains a dictatorship, which in the optimal situation is practised via the primacy of ideology, but founded on the concentration and threat of physical force. In this sense, the army represents and is a kind of embodiment of the final nature of the state, that of being a form of domination.

The state cannot be reduced to this alone. In reality, the modern state is the organization of a general power structure that exercises leadership and

---

21 René Zavaleta, 'El fascismo y América Latina', *Nueva Política* 1 (1976): 191.

sovereignty in society through the primacy of ideology. In the case where the armed forces occupy the central functions of the state, that is, they take over the government, this implies that the state has failed in the ideological construction of its domination. It is an index of the lack of correspondence between the state and civil society. The state then has to show its dictatorial face.

It can also happen that a collective subject within civil society is able to embody the larger social whole. In the Bolivian case, Zavaleta thought that the workers' movement and its organization, the COB, were a kind of embodiment of civil society at that moment, opposed to the army, as the embodiment of the state. This is a situation of lack of correspondence, of open confrontation between the essence of civil society and that of the state. It is an extreme and general misalignment in the composition of a society.

This weak and conflictive articulation makes these societies more vulnerable to external determinations, in this case the imposition of a political regime by the US. Zavaleta's view of this is: 'Fascism as state mechanics is here a by-product of imperialist domination. Antifascism thus has to join the struggle against imperialism as a whole.'[22]

Many students of Latin American dictatorships have been led to characterize these regimes as fascist because they were installed with a project of authoritarian remodelling of society, they practiced terror against the workers' movement and were linked to the movements of monopoly capital.[23]

Although these authors recall that the first fascist experiences in European history emerged from the conjunction of monopoly capital and the national question, they forget this second component in the analysis of recent Latin American histories. This is a key point in Zavaleta's analysis, in at least two aspects.

The other authors mentioned examine the processes of trans-nationalization of the economy and the resultant dismantling of the national economies, their internal markets and local sovereignty. The analysis considers both the changes in the patterns of accumulation in the world economic

---

22 René Zavaleta, 'Bordaberry y el fascismo', *El Excelsior* (20 April 1976).

23 Representative works are those of Agustín Cueva, 'Fascismo y sociedad en América Latina', and 'Teoría social y procesos políticos en América Latina'; Álvaro Briones, 'Ideología del fascismo dependiente'; Vania Bambirra and Theotonio dos Santos, 'Dictadura militar y fascismo en Brasil'; Alvaro Briones and Orlando Caputo, 'América Latina: Nuevas modalidades de acumulación y fascismo dependiente'. All these texts are included in ILDIS, *El control político en el cono sur* (Mexico City: Siglo XXI, 1978).

system and the types of military action taken. They do not analyse the relations and mediations between the state and civil society and a longer social and political history in order to account for this.

The national question is key in illuminating the difficulties that these regimes encounter in constituting a mass fascist movement. Since this was not an endogenous project but, rather, one imposed by US imperialism, there was no possibility of mobilizing intermediate sectors around the national question.

Zavaleta thinks that fascism is a side-product of imperialist domination, that is, an external determination, but that even so one always has to analyse the internal political composition of each society, to see how that society receives external determination. This allows one to elucidate how, notwithstanding the presence of a fascist project elaborated within the society, the recent and remote history of that society may give rise to a general articulation and local historical accumulation such that it does not receive this project in such a way as to generate the corresponding reactionary mass movement. Fascist forces may come to dominate the state apparatus, but if they do not manage to organize society in an adequate way they will not configure what Zavaleta calls a power structure.

One of the principal characteristics of these dictatorships is that they dismantle the principal structures of mediation which existed between the state and civil society, which had generally been organized in the Bonapartist, populist and nationalist periods of the preceding decades: 'What is fundamental in the authoritarian dictatorships with fascist projects actually in power in the region consists in the strangling of the state mediations that enabled some level of bourgeois democracy in these countries.'[24]

From the state, they tried to reconstruct a group of corporative mediations which in most cases turned out to be artificial and were rejected by society. The earliest case of this is precisely in Bolivia. The fascist project soon collapsed and, clandestinely, the structures of union organization were rebuilt, ultimately leading to the crisis of the dictatorship in the late 1970s.[25]

24 Zavaleta, 'Fascismo, dictadura y coyuntura de disolución': 84.

25 Zavaleta analyses what he calls worker disobedience under the Banzer dictatorship in a series of articles. Among the most important are 'La dictadura de Banzer. Desacato de los obreros' (14 November 1976); 'Juan José Torres. El sistema de mayo' (5 June 1976); 'Militares y campesinos. Crisis en Bolivia' (6 June 1974); 'Mayo minero. Riesgo que vale un destino' (5 May 1976); 'Juegos de Banzer. El nuevo orden' (19 November 1974); 'Bolivia. Las luchas mineras' (2 March 1975); 'La huelga de masas' (29 June 1976);

Another aspect of these dictatorships was the precipitous destruction of the structures of representation and the political freedoms of organization and expression. With this the state no longer had the means to take the pulse of its society, to know what it desired, what it thought, what it did, who was acting. The previous systems of mediation and, above all, the existence of a representative democracy allowed this state knowledge to function.

These dictatorships roll back state power to the armed forces. They exercise greater vigilance over society but they know it less. All together, these characteristics made it impossible for them to carry out their objective of an authoritarian and vertical restructuring of society.

Both the US and the military thought that it was enough to have a plan and the necessary force to implement it—not only that of the local armed forces but also that of the imperialist power—without taking into account local history, that is to say, the conditions of reception both of the ideological production of the authoritarian project by the local state and of the external determination of the US political model.

This refers to general tendencies: in the Chilean case, for example, there was some measure of reactionary mobilization in civil society. It is the case that came closest to constituting a fascist regime on the continent. In practice, the terror prolonged over time ended up modifying these societies, as has come to be known after a few decades.[26]

I have not attempted to reconstruct in detail what Zavaleta wrote on Bonapartism, populism and fascism, but, rather, to call attention to two things—that Zavaleta was a political thinker who constantly followed the political history of Bolivia and other countries of the continent, and on that basis developed his theory of the state, politics and social science in times of

---

'Bolivia. La crisis de 1971' (26 August 1975); 'Bolivia. La división trotskista' (4 November 1975). All were published in *El Excelsior* in Mexico.

26 See the following articles by Zavaleta: 'Detrás de las fuerzas armadas. La crisis nacional en Chile' (25 February 1975); 'Chile y Perú. Los motivos militares' (8 October 1974); 'Los idus de marzo. El golpe en la Argentina' (23 March 1970); 'Allende y Pinochet. La democracia de clase en Chile' (9 September 1975); 'Las ideas de Leigh. La fascistización en Chile' (29 August 1975); 'Golpes tranquilos. El sueño del pasado' (15 June 1976); 'Perspectivas de la represión. El terror ineficaz' (28 January 1975); 'El fascismo en Chile. La provocación inminente' (3 December 1974); 'Church y el fascismo chileno. Cómo sucedieron las cosas' (2 December 1975). All likewise published in *El Excelsior*.

capitalist modernity, but also of the more specific problems of the type of complexity of our societies characterized by a disjointed diversity.

Zavaleta thought of journalism as more or less his second profession, since he made his living as a journalist at various times: in the 1950s in Bolivia, in the 1960s in Bolivia and Uruguay, in the 1970s in Mexico. This led him to criticize the way in which journalists present political events. In an interview he expressed the opinion: 'It must be said that what in the parlance of the trade is called journalistic objectivity, not without a certain pretentiousness, turns out in practice to be an act of pulverizing or disintegrating reality.'[27]

He opposes this to what he calls the total perspective. Even in his journalistic work he insisted that state theory cannot be developed without analysing specific histories: 'Any attempt to do state theory without the analysis of historical cases is bound to fail, since in reality one cannot talk of the theory of the state as such but only of an optimum or a social system in a determined space and time.'[28]

For a long time, Zavaleta was primarily concerned with contemporary history, thinking through events almost as they happened. He would return to macrohistorical analysis in *Lo nacional-popular en Bolivia*, where he aims to study the constitutive moments of the society. The analysis of the conjuncture, macrohistorical analysis and that of constitutive moments are complementary. Finally, politics cannot be explained by itself. It is necessary to have recourse to a vision of the organization of society as a whole and in its different dimensions. Although politics appears as a condensation of society, it has to be explained going beyond it to the composition of society as a whole in historical terms.

---

27 René Zavaleta, 'Todo lo que Bolivia es hoy no es sino el desplegamiento de 1952', Interview with Mariano Baptista Gumucio, *Ultima Hora*, 1983.

28 René Zavaleta, 'Sobre problemas de la teoría del estado', unpublished manuscript.

CHAPTER ELEVEN

Anti-Imperialism and Sovereignty

The exercise of freedom is somewhat difficult in Latin American societies since they not only have to produce the internal conditions for the existence of historically recognized individuals and collective freedoms, but also have to resist external powers that try to reduce or control and dismantle those liberties, above all the general exercise of the political freedom of a society, which is national sovereignty.

Here and elsewhere in the periphery, the collective construction of political unity is more necessary, even for the exercise of individual liberties. The exercise of freedom has been and is everywhere something that has to be won. But in some societies, those which dominate the world once these freedoms have become part of social life, recognized and made possible by their cultural and political structures, their maintenance becomes more a question of self-development, since, as Zavaleta understood, in order for freedom to exist it must be constantly renewed, reconquered and developed.

In other societies, in contrast, the maintenance of historically conquered liberties is a permanent struggle with internal powers that attempt to restore exclusive privileges, and above all with external powers that have based part of their exercise of liberties in the submission of other societies of the world.

This chapter explains some of Zavaleta's ideas about sovereignty. Although he always privileged the idea that in order to explain our local histories one has to take into account the internal accumulation of events and the specific historical and political composition of the state and society, this does not exclude imperialism from the context of analysis. The question is to reach it via what he called the internal horizon, since strictly speaking one only knows from that position.

Zavaleta's work does not study the economic and political structures of imperialism in general but rather its mode of intervention in Latin American histories, the political model that it has installed in different phases in Latin American politics. Above all he analyses how this external determination is carried out in several local Latin American histories, how it has dominated these societies but also how it has been resisted.

He studies the production of imperialist policy and its reception by each primordial form (that is, formation composed of each local state and society) and, no less importantly, the forms of resistance, that is, the anti-imperialist struggles.

While Zavaleta is a thinker of the local or internal horizon, he is also, for that reason, an anti-imperialist thinker. He writes: 'The fundamental enemy of the peoples of Latin America is Yankee imperialism.'[1]

Latin American societies have been the object of several projects of domination, but our era is marked by the predominance of this imperialism in our region. Zavaleta defines imperialism as follows: 'Imperialism is a result of monopoly capitalism. In politics it corresponds to the advanced phase of the nation-state of the oppressing country which impedes the construction of the nation-state in the oppressed country.'[2]

Imperialism is the result of the conjunction of a world market and a world political system, through which the appropriation of surplus value by the dominant countries and its investment in expanded reproduction and the construction of a system of government institutions and of political mediation, including representative democracy, feeds off the economic exploitation of the periphery of this world market. The nation-states with representative democracy , in the central countries of this system feed off the surplus of the periphery and block the constitution of nation-states with collective local sovereignty in those societies.

Imperialist intervention in the continent has not allowed Latin American countries to achieve autonomy in the reproduction and expansion of their economic systems or independence in the organization of their respective state structures and processes.[3]

What it has produced as a general condition is the semi-colony, from which the countries of the area have not managed to escape even in their moments of greatest social struggles.

Zavaleta finds Lenin's characterization of the semi-colony to be pertinent to the situation of our countries. Semi-colonies are countries that on the formal political level appear as independent but are highly subordinated to the financial, political, diplomatic and military power structures of the imperialist powers, in addition to their economic dependence.

---

1 René Zavaleta, 'La razón de la soberanía', unpublished manuscript, p. 1.

2 René Zavaleta, 'Las luchas antiimperialistas en América Latina', *Revista Mexicana de Sociología* 27(1) (January–March 1976): 12.

3 Zavaleta, 'Las luchas antiimperialistas': 17.

In the semi-colony, political sovereignty is weak, sporadic and partial. This has to do with the long-term incapacity of the local bourgeoisies, in particular that of Bolivia, to retain the surplus produced in their society and transform it into investment in a state to produce the unity of the dominant class and the society as a whole, which would then be able to exercise national sovereignty.

This weakness produces what Zavaleta calls the transfer of phases of the state from the centre to the periphery. This penetration begins with multinational companies that, installed in peripheral societies, become a power superior to the weak local state structures. This transfer of state forms increased in the period that he called that of the installation of authoritarian dictatorships with a fascist project, in which the transfer took place at the level of the repressive apparatus of the state, that is, of the armed forces, which also became the state bureaucracy.

Zavaleta writes: ' [. . .] here, the very heart of sovereignty (its defence) is occupied by our enemies as much as in the bleakest and most chaotic moments of civil society.'[4]

That one state can transfer its phases to another is an indication that the latter does not, strictly speaking, exercise political sovereignty. This is, in turn, an index of the failure to construct a nation through relations of correspondence between the state and civil society, and shows that the dominant part of society and the state has opted to receive external determination and the validation of their domination from outside, not from within its society.

The dominant bourgeoisies' incapacity for national construction implies that they seek validation and support for their form of domination through the acceptance of the transfer of phases from the imperialist states.

In this sense, anti-imperialist struggles put forward the unsolved question of the nation. Not only do they have to assume the expulsion of the political and economic imperialist powers located in their society, but, in order to do this, they also have to confront the problem of not having achieved the construction of the nation, that is, the unification of structures of economic and political power in a nation-state with a capacity for self-determination and resistance to external determinations.

Zavaleta considers that what independence there is or has been in Latin American countries is the result of the struggles of their peoples. For several decades, anti-imperialist struggles have had what he calls localized objectives.

---

4 René Zavaleta, 'Las costumbres militares', *El Día* (June 1979).

Several have been successful. They have recuperated economic control of some strategic areas such as petroleum and mines; they have even built significant structures of industrialization and an internal market. But they have not been able to dislodge imperialism in so far as the greater part of these struggles have had national-bourgeois objectives.[5]

These struggles, despite their partial success, did not procure the development of a firm national bourgeoisie that could direct a sovereign state; as nationalist processes, they have been accompanied by Bonapartist regimes, popular mobilizations and processes of redistribution of wealth and economic power. Most of the bourgeoisies have reacted to these processes in such a way as to block the articulation and construction of the nation, turning to new alliances with the imperialist power.

The bourgeoisie has been the first to abandon the construction of the nation and the first to form alliances in preparation for the transfer of state forms from other societies, which ends end up perpetuating the semi-colonial condition. The most general tendency of the dominant classes in Latin American societies is to reconstitute their political power adapting to and following the political models that imperialism prepares for the region. Many bourgeoisies and bureaucracies have displayed an incapacity and unwillingness for local political construction, since this seems to imply a group of economic and social reforms that would reduce their power, as is most evident in Bolivia.

The people, in contrast, have no choice but to insist on the political construction of their society as nation and on the conquest of political freedom or sovereignty. In our countries, it is more difficult for the subalterns to exercise individual liberties when they cannot exercise them collectively and a political space of local self-determination has not been produced; a society exercises freedom in the world system according to its location within it. But this location is not simply the place assigned to a society and its state by the world power system. It also depends on how each society and its state assumes these determinations. There are different ways to accept the determinations of the world system and imperialism and of situating the country within world power systems and structures.

The analysis of imperialist presence in Latin America is a mode of thinking the problems of the theory of the state on the level of inter-state relations. There are unequal relations between states, which can be thought on the basis

---

5 Zavaleta, 'Las luchas antiimperialistas': 11.

of the internal composition of each of the states involved. An imperialist state has unified its dominant class, which has in turn unified the other classes. It is therefore capable of exercising its sovereignty by transferring its phases to other states, and this becomes a relation of domination.

States in the periphery have difficulties in constructing their nations due to the presence of imperialism, in addition to the internal obstacles that result from the relations between their social classes. Sovereignty can be analysed on two levels: the internal composition and organization of the state in each society, which can give rise to internal sovereignty, and the possibility that this totalization allows the exercise of sovereignty in relation to other states, that is, external sovereignty.

In the semi-colonial condition in which imperialism has maintained Latin American societies, external sovereignty is intermittent or simply does not exist. Internal sovereignty is also partial in so far as these are occupied states, since the transfer of imperialist state forms has blocked local sovereignty.

Zavaleta thinks that in another dimension, in spite of these external determinations and the semi-colonial condition, sovereignty exists in the heart of our peoples. He writes:

> Sovereignty is the soul of the people and the reason for the nation. Popular sovereignty is the foundation of the modern world and the basis of civilization. It is not only the political and moral foundation of our time; it is also the condition for peace. [. . .] The men of our America have been born in the school of reason of the sovereignty of the people.[6]

Sovereignty is the soul of the people in the sense that its collective life can only develop in so far as it is self-determined. Popular sovereignty is fundamental to the modern secular and anthropocentric world and also the condition of peace in so far as it implies a local construction of politics, of the collectivity as a form of unity and self-government.

The generalization of liberty can only occur when there is a local construction of politics, although with universal or universalizing contents. Popular sovereignty or the exercise of collective liberty does not imply the unfolding of an ahistorical essence, but rather historical processes of social and political democratization. It implies what Zavaleta calls the emergent formation of power. This, the most radical form of democracy, is always a local production.

---

6 Zavaleta, 'La razón de la soberanía', pp. 3–4.

In Bolivia and similar countries, the local formation of power structures does not only imply collective organization, but also a defensive policy. Referring to the relationship between Latin American countries and the US, Zavaleta writes: 'Their relations with that country can only be defensive. Each sovereign act of our countries is an aggression against US national interests and therefore we will not exist unless US policy ceases to exist within our policies.'[7]

The practice of sovereignty, above all of popular sovereignty, is an emergent formation of power as a process of self-development. It is the mode of defence of the form of the community or society and its objectives. The best way to defend the society and the forms of community that characterize a nation and its state is through a process of emergent formation of power, and this is basically democracy with its dimensions of representation and participation.

In this sense, anti-imperialist struggles are linked to the construction of the nation, which is not realized as long as there is no sovereignty. In the same way, they are linked to the democratization of their societies. Their success has to be based on extensive processes of democratization and nationalization (in the general sense of becoming a nation and not merely declaring state ownership of resources).

A final consideration on the relation between anti-imperialism, sovereignty and local knowledge is that imperialism, which impedes the independence of peripheral countries by denying them sovereignty, also has consequences for the limits to self-knowledge and the way in which each society creates its self-image.

When a society is penetrated by state forms transferred from other states and is therefore not self-directed, the self-image that it creates does not produce a local emergent formation out of the experience of its reality but, rather, responds in part to the vertical redefinition of its self-image by the dominant society, whose ideological discourse becomes a more or less important component in the local recognition of its history and its social and political reality. It has the greatest influence in the dominant part of the local society, which conceives and defines its society through the internalization of the conscience of the master in the subordinate or slave, to use Hegel's metaphor, of which Zavaleta was fond.

---

7 René Zavaleta, 'Chile, Kissinger, libertad. Sobre idiotas y ratones', *El Excelsior* (25 November 1974).

The dominant blocs or oligarchies tend to define their societies through the ideology of the imperialist society that has been transferred to the semi-colonies.

Without political sovereignty, the societies' self-image and self-knowledge are incomplete and distorted, precisely due to the exercise of the sovereignty of other states in their internal politics, and also due to the politics of the local dominant group, formulated in the master's terms, as a result of their subordination to the networks of imperialist power.

Anti-imperialist struggles therefore also entail redefining the self-image of the local society and of the regional reality, through the channels of local sovereignty that they have been able to conquer, which are the principal political and social conditions of self-knowledge.

Thus, they also have an ideological dimension, which is generally not recognized in talking about anti-imperialism. It has to do with the production of a local self-image on the basis of an intellectual and cultural systematization of the internal horizon in its own terms, as a substitute for and critique of the ideology of the dominant bloc, which is articulated in part by the definition and ordering of reality established by the imperialist power.

Zavaleta thought that there cannot be equal relations between unequal countries,[8] and in consequence there cannot be peace. A possible interpretation of his position is that sovereignty is the condition for peace in so far as, when it exists in each society and is recognized and respected by other societies and their states, this is the only kind of equality that does not also mean the homogenization of the cultures, histories and political objectives of each national or multinational community and society. Popular sovereignty as the condition of world peace can only mean the development of the capacity of the emergent formation of power or local construction of politics in the different societies and communities of the world, and its recognition and respect as the norm between societies living together.

---

8 Zavaleta, 'Chile, Kissinger, libertad'.

CHAPTER TWELVE

Democracy

Research Programme and Intellectual Synthesis

There are topics that allow one to sum up a whole intellectual trajectory and at the same time a broad spectrum of reality. Zavaleta does this in his essay on four concepts of democracy. He finished writing this text in 1981 and it was published for the first time in 1982, two years before his death; it is a concise exposition of his mature theoretical production.

First, it encapsulates his development up to that point, from the idea of class and proletarian centrality to the idea of the masses and of intersubjectivity. Second, it incorporates an analysis of the process that begins with the establishment of the capitalist mode of production or the phases of its constitutive moment, which follow the logical sequence factory—union—party—power, in the case of the working class, and, more broadly, the logic of the factory—internal market—nation-state—bourgeois representative democracy.

It is also a moment of theoretical maturity in so far as this dense and rich essay contains a kind of programme of research for the future. On summarizing previous results, it does not close with the limits of a certain strategy and programme but, instead, in carrying out this review, sketches a new horizon for continuing with his theoretical production and historical and political analysis. He would continue with this research programme until his early death in 1984.

His texts 'La reforma del estado en la Bolivia posdictatorial' [The reform of the state in Bolivia after the dictatorship], 'La fuerza de la masa: Forma clase y forma multitud' [The force of the mass: class form and multitude form] and 'Problemas de la participación popular' [Problems of popular participation] apply this research programme in order to think the contemporary problems of Bolivia. I will later explain how he made use of it.

At the end of the 1970s and the beginning of the 1980s, the topic of democracy became a central concern in Latin America, a trend that continues with growing intensity today, although its depth is something that I will problematize on the basis of this analysis of Zavaleta's work.

Movements within civil society in Latin American countries were demanding a transition to regimes that respected basic political rights. This put the dictatorships in crisis and made possible the transition to regimes of representative democracy. Research on democracy responds to the history of our societies in that moment when the dictatorships began to experience more or less generalized crises.

In Latin America, writers began to describe these processes of transition and to elaborate some analytical models of the transitions to democracy which, while recognizing shared elements, also account for the variants of the different cases. The most systematic results of this are the books compiled by Guillermo O'Donnell, Philippe C. Schmitter and Laurence Whitehead, in particular the conclusions by these three authors.[1]

From an analysis centred on the political actors and the variables of integration and participation, there is a passage to an intellectual labour more focused on the type of political regime and the problems of institutional reform, governability and electoral processes, systems and laws. The system of political parties and bureaucracy are frequent subjects in this literature.

I summarize some features of this process so as to propose a hypothesis on Zavaleta's work. Although it is part of this current and the intellectual turn of the time, his theoretical mode and findings are different, which has to do with what I will call the depth or degree of articulation of various dimensions of historical reality.

Zavaleta does not offer a political model for the transitions and the processes of consolidation, which, in any case, he did not live to see; nor does he deal with the relation between the transitions to democracy and the dynamics of world capitalism, or the relation between these processes and US foreign policy in terms of cause and effect.

It is an analysis on the level of what could be called social totality, in a double sense: that of its actual articulation, which he sums up in the notion of the primordial form, and that of its history, which includes its constitutive moments and their subsequent restructurations. It connects the analysis of

---

1 Guillermo O'Donnell, Philippe C. Schmitter and Laurence Whitehead (eds.), *Transitions from Authoritarian Rule: Comparative Perspectives* (Baltimore, MD: Johns Hopkins University Press, 1986). Available in Spanish in four volumes: *Transiciones desde un gobierno autoritario, Volumen 1: Europa meridional; Volumen 2: América Latina; Volumen 3: Perspectivas comparadas; Volumen 4: Conclusiones tentativas sobre las democracias inciertas* (Barcelona: Oniro, 1994).

the economic base with that of the configuration of the state, and the relation between the state and civil society and its system of mediations. In doing this, he takes into account the local histories. It can be taken as a study of the problem of representation.

State of Separation and Representation

Representation appears on the level of mediations. It is a central element of democracy. Under the dictatorships, civil societies reached a moment in which they did not only need to represent themselves in the instances of political power of the state but also had the organizational capacity to put the dictatorships in crisis. Representation appears as a result of the struggles to restore political rights and freedoms that, after electoral processes of transition, succeeded in establishing forms of representative government.

The transitions to democracy can be seen as a kind of liberation of civil society, as the creation of conditions for and elimination of obstacles to its self-representation in political life through a specific channel, the system of political parties.

Representation is thus thought in relation to political liberties and political participation within modern states. The first relation is the structural determination established between the equality of men on the level of the capitalist mode of production and its ideological correlate as formal legal equality on the level of politics and ideology. In this sense the rule of law and representative democracy are forms of optimal correspondence with capitalist society.

Democracy is a form of representation of men who are equal or equalized and individualized by capitalism. They are individuals who are and represent the same type of social substance. Strictly speaking, the bourgeois organization of democracy is a form of representation of differentiated particular interests, and not of different qualities, that is, not of different types of culture, society and politics. The elections of this type of regime serve to choose who will govern society, what will be the composition of the representation of interests of groups, classes and individuals, who will incarnate their feelings, proposals and demands within the horizon of this type of society.

Representative democracy in capitalist society represents the differences within a unity which is the homogeneity of the base or social substance that constitutes it. As Zavaleta would say, bourgeois democracy includes or represents what is representable in the framework of its constitution. It is the

political form of a society that has produced de-communized individual subjects who, if they have undergone the processes of real subsumption, belong
totally to capitalist society. Democracy is a framework for the representation
of this type of individuals. Democracy responds to a more general process of
modernity, which Zavaleta calls democracy as the general movement of the
era. This consists in a set of social processes that produce the equality of men
in the transformation of the productive moment. It also develops the ideology
of equality among men at the political and cultural level. Zavaleta writes:

> It could be said that the primary productive force of this moment of
> civilization that is capitalism is the free man. [...]

> One is only free if he is among free men and, in the last instance, one
> is only relatively free if freedom is not a fact that includes all the men
> in the setting of one's existence. [...]

> Surplus value is no more than a historical form of surplus that pro-
> ceeds from the fusion of promised liberty and the socialization of
> production. [...]

> The assignment of value itself is the parallel in production of the legal
> extension of individual equality. Man has thus applied his measure,
> which is value, to all material units.[2]

This axis that links freedom in the productive moment with freedom in the
political moment is the core of the analysis of democracy. The acquisition of
this individual liberty which becomes the first modern productive force
implies, according to Zavaleta, a first loss of the collective self and the acquisition of the individual self as a product of the loss of peasant status and the
dissolution of community. From this comes in part the initial atomization of
modern social life. If modern man initially experiences his individual freedom as separation, as solitude, there is a second moment in which the individual once again loses his freedom in the moment in which he compromises
his individual freedom in the sale of his labour power and in its productive
consumption through capitalist transformation of material substances.[3]

Here, men do not experience freedom because they exercise it but because
they lose it. This moment of loss or subsumption creates the conditions for
the reconstitution of a new self in collective terms. The socialization of the
productive forces that capitalism produces in turn produces the collective

---

2 Zavaleta, 'Cuatro conceptos de la democracia': 12.

3 Zavaleta, 'Cuatro conceptos de la democracia': 12.

worker and the conditions for the constitution of a class subject on the basis of these new structures of production. Through this constitution of the collective worker we experience a new development of freedom as democracy, no longer only as formal juridical recognition by the state. This is an intersubjective recognition between individuals in which the identity and the conception of equality between men is constructed not only on the basis of the abstract reference to the law of the state but on the basis of the socialization given in the productive moment, which tends to generate increasing degrees of self-reference, above all among the collective of workers. With respect to this Zavaleta writes:

> Recognition is, then, the second function of the logic of the factory, although it is also the most transcendental [. . .]. It follows from this that the mechanics of the action that we call 'being free' consists first in the recognition of the freedom of the other (not as a mental act but as an imperative internal to the self, although provoked by the other). Class consciousness, then, is no more than democracy for us; in that moment it ceases to be part and object of others' democracy and assumes the moment of self-reference.[4]

This means that the sense and mode of democracy is different in the state and in civil society. In the state it exists as formal juridical equalization of men and as a space that allows the quantification and instrumental knowledge of its society. Democracy as a state instance is a dislocated and abstract referent of identification, because it occurs precisely in that form which has separated itself from society and aims to synthesize it. In contrast, within civil society, democracy for us, as Zavaleta calls it, is a mode in which we begin to construct and reconstruct a collective form of social life, which even has some communitarian dimensions, and which begins to modify the atomization and individualization produced in the primitive moment of capitalism.

Democracy as a state instance serves to reproduce and expand a mode of production that established the separation between the productive moment, political life and state power. Democracy as a moment in the life of civil society is rather practiced as a way to rearticulate once more the productive moment and political life, a process that tends towards the reabsorption of the state in civil society.

We can make the following general assessment of this tendency. The degree of development of democracy within the state is an index of the degree

---

4 Zavaleta, 'Cuatro conceptos de la democracia': 14.

of separation between the state and civil society, and of the attainment of an optimal degree of representation of that civil society in the state under the form of separation. The more representative that democracy, the greater the separation of politics.

The development of democracy within civil society, which occurs first of all within the working class, can be taken as an index of the creation of conditions for reversing the separation of the state and civil society. This can only occur once the separation and the development of the moment of representative democracy has taken place. The moment of representation is the optimal moment of the relation of separation.

Democracy, Motley Societies and the Apparent State

The problem of the relation between democracy and motley societies is a central concern for Zavaleta. This is his principal contribution and he is one of the few theorists who has grappled with the difficulties proposed by the establishment of representative democracies in societies that are highly heterogeneous and are not articulated in an organic way. His work on this subject results in an analysis of the problems of the political construction of state unity.

Democracy is a form of representation in societies where a process of separation of the state and civil society has been endogenously produced, a product of the constitution of capitalism; that is to say, where there was primitive accumulation and production of free men, and thus de-peasantization, the dissolution of community and a process of social atomization. This results in the substitution of local and traditional forms of authority on a micro level by the authority of the new nation-state under construction.

A motley society is one that is not organically connected. There is an inorganic coexistence, product of incomplete penetrations and transformations. The result is the existence of various forms of sociability in the same territory in which a state claims to govern.

'On one extreme there is a degree of disconnection or lack of articulation among the elements and one thus speaks of an apparent state because civil society is not internally linked on an organic level.'[5]

This implies that there are other locally existing forms of production and there are peoples and cultures with their own languages and customs and,

---

5 Zavaleta, 'Cuatro conceptos de la democracia': 18.

above all, for what concerns us here, with their own structures of authority and political life. Not all the communities and populations of the country have passed through an endogenous process of separation between the state and civil society; rather, they are in a situation where they still have local forms of government, which effectively govern civil society. On the other hand, there is a supposedly national state superposed on these structures of local authority which, in consequence, generally appears as a form of external domination. Hence this state is recognized only partially or not at all.

For many of these communities, the separation between the state and civil society has occurred in another place, dislocated from their territory. In so far as this separation is not an endogenous process it does not create firm bases for its legitimacy, much less when local authority structures persist.

All this also means that the processes of nationalization of the state are highly partial and weak. This is the situation that Zavaleta calls the apparent state. This is a political power that pretends to be valid in the entire territory of a country in which, nevertheless, various forms of society exist, that is, various forms of relations of production and diverse forms of local political life that are more valid than the supposed national state, which in any case is felt to be an external power. In many places the articulation of the primordial form still has a local and regional character, and this has more force than the primordial form on the national level, or in any case, there is a superposition in the composition of the primordial form at the national level in which the state that emerges from this is ultimately an external determination in relation to various local societies that exist in its territory.

The apparent state is an inorganic state, that is, a state that does not correspond to the ways of life that it governs and dominates. Strictly speaking, the state in its modern form of separation of political power can only be organic where the capitalist mode of production has been established. As Zavaleta sees it, where the capitalist mode of production has not penetrated and replaced other ways to organize the relations of production, the conditions for the representation of those societies and communities in democracy do not exist. As he would say, in democracy only that which can be represented is represented. That which can be represented is that which shares the same quality or social substance, that is to say, where the abstraction of labour time, of the equality of men and of political power in the form of the state has been produced.

The representation of the rest is only partial or else a representation that modifies the sense of what it represents, that is, that which is called bourgeois or liberal representative democracy can only adequately represent that which has been equalized by the productive moment and state legality.

Democracy is a way to represent that which has already been equalized in the base. In this sense it cannot adequately represent that which is not equal, above all that which proceeds from other ways of organizing the moment of production and from other forms of relation between production and politics within each community. In so far as these other forms of society aim to represent themselves within a liberal bourgeois democracy, they end up representing only that which is common to any other member of that nation-state: their abstract condition of being a citizen who recognizes and obeys the laws of the constitution of the state.

That which is left out is that which is, effectively, qualitatively different. The more symbolic forms of those differences may circulate, but what is excluded are the local forms of political authority, since this is the point of conflict and the cause of the inorganicity of the nation-state in relation to some collectivities in its country.

In relation to these collectivities, democracy will only produce the illusion of representation of the form of their social being and their interests. It can only represent that for which the state and its democratic moment are organized, and that is what is common to all the inhabitants of the country, not their differences.

Democracy cannot adequately represent, and in the last instance cannot represent at all, that which has not experienced internally the production of representation, which is generated by the process of separation of politics. Hence, the apparent state is inorganic in relation to those contexts where the processes of separation of politics have occurred only partially or not at all, although this may be lived as a kind of external determination. There may be a habit of subordination due to the fact of colonial and republican domination, but not an experience of internal separation of politics. Where this has not occurred, the national state is a more or less external form of domination and not a political form internal to each locality.

This mode of thinking a motley society that gives rise to an apparent state proposes that it is almost impossible to produce an organic national state where the nucleus of capitalist social life has not been established. Intimately related to this is the problem of the conditions of possibility, validity and efficacy of democracy as representation.

This argument elucidates some of the central problems in Bolivian history. The incomplete totalization of this society in capitalist terms translates into a weakness in the construction of the nation-state and in the organization, legitimacy and efficiency of representative democracy in the country. The initial feeling is one of pessimism with respect to the possibilities of political construction in the future. If the installation of the capitalist mode of production with all its consequences is the basis for the organic foundation of the nation-state and representative democracy, then Bolivia is more or less condemned for a long time, if not forever, to be an incomplete society, that is, motley, with a composition in which the lack of correspondence and disjointedness predominate over organic relations of correspondence.

There have been three axes of nationalization in Bolivia. The first is nationalization as restitution or conquest of local sovereignty over natural resources: nationalization of the mines and of petroleum. Another is what Almaraz called the nationalization of its own government. A third would be the expansion of capitalism on the basis of the nationalized mines which financed its extension to other regions of the country, breaking with the enclave modality that previously existed. One could add a fourth process on the cultural and ideological level, which is what the nationalists called the development of national consciousness. The latter preceded and paved the way for the 1952 revolution, which led to the first three axes. In the case of the nationalization of oil, there was a precedent in 1931.

After these three processes, there was another phase of development of national consciousness, in recognition of the new state and the new composition or relation between the state and civil society. The basis of these processes is state capitalism, which was organized after 1952 around the nationalization of natural resources and the establishment of state enterprises to exploit them. It is a phase of nationalization without a bourgeoisie that could construct hegemony on the basis of these processes.

As Gramsci said, the construction of hegemony is another form of nationalization. It is the form of organization of modern nations. This has not occurred in Bolivia, or it has occurred only in a very weak and partial way. Nationalization in Bolivia is a demand that emerges from within civil society and has as one of its consequences and causes the 1952 revolution, which gave rise to a process of nationalization on the basis of the state. Speaking exclusively of nation formation, it can be said that this process, which culminated after a decade in the installation of a military dictatorship in Bolivia, was one in which nationalization advanced from the state and civil society until the moment in which the state fell behind and came into contradiction with the demands of civil society and, in consequence, became a dictatorship.

It then began a new phase of de-nationalization with respect to sovereignty, that is, both the government and natural resources were de-nationalized.

Turning to the other dimension, that of democracy, in his essay 'Las masas en noviembre' [The masses in November], Zavaleta affirms that in the crisis of political power at the end of the 1970s, the workers' movement and civil society came to assume representative democracy as a demand and as a necessity, as a project. Before this, the programme of civil society was the construction of a sovereign nation-state. When, in the 1970s, the state resulting from the revolution had become a dictatorship, and as such a form of internal domination, in the course of the reorganization of the popular sectors in the resistance to the dictatorship a demand matured and emerged in the form of representative democracy, which had thus been internalized.

I want to comment on this in relation to the motley nature of society, which implies that democracy would not be capable of representing its diverse social qualities.

First, Bolivian civil society internalized or assumed representative democracy from the workers' movement, that is, that sector which belonged to the capitalist mode of production and, in consequence, could be organically represented in democracy; even though its process of constitution as a political subject corresponded to what Zavaleta called a composite medium, in so far as the proletariat, above all the miners, had its origin in peasant communities.

The adoption of representative democracy corresponds, *grosso modo*, to the sphere of the COB. It was adopted with meanings that do not correspond to the structural equivalence between the capitalist mode of production and the political state. The demand for democracy contained, on the one hand, the claim to recognition of political rights and liberties, and on the other, to participation and, therefore, representation.

In other words, representative democracy was not taken up assuming the separation of politics with respect to society and demanding rational organization but, rather, in the belief that through the transition to that type of regime it would be possible for the state to become closer to civil society, from which it had been brutally separated by the dictatorships. This approach would have to be promoted by the inclusion of the political parties, formed within civil society, in the structures of state representation, and also by the recognition and participatory incorporation of other forms of political organization from within civil society, above all the unions, in the representation of interests and in government policies.

It is worth recalling that the recognition and defence of elections implying a party system is something that has force above all in the moment of transition. Once the first steps had been taken in this direction, the demand for democracy appeared as a proposal for the incorporation of the COB in government, that is, the entry of the unions into the national government; this obviously does not imply the abstract representation of citizens but, rather, the representation and participation of concrete interests in the state.

The years after the transition, as far as Zavaleta lived to see them, reinforce the more structural elements of his analysis. After a first moment in which the transition to democracy was a kind of liberation of civil society, or a conquest of rights and political liberties, the development of representation in Bolivia is linked to the development of capitalism. The parliament and the state as a whole have tended to homogenization, that is, to represent less the differences that appeared in some way in the period of transition and the UDP government, and to become a form of abstract quantification of that little which is common to all Bolivians, their quality of abstractly homogeneous citizens.

Homogenization within a party system would improve representation in a society highly totalized by the capitalist mode of production and its resultant superstructures. In a society that is not so totalized, like the Bolivian, the party system becomes less representative in so far as it is less organic. Basically, it is an instance of competition between elites, as Schumpeter would say,[6] reconstructed from above, which is a way in which representative democracy tries to find and delimit what it can represent. From the start the representation of different cultural and political matrices has no place, and it also aims to eliminate political and ideological options within the modern part of society, with the short term aim of what is called governability.

In the moment of transition, representative democracy was presented as if it could offer more than it really could, because among other things there was a wish to convert it into a more participatory democracy and reduce the separation between the state and civil society, which among the populace had never been internalized except as external domination, not as an internal necessity. There was no interest in a definitive and rational organization of the state.

Zavaleta's analysis puts forward a much broader problem for the future of societies like that of Bolivia or motley societies in general. How can a form

---

6 Joseph A. Schumpeter, *Capitalism, Socialism and Democracy* (London: Harper Perennial Modern Classics, 2008[1942]).

of state or unitary political government be constituted for societies that are not unified? The problem is that, even in the most democratic moment of deliberation, election and constitution of that political power, it might not be possible to resolve the lack of unity in the base. Let us suppose that different peoples, cultures and hence modalities of constitution of political authority are gathered together to freely debate the form of belonging to one and the same national society and, in consequence, to constitute their political government. In the moment in which that form is decided on and configured, it will cease to correspond in terms of organic articulation to each of the social components that participate in the new union. It will only represent them partially, to a greater or lesser degree. According to the level of democratization present in the constitutive moment of this political unit or unity, it will be more or less oppressive for some or others and also more or less representative. It will always contain unequal and partial degrees of recognition of each component and degrees of denial or ignorance of each one of them.

These are the structural limits to the construction of political unity or the state form for the government of societies that are not equal nor unified in their base. It seems that motley societies are more or less condemned to some degree of inorganicity of political power. What remains as a proposal is a set of processes of reform that extend the degree of democratization although they cannot provide a total solution to this problem of lack of correspondence between the state and society at the general level.

Xaver Albó, in an essay entitled '40 naciones en una' [Forty nations in one],[7] has a more optimistic view of living together in difference in a country that, according to him, includes at least 40 nations, which nevertheless could maintain and develop their cultural and political identity alongside a collective national identity that would not be exclusive and oppressive to those which preceded it. This optimistic perspective, which should be insisted on in any case, is premised on Albó's assumption of the possibility of the construction of collective identities in which societies can imagine things beyond what their material bases and their social structures allow.

The problems noted by Zavaleta proceed from his analysis of this determination by the social base. They concern the deepest structural obstacles in a chain of causality that shapes the various levels of articulation and differentiation of the social totality, but this does not make it a partial diagnosis. We must try to integrate the conceptions of the problems that political

---

7 Xavier Albó, '40 naciones en una', *Cuarto intermedio* 6(1) (1988): 19–44.

construction must face in a country like Bolivia elaborated by Zavaleta, Albó, Silvia Rivera and others, products of the political emergence of various peoples and cultures in Bolivian society that are advancing their political positions.

Another comparison that it is worth making with respect to this problem is the consideration of the model called consociational, which various European countries have experimented with as a way to resolve conflicts due to religious, linguistic and plurinational diversity within some of these societies. Without going into detail, the point that concerns us here consists in a political response that incorporates, not only in the legislature but also in the executive power, representatives of each of the different social groups in terms proportional to the votes that express their existence in the country.[8]

This type of political solution has a significant degree of success in the resolution of conflicts, and hence of representativity, because it is based on populations where the capitalist mode of production has been established in their base. Their differences have more to do with differences in the superstructure that have persisted after the development of capitalism due to local expressions of different aspects of social life. The consociational model can solve problems of ethnic, linguistic and religious heterogeneity because the unified base favours it. There is juridical equality in the state despite cultural diversity. Strictly speaking, the state is not apparent although it needs to be plural. It is organic with respect to society and more so because it incorporates this pluralism in legislative and executive representation.

The problem with the incorporation of this model in other societies in Africa and Latin America, in particular in Bolivia, is precisely that this unity in the base does not exist. The difficulty is more serious in so far as the state is more apparent and inorganic, as previously explained.[9]

---

8 Arend Lijphart, *Democracias contemporáneas* (Barcelona: Ariel, 1998).

9 Gonzalo Rojas Ortuste has argued for a combined variant of the consociational model for Bolivia in *Democracia en Bolivia. Hoy y mañana. Enraizando la democracia con las experiencias de los pueblos indígenas* (La Paz: CIPCA, 1994). In Lijphart's book, the argument is that the consociational model (which he calls 'shared power') is a way to resolve political problems in multi-ethnic societies. This solution, which seems at first to be a good one, runs into problems in what Zavaleta calls motley societies, because it is a model constructed on the level of the superstructures, and seeks a solution on that level. It does not consider the production of equality in the structures of the base. See Arend Lijphart, 'El enfoque de poder compartido para sociedades multiétnicas', *Autodeterminación* 12 (1994): 153–89; 'The Power-Sharing Approach' in J. V. Montville (ed.), *Conflict and Peacemaking in Multiethnic Societies* (New York: Lexington Books, 1991).

Zavaleta's first definition of democracy is a general movement of the era that consists in the processes that he refers to as social democratization followed by the political democratization that this demands. He explains this as follows:

> As a conclusion to this part on democracy as a condition of the era, we will still say that the process consists in: the advent of the self; the compulsion or anxiety for the productive surrender of the self; and the collective reconstruction of the self on the basis of the operation of the logic of the factory by the class or of the sequence factory—union—theory—party—power. This is, finally, how we should explain the relation between the law of value and the construction of the modern state. In other words, the freedom of social democratization contains at the same time the grandeur of capitalism, capable of generating masses of individuals identified as members of the nation, and capitalism's perdition, because the socialization of production paves the way for the socialization of power.[10]

Knowledge in Democracy

Zavaleta complements this discussion of democracy as a general movement of the era with the idea of democracy as a space and method of state knowledge. The problem of knowledge is proposed as the vertical application of representative democracy as a requisite of the era:[11] 'Democracy is, in this sense, the bourgeois calculation or registration of society, a function comparable to that of the law of value with respect to historical materialism.'[12]

The level of representative democracy present in a society corresponds to the efficacy with which the society can be observed, listened to and known. The respect for political liberties such as free association and freedom of speech allows society to express itself and the state, in consequence, to be advised or informed of its demands, its plans, which political and social subjects are being constituted, in which directions they are moving and to what end. On this basis the state can prepare its intervention so as to orchestrate its general reproduction.

Zavaleta's analysis continues to be anchored in the influences and consequences of the installation and development of the capitalist mode of

---

10 Zavaleta, 'Cuatro conceptions of democracy', pp. 15–16.

11 Zavaleta, 'Cuatro conceptions of democracy', p. 19.

12 Zavaleta, 'Cuatro conceptions of democracy', p. 20.

production, in this case on the level of the superstructures, centred on democracy as a problem of knowledge in terms of the necessity of the process of expanded reproduction of capitalism: 'Democracy is the practical expression of reproduction on an expanded scale.'[13]

While the capitalist mode of production tends in itself to expanded reproduction, this has to be prepared for and this preparation is the task of the state. Representative democracy is the most rational form of organization of the state–civil society relation in capitalist societies, where the separation of politics via the representative state provides a distance that permits it to see its society beyond the mere particular interests of localized domination, and to view it from the perspective of the reproduction of society in general.

This is achieved when what in Marxist terms is called the autonomy of politics has been produced, that is, with the appearance and development of a bureaucracy that, although it governs in order to reproduce bourgeois society, has at the same time a distance with respect to particular attributes of the members and fractions of the dominant class: 'The appearance of bureaucracy in the modern sense is the classic outcome of the perplexity of the bourgeoisie as dominant class with respect to expanded reproduction and the cycle of crises.'[14]

Politics is thus freely revealed democracy, that is, society decrypted. The visibility of the conjuncture, which is the primary interest of bourgeois domination, is conditioned by the separation of society and the state.

This implies that societies that are already divided into classes but have not yet developed a clear separation of politics cannot achieve this degree of visibility that is developed in conditions of democracy and representation. When the separation of politics has occurred, the conjuncture is visible through representation.

Returning to a previous problem, if visibility is basically due to representation, the conclusion is that what is visible is that which can be represented, and that which can be represented is that which has passed more or less substantially through capitalist totalization. The degree of this totalization conditions the scope of visibility present in democracy. More is known through representative democracy in societies that have been more homogenized or unified in processes of social democratization than in motley societies.

---

13 Zavaleta, 'Cuatro conceptions of democracy', p. 22.

14 Zavaleta, 'Cuatro conceptions of democracy', p. 22.

But the state does not cease to exist in motley societies, however inorganic or apparent it may be. Democracy continues to be a condition of greater visibility, although more restricted, since that which possesses a different social quality, when it tries to present and represent itself in the democratic framework, in some way ends up reducing its contents to the code that the state form uses to see them. Something similar occurs in the opposite direction with respect to how the different cultures see the state.

Democracy as representation is not an open and unstructured space of visibility of society, but rather an organized and encoded space for the knowledge of society. In this sense, the subjects who make use of democracy to produce knowledge translate the representation they make of other social qualities into the abstract codes of formal equality of the structure, which exists in order to reproduce the higher level abstraction of the law of value.

Once the representatives of other cultures, peoples or political and cultural matrices enter the framework of representation of bourgeois democracy, they end up representing what is more or less common to every citizen of this state. For example, in Bolivia, during the 1993–97 government, Víctor Hugo Cárdenas, an Aymara *katarista* leader, was incorporated as vice president.[15] Various parts of society and above all the state argued that, at least symbolically, he represented the Aymaras and other indigenous peoples and cultures. Supposing that this were the case, which is debatable, Cárdenas ended up representing the Aymaras and the rest but in those aspects which they had in common with other Bolivians who lived another type of culture, that is, he represented them as abstract individual Bolivian citizens, since in the last instance if the elections are used to read the country, this reading reduces them to numbers of votes and, in consequence, eliminates the differences between those who have voted. In this process, Cárdenas, rather than

---

15 *Katarismo* was a political and ideological movement which began in the early 1970s in Bolivia among militants of the peasant syndicalist organization and their intellectual sympathizers. They argued that the exclusively class-based positions of the popular movements were inadequate to account for the oppression of the indigenous peasantry and, by extension, large portions of the urban lower classes that maintained cultural forms inherited from their peasant origins; it was necessary to consider the ethnic aspects of their oppression as bearers of Aymara and Quechua indigenous culture, subordinated to the creole–Hispanic–European culture which the dominant classes claimed to bear. The name *katarismo* (hence their militants were *kataristas*) was taken from the name Tupac Katari or 'Resplendent Serpent', assumed by Julián Apaza, leader of an anticolonial rebellion in 1781. [Trans.]

a representative of those peoples and cultures in an empowering sense, ended up becoming a mediator of the state in a neutralizing sense.

The crucial political point is that Cárdenas' inclusion in government did not bring with it the inclusion of political forms of authority in those peoples who were supposedly represented by him in the national state. Strictly speaking, he did not present nor represent those cultural matrices in their political forms, but only the participation of Aymaras and others in the general forms of the Bolivian state in so far as they were abstract citizens.

Here, it is not so much representation that permits certain cognitive functions, but rather the existence of political rights and their exercise by other peoples and cultures that exist in the Bolivian territory. The exercise of these liberties allows the expression of differences and the persistence of other cultures as it allows knowledge of their existence, knowledge that they have certain demands and projects, but in the moment in which they are incorporated in the framework of state representation they tend to lose their differential quality and appear as does any other Bolivian citizen, subjects under the rule of law in general and not as members of a particular culture.

Democracy is, despite all these limitation, a space of organized openness to the recognition and knowledge of movements within a social totality. Zavaleta writes: 'Democracy [. . .] immediately registers the palpitations of the sites of society; the mediators convert these contractions into state material. In other words, democracy hears the sound of the social body.'[16]

For democracy to be able to hear this sound and turn it into state material, that is, a set of mediations and government policies for civil society and for the internal organization of the state, it needs a subject capable of processing this transformation, that is, a rational bureaucracy.[17] This takes us to another dimension of the problem, which is the local or national capacity for retention of the surplus produced in society.

Democracy, as a group of institutions of representation, has to be financed. It has costs, hence it depends on the surplus that can be collected

---

16 Zavaleta, 'Cuatro conceptions of democracy', p. 22.

17 Zavaleta's notion of bureaucracy combines Weber and Marx. The idea of rational administration comes from Weber, but he unites it with the idea of bureaucracy as the subject of state direction and strategic rationality or the total capitalist, who handles state secrets, that is, the final ends, ideas taken from Marx and contemporary Marxists. Weber considers that the ideal is the separation of rational bureaucracy and political leadership.

and retained by the state in order to invest it in representation which, at the same time, is an investment in knowledge of civil society. In this sense it is an investment in the conditions of reproduction of the state itself and in its type of society, that is, also in the productive nucleus.

On the other hand, the existence of a more or less rational bureaucracy is also linked to the capacity of a state for investment in its internal structure. Societies like Bolivia, whose internal composition generates weak sovereignty and which occupy a subordinate position in the networks of world power, face serious difficulties in the development of a rational bureaucracy, in financing democracy, and finally, in producing knowledge of their own societies.

These things do not necessarily have to occur together. Observing the countries of Latin America, it can be seen that rational bureaucracy is most developed in Mexico and Brazil, the countries with the greatest capacity for retention of the surplus that their societies have produced, which implies a significant degree of nationalization and nationalism. However, it can be observed that this has not occurred in parallel with the development of representative democracy.

In order for democracy to carry out its cognitive functions and produce state results, an endogenous process is necessary, which generates organic relations between the separation of politics, the articulation of mediations and institutions of representation, and bureaucratic-state rationality. If some facets of representative democracy are no more than the transfer of state forms from another country, without the accompanying internal mediations and state bureaucracy, they will not have good cognitive results.

Zavaleta considers democracy as a state method:

Here democracy appears as an act of the state. It is, thus, the consciousness of the state calculating the reverberations of civil society. In this gnoseological phase, civil society is only the object of democracy, but the democratic subject (so to speak) is the dominant class, that is, its personification in the rational state, which is the bureaucrat. Democracy therefore functions as the cunning of the dictatorship. This is the undemocratic moment of democracy.[18]

Civil society can become the object of knowledge of the state because the latter is politically separate. On becoming an object of knowledge, civil society also becomes an object of manipulation or transformation from outside. In

---

18 Zavaleta, 'Cuatro conceptions of democracy', pp. 22–3.

this sense, the knowledge produced is basically instrumental. Via democracy it is possible to know who is acting in society, with what ends, who meets whom, and in consequence what dangers some of these movements may present for the reproduction and stability of the state, and also which movements can be used to provide support, consensus, and legitimacy; in general, what problems have to be solved. This is democracy used in preparation for the reproduction of the type of domination that the state exercises. It is what Zavaleta calls the undemocratic moment of democracy.

This instrumental knowledge is a knowledge that one subject uses in order to act on that which is known. It is not a knowledge that civil society itself can use in order to develop its life. The knowledge that the state produces using democracy as a method is a partial and superficial knowledge of its society. It is achieved by converting society into a thing, into the object of knowledge. In so far as it goes beyond the superficial, it tends to be a mechanical knowledge of how social objects function.

The state appears as a synthesis of society since it is that which in some measure organizes the social totality, and appears as part of its necessary internal ideology as the general representative of society. On this basis it aims to produce knowledge of society. It is supposedly the central, privileged site from which to view society in general. But, as Zavaleta says, the state is a qualified synthesis of society, that is: 'The state, as counterpart, is never the form of unity of society but rather the expression of its internal differentiation, that is, the way in which the dominant side dominates.'[19]

Democracy as a state method functions to facilitate the domination of this internal differentiation. While democracy can appear, in the first instance, as a moment of intersubjective expression of various subjectivities within civil society, the knowledge that the state produces as it collects the noise of civil society is basically in the form of a monologue. The state generally has neither interest in nor methods for a dialogue; rather, its instrumental interests lead to a monological rationality.

The state organizes and uses representative democracy, which is a moment of intersubjectivity, to capture the movements of civil society. The intersubjective democratic moment is the moment in which it collects the raw materials that it uses to produce state knowledge. However, this knowledge is not produced in the representative moment of the state but rather in its other dimension which, in Zavaleta's terms, is that of the development of

19 Zavaleta, 'Cuatro conceptions of democracy', p. 18.

political autonomy as the rational state bureaucracy, which takes the form of a monologue.

Although this discourse is a monologue, this does not eliminate its dual character. This is due to the other structural tendency of the capitalist mode of production, which consists in the production of apparent forms. Since it arises through viewing the separation of politics from above, state knowledge tends to acquire some features of fallacious recognition of data on civil society. There is a tendency to convert a part of reality into the truth about the whole. The selection of that part which becomes the core of the production of the discourse on reality through its generalization as a complete explanation corresponds to what Zavaleta calls necessary ideology. It is the part of social discourse or consciousness that recognizes reality in the modality of self-justification of the position of the dominant group. Those who exercise domination necessarily have to believe a great many things in order to be able to do so.

The state knows on the basis of the illusion of its epistemological superiority over the rest of society. It feels capable of a more global knowledge. In these lines of reasoning and practice, civil society is converted above all into an object of knowledge. The knowledge that is thus produced tends to be instrumental and to be used in the service of the manipulation of this object.

The passage from democracy as a method of knowledge employed by the state to the another mode of democracy as possibility of knowledge within civil society makes it possible for society to pass from the condition of being the object of knowledge to that of being the subject of knowledge, that is, of self-knowledge.

Only when someone passes from being the object to being the subject of knowledge can one speak of self-knowledge. When democracy can also be exploited within civil society in order for it to know itself, the broader conditions are created for what can properly be called social self-knowledge. This democratic self-determination of the masses within civil society, as the political form of their unification, is what in different historical moments has created the conditions for what spaces of knowledge exist today in Bolivia.

If the state is an apparent form, the knowledge that it produces, consciously and unconsciously, follows the patterns of expanded reproduction, to produce an ideology that tends to obscure the reality it reproduces.

To know from the state is to know from the core of production of the principal apparent forms or illusions of capitalist time, no matter how pragmatic its bureaucracies aim to be. The separation of politics in the state produces the illusion of something general and, in consequence, a large part of the knowledge elaborated by the state tends to participate in this illusion of generality. With these characteristics it may be the case that for a long time the state maintains superiority in terms of knowledge with respect to its society because that society is not organized and has not produced an intersubjectivity capable of self-knowledge.

That the state is superior in knowledge of its society indicates that society's knowledge of itself is highly instrumental.

Following Marx, Zavaleta thought that capitalism makes possible social science, that is, critical knowledge of society. This state of separation has different degrees and phases of epistemic productivity. One of them is precisely the knowledge practiced and produced by the form of separation of politics which is the state. However, both authors seek for that condition of separation to be exploited as critique in the radical sense, not on the part of the state but by that core which has produced the separation, that is, by and within civil society.

In this sense democracy can be thought of as one of the modes of re-appropriation of knowledge inside civil society and of its socialization in the new collective conditions created by the capitalist mode of production. Zavaleta thought that the self-determination of the masses was a method of civil society.[20] But on saying this he was not thinking so much of problems of knowledge but rather of politics in the strong sense, which is at the same time a form of synthesis.

Self-Determination: The Foundation of Liberty

The following passage demonstrates the scope of the implications of Zavaleta's conception of this question:

> The true school of the entirely free man is mass action and the principle of self-determination defines the manner in which all the other concepts of democracy occur [. . .]. Insofar as it is a desire proper to all eras, the self-determination of the masses is, without doubt, the principle of world history. We therefore consider it to be the core of the question of democracy. If it is true that it is man's business to debate the propositions of the world, self-determination is the application of this practice on the part of the masses. In this sense what is

---

20 Zavaleta, 'Cuatro conceptions of democracy', p. 28.

human in man is what is democratic, because in this he contests everything that exists.[21]

Democracy as self-determination of the masses is a kind of synthesis or concentration, because it is like the movement of society in its moments of greatest sovereignty, both in the general sense as a society in relation to others and in its horizontal internal exercise. It is a kind of reabsorption of the state and an overcoming of the separation of politics within civil society. It is a synthesis that overcomes or negates the abstraction of the state or the abstraction of politics as the state.

A couple more passages explain this desire:

The masses are civil society in action, that is, a pathetic, sentimental and epic state of unification.[22]

[...]

The history of the masses is always a history made against the state, in such a way that here we speak of structures of rebellion and not of forms of belonging. Every state in the last instance denies the masses, although it may express or wish to express them, because it wants to insist on its being which is that of being a state, that is, the substantial form of social material. [...] It can be said that in this case democracy for the dominant class is replaced by democracy for itself.[23]

In thinking the masses as the epic moment of unification, one thinks of a condition that overcomes the normal and everyday atomization of social life produced by the capitalist mode of production and the separation of politics. The state, as it reproduces that reality, tends to reproduce that atomization. It is in this sense that the masses become a form of suspension of that form of domination, since what Zavaleta calls forms of belonging to the state tend to be organized through institutional and ideological mediations that try to avoid the constitution of masses. In so far as they do arise within a state, the masses are the bearers of some form of crisis and suspension of the dominant ideology, which ceases to be such at least in part when this happens.

---

21 Zavaleta, 'Cuatro conceptions of democracy', p. 29.

22 Zavaleta, 'Cuatro conceptions of democracy', p. 27.

23 Zavaleta, 'Cuatro conceptions of democracy', pp. 26–7.

The masses embody a type of political action by civil society. In this sense they represent a kind of suspension of the monopoly that the state in general tends to exercise over politics. The frequent or permanent presence of active masses indicates that the state has not consolidated or constructed its hegemony. This history of the masses of which Zavaleta speaks and the structures of rebellion that they manage to organize, reproduced and renewed over time, can elaborate what he calls the foundation of liberty: 'The foundation of liberty, that is, the establishment of self-determination as an everyday custom.'[24]

This idea of democracy as self-determination of the masses corresponds to the re-absorption of the state within civil society, which is how Gramsci thought of the revolution or how Marx thought of communism.

Self-determination as a daily habit is the political objective in the broader democratic horizon. It implies collectively produced structures of participation, of deliberation and direction; but for these structures of collective sovereignty to predominate in society there must be a history of struggle. It is about organizing structures of rebellion, which means in part reversing the separation of politics as a state abstraction.

In this perspective it is not a negation that replaces what preceded it but, rather, a Hegelian process that overcomes the actual form incorporating the work developed by consciousness and the social body to criticize the present and make visible the form, or various alternative forms, of unfolding humanity and politics.

Zavaleta's work has a liberatory concept of democracy.

The analysis of various facets of democracy as genetically and organically linked to the development of capitalism in several dimensions does not conclude with the closure that identifies capitalism with democracy, claiming that the latter can only exist in the framework of the former, as is the case with liberalism.

Zavaleta concludes his analysis drawing on the most radical wing of the history of democracy, as the everyday practice of freedom. One cannot be free in a society where others cannot be free, he said; that is to say, there are collective conditions that are necessary for the exercise of individual freedom. It has to be a generalized condition.

Zavaleta analyses how democracy has been expressed in the process of separation of politics, that is, in the construction of the modern state as the

---

24 Zavaleta, 'Cuatro conceptions of democracy', p. 30.

rational form of organization of power, representation and mediation in the civil society that produced it.

All his analysis only makes sense from the liberatory and communist perspective of reversing that separation of politics and therefore of negating that state as a form of domination.

Democracy as self-determination of the masses is the way in which Zavaleta thought, above all on the basis of Bolivian history, of the process in which local struggles, which aim to construct a self-referential form of constitution of their primordial form, have throughout our history resisted colonial, patrimonial and legal-rational forms of domination, at the same time incorporating some modern elements that permit the overcoming of those modalities of domination, not only as a mere reinstatement of what came before, which did not contain democracy, but as a form of liberty in the new collective conditions of our society.

PART D

The Production of Local Knowledge

CHAPTER THIRTEEN

The Masses in November:
Self-Transformation of the People and Crisis of the State

From the Centrality of the Proletariat to the Self-Determination of the Masses

At the end of the 1970s Zavaleta took another step towards maturity in his thought, focusing on the most recent events in contemporary Bolivian history, in particular the crisis of the state that reached its climax in November 1979.

Between 1980 and 1984, the year he died, he published a series of texts on contemporary processes in Bolivia, the most important of which are 'Las masas en noviembre' [The masses in November] and 'Cuatro conceptos de democracia' [Four concepts of democracy]. The first is a text that ripened as it circulated for some years in different versions, as he revised and expanded it.

In a seminar on democracy and popular movements in November 1980, he presented, under the title 'Bolivia. Algunos problemas acerca de la democracia, el movimiento popular y la crisis revolucionaria' [Bolivia: some problems concerning democracy, the popular movement and the revolutionary crisis],[1] points that would later form part of 'Las masas en noviembre' and some sections of 'Cuatro conceptos de democracia'. In 1981, in some seminars at the UNAM on the conjuncture in Bolivia, Zavaleta circulated mimeographed copies of both these texts.

In 1983 'Las masas en noviembre' appeared at the beginning of a compilation of essays edited by Zavaleta on contemporary processes in Bolivia, written by some of the principal researchers in the country.[2]

---

1 René Zavaleta, 'Bolivia. Algunos problemas acerca de la democracia, el movimiento popular y la crisis revolucionaria' in *América Latina 80. Democracia y movimiento popular* (Lima: DESCO, 1981), pp. 373–80.

2 In René Zavaleta (ed), *Bolivia, hoy* (Mexico City: Siglo XXI, 1983), pp. 1–30. 'Las masas en noviembre' also appeared as 'Autodeterminación y democracia en Bolivia (1978–1980)' in Gonzalez Casanova (ed.), *No intervención, autodeterminación y*

In this chapter I will focus on his analysis of the horizon of proletarian centrality as self-determination in relation to the conjuncture of the crisis of the state in Bolivia. I am interested in how this explanation unfolds in 'Las masas en noviembre' and the conception Zavaleta had of Bolivia in the last years of his life.

In the 1980s Zavaleta wrote and edited a series of essays that responded almost immediately to the development of events in the country, grounded in the entire structure of explanation of Bolivian history that he had been elaborating throughout the 1970s.

Apart from 'Las masas', this series includes 'Forma clase y forma multitud en el proletariado minero en Bolivia' [Class form and multitude form in the mining proletariat in Bolivia];³ 'La fuerza de la masa: Forma clase y forma multitud' [The force of the mass: class form and multitude form];⁴ 'El largo viaje de Arze a Banzer' [The long journey from Arze to Banzer]⁵ and 'La reforma del estado en la Bolivia posdictatorial' [The reform of the state in Bolivia after the dictatorship];⁶ finally, one could include the text 'Informe acerca de la participación con relación al plan de rehabilitación y desarrollo' [Report on participation with respect to the plan for rehabilitation and development].

In these texts, in particular those compiled with 'Las masas', Zavaleta studies the expansion and development of proletarian centrality into a new type of intersubjectivity, explained by two types of process. The first is irradiation and accumulation within the working class. The other is crisis as the moment of emergence of a new type of intersubjectivity or collective subject, which is the masses, of crisis as a moment of knowledge in motley societies.

After the 1952 revolution, the Bolivian working class developed proletarian centrality in the organization of civil society. This, according to Zavaleta, allowed it to acquire epistemological centrality for social science in Bolivia.

---

democracia en América Latina (Mexico City: UNAM / Siglo XXI, 1983), pp. 159–71, and gave its name as title of a collection of Zavaleta's essays published by Juventud in Bolivia in the same year, which also included 'Cuatro conceptos de democracia'.

3 Also published in the aforementioned Bolivia, hoy.

4 In Cuadernos de marcha 3 (1980): 29–42. It also appeared as 'El proceso democrático en Bolivia' in América Latina: Proyectos de recambio y fuerzas internacionales en los 80 (Mexico City: Edicol, 1980).

5 In Bases. Expresiones del pensamiento marxista boliviano 1 (1981): 101–24.

6 In Cuadernos de Marcha 5(26) (March–April 1984): 3–8.

The development of the working class as irradiation took place above all via the trade union form, which was extended to other forms of labour in the country, and was adopted to represent its interests and incorporated in the central national organization of workers, the COB. This led Zavaleta to think that the COB was the synthesis of civil society, just as the armed forces were the synthesis of the state, in a post-revolutionary period in which the state entered a cycle of military governments that were basically anti-worker.

What Zavaleta called accumulation within the class was what allowed the Bolivian workers' movement to resist the long Banzer dictatorship in the 1970s and reorganize itself as the foundation of the mobilization within civil society that put the dictatorship in crisis at the end of the decade, when it demanded elections, initiating the process of transition.

Zavaleta understand accumulation within the class as follows:

In the analysis of the Bolivian workers' movement, within our modest sociological tradition, the concept of accumulation within the class has been used to describe the relation between collective memory, suppression-consecration and active enunciation, that is, it is a metaphor that refers to the mechanisms of positive and negative selection in the movements of collective consciousness. [...]

This supposition, that of accumulation within the class, affirms that the hypothesis is not valid if it is not acquired, that is, if it has not become part of good common sense or popular prejudice after its selection.[7]

This conception is completed as follows:

The union dogma is something upheld to its final consequences. The history of their ascendant period has made the miners into men of sudden action. This is because the initiative of the masses and of each individual within the masses has to do with the premise of the total worker which is derived from the condition of their leaders as surrogates and subject to trial. The assumption is that disorganization is not proper to the workers.[8]

All this forms part of an idea of the class conceived as a structural location plus its history. The class is a process of constitution and development as a

---

7 René Zavaleta, 'Forma clase y forma multitud en el proletariado minero en Bolivia'.
8 Zavaleta, 'Forma clase y forma multitud', p. 279.

political subject on the cultural level, on the basis of the determinations of the base or infrastructure.

According to Zavaleta, in November 1979, with the great popular mobilization to resist the Natusch Busch coup that interrupted the transition to democracy, a new type of intersubjectivity was revealed that acquired the form of the masses. It transcended the organization and movement of the working class, but it was made possible by the many years of the development of workers' centrality in the history of the country.

In that month, the COB, as the soul of civil society,[9] called a general strike. Zavaleta believes this was the first time when the peasantry supported a general strike called by the working class. One of the most important aspects of the 1979 crisis is a reconfiguration of Bolivian society that has to do, above all, with the encounter between the working class and the peasantry:

> This is an axis of constitution of the multitude, so to speak, of a historic bloc. It is the re-composition of the alliance of 1952. [. . .] In what is still more important as accumulation of the masses, the classic methods of agrarian struggle are incorporated into the pattern of working class insurrection. [. . .] It is a case of proletarian interpellation of huge pre-capitalist masses.[10]

In November 1979 there are two important confluences around proletarian centrality that determine its extent. One of them is this axis of articulation between workers and peasants and the fusion of their methods of struggle. The other consists in the incorporation in this conjuncture of representative democracy in the configuration of intersubjectivity that was taking place in the working class and in the larger horizon of the masses. Zavaleta explains:

> The masses, who had always been clandestine with respect to representative democracy, now went into assault under the standard of representative democracy, which they incorporated into their mass memory or accumulation within the class. Whatever one thinks of the question of the workers in general, here there is no doubt that the masses were constituted on the basis of proletarian interpellation.[11]

---

9 Zavaleta, 'Las masas en noviembre', p. 21.

10 Zavaleta, 'Las masas en noviembre', p. 21–2.

11 Zavaleta, 'Las masas en noviembre', p. 22.

Proletarian interpellation at that point in time had a capacity for political constitution as a result of the long years of irradiation of the working class. The action of the masses therefore does not appear as a simple following or imitation of proletarian action but, rather, as a group of autonomous or specific initiatives of each of the groups, which nevertheless are organized by proletarian leadership, as the product of a prolonged historical accumulation.

November 1979 expresses a new fusion, a reconstitution of Bolivian society that had been in the works for a long time. One of the components is the re-emergence of the peasantry in Bolivian politics. In the post-revolutionary process, the state established an extensive peasant sector as social base for its bourgeois reform project, as a counterweight to the workers' movement, which was considered dangerous because of its capacity to develop political autonomy. During the Barrientos dictatorship, for at least a decade, part of the peasant union movement was incorporated in the Military–Peasant Pact as the political basis of the dictatorial phase of the state of 1952. This begins to disintegrate with the massacres of Tolata and Epizana in 1974.[12] This is when the process of separation of the peasantry with respect to the axis of legitimacy of the state began.

In November 1979, the peasantry appears in a new and radically opposite position—in the worker-peasant axis around the COB's proletarian interpellation. According to Zavaleta, this axis would one day allow the workers' movement to emerge from its corporative enclosure, which was clearly expressed in its moment of greatest autonomous political unfolding, the Popular Assembly. He writes: 'The November crisis is without doubt the greatest separatist action of the fundamental masses in relation to the hegemonic mould of the state of 1952.'[13]

---

12 Tolata and Epizana are communities in the valley of Cochabamba. In 1974 the Banzer dictatorship declared sharp rises in fuel prices while freezing the prices of food products in the cities. This hurt peasant incomes since they would have to pay more to transport their produce to market but would not be paid more when they sold it. They blocked the highway in those two places and demanded negotiations with the government. Previous dictators had agreed to negotiate peaceably with them in the recognition of the aforementioned pact in which the peasants supported the government against the miners. However, this time the army detachment that arrived at the roadblock did not negotiate but immediately opened fire on the crowd. The number of dead has never been determined; official figures admitted to around 20 but in reality probably more than 100 people died. [Trans.]

13 Zavaleta, 'Las masas en noviembre', p. 22.

This is the most severe crisis of the 1952 state since those who were at one point components of its social base are now engaged in a process of constitution of a new historic bloc, ideologically and politically separate from that state. The crisis is more profound because at the same time there is an element of construction of national politics, which consists in the constitution of this new worker-peasant bloc.

It is in this series of texts that Zavaleta incorporates the general conception of politics and the theoretical categories of Antonio Gramsci, such as historical bloc, hegemony, moral and intellectual reform. This broadens Zavaleta's conception of Marxism and his understanding of the expansion of the social and cognitive horizon in Bolivian society.

The idea of the masses as a kind of composite subject and intersubjectivity is elaborated on the basis of the idea of class and proletarian centrality in addition to Gramsci's idea of the historical bloc. For Gramsci, a historical bloc is configured around one of the fundamental classes, that is, those which occupy the poles of a mode of production, which in modern societies are the bourgeoisie and the proletariat. What is constructed around one of these classes is not a simple alliance between classes, but rather a composition of classes and subaltern groups via the organization of culture that this class carries out in a process of fusion and articulation around a project of civilization and state. It is a process of integration and participation in a conception of the world and, therefore, of consensual participation in social organization when this conception and world order are hegemonic, or of participation in the construction of an alternative project of civilization and state around a historical bloc that is alternative to the dominant one.[14]

The masses are one of the forms of appearance and existence of a historical bloc. They are not a permanent condition of existence of the forms of organization of the social subjects who arise in the construction of a historic bloc. The masses are constructed above all in conjunctures of crisis. Zavaleta defines the masses as follows: 'The masses are civil society in action, that is, a pathetic, sentimental and epic state of unification.'[15]

The masses are constituted when there is a suspension of the normal atomization which is one of the characteristics of civil society and the normal domination with its effective ideology. They are constituted when the system of mediations shatters and another set of alternative and separatist mediations

14 See Antonio Gramsci, *Cuadernos de la cárcel*.

15 Zavaleta, 'Cuatro conceptos de democracia': 27.

is configured. They appear in the crisis as the expression of new configurations in the composition of society and as an index of the decomposition of the form of domination, that is, the state and its mediations.

Masses in action do not appear in any and every crisis. They appear when history has prepared the necessary conditions and subjects. If the masses are separatist and anti-state, as Zavaleta believes them to be, their separation can only arise following a preparation for self-development that overcomes the condition of ideological and political subordination. In this sense the masses are only possible on condition of the accumulation within the Bolivian working class. As Zavaleta says, the masses always have a high degree of spontaneity, but this spontaneity only unfolds around the core structured by accumulation within the class.

The masses are not the negation of class but rather its unfolding and explosion in the moment in which the class shifts from its location totally internal to the mode of production as dominated class to a moment of rebellion and separation. This is when they shift from being a component of the development of the forces of production and of capital to a moment of self-development for itself, as a class or collective subject that organizes, in the moment of its separation, other subalterns around another project or conception of society.

The masses are the appearance in the crisis of the national-popular bloc in process of political construction. There are various components that I want to make explicit here. First, there is the class component of the historical bloc. Gramsci conceived this in terms of articulation around a fundamental class. Zavaleta thought that the national-popular historical bloc was likewise organized around proletarian interpellation, which was based on the development of accumulation within the class. Around this core, the peasants were articulated with their own forms of struggles and demands, but following the leadership of the workers. Some of the middle strata, other forms of labour and subalterns in general were also incorporated.

The masses that emerge from this process do so with a certain level of self-determination. If the masses are a mode of separation from the everyday structures of domination, which is what puts the state in crisis, this implies that in separation they begin to live in themselves and for themselves, that is, with a degree of self-reference. Since the masses are a form of political action, their existence is a form of self-determination.

The masses are a moment of fusion of the subalterns around structures of rebellion that some of them have elaborated and arduously articulated over time. In the contemporary history of Bolivia, the structures of rebellion have been organized by the working class. The multiple forms and the vast scope of the November rebellion were constituted by the various subaltern groups, which, in that moment of fusion, configured and recognized at one and the same time a new identity, or an extended historical identity: the national-popular identity as the form of consciousness of the masses in November.

In so far as the historical bloc is a composite subject, its forms of organization, mobilization and struggle also tend to be composite and multiple. There is another current of structures of resistance present in November 1979 that corresponds to the *katarista* tradition of Aymara and Quechua rebellions, and these communities' forms of occupation of territory and of making war. The deep history of Bolivia rebels against the form of apparent unity that the Bolivian state never ceased to be, despite and throughout the 1952 revolution, which had a short period of articulation of partial but significant relations of correspondence between the state and civil society.

In various places in 'Las masas en noviembre', Zavaleta uses the term 'multitude' almost as a synonym for masses or for this new historical bloc under construction. For example, he writes that as a product of this set of changes in the crisis of the 1952 state, politics as a whole was obsolete because there was a new multitude.[16] This new multitude is that which he also conceives of as a historical bloc with a class core.

In another text that addresses these topics, 'Forma clase y forma multitud en el proletariado minero en Bolivia', although it does not define the concepts explicitly, the reasoning is somewhat different. In this essay he tries to establish the following distinction. The class form corresponds to the process through which a collective subject is constituted on the basis of its structural location, in which it develops a history of organization and political and ideological maturity, its own political horizon. The multitude form refers to those spontaneous and messianic moments of that same worker subject or of other subaltern groups.

'The workers' movement was capable of selecting the moments that constituted its memory, that is, it was the moment of the superiority of the accumulation within the class over the spontaneous self-conception of the workers as a multitude or as the plebeians in action and not as a class.'[17]

He said this with reference to the 1971 Popular Assembly. With respect to a conjuncture of workers' mobilization and resistance in 1976, when the

---

16 Zavaleta, 'Las masas en noviembre', p. 23.

17 Zavaleta, 'Las masas en noviembre', p. 235.

miners' federation managed to organize a clandestine congress at the height of the Banzer dictatorship and resisted military siege for seven weeks, he wrote:

'It imposed the line of spontaneous and maximal action that proceeded from the tradition of 1952, that is, the self-reflection of the mining proletariat as revolt and its organization as a messianic multitude.'[18]

In this text the multitude is the plebeians and not the historical bloc in action. In comparative terms, the multitude is the fusion of the subalterns without a historical bloc in construction (although with elements of traditions of rebellion) and, in consequence, without class or proletarian centrality. The multitude is the fusion of the people and thus the plebeians in action. The masses are civil society in action, which connotes a level of organization that underlies or provides the conditions of their possibility.

It should be recalled that Zavaleta is using here the notion of civil society taken from Gramsci, which implies the set of institutions or forms of organization through which individuals participate in public life. This tension between the differentiation that I have just mentioned and the identification, above all in 'Las masas', between masses, historic bloc and multitude, is not resolved in Zavaleta's work, even though these divergent uses appear in essays compiled in the same book.

A final category that comes into play here is that of the composite medium.

'While social class is understood as a logical and formal object, the composite medium is the context in which classes and non-class strata occur, that is, it refers to something hybrid.

'What is important, then, is what composes the medium, because it is presumed that the difference between the factors will be resolved in a hegemonic unity.

'The compound is its structural or productive location plus the nature of the constitutive interpellation.[19]

Irradiation has constituted the class bloc far beyond its 'limited numbers'.[20]

Finally, the concept of irradiation shifts the analysis from structural description to the systematization of politics as a logic of conjunctures. The idea of the composite medium is not only a static image of the differentiation

---

18 Zavaleta, 'Las masas en noviembre', p. 236.

19 Zavaleta, 'Las masas en noviembre', p. 225.

20 Zavaleta, 'Las masas en noviembre', pp. 225–26.

of society but also corresponds to the movement through which a class subject irradiates its history into other groups, configuring a new reality, a bloc. A composite medium tends to articulate a composite subject. At the same time this medium is a product of the articulation that a subject has carried out in the horizon of a heterogeneous society or in social diversity.

The idea of the composite medium corresponds to class analysis on the level of the socioeconomic formation and to that of a motley formation, which I will discuss later.

With these ideas of accumulation within the class, composite medium, historical bloc and masses, Zavaleta arrives at the notion of intersubjectivity. The composite medium configured through the development of a historical bloc around proletarian centrality and the fusion of the subalterns in the November crisis possessed an expanded and deepened intersubjectivity. It also had worker consensus in its legitimation and emergent peasant unionism, which brought with it what Silvia Rivera calls its long memory and short memory, that is, the memory and revival of its ancestral cultural matrix with its worldview and social organization (long memory) and the recollection of its participation in the revolution and state of 1952 (short memory).[21]

The new intersubjectivity corresponds to the constitution of the masses, which is a form of totalization that arises in the moments of state crisis. In crisis, the mediations are suspended and hence the irradiation of the proletariat has effects that constitute the masses and form an alternative historical bloc. There is a reorganization of society that undergoes moments of fluidity, and the alliances and fusions of social and political subjects are recomposed.

The basic intersubjectivity of 1952 was organized around revolutionary nationalism as the dominant ideology,[22] which proposed the necessity of constructing a nation-state that would represent the national classes; it was to represent them, not to contain them. November of 1979 is also a moment of crisis in the articulation of revolutionary nationalism, in so far as it is a separatist moment on the ideological level. The masses construct themselves so as to represent themselves in opposition to that apparent form of representation of the nation which is the state of 1952.

---

21 See Silvia Rivera, 'Luchas campesinas contemporáneas en Bolivia. El movimiento katarista, 1970–1980' in *Bolivia, hoy*; and *'Oprimidos pero no vencidos'. Luchas del campesinado aymara y qhechwa de Bolivia, 1900–1980* (La Paz: HISBOL/CSUTCB, 1984).

22 See Antezana, 'Sistema y proceso ideológico en Bolivia'. Also in *Bases. Expresiones del pensamiento marxista boliviano* 1 (1981).

The 1979 crisis is a moment of suspension of that dominant ideology, although it did not yet overcome it; it was recomposed after the crisis, because it continued to exist in the common sense of the popular organizations and subjects.

'Las masas en noviembre' is an explanation of how this new intersubjectivity was constituted historically in Bolivia and a reflection on the implications of this as a condition for knowledge.

Self-Knowledge in the Crisis and Nation Formation from Civil Society

Thus far we have analysed the masses as a form of appearance of the historical bloc in the conjuncture of the crisis. According to Zavaleta, the lack of conventional unity in the object of study constitutes a serious obstacle to knowledge of Bolivian society.[23] Bolivia's social diversity cannot be represented by homogeneous images, models and discourses. Unity is not possible in the representation because it does not exist in social life. Zavaleta speaks of this in terms of the notion of a motley formation:

> If it is said that Bolivia is a motley formation, this is because in it not only are there superimposed economic eras (those of the common taxonomy) without much combination, as if feudalism belonged to one culture and capitalism to another and nevertheless they occur in the same territory, as if one country was under feudalism and the other under capitalism, superimposed in a disjointed way.[24]

In societies whose components have little contact in their everyday life, communication between them occurs only in crisis and not in their normal state of apparent unification:

'The crisis is the pathetic form of unity in diversity.'[25]

'The only time common to all these forms is the general crisis that incorporates them, that is, political time. The crisis thus not only reveals what is national in Bolivia but is also in itself a nationalizing event; the diverse temporalities are altered by its eruption.'[26]

In these moments of nation formation or of political fluidity, society is synthesized more than in its normal life. A motley society does not live all its

---

23 Zavaleta, 'Las masas en noviembre', p. 17.

24 Zavaleta, 'Las masas en noviembre', p. 17.

25 Zavaleta, 'Las masas en noviembre', p. 18.

26 Zavaleta, 'Las masas en noviembre', p. 19.

components in a complete and permanent manner. There are moments of synthesis in which a broader spectrum of its reality is lived and made known, a reality that is potentially contained in the coexistence of this social diversity:

'Crisis is thus postulated as the phenomenon or the externality of societies which do not have the possibility of an empirically demonstrable cognitive revelation, societies that require a synthetic acquisition of knowledge.'[27]

This does not only mean that knowledge of such societies has to be constructed in synthetic moments like those of crisis, but that these are also societies that are not normally lived as totality or totalization. They lack an extensive formation of the nation, whether via the homogenization of social substance or via the organization of their social diversity, above all via the development of an identity or an intersubjectivity that at times can exist prior to the material conditions of unity.

The more extensive the participation of the diverse subjects in the moment of crisis, the deeper the process of nationalization or the generalization of the events. This depends on the capacity for mobilization of the subjects who take part and on the existence, or absence, of a project capable of articulating or re-articulating society.

Zavaleta's historical research and theory is based on the idea that the knowledge possible of and in a society is determined by the social conditions, which allow or impede the self-knowledge of a society to different degrees. One of these social conditions is the articulation of social diversity, something that is only partial where different productive and political temporalities are lived within society.

In 'Las masas en noviembre', Zavaleta also argues that the constitution of a certain type of intersubjectivity is also a kind of social materiality. Although the modes of production, political structures and world views are not fundamentally unified, a feeling of identity with reference to the nation can arise on the basis of great social encounters that occur in the moments of crisis in Bolivian history and in motley societies.

This would have occurred in Bolivia in the Chaco War in the 1930s, in the 1952 revolution and in 1979, that is, in the moment of crisis of the oligarchic seigneurial miner state, in its final moment of crisis which was the 1952 revolution, and in the moment of crisis of the state established after 1952. The articulation of more extensive intersubjectivities occurred above all in the Chaco War and in 1979. 1952 was probably the only moment in

27 Zavaleta, 'Las masas en noviembre', p. 17.

which these processes of nationalization pervaded civil society together with a state policy that aimed to correspond to these great tendencies in society.

In the Chaco crisis and that of November 1979 what occurred was nationalization on the basis of encounters within civil society, although in the first case this occurred in the midst of a war. In a society in which the dominant classes have generally not attempted to organize the state in such a way that it includes the dominated or to arrange a consensus through an organic system of mediations, the major processes of nationalization in Bolivian history have occurred in moments of crisis and through the movement of civil society. Thus the type of intersubjectivity produced was a national identity with reference to Bolivian society and not the Bolivian state.

The process of nationalization in November 1979 was profound in at least two senses. On the one hand, it recovered roots or traditions, in particular those of the workers' movement which is a more recent history, but also the tradition of *katarista* rebellions. On the other hand, it grew roots as a process of configuration of a new historical bloc. It was a moment of fusion and in this sense, founded social groups. It was a fusion in which workers, indigenous peasants and broad sectors of the middle strata concurred.

This is a process of nation formation from the base, from civil society and the deep history of the country, of the nationalization of something that the state had not nationalized on the level of general political power. It moved against the state which did not include, represent or correspond to the social diversity that lived its moment of political encounter in November 1979, a moment made possible by conditions that developed over the long histories of the subjects who took part in it.

What is important in the crisis of November 1979 is not that there was a plurality of protests from the most diverse sectors of Bolivian society, but rather that there was an alliance of the subaltern groups around the core of proletarian interpellation. At the same time, it was a moment of fusion in which different identities came into view and expressed themselves forcefully. The Bolivian people lived their unification in an experience that recognized, with more force than in any prior conjuncture, that it was a people composed of many identities, subjects and histories, but with a common feature, that of being an organized working people. They were different but could unite; they had to unite.

November is a moment of nationalization without the veil of nationalist ideology, that is, without the premise and objective of unity as homogenization of something that is supposedly common to all but has not been historically constructed. It showed that if the Bolivian nation existed, it was a proletarian and indigenous nation, which existed against or beneath a highly apparent state and a dominant class that was also seigneurial and authoritarian.

As a constitutive moment, it presents a new synthesis of what history had been preparing. But as a new synthesis it is also the beginning of a new history. It exhibits certain features that would mark some of the axes of later history. The November bloc displays two significant features. The first is the peasant and indigenous presence with its own forms of political action under proletarian leadership and interpellation. At the same time, while it is a mobilization within the horizon of proletarian centrality, it is the beginning which establishes the basic historical and political conditions for the critique of the corporative features of that proletarian centrality.

The workers' movement has the strength to interpellate the fundamental sectors of society in order to articulate a new historical bloc, but in so far as this relation is effective and mobilizes other sectors, it creates the conditions for its own overcoming through the configuration of a broader and more complete identity. In the last instance, it creates the bases for the diffusion of class centrality through democratization and pluralization of the core of organization and leadership of the new historical bloc. This appears as program and possibility in November and tends to develop in a discontinuous fashion with advances and retreats in the following years.

Moral and Intellectual Reform: Self-Transformation, Desire and the Conquest of Democracy

The other component that appears in the November crisis is what Zavaleta calls the incorporation or assumption of representative democracy by the working class and the masses. This is somewhat complicated. One can start with the most evident features in the conjuncture, although they have tended to be ignored afterwards in Bolivian politics.

There was a demand for representative democracy within Bolivian society, which at that time was basically organized around the COB, and to a much lesser degree, around the confederations of private enterprise. In the COB pole, which is what we are interested in here, representative democracy was conceived in a key in which union freedom was the central concern. The political setting was one in which it was thought that representative democracy was a means to recover political and organizational freedom in general, so as to then extend the organizational experience of the unions and their way of doing politics on the basis of civil society towards the state.

It seems that there was a sort of diffuse common sense in the popular movement of the period in which democracy was conceived as kind of fusion, transformation and co-existence between the unions, taken into the power structure of the national state, the parliament and the system of political parties.

Other, less evident, implications have to do with the relation between the incorporation of representative democracy in the ideological and political sphere in the conjuncture of the constitution of the new historical bloc and the history of its development and the conditions that it aimed to overcome.

Representative democracy as formally recognized in the 1952 state established structures of mediation with the workers as a form of partial integration, as part of the social base of the state but not as part of its power. This led to the dictatorial phase.

With the demand for representative democracy in the November crisis, the new historical bloc was trying to overcome this type of representation in the nationalist state and replace it by self-representation. It was a vision of the possibility and necessity of a reform of the state in which representative democracy would be the context of self-representation of the social classes.

The modality in which the masses in November assumed representative democracy, and the political program this represented, has much more profound implications than has been recognized.

In brief and strictly speaking, this assumption of representative democracy was not only about the demand for elections and respect for constitutional political liberties, linked to a system of political parties for the election of those who would govern, who through these mechanisms ended up substituting and excluding the collectivities and individuals who make up this country.

The program of the masses did not consist in restoring substitutive representation in the liberal sense, but rather in overcoming the abstract representation of the state, which did not change substantially through the mediation monopolized by political parties. Its aim, rather, was to introduce self-representation of social diversity in the state, and moreover, as the form of real power of that state. That is to say, it implied a radical reform of the state.

In Bolivian history, self-representation has taken the form of the trade union. Representative democracy as self-representation was thus the introduction or transfer of the unions to the state to share in political power, which had an expression and even a concrete slogan: co-government with the COB.

The COB is a structure of representation above all at the national level, but, in any case, it is a structure of representation of workers by workers and thus of self-representation. In the history of Bolivia, the unions have predominated over parties, except for the phase of the 1952 revolution when union leaders were also members of the MNR party and this second membership weighed more than the first. Descendent state mediation circulated more than ascendent mediation. Afterwards, left-wing parties generally worked for the unions and legitimized their existence as part of the more general activity of the workers' movement, whose leadership was in the COB and not in the parties.

The demand for representative democracy took the form of a demand for co-government with the COB, since the new historical bloc had not matured to the point of hegemony over society as a whole. The most representative structure in the country at that time was the COB; therefore, any democracy that aimed to be representative had to take it into account if the state was to correspond to the history and movements of its society and not invent artificial structures, adopting models widely recognized in other places but that had not been incorporated and produced by local history.

While the masses in November did prevail over the military coup, they did not manage to overcome the dominant bloc that would ensure that the political organization of civil society would follow other routes and end up serving the constitution of its form of domination. Zavaleta sums up the incorporation of democracy in the constitutive action of the masses as follows.

'The construction of democracy has been without a doubt a national victory but above all because it has been an ideological act of self-transformation of the people.'[28]

This self-transformation of the people implies fusion, which overcomes the separation and particular corporativism of each of these subjects, or at least begins to overcome it. It is also self-transformation in that it is constituted as self-determination, that is to say, something done for oneself, by oneself, assuming responsibility for the change that is produced.

Democracy is not a change that comes from outside the Bolivian people, imposed by the state or external powers, but rather a transformation that the people themselves have generated.

What Gramsci called moral and intellectual reform was taking place in Bolivia at the time. Zavaleta proposed to respond to the tasks put forward by

---

28 René Zavaleta, 'La reforma del estado en la Bolivia postdictatorial', *Cuadernos de Marcha* V (26) (March–April 1984): 8.

these transformations in contemporary Bolivian history. In the Introduction to the journal *Bases. Expresiones del pensamiento marxista boliviano*, he defined the challenge as follows:

'[N]ow an imminent necessity of Bolivian society: the strike as organic ideology of the accumulation of the national-popular throughout its history.'[29]

The journal *Bases*, in which an important group of Bolivian intellectuals and politicians collaborated, is part of this task, which Zavaleta conceived as collective. The Bolivian people was organized, mobilized and was producing new realities; intellectual work had to respond to the dynamic of the changes, and cognitively exploit the horizon of visibility extended by the constitution of the masses in November, whose contemporary historical foundation was the constitution of a new historical bloc.

Zavaleta is the organic intellectual of this national-popular historical bloc formed around democratized proletarian centrality through the constitution of the masses produced by the bloc. He expresses this in the social explanation of the conditions of possibility for the bloc's existence and for Bolivian society's consciousness of the transformations. He elaborates an explanation of the crisis of the state and the expansion of the horizon of visibility, which broadens the possibilities for self-knowledge and self-transformation. The constitution of subjects in such a conjuncture allows for more democratic and diversified possibilities.

In other words, the changes in the history of the country would be marked more by the presence of democracy and social diversity, which emerge from the forms of negation and exclusion, to reform the relation between the base of Bolivian society and its state.

Moral and intellectual reform implies changes in sentiments and world views, in addition to actions or practices. An important aspect of the processes that Zavaleta is thinking about is the feeling of belonging. The masses in November generate a feeling of belonging to a new social and political unity, to a deep history and a deep homeland. This is a reform that implies distance from the ideology of revolutionary nationalism. There is a national sentiment that is no longer that of the state of 1952, but rather perhaps that of the democratic movement of the 1952 revolution and its subsequent history.

Another important component of the moral and intellectual reform is that of self-transformation, the feeling that one is personally changing reality

---

29 René Zavaleta, Introduction to *Bases. Expresiones del pensamiento marxista boliviano* 1, Mexico City, 1981.

and changing one's own self. In November, as Zavaleta says, there is a self-transformation of the people which has to do, among other things, with the feeling that politics is no longer done only by the state but also by each and every one and with a perspective that implies overcoming at least in part the condition of subordination or the passive condition of the dominated.

In November, there are a group of glimpses or seeds of a more general moral and intellectual reform; there are also some more developed elements that make possible that moment of fusion, among them, in particular, proletarian centrality. November is a sort of constitutive moment in civil society, a first moment of fusion of a new historical bloc which throws into crisis the state structure of 1952, which was already dictatorial. It is not a constitutive moment that reaches the whole of society, that is to say, it does not go so far as to found a new state. It is an organic crisis produced by these new realities, but not yet a revolutionary crisis.

The necessary intellectual reform of which Zavaleta speaks in *Bases* implies a change in the conception of Bolivia, the ideas about the country, and above all in the type of explanation that can be given of the country and its history. 'Las masas en noviembre' is part of this reform. It gives us a more complex and dynamic image in which the social diversity that has historically existed appears with more force. But above all it represents a historiographical change that corresponds to the transformation of the social and political conditions of self-knowledge produced by the movements of society. Zavaleta is an organic intellectual in this sense too, in thinking in parallel with or immediately following the events to develop a new conception of the country.

Reform of the State and Oligarchic Recomposition

Some years later, in 1984, Zavaleta wrote a 'Report on the Problem of Participation in Relation to the Plan of Rehabilitation and Development' during the government of Democratic and Popular Unity (*Unidad Democrática y Popular*, UDP). This text, probably one of the last he wrote, takes as its central problem the incorporation and legalization of the forms of participation developed within civil society in the reform of the state. He reviews historical processes, at least since 1952, that are present as conditions of contemporary political practices, and analyses the possibilities and tasks of reform of the state in relation to four strategies of development. This is where Zavaleta talks most explicitly of questions of political construction and, therefore, of the reform of the state in Bolivia, in a mode of social science in the service of the specification of political tasks and alternatives, that is, as an organic

intellectual in the sense that implies thinking about the direction and organization of politics, and therefore culture as well, as part of the process of
constitution of a historical bloc.

In 'Las masas en noviembre' and his later writings, Zavaleta also analyses
how the UDP's political front was a result of the widespread mobilization,
above all of the unions, at the end of the 1970s, which secured its victory in
three successive elections, in 1978, 1979 and 1980. After military coups that
tried to block the UDP from taking power, at the end of 1982 the UDP finally
formed a government. In his analysis of the period when this political front
took over the government, I want to focus on two topics: the incorporation
of participation as the core of the reform of the state, and the reconstitution
of oligarchic forms of politics in Bolivia.

The Bolivian state has generally disorganized and excluded the masses
throughout its existence. Zavaleta thinks the masses' forms of participation
have generally ended up disorganizing the state. Responding to the generally
authoritarian and exclusive character of the state, their political participation
has been 'rebellious, tactical and provisional'. According to Zavaleta:

> For the Bolivian case, the following circumstances should be taken
> into account:
>
> (a) The aforementioned attitude of resistance and non-disorganis-
> ability of the masses, a powerful force of preservation of their par-
> ticipatory structures.
>
> (b) The authoritarian period was brought to an end by widespread
> mass mobilizations. This is an important social fact, and displays the
> weakness of the authoritarian project of reorganization of social
> forces [...]
>
> (c) The strong participation in the subsequent elections reveals [...]
> a new state of mind, an ideological acceptance of representative
> democracy, which configures the structural base on which the reform
> of the state has to be proposed.[30]

But since there has been little correspondence between society and the state
in Bolivian political history, the way in which these civil society movements
propose the reform of the state does not coincide with how the state proposes
its self-transformation. While on the part of the former there is fluidity,

---

30 Zavaleta, Introduction to *Bases. Expresiones del pensamiento marxista boliviano* 1
(1981): 10–11.

rigidity prevails in the state, which almost entirely lacks traditions of reform via integration. The traditions of the state are not those of civil society. Zavaleta describes the tasks of the state as follows:

'The Bolivian state must confront two central questions of participation, which are the reform of the state, that is, the transformation of the mechanisms of reading and correspondence with society, and the construction of new apparatuses of mediation that would allow the transformation of the strong participatory impulse of the masses into material effects within the state'.[31]

This is not an easy task, since the COB, as the hub of the popular sectors' practices of organization and participation, has, according to Zavaleta, defects in its proposals. It has a great capacity for resistance and organization, and for persisting and maturing over long periods, because it has generally had to become a site of resistance to the state in its authoritarian and dictatorial forms. It does not have a continuous history of proposing the reform of the state as a process of political construction.

This same history means that its capacity for proposals is weak and deficient. The COB did not have a project that responded to the transformations of the conjuncture apart from the memory of co-government. The slogan 'All power to the COB' was the proposal of only a part of the COB and not a majority decision, a proposal to convert the form of organization and national irradiation of the working class into the form of general political power, and, therefore, a form with corporative tendencies.

Likewise, the parties were not in a position to reform the state or to propose a new institutional system that would legalize the forms of political participation, both traditional and those emerging from the conjuncture. Many parties barely managed to adapt to the rules of the game of a representative regime, which were contained in the constitution but which did not correspond to the political and historical reality of the country.

This led to what Zavaleta called the furtive forms of rebirth of the oligarchy and the under-representation of the majorities of the country:

If one registers the effective participation according to origin or extraction in the entities of representation (from the executive to the parliament and the political leadership), it is obvious that the real majority of the country is under-represented. That means two things: first, that in practice the superstructures of representation have

---

31 Zavaleta, Introduction to *Bases. Expresiones del pensamiento marxista boliviano* 1 (1981): 18.

turned out to be almost as exclusive or oligarchical as the previous forms of representation prior to universal suffrage, and second, that since these vast sectors are relegated in a lateral or indirect way, they are obliged to assume a corporative or oppositional and not representative role in relation to the state.[32]

While on the one hand the political movements of civil society propose a definition of democracy in terms of participation, on the other the re-establishment of representative structures within the state begins to reconstitute, under new conditions, the oligarchic concentration and organization of politics. The two do not correspond to one other in the process of democratization.

From the beginning there are two ways of thinking and acting in the process of democratization in the country: as participation and as representation. The former is the predominant tendency among the subjects in civil society. The latter predominates as strategy and vision among the subjects who act in the reorganization of the state, and serves to restore the political power of the oligarchy. There is no proposal of institutional reform that would integrate the participation of the masses so that democratization would lead to a social optimum.

These are the conditions and challenges that Zavaleta recognizes in thinking about the central task of the moment:

'The legal systematization of the self-determination of the masses, both in the political system and in the regional organization of power, thus acquires the value of an authentic principle.'[33]

Part of the Left refused to talk about the reform of the state adopting a more revolutionary language or discourse, but without proposals for the solution of the political tasks of the moment, which were not those of a revolution but precisely those of reform. Other political forces within the government talked about political reform but without proposing an institutional reform of the state. Zavaleta declared frankly that what was necessary was a reform of the state that would integrate the recent developments in the participation of the masses.

The Left did not consider incorporating the participation of civil society in order to generate forces and resources for reform of economic and social

32 Zavaleta, Introduction to *Bases. Expresiones del pensamiento marxista boliviano* 1 (1981): 25–26.

33 Zavaleta, Introduction to *Bases. Expresiones del pensamiento marxista boliviano* 1 (1981): 37.

policies, but rather located the problem on the level of the simple formulation of economic policies that would supposedly benefit popular sectors but would not integrate them in a significantly reformed political structure of the state.

However, Zavaleta does not have a proposal for how this participation would be legalized and institutionalized in state reform. He posed the problem more clearly than anyone else at the time, but perhaps did not have the time to develop this into a political proposal, due to his early and sudden death in the middle of this process, in November 1984.

While Zavaleta's work combines social science and strategic political analysis in his work, his approach also represents a certain overcoming of Jacobinism or left-wing vanguardism, those positions which consider that one of the tasks of the intellectuals of the party is to elaborate proposals and political projects for the masses of the country, in a form more or less independent of the developments in the political struggles and forms of organization and reflection on their political life on the part of the masses themselves.

Zavaleta follows the movements of his society to explain them in terms of causality and historical accumulation, reflecting on them politically to pose synthetically what the problems are for political construction in the particular conjunctures, and to recognize the potential of the movements and their repercussions at the general level of society. He is an organic intellectual who writes speaking to his society, in particular to the historical bloc in formation, about what it is doing, the effects it is producing, the problems that must be resolved. But he does not set himself the task of saying what should be done. He is not exempt from this, but he seems to think that the questions of what is to be done, what is to be constructed and how to do so involve a collective task suited to the practices and participation of the subjects who constitute themselves in the movement and in the encounter with social diversity. The intellectual is one among many and not the one who must propose the political truth as a project for the people.

From 'Las masas en noviembre' to the reflections on participation and the plan for development, Zavaleta shifts from the moment of fusion of the subalterns in a new historical bloc which conceives of democracy as participation to the moment in which the reorganization of the state as representative democracy is unable to legalise participation and construct a social optimum or rapprochement between civil society and the state. Once the state separates itself from society, it generally despises it in so far as society does not match the oligarchic nucleus represented by the state.

CHAPTER FOURTEEN

The Primordial Form: Strategy of Explanation

Theoretical synthesis is the product of a more or less prolonged process of elaboration, of work, of putting into practice the ideas and orientations that are productive for thought, until one arrives at the categories that organize these ideas into broader conceptual constellations, within which they achieve coherence.

At the beginning of the 1980s, in an essay titled 'Problemas de la determinación dependiente y la forma primordial' [Problems of dependent determination and the primordial form],[1] Zavaleta arrives at a synthesis of the way in which to study politics in Latin American societies. In this text, he performs a comparative study of Latin American histories, a method that he had already practiced for some time but which had not so far been subject to theoretical and methodological reflection.

The notion of the primordial form and how one should study dependent determination in relation to it allows Zavaleta to make more explicit what he had previously done in *La caída del MNR* [The downfall of the MNR] and other writings from the late 1960s and early 1970s. This was to study the internal articulations of society in terms of social classes and political, economic and ideological structures in order to explain the history of the country in moments when it appeared that an imperialist power determined everything.

Starting from something already present in 'Las formaciones aparentes en Marx' [Apparent formations in Marx], that is, the idea that on a global level the mode of production or the material base is what provides lines of unity and homogenization while the superstructures display the diversity of histories, and then going on to argue that on the level of a particular society the state is that which unifies and diversity appears rather at the level of the different forms of production, that is, in the base, Zavaleta arrives at the idea that the primordial form is local historical causation within each social formation.[2]

---

1 René Zavaleta, 'Problemas de la determinación dependiente y la forma primordial'.

2 Zavaleta, 'Problemas de la determinación dependiente y la forma primordial', p. 57.

There is a methodological strategy in the idea of the primordial form, which I will call a matrix of explanation. Zavaleta's idea or strategy proposes that the explanatory core of each society, of each local study, consists in making explicit the analysis of how, within each society, the causal processes that correspond both to the forms and practices of production and to the specific articulation of the superstructures, which correspond to local history, have been structured.

How a society is internally structured is the basis for an explanation that includes how external determinations act, once one sets to thinking about this society in the context of broader realities, regional and in the world system.

The internal articulation of a society configures what Zavaleta calls the mode of reception of external or dependent determinations. The point is not to think of the primordial form as a mere complement to the dependent determination, but rather to consider the primary causal force within the local articulation.

The internal articulation of a society is a question of political construction. This general thesis, which has the primordial form as explanatory matrix, is developed by way of other complementary ideas such as that of the state axis. Zavaleta understands the state axis as follows:

'We understand the state axis as the type of relationship that exists between civil society, the structures of mediation and the political state. The optimum is adaptation and correspondence between these two orders.'[3] One studies the primordial form by analyzing the articulation between state and civil society and the mediations carried out in each case.

The distinction between state and civil society and the problem of the mediations comes from Hegel in his *Philosophy of Right*, followed by Marx and later Antonio Gramsci. Zavaleta's works from the late 1970s and the 1980s incorporate the thought of Antonio Gramsci, whose categories begin to articulate Zavaleta's analysis and historical narrative.

I will briefly summarize the steps in this trajectory from Hegel to Gramsci, which Zavaleta takes up, as a point of reference in order to better explain this idea of the primordial form. For Hegel, civil society was the realm of the necessary, or the particular, and therefore, the context where particularities confronted one another and competed among themselves; the political state, or the objective spirit, according to Hegel, incarnated the general consciousness, that is to say, the consciousness of the society in contraposition to the

---

3 Zavaleta, 'Problemas de la determinación dependiente y la forma primordial', p. 82.

consciousness of the particularities that existed within civil society. The mediations carried out through the encounters between corporative representations of civil society and the bureaucracy had as their objective the transmission of the general consciousness to civil society, without eliminating the particular, that is to say, as a meeting point between the general and the particular which does not dissolve them into a single dimension but rather maintains their differentiation as moments of a unitary totality, self-conscious in the moment of its synthesis. Marx takes up this distinction but uses it to explain something a little different: the idea that state forms are produced by the kinds of social relations that men establish in civil society. The state, as a political form separated from society, is produced by the separation that is engendered or developed within what, on the basis of this separation, can be called civil society.

This state is what is called an apparent formation, that is, it appears as the representation of the general interest while it is in fact the representation of a particular interest, that of the dominant class. Thus, the state does not incarnate a universal consciousness, although it does produce a fallacious discourse concerning the generality of its existence.

Marx, unlike Hegel, does not pay much attention to the dimension of the mediations between the state and civil society, but rather as a rule is dedicated to emphasizing the contraposition derived from the contradiction that exists between the two in analyzing the class struggle in various conjunctures and also as a general conception. First of all, he explains the rise of the modern state in terms of a genetic process originating with the development of civil society, but once this is done he goes on to analyse the phase in which the state exists or functions as an apparatus of domination.

Although Marx proposes that there is a unity of base and superstructure, he does not develop a theory of how this is articulated, although he does carry out various complex analyses of the articulation in specific histories and conjunctures, such as, for example, the famous *The Eighteenth Brumaire of Louis Bonaparte*. Nevertheless, he does not provide the categories for such an analysis.

Antonio Gramsci, in the early twentieth century, elaborates a set of categories that are concerned precisely with considering the articulation of base and superstructure as a process of constructing the nation. He recovers the problem of mediations in a much more complex manner, abandoning the sense they had in Hegel—that of mediation from above to below, from the general to the particular—and develops the other sense, found in Marx, concerned with how it is that civil society is the site of production of the domination and direction of society that is concentrated in the state, and which can only be explained by that previous configuration.

The concepts of historical bloc, hegemony and the very rethinking of civil society and its relations with the state correspond to this way of thinking about this problematic. While Marx analyses historical and local causation, strictly speaking, it is Gramsci who provides the set of categories, that is to say, the methodological and theoretical framework for considering the historical, national articulation of base and superstructure.

Zavaleta takes up this line of theoretical development, which includes Marx himself, and contributes within the Marxist tradition what we are calling a theory of the primordial form.

Gramsci focused on problems of the construction of hegemony within a social formation, that is to say, the problems of constructing a nation. The idea of the primordial form is one more step in this direction. It is a step taken when this kind of analysis is considered in the context of national and global reality.

Of course, it makes sense that this kind of theorization comes from the periphery, because the countries of the periphery are those which experience the determination and the power of the central countries of capitalism. Zavaleta does two things at once: he establishes a sort of epistemological privilege of the primordial form, and he studies the local articulation of societies even as these societies are considered in the context of regional and global power, without dissolving the former in the latter. The primordial form has primacy, since it is an explanatory matrix.

In many peripheral countries, Marxists often thought that carrying out an analysis of the conjuncture and the country basically required understanding the dynamic of the central imperialist countries and then deriving results in local histories from this. Zavaleta was concerned with analyzing the level of self-referentiality and the degree to which it has been possible to establish sites of self-determination in thinking our countries.[4]

From there he begins to work in a direction contrary to that taken by dependency theorists, who rather derive the degrees and forms of dependency of national formations from the world system and its centers of economic and political power.

---

4 Zavaleta, 'Problemas de la determinación dependiente y la forma primordial', p. 58.

The question that guides the analysis is not in what measure or in what way are we dependent, but rather what margins and conditions exist for thinking for ourselves and constructing a local identity—what are the necessary conditions for thinking political self-determination? If these are not present, then, what are the conditions that have to be politically constructed?

Dependency is a result as much of the form in which historical processes operate as it is of the process of political and historical exploration and investigation; it is not the starting point of this investigation.

The idea of the primordial form is a way to theoretically construct self-referentiality in order to explicate our history, although with a level of generality that serves to analyse modern societies that go through processes of local-national construction and articulation in a context of transnationalization of political power, ideology and economic relations. At the end of 'Problemas de la determinación dependiente y la forma primordial', Zavaleta writes: 'The national continues to be the only recognizable form within the terms of transnationalization.'[5]

This means that the epistemological primacy of the primordial form does not imply the annulment of the consideration of external determinations. It implies only the development of a matrix of explanation around which to organize our understanding of these determinations.

Zavaleta also writes that imperialism obstructs and disorganizes the local apparatus for reading societies, and thus impedes the existence of an state optimum in them. This means that the understanding of motley societies like Bolivia has to confront not only the obstacles presented by the lack of homogeneity of the social substance, which translates into illegibility, but also that due to imperialist policies it also has to confront problems of distancing between the state and civil society which become obstacles for social self-knowledge.

The lack of a state optimum is caused not only by imperialism, but also results from the articulations of local history. The state optimum is precisely the lens through which one attempts to study the local articulation. Zavaleta approaches the problem of analyzing the articulation of state and civil society in the context of interstate relations and the transnationalization of the world system with this idea of the primordial form.

This is a problem of particular importance for intellectuals in the periphery. The thinkers who proposed this set of categories of analysis of the relation

---

5 Zavaleta, 'Problemas de la determinación dependiente y la forma primordial', p. 78.

between the state and civil society—Hegel, Marx, Gramsci—were thinking of the societies that they believed to be at the center of world history and, therefore, they thought of the articulation between the state and civil society on the level of a social formation and a national society. This is clearly evident, for example, in Gramsci; Marx was the most internationalist of all.

I have indicated that Gramsci's contribution was to provide a set of categories precisely for the consideration of the articulation of the state and civil society, that is, the development of the intermediate levels of analysis that were lacking in Marx's thought. What Zavaleta does is to think of this level of articulation, in addition, as a matrix of historical explanation within the horizon of a reality composed of various social formations and various national societies, where some exercise greater determination over others.

I turn now to review the idea of the primordial form as the basis for the analysis of the equation of the state axis, that is, of the articulation between the state and civil society in relation to democratization. An state optimum is given when, historically, there has been a process of social democratization, on the one hand, and on the other, a process of political democratization. The idea of social democratization[6] that Zavaleta uses here refers to a process of growing integration and socio-economic equalization, a result of the processes of modernization of the economy, the expansion of the relations of the labour market and consumption. It also involves the redistribution of wealth, which is where political and social democratization generally coincide.

On the political and ideological level, the capitalist mode of production tends to require the juridical equality of men. This element is developed as processes of political democratization, as processes of increasing incorporation of subjects as citizens, the expansion of political participation and, through it, the demand for redistribution of wealth, that is, social democratization.

A degree of self-referentiality and self-determination is produced when societies undergo these processes of both social democratization and political democratization. The greater the level of correspondence, the better the conditions both for self-knowledge and for self-determination or self-government. In the Latin American societies studied by Zavaleta, there are relations of non-correspondence between these two processes.

This way of seeing the correspondence between the state and civil society through the ideas of social democratization and political democratization implies that a key theme or dimension in matters of political knowledge and

---

6 The idea of social democratization proceeds above all from Tocqueville and Weber.

government is that of equality. Hence, the most egalitarian and democratized societies tend to know themselves better and are more self-determined.

Zavaleta distinguishes between what he calls models of regularity, which, strictly speaking, can be elaborated with relation to the base or the core of society, and political models, which are not models of regularity. In 'Problemas de la determinación dependiente y la forma primordial', Zavaleta analyses the political model that the US attempted to introduce in the region, above all in the period of installation of authoritarian regimes in the Southern Cone. That is, the determination arises from the imperialist policy that aims to impose homogeneity in the region through a common political model for all the societies. Here it is clear that the political model is not an explanatory theoretical model but rather a normative model, with the aim of organizing society, in this case, on the basis of the assumption that Latin American societies taken as a group are homogeneous and therefore, that this implementation can be successful, even when one ignores local conditions.

In this case, the US political model is an attempt to homogenize from above, on the level of the superstructures, that of the political regimes.

It is by studying this kind of strategy that one can also determine the limits of the elaboration of models of regularity for thinking politics. This case deals with the imposition of a common model on a group of countries, but the result is not the same in each local society. This strategy failed to produce homogeneity among these societies. It is not possible to think politics in terms of models of regularity except in relation to certain forms of correspondence already indicated by Zavaleta in his study of the problem of democracy, namely the sequence capitalist mode of production—logic of the factory— internal market—nation-state—bourgeois democracy.

Zavaleta argues for the necessity of considering these societies starting from the explanation of their primordial form, precisely at the moment when imperialism is trying harder than ever to impose a common political model on the whole region. This is not, therefore, an idea that can only be applied in conjunctures in which some society in our region exercises a significant level of self-determination. Even in the moments of the strongest imperialist determination one must think starting with and on the basis of the elucidation of the primordial form.

Zavaleta characterizes this imperialist political model on the basis of four components, which in very summary terms are as follows:

(a) The capitalist reorganization of society, the objective of which is to restore governability.

(b) An economic strategy based on the dogma of the world system, which implies the transnationalization of the act of production, distancing it from a national logic.[7]

(c) The doctrine of national security as official ideology, which tries to exploit reactionary elements present in the collective unconscious of these societies.

(d) A process of ideological reconstitution of the society through generalized terror or the terror that produces a negative hegemony by changing the ideological referents, destroying the previous ones.

I will not go into details in the description of this model. I am interested in citing it in order to propose the following: Zavaleta does not elaborate the characterization of this model in order to then make use of it in the description of each society of the region in terms of the subsumption of the political life of each one of them under this general model. He intends, rather, the opposite: to show how even in the case of the imposition of a common political model on the part of the greatest world power, the local or national results are different. That is to say, local history or historical causation is irreducible and that is what explains the differences. These differences are produced on the level of the superstructures. It is therefore impossible and irrelevant to elaborate models of regularity that could pretend to universal validity, since they only partially solidify, penetrate or are accepted by local societies, when they are exogenous to these societies. The results are more diverse when the construction of politics in the society has achieved a greater degree of self-referentiality.

This idea of the primordial form, this reflexive strategy, this matrix of explanation enters into a polemic with dependency theory. It does not eliminate the problem of dependency, nor does it deny that it exists in our countries. What changes is the way in which it is explained. To explain dependency, it does not proceed by studying the configuration, structure and dynamic of metropolitan capitalism and explaining in an almost deductive manner how the characteristics of local history correspond to the determinations of that global history, which supposes that external determinations of an imperialist type have penetrated to the roots and in every corner of national life, that they are the exclusive or almost exclusive determinants. Dependency is explained as the confluence of two lines or causal processes. One is effectively the dynamic of imperialism, of global capitalism. The other

---

7 Zavaleta, 'Problemas de la determinación dependiente y la forma primordial', p. 63.

line of causality is the local aggregation, the mode in which the state and civil society are articulated within the social formation.

In order to synthesize the implications of the idea of the primordial form, I will make some remarks on the idea of history and its implicit conception of politics. Let us begin with politics. The primordial form is a way of thinking through the articulation of base and superstructure in a specific local history through the articulation of the state and civil society, which is a political fact. While the productive moment or base is the core of determination of a society, the superstructures are what articulates the social totality. In other words, the articulation of the totality is political and ideological.

The act of privileging the political form in the analysis implies that political-ideological analysis becomes an entry point for the study of the social totality, because politics is what articulates the social totality. The analysis of that dimension becomes a point of entry, although what is called the core of society is what provides the core of the explanation. It is therefore necessary to distinguish the point of entry from the core of the explanation.

The primordial form is a conceptual tool for thinking the structuration of history by politics. It is a way of thinking the composition of societies in historical terms, in terms of process.

The idea of the primordial form implies a plural idea of history, that is to say, there is no unique global history that characterizes social reality, but rather various histories with diverse forms of configuration, with different degrees of force and depth in their capacity to articulate structures and produce cultures. There are various histories, and the way in which they are articulated or encounter each other depends on the internal composition of each and the power they can generate internally in order to determine others.

The idea of the primordial form requires us to think of the mode of reception of external determinations on the basis of the internal composition, which is at the center of Zavaleta's project. It might seem to be conceived for Latin American societies, but it also implies that the internal composition is the origin of the power and the form of determination directed toward other societies. The idea of the primordial form also allows us to think of the articulation of histories on the international or interstate level, starting from the depth of each local history, and not on a superficial level that only takes into account a few points of contact between societies or the dynamic of the dominant powers or societies.

Thus, the idea of the primordial form is not only a key for thinking local history but also a for thinking the articulation of global history with attention to local histories, that is to say, its manner of thinking world or international history arises from the historical depth of each society and not from the surface of interstate articulations and data on world economy on the level of exchange or the market.

The idea of the primordial form implies a conception of politics not merely as a reflection or reproduction of the dynamic of the productive moment, nor is it merely the dynamic of a set of government institutions and the bureaucratic administration of society, nor merely a system of mediations in terms of government apparatuses, but rather it implies in its broadest sense a collection of practices that constitute the social totality. It is in this sense that Zavaleta recalls the idea of the state as a synthesis of society, as proposed by Lenin and Marx.

Together with this idea of the capacity to articulate the totality as a political construction, the idea of the primordial form leads to another dimension, which is that of sovereignty. The primordial form is the political composition of each society and of the degrees of sovereignty it is able to produce. At the same time, it is an indication of how sovereignty is produced, through the articulation between the state and civil society.

In analyzing the composition of the primordial form, we can see what type of sovereignty is internally produced. If the sovereignty of the state over its civil society is produced on the basis of organic non-correspondence, this generally propitiates a weakness in the face of external determinations. If the society articulates locally a certain degree of organic correspondence between the state and civil society, there is greater probability of resisting and even rejecting external determination due to this internal consistency.

The description and analysis of a primordial form is a type of political analysis that privileges two dimensions: that of the articulation of the social totality, and that of the production of sovereignty and the types of sovereignty that are produced by the composition of each society.

This analysis implies making a complete or general map of the dimensions of politics in the society, including the state, the forms of politics practiced within civil society and the institutional mediations between these dimensions. This is what Zavaleta calls the state axis or the political system, taking up the sense from Gramsci, which seems more adequate for its greater breadth.

The notion of the state axis resonates with Gramsci's conception of the integral or expanded state, as the unity of the state and civil society. The notion of the state axis has narrower connotations because it can also be understood as dealing only with the group of state and para-state apparatuses and institutions. In contrast, the notion of the political system appears more adequate, since it implies that politics is done not only within the state but also in other dimensions or contexts of civil society. It is a better expression of this wider universe in which political ideas and practices can arise and take place.

The idea of the primordial form is a kind of synthesis, which implies a labor of analysis and composition of levels of previous analyses. The idea of the primordial form on this level presents a synthesis of those articulations and, thus, of the global political and economic results of those articulations. The primordial form is not only a manner of synthesizing levels of analysis that correspond to the type of structures of social life; it is also a kind of synthesis of the history of a society.

Taking account of the primordial form of a society in a given moment implies the review of the genesis of the social forms and contents that enter into its composition. This does not mean tracing the history of a society, but rather producing a synthesis of the present or past configuration that corresponds to the moment under analysis. But it is a method that always takes into account a society's process of formation, its constitutive moments.

Finally, while the primordial form, as an explanatory matrix, is a category of synthesis for the analysis of societies and for thinking these societies in the international and global context, it is an idea that can also serve as a regulatory idea for political construction; that is to say, we can use it to think forms of political articulation or construction where one of the central objectives would be the production of national sovereignty. One can make conscious and explicit political use of an idea that in its origins was theoretical, explanatory and methodological. For example, to articulate the primordial form democratically can be a political banner with a cognitive content or basis.

The idea of the primordial form corresponds to the explanation of the processes of totalization of base and superstructure in each local society in the context of global imperialism. It reveals the limits of the models of regularity by accounting for structural causation in each history.

CHAPTER FIFTEEN

Constitutive Moments

Zavaleta's theoretical production is centered on the genetic explanation of states, connecting the idea of Marx that the state is produced in civil society with that of the primordial form as the type of relation between civil society, structures of mediation and the state. This led him to formulate the idea of constitutive moments. He writes: 'What one has to analyse is where this way of doing things comes from: the original reasons. There is a moment in which things begin to be what they are, and that is what we call the ancestral or arcane constitutive moment.'[1]

First, I will analyse the idea of the constitutive moment in relation to political theory. I will then consider it in terms of the matrix of historical explanation.

There are various constitutive moments: a constitutive moment of the nation and a constitutive moment of the state. They can be thought of as the moments in which a state axis, the relation between the state and civil society, is articulated historically with force and novelty. It is a moment in which the program of a civilization or an era is constituted, in so far as it refers to an articulation of base and superstructure, the type of internal life and culture, that is, the values and meanings with which forms of production and social relations are seen and experienced.

Societies change; at times, they pass through several constitutive moments, some of which are reconstructions of preceding ones. The most recent constitutive moments do not wipe out their past, even when one of their characteristics is the situation of receptivity and ideological substitution in circumstances of fluidity, generally produced in situations of crisis.

Here I analyse the idea of the constitutive moment as the historical origin of a primordial form, which is related to what Zavaleta calls the state axis. It is a problem of the articulation of the state and civil society in the origins of local histories, which will mark the character of their history for a long time.

---

1 Zavaleta, 'El estado en América Latina': 68.

It resembles the origin or starting point of what Braudel calls the longue durée.[2]

The concern with constitutive moments comes from the idea that in order to explain political and social life in the present, keys can be found in the study of historical origins, rather than in the detailed description of how structures and institutions function and how subjects act in the present. It opposes a genetic historical analysis to a systemic vision of the present.

According to Zavaleta, the constitutive moment conditions and gives meaning to the events that follow it for a long time, even when the character of the society and the state changes. It is the birth of a destiny, but a destiny that can be modified, if that destiny is a decision freely taken by men, which is how Zavaleta considers democracy and intellectual and moral reform in modern times.

Zavaleta's conception of modern history, implicit in his writings, is that there are genetic historical moments, constitutive moments in which the members of society meet in a state of fluidity, producing an ideological vacancy. These situations are generally produced by crises, war or violence. On this basis, a new program of society is established. This implies that constitutive moments are moments of exercise of freedom, at least on the part of those who take the initiative in the reorganization of society.

A constitutive moment is a moment of political construction and ideological production. It is the factory of an era, because in that moment the society in which a people will live for a long time is produced, not inside a workshop but in an open field where all the social forces are in movement. It is a political and ideological construction in action; but it can only be produced in action by those who are adequately positioned to so.

For modern societies, this mode of restructuration in the constitutive moment has the force of a massive event, which is what Zavaleta calls intellectual and moral reform. It is the development of degrees of self-knowledge and self-determination.

Metaphorically, a constitutive moment establishes a world in which one will live for a long time, but also a kind of prison from which there will be no escape until great changes have been produced within it. It is a prison of historical time for the societies that experience it, and its restructuration can only be given by the exercise of new forms of liberty. In the following passage, Zavaleta presents the phases of the constitutive moment of the modern state:

---

2 See Braudel, *La historia y las ciencias sociales*.

A typical constitutive moment is without doubt that of primitive accumulation. We must distinguish at least three stages in this: first, the massive production of alienated men, that is, free and legally equal individuals, a negative moment of accumulation, which supposes vacancy or the state of receptivity. Then comes the hour of formal subsumption which is the real subordination of labour to capital. Here is where interpellation should arise, that is, the suppression of vacancy from a determinate point of view. Without a doubt this is the moment of foundation of the state. In third place is real subsumption, that is, the application of conscious gnosis as well as the force of the masses and other qualitative forces superior to the two previous factors, capital as effective command and free men in the condition of masses.[3]

This implies that the constitutive moment is a moment of destruction of other forms of social life, which produces ideological receptivity, followed by formal subsumption, which is the existence of workers under the new capitalist relations of production, although they still employ prior processes of production. This is the moment of foundation of the state, of a new articulation of the base and superstructure, a new superstructure for this type of society.

It is not only the case that the new mode of production has produced or managed to derive the form it requires on the level of the state. If we look back, primitive accumulation is produced by the exercise of political power, in forms that strictly speaking are neither of the state nor modern. It is produced by forms of violence on the part of political powers that have to transform themselves in order to create the adequate superstructure, the foundational unity, which corresponds to the new type of society. After this, the state becomes an ideology implanted in society, via its internalization in individuals, operated with greater force through the law of value.

In the phase of real subsumption this becomes the construction of hegemony, combining Marx and Gramsci. The problem is the extension and universality of real subsumption and also its degree of intensity: to what extent the masses have internalized the anthropocentrism, calculability, rationalism and all the rest of the intellectual reform that configures the capitalist mode of production as a secular civilization.[4]

---

3 Zavaleta, 'El estado en América Latina': 68.

4 Zavaleta, 'El estado en América Latina': 68.

The construction of hegemony is a shift in the command of production and the expropriation of the workers' productive knowledge; it is the creation of new knowledge as a productive force. This moment of total change in production is then accompanied by the organization of everyday life in civil society as the extension of its principles into the rest of social life, or, at least, as the re-adaption of prior cultural elements.

Zavaleta's process of historical explanation seeks to determine the constitutive moments of the society under study. This is a question asked in moments of crisis, in which one seeks the origins.

Between the constitutive moment and the crisis come the moments of reform. The key to these moments is real subsumption, which is:

> [. . .] the incorporation of the principle of scientific rationality in the customs of collective production. Real subsumption certainly means—if it means anything—science as a mass act, that is, constructing a rational view of the world. The democratic revolution, in this sense, occurs when the masses acquire a scientific perspective.[5]

Real subsumption is the moment of the process in which there is a change of civilization and mentality, of forms of life. It is the moment in which the change in the relations of production culminates as a change in the type of productive knowledge. It is the total integration in the type of society that capitalism contains as program.

It is at this point that Zavaleta believes that the conditions arise for the construction of hegemony, that is, for the dominant class to organize civil society and the state in a manner corresponding to the capitalist mode of production. Here he unites Marx's idea of real subsumption with Gramsci's idea of the construction of hegemony.

Real subsumption is the point of qualitative and almost total transformation of the core of the productive moment. Those who have undergone this transformation are in conditions to create hegemony, that is, to articulate the subalterns around their project of unity of base and superstructure or unity between the life and organization of civil society and the project and direction of the state.

In Gramsci's theory of hegemony and Zavaleta's idea of the constitutive moment, the process is above all one of the articulation of existing cultural

---

5 René Zavaleta, 'Notas sobre la cuestión nacional en América Latina' in Juan Enrique Vega (ed.), *Teoría y política en América Latina* (Mexico City: CIDE, 1982), p. 288.

and ideological elements around the political project of a historical bloc, and of the articulation of all this with the productive moment of the society.

Marx thought of intellectual reform primarily on the level of the moment of production and in terms of science as a productive force. In this he did not cease to consider the form of community, that is, the form of totalization of the relations of production, which also propitiates changes in the intellectual universe. Gramsci thought the problem of intellectual reform on a more political, ideological and cultural level, which corresponds to the construction of the nation or the nation-state. The changes in the moment of production imply that they are expressed as juridical equality, which implies political democratization, which Marx thought of more generally as the global process of modernity or the transition to modern societies. Gramsci thinks the problem of equality as the construction of the nation. The community that fills the political and ideological vacuum produced by de-peasantization cannot be the state in the abstract, but rather something more flesh and blood, a group of beliefs with which one can identify.

Marx gave little importance to the problem of nationalization. He thought that the development of capitalism would be such a huge determinant that, on the ideological and political plane, it would not be necessary to produce cultural elements that would give rise to concrete social formations with differentiated political identities. In other words, real subsumption would translate into the rational condition of individuals in large part without community and without a nation, in the context of a more international and, thus, more homogeneous reality.

Gramsci was concerned with the construction of the nation in capitalist modernity in terms of intellectual reform, which no longer referred solely to the conversion of science into a productive force and its massification in the moment of production, but also to the production of culture, which is transformed as it produces itself, incorporating elements of the past.

The nation is not a social substance that exists before the state. It is something that is politically constituted by articulating a project of the state and of civilization. It is better to think of the nation as a process of nation formation or nationalization. Nationalization should be thought of as a type of constitutive moment that establishes a significant level of correspondence between the state and civil society, in which the state produces and contains a project for the society that it directs and dominates.

Democracy, in Zavaleta's terms, is the intermediate level in which the superstructures, in this case in political life and in the state, correspond to a model of regularity, although they do not form part of it. This is the relation between the law of value and democracy. Both are international processes or tendencies.

Science is the most general level of intellectual reform, democracy is the intermediate level and the national question is the most concrete and specific level.

In Zavaleta's scheme, democracy does not appear as a component in any of the three phases of the constitutive moment of capitalist societies derived from primitive accumulation, although the question of equality does appear. This is above all formal equality, both in labour, time and juridical equality. Democracy, then, is not present in the constitutive moment of capitalist societies, at least in the first among them. Democracy appears in the moments of restructuration of the constitutive moment. In contrast, the nation tends to appear in the foundational moments of the state, that is to say, some constitutive moments are also moments of nationalization.

According to Zavaleta, in the processes of development of capitalist society in general, the moment of nationalization has preceded that of democratization. Democracy corresponds to those moments of reform or restructuring of the constitutive moment. This is not always the case. For example, in Bolivia the constitutive moment of capitalist society as such, that is, as the character of the totality of our society, was a moment of intense nationalization but it also had a component of democratization, above all within civil society. This explains why it is a society with a great capacity of resistance and a state that has not been nationalized or democratized to the same degree as society.

The task is to incorporate nationalization or democratization in the analysis of the constitutive moment, as well as to explore to what extent they have occurred within civil society and the state. The analysis is completed by determining the degree of correspondence between each of these or their uneven development. Zavaleta makes a comparative analysis of Latin American countries, especially those he knows from within, on the basis of this approach.

I add another element to this analysis, that of surplus value in relation to nationalization, democratization and sovereignty. According to Zavaleta, the economic surplus enables the organization of mediations between the state and civil society. It also influences the development of science and in the organization of democracy as an institutional apparatus for political life. The key is the capacity of each society to retain the surplus produced within it, that is, the degree of nationalization of its own surplus. This is related to the degree of self-determination exercised by a society, which is correlated with the degree of democratization.

This is only a tendency, and there are forms of national self-determination which are not necessarily democratic. There are authoritarian forms of nationalization, which have been common in our national histories. National self-determination with democratization is the ideal, but it is not the most frequent modality.

In so far as society retains more of its surplus, it is probable that formal and real subsumption will be extended in its territory. Another function of economic surplus is to finance and organize the mediations between the state and civil society. In so far as the political state predominates in the composition of the primordial form, this surplus enables the organization of mediations via the state bureaucracy, but this does not automatically occur. It depends on the political initiative of the subjects, and in this case the on process of construction of hegemony.

If civil society's capacity to capture the surplus predominates in the composition of the primordial form, this gives more force to mediations of a corporative type and one result of this may be to obstruct the operation of the state. Zavaleta thinks that some constitutive moments can restructure previous ones and that in this sense their depth can vary. This is evident in comparing Latin American histories. For example, Mexican society had a deep and extensive constitutive moment in an intense civil war during the revolution at the beginning of the twentieth century. In contrast, Argentine society had a history with an ample surplus but less profound constitutive moments.[6]

One possibility that Zavaleta considers is that profound pre-capitalist constitutive moments block subsequent moments in which there are attempts to configure a capitalist society and, via its organizational principle, a nation and a nation-state. Where the pre-capitalist constitutive moments have been more profound, the constitution of a capitalist society has been a much more difficult task and, at times, has been impossible.[7]

While modern history is one of constant changes and ceaseless self-transformation on the part of societies that have taken on the organizing principle of capitalism, that history involves changes set locally or nationally by the constitutive moment.

---

6 See Zavaleta, 'El estado en América Latina'.

7 See Zavaleta, 'Notas sobre la cuestión nacional en América Latina'.

To summarize this section, I sketch out here the constitutive moment as a matrix of explication. Normally one arrives at it starting from the moment of crisis, so that it involves an element of genetic explanation, but it also becomes the center of synthetic explanation.

The key is explaining the composition of the primordial form in the constitutive moment, that is, the composition of civil society and the state, and how and to what extent each participates in the primordial form's original articulation. To analyse this composition, one has to think of the level in which processes of nationalization, democratization and self-determination have taken place in the state and civil society. The degrees of correspondence or non-correspondence in this composition is key for the explanation of the events and subsequent processes. As a complement to this explanatory framework, one must consider the processes of reform that have been carried out in the history of the society under analysis.

This explanation is causal, considering multiple determinants. It deals with determination by the social totality and more specifically with determination by the historical genesis of that totality. The genetic element here does not refer to the first origin of the societies but rather to those moments of foundation of a historical character.

Zavaleta conceives of history as an unfolding of programs of life for society as a totality, given to and by society in the determinations of the constitutive moment. The change in the conception of history, in relation to the moment of nationalist historical revisionism, is that history is no longer thought as the dynamic of macro-subjects in the framework of the duality nation–anti-nation, but rather as a process of totalities in which collective subjects organize the structures but do so in configurations which then determine them as subjects. Men organize structures which later or at the same time are their own determinants.

The introduction of the idea of totality implies that the destiny and orientation of a local history is not configured by only a part of society, as in the duality nation–anti-nation, but rather all subjects who live in a society, in different ways, participate through their practices in the articulation of the global composition of their society, which becomes a kind of complex structural causality.

The idea of programmes of life in society, programs that emerge in the moments of refoundation of society when there is fluidity, substitution and emergence of new forms and contents, does not refer to programs that exist in a completely conscious manner in society as a whole, or even in a part of it. They are programs that are concentrated in certain nuclei and contexts of society, but also dispersed in other parts of it. They consist in a series of elements that are found in what can be called society's subconscious. The constitutive moment generates a collective subconscious which is only revealed in moments of crisis.

A life program is generally not substituted until it has exhausted all its possibilities, or at least the principal ones, that is, until it has experienced its limits. Constitutive moments are programs of life of the totality that are reformed or restructured within the same political and cultural horizon.

The idea of the primordial form is a point of reference around which to articulate the recognition of differences within each society and differences between societies. It also distinguishes degrees of profundity and of historical accumulation. Each present lives its constitutive moment in a more or less reformed manner with more or less force, that is, each present simultaneously lives part of its past, that which was constituted to ensure the preservation of the program of life generated by the society.

The constitutive moment is not only a moment of political and ideological enunciation. It is a moment of organization of economic and social structures, and above all of the structures of the relations between the economy, politics and ideology, as social totality.

The burden of the past that is lived in each present can be an index of the depth of its historical structures. The idea of the constitutive moment implies that the lives we live are structurally determined in a much more powerful and profound manner than that which we could conceive through a merely sociological focus. It implies that we are not only determined by the actual economic structures and the actual set of political institutions and discourses, but that we also suffer determinations of the genetic moment that constitutes us and the social context or reality in which we live.

There is an idea that there are levels of profundity in historical and social determinations. The idea of the constitutive moment implies that there are great moments of social creation, and also that men are slaves for a time of their great creations. Those creations provide the conditions for the type of social life that they will live for a long time.

In terms of politics, the idea of the constitutive moment implies that the set of determinants of a society constitute a political articulation. Describing this as articulation implies that politics is the means by which the composition is carried out, although perhaps not all its substance is politics.

Politics is a means of organization of the social, but it is at the same time is a synthesis. At the origin or foundation of a society is the type of political synthesis that founds or re-founds it. The political synthesis of the constitutive moment configures the type of domination and freedom that the society will live out and the forms in which these are combined.

The constitutive moment gives a direction to society, which comes from the way in which everything participates in its new fusion. Politics is the conscious or deliberate part of that direction; hence it is also one of the principal forms of modification of that destination that is generated in the constitutive moment. The reforms of the constitutive moment are also political and ideological forms. The first among them is democracy, which is the way in which freedom tries to reform the forms of domination.

The way in which politics is incorporated in the idea of the constitutive moment implies that politics is not conceived as the simple activity of administering government or of domination, which corresponds to the idea of working with what has already been constituted. Political theories that move within those horizons or limits are theories that lack a genetic dimension and do not recognize that politics has a capacity to construct or produce society, as Zavaleta thought it did in its most intense or constitutive moments, when politics is the concentration of the force of creation of society, its mode of articulation.

CHAPTER SIXTEEN

Time, History and Motley Society

Historical Time

Zavaleta characterised the type of complexity that exists in Bolivian and similar societies as national-popular. These socities have been structured in part by colonial domination and then by the development of capitalism, but at the same time have maintained previous social and political forms. Zavaleta proposed the category of motley social formations to account for this type of reality.

The motley can be characterized on the basis of *Lo nacional-popular en Bolivia*. Zavaleta considers two axes—one is the temporality of history, and the other is politics. First of all, I will deal with the dimension of time in history. Zavaleta thought conceived of historical time on the basis of the productive moment of a type of seasonal temporality that characterizes the agrarian civilization that developed in Andean societies.

Zavaleta thinks of a determination, produced on the level of the productive moment and exercised on the organization of the rest of society, in terms of its rhythm of reproduction. While historical time is generated in the moment of production, it corresponds to the conceptualization of the processes of reproduction of the totality as well as to the articulation of other processes with the time or rhythm of reproduction and development of the mode of production. In consequence, historical time partially defines politics.

Zavaleta sees the constitutive moment of Andean societies as follows:

The originary event of this society makes space predominate over time. Adaptation to the harsh environment marks its elemental historical time. [...]

The unity of space, therefore, is but an extension of this historical time, which is not that of capitalism (which does indeed break with agricultural time), but a local form of seasonal agricultural time. Here political unity is derived from the necessities of subsistence and subsistence itself can only be conceived as collective time. The first consequence of this is that intersubjectivity is a precocious and violent event.[1]

In order to survive, Andean peoples had to organize themselves by occupying various spaces in order to satisfy their needs; this is what has been called the archipelago or vertical control of a maximum number of ecological tiers according to Murra's study,[2] or macro-symbiotic complementarity according to the earlier work of Ramiro Condarco Morales.[3]

This control of a maximum number of ecological tiers[4] corresponds to the seasonal time of Andean culture and also to the form of the state. The men or culture of these difficult lands, in order to survive, had to be organized not only locally but also via a group of ecological levels that would allow them to satisfy their needs. Hence, the need for political organization arises. The state is necessary for this kind of agricultural production, and it is organized in accordance with the patterns of seasonal historical time of Andean agriculture.

On a more general level, Zavaleta distinguishes two types of temporality or historical time. One is seasonal agricultural time and the other is the historical time of the capitalist mode of production. Seasonal agricultural time covers several modes of production, that is, several types of juridical property

---

1 Zavaleta, *Towards a History of the National-Popular in Bolivia*, p. 25.

2 See John Murra, *Formaciones económicas y políticas del mundo andino* (Lima: Instituto de Estudios Peruanos, 1975).

3 See Ramiro Condarco Morales, *El escenario andino y el hombre* (La Paz: Imprenta y Librería Renovación, 1971).

4 In the Central Andes, climate varies according to altitude, from the tundra-like *puna* at 4,000 and more metres above sea level, cold temperate climates around 3,500 metres, so-called 'valley' or warm temperate climates from about 2,000 to 3,000 metres, subtropical 'yungas' from 1,000 to 2,000 metres, and fully tropical climates below 1,000 metres. The two highest levels are characterized by herding (llamas, alpacas, and after the Spanish conquest, sheep and some cows) and potatoes (which are native to this area of the Andes); 'valley' levels produce maize, vegetables and temperate fruit; the 'yungas' produce coca leaves, hot peppers and tropical fruit, and the lowest levels produce fine hardwood and tropical crops such as bananas and manioc. According to Murra's theory, the pre-conquest ideal was to have direct access to land on all or most of these levels in order to obtain the corresponding products; the area which each social group controlled on each level could be separated from their lands at other elevation levels by a distance that took several days or even weeks to traverse on foot, hence the appellation 'vertical archipelago' (translator's note).

rights and of social division among men, around one basic modality of transformation of nature. Zavaleta writes:

> Modes of production would come and go without interrupting the
> repetition of the productive patterns of Andean agriculture, and
> would merely be translated into juridical forms of circulation super-
> imposed upon local practices of the transformation of nature. The
> old state had retracted into the moment of production itself and,
> therefore, the apex of the state in relation to this would never be more
> than a weakly supported facade. Strictly speaking, the local mode of
> production would not change over the course of several juridical
> forms, from Asiatic despotism to commercial capital, from gamon-
> alism to simple mercantile production, which only concealed or
> masked it.[5]

These patterns of agricultural production would have been transmitted from
the colonial period to that of the independent republic. Even today, their persistence does not only mean the persistence of certain techniques of agricultural labour, but also the persistence of a form of social organization, which
in the Andean part of Bolivia is the *ayllu*.[6] This implies a local system of
authorities, that is, a form of organization of production on the basis of a
social and political organization.

In so far as the new juridical means of domination have not transformed
these two dimensions—the productive pattern and the local system of authorities—moreover, in so far as they have not been substituted by another type
of historical time and political unit, we have what Zavaleta called an apparent
state: that is, a political power that is the juridical sovereign in a determinate
territory, but that does not have an organic relation with the populations it
claims to govern.

---

5 Zavaleta, *Lo nacional-popular en Bolivia*, p. 29.

6 *Ayllu* is a Quechua term whose original meaning was probably a kin group. In fact, it
was introduced in what is now Bolivia by Spanish colonial authorities, to denominate
a peasant community or population group which, in the ideal interpretation of early
colonial data, covered various 'islands' of productive land in different ecological zones,
intercalated with the lands of other *ayllus*. These 'islands' often fell into different Spanish
and republican administrative divisions and as a result very few *ayllus* managed to retain
control over more than one of them: hence, by the nineteenth century, *ayllu* came to
refer basically to one local peasant community with a unitary territory (translator's
note).

Local systems of authority exist that are not part of the descendent and de-centralized structure of national government, but rather are locally articulated and generally lived and transmitted across the generations. These local systems persist more where the process of primitive accumulation of capital or formal and real subsumption, that is, a change of historical time, has not occurred.

A change of historical time occurs with what Zavaleta, based on Marx, calls real subsumption—the moment in which not only the juridical relations between workers and the means of production change, but the mode of trans-formation of nature also changes, generally when industry comes to predom-inate over agriculture. With industry comes the predominance of the collective worker in mass production, which is produced by capital, in which each one of these workers no longer controls the productive process but instead is subjected to the new technical and social organization under the command of capital.

The predominance of real subsumption in the productive moment implies a change in the rhythm of social and economic reproduction; in con-sequence, it implies an acceleration and concentration of time in which the aim is no longer to reinstate the previous conditions of production above all in terms of a set of use values, but rather to expand reproduction in terms of a time of abstract value. In this way, it tends to introduce, in modernized soci-eties, a more lineal conception of time or a conception that conceives of time as looking to the future. As real subsumption penetrates societies, this tends to replace more or less cyclical conceptions of time.

Motley Social Formation

Here I present an initial characterization of the notion of a motley social for-mation, one of Zavaleta's commonly cited ideas, which has been used in Boli-vian social science from the 1990s onwards, but whose complex content has not necessarily been understood.

Zavaleta works off of the notion of socio-economic formation in Marx-ism,[7] and in particular in the work of Emilio Sereni.[8] Here social formation is a unity of base and superstructure in which different modes of production are articulated as a historical bloc in a given society.

---

7 Luis H. Antezana elaborates this point in *La diversidad social en Zavaleta Mercado*.

8 Emilio Sereni, 'La categoría de "formación económico-social"' in Cesare Luporini, Emilio Sereni, et al., *El concepto de formación económico-social*, Cuadernos de Pasado y Presente 39 (Mexico City: Siglo XXI, 1976).

In the traditional notion of a socio-economic formation there is the idea that one mode of production, generally capitalism in modern times, dominates the rest and ends up re-articulating them into a totality in a way that serves its pattern of production and expanded reproduction.

In general, the concept of socio-economic formation aims to account for the co-existence of several modes of production, or of heterogeneity on the level of the moment of production. This category has also been conceived as the union of base and superstructure, where the superstructure provides unity for the diversity of modes of production. Some have seen the state, which provides unity at the level of the superstructure, as containing elements of previous traditions, re-purposed for capitalist society, which end up forming part of a new political and social quality.

Zavaleta's notion of the motley takes up the problem of the lack of articulation of modes of production, and above all of other dimensions in social life, principally in politics, in societies like the Bolivian, where the development of capitalism is weak and, in consequence, the transformation and articulation of other social qualities has only partially occurred. Political unity at the level of the state is, therefore, to a large degree only apparent, as Zavaleta asserts.

A motley social formation is characterized in the first place by the co-existence of various temporalities or historical times. It should be noted that the notion of historical time is not identical with that of mode of production, since various modes of production fit into what Zavaleta calls the seasonal time of agriculture. Capitalism initiates a new type of historical time, but only in its mature phase—that of real subsumption. This means that capitalism also exists before this transformation of historical time, and prepares it.

In a motley social formation, not only do various social and juridical relations of production coexist, but also, and more fundamentally, there are heterogeneous historical times. This involves profound diversity, with more or less irreducible differences in political structures and general culture.

In consequence, while on the one hand a national political state exists with more or less modern features, on the other hand there is a group of local structures of authority, diverse among themselves, which do not correspond to the local representation of the national government nor are designated by it, but are rather the endogenous local and more or less ancestral forms of organization of social life. In most cases in these territories, there is not yet an endogenous separation of the political. This occurs with the national state which is configured at a remove from these communities, or with a high degree of exteriority and hence imposition.

In large part, many of these communities exist as they did prior to the state and, in consequence, there is an apparent state. The abstract rational state representing formal equality which corresponds to the capitalist mode of production holds political validity or efficacy where it comes from an internal process of separation of the political, dismantling the elements of life and political practice within society and transferring them to the state. Where local structures of authority persist, the national state holds less validity, efficacy, or legitimacy.

The separation of politics as a state has not been fully achieved in the national territory, because the society has not undergone the other process of separation that leads to the formation of free men under capitalism, that is, the process of primitive accumulation. This has not occurred in Bolivia because what Zavaleta called Andean patterns of agricultural production, and others, persist. In so far as capitalism has not expanded into the whole of the territory, there is no basic separation of the state or political conditions for state validity.

Thus, we have a state constitutionally organized according to principles that correspond to the organization of the capitalist mode of production, which claims to be valid for a territory and a group of communities that are not organized according to those principles and, in consequence, have not experienced internally the processes that would lead them to live capitalist historical time and experience a representative state which is its optimal organic form. This, in turn, means that the state has great problems in acquiring legitimacy and constructing hegemony, which are conditions for the real validity of the state.

Complete unity is not possible on the political and state level because the economic and social substance is not unified. A motley social formation is the combination of high levels of disarticulation, with processes of articulation of various modes of production and processes of articulation of structure and superstructures, in the traditional Marxist sense of these terms. It is, therefore, an incomplete or partial process of totalization; incomplete both with respect to the domination of one mode of production over the other forms of production, and with respect to the unification of the existing types of historical temporality. It is also an apparent process of unification. That which has not been transformed in terms of the structure of historical time and homogenization of social substance is unified only apparently at the superstructural level of the political state.

In so far as such societies have an apparent state and a diversity of cultural communities of production, they are also societies where the processes of construction of the nation on the cultural and above all on the political level are likewise unfinished or partial. It has not been possible to substitute local structures of authority and superimpose on them a new national identity and authority, in terms of loyalty, belonging and legitimacy.

Diversity of Histories and Historical Times

A motley society, which is the confluence of various social and cultural matrices, is also the confluence of various histories, that is, of the movements of these societies, of the hits and misses they have passed through, and of the forms of domination structured by these relations.

Capitalism tends to create a world system, composed of national totalities, at least for a time. These local national totalizations give rise to differentiated histories. This level of analysis deals with the recognition and differentiation of histories between countries and nation-states, that is to say, a history of France is different from a history of Chile or a history of Mexico.

In the case of a motley social formation, a society contains several histories and temporalities. Hence there is a diversity of histories within capitalist historical time itself, that is, between the histories of different nations and nation-states, but there are also different histories within the historical process of a motley society.

We need to make a distinction here. History is not a synonym of historical time. Historical time expresses the movement of societies on the basis of the organization of their productive moment or pattern of transformation of nature. It is a kind of rhythm and direction of the social matrix. It is not the sequence, concatenation or articulation of their collective events.

Histories are the movements of societies in their processes of totalization, both in the continuation of the past, and in present innovations and projects; they are the totality of their events, which occur in the framework of organization that is their historical time.

There is a plurality of histories because there is a plurality of capitalist societies, but in motley societies there is not only a plurality of histories but also a plurality of historical times; in this sense, they are more complex.

The diversity of a motley society is multiple: diversity of historical times and histories, of political forms or structures of authority, which implies cultural diversity or, in a more general sense, diversity of civilizations, which nevertheless coexist or form part of what is recognized today as a society that is more or less a nation or a country.

This multiple diversity is differentiated and categorized by Zavaleta. The motley does not simply mean diversity and coexistence. Rather, his thinking is a structural and historical-genetic analysis of the types of diversity and the margins of articulation and disarticulation.

While the notion of a motley social formation is based on the category of socio-economic formation in Marxism, it is not only the application of this category to societies that are weakly and partially articulated and transformed by capitalism. Rather it relativizes the concept of a socio-economic formation in which one mode of production dominates others while articulating them under its own principles. It refers to the partial and apparent domination of the dominant mode of production, without supposing that this mode carries out a reorganization of the other modes of production present; it does not transform them in accordance with the organizational principle of the dominant mode. It is a way of thinking about disarticulated domination, which is domination nevertheless.

Though Zavaleta drew on the idea of the socio-economic formation as the unity of base and superstructure, as a sort of historical bloc in the Gramscian sense,[9] he also considers the limits and slippage in this unity. The notion of motley social formation thus relativizes and notes the limits of the category of socio-economic formation, as well as its utility.

The idea of motley social formation is a theoretical space to think the articulation between the moment of production and the state political form, and it reveals that where there is diversity of historical times, there is a diversity of local structures of authority, and thus apparent unity between politics and production.

Framework of Reception and Incorporation of Other Histories

In his treatment of the plurality of histories in *Lo nacional-popular en Bolivia*, Zavaleta presents a sort of framework of reception of other histories. The motley society is not the parallel co-existence of Aymara, Quechua, Guarani or any other people and culture that live in Bolivia, but rather their disarticulated confluence.

The framework of reception of these other, particular histories is composed of the categories of motley social formation, constitutive moments, crisis

9 This is the formulation of Emilio Sereni in the article cited.

as knowledge, the primordial form and the social axis or equation. These categories emerge from a Marxist framework and thus use categories elaborated to conceive of the capitalist mode of production and its levels of superstructural correspondence.

The idea of motley social formation and the analysis of the national-popular in Bolivia draw from notions such as primitive accumulation, formal and real subsumption, the logic of the factory, the collective worker, the capitalist state or total capitalist. They refer to the separation from the moment of production that gives rise to the state form, formal equality, representation and their correlates in the process of real subsumption. Such categories serve for thinking the regularity of world history in capitalist time.

Zavaleta considers their relation to the histories of our peripheral societies, and on the basis of what is considered to be universal in the framework of world history, considers what has not been incorporated in that history or has been denied or ignored by it. Above all in *Lo nacional-popular en Bolivia* he is concerned with the incorporation of the history of the rebellions of the Aymara and Quechua peoples. I will first consider his sources, and then the theoretical structure he applies.

Zavaleta is not a professional historian who works with primary sources; a large part of his work relies on secondary sources, that is, histories written by other scholars. His contribution is a theoretical structure, a matrix of articulation of historical events, documented in various written histories and treated in different ways in each of these narratives. He provides a new understanding of the same events and documents present in these studies, attentive to the conditions of self-knowledge that Bolivian society has progressively produced and the limits within which it has exploited these horizons of visibility.

In particular, in the chapters on 'El mundo del temible Willka' [The world of the fearsome Willka] and 'El estupor de los siglos' [The torpor of centuries], Zavaleta focuses on moments of crisis that became constitutive moments with the participation of the indigenous population, above all the history of the Aymara rebellions documented in the important work of Ramiro Condarco Morales[10] and the contemporary work of Silvia Rivera on peasant unionism and the *katarista* movement.[11]

---

10 See Ramiro Condarco Morales, *Zárate, el 'temible' Willka. Historia de la rebelión indígena de 1899 en la República de Bolivia* (La Paz: Talleres Gráficos, 1965).

11 See Rivera, *'Oprimidos pero no vencidos'*; Silvia Rivera, 'Memoria colectiva y memoria popular. Notas para un debate', *Bases. Expresiones del pensamiento marxista boliviano* 1 (1981).

Zavaleta does not write the histories of other peoples in this motley society, but rather incorporates their histories into a global analysis of the history of Bolivia. He incorporates these histories into the explanation of the moments of configuration of the deep structures of Bolivia, rather than incorporating them into a general national history in terms of a more or less sequential relation. He relies on the work of historians at the forefront of the field at the time he was writing; for indigenous rebellions, above all Condarco and Rivera, and in the case of mining, Antonio Mitre's work from those years.[12] For the subject of Andean agriculture and its territorial occupation, he used Murra's and Condarco's previously cited theories of ecological tiers. Zavaleta was the first to incorporate the most innovative work in various social disciplines into the analysis and explanation of Bolivia as a historical totality, synthesizing research that was in itself diverse. No one has since made these kinds of broad connections.

Lo nacional-popular en Bolivia is not an eclectic synthesis of various studies, but rather a complex and structured framework that aims to explain social and historical diversity in which the results of these studies are incorporated.

I will explain how the incorporation of other histories within a motley social formation operates by reviewing how Zavaleta treats the problem of the indigenous population or the Indians, in terms of structure and explanatory process.

Above all in the second chapter, 'El mundo del temible Willka',[13] Zavaleta analyses how the presence or emergence of the Indians in history and political life overdetermines the ideology of the dominant seigneurial caste in Bolivia.[14]

---

12 See Antonio Mitre, *Los patriarcas de la plata* (Lima: Instituto de Estudios Peruanos, 1981).

13 'Willka', which is the archaic Aymara world for 'Sun', was adopted by the late nineteenth century Aymara leader Pablo Zárate, and others who accompanied him, as a military title when the Liberals, headed by José Manuel Pando, recruited Indian irregulars to support them in their civil war against the Conservatives. The irregulars got out of hand and ended by committing various massacres, which were interpreted at the time as the expression of a race war, although recent studies indicate that they had more to do with internecine struggles within the creole elite and indigenous tendencies toward political autonomy. Zárate Willka did not take part in these massacres but was nevertheless held responsible for them, put on trial, and shot supposedly while trying to escape in 1903 (translator's note).

14 *Casta*, which translates as 'caste', should not be confused in this context with the Indian caste system. In the colonial period in the Andes, 'the castes' referred to groups

Colonial domination and the subsequent republic were based on the policy of exclusion and denial of the indigenous population as part of the citizenry, in politics and ideology.

This domination was based on what Zavaleta calls a seigneurial articulation:

> [...] the seigneurial articulation is that which is based on an originary hierarchical pact, which can be factual or contractual, that is, it is not founded on equality but on an essential inequality among men. This is at once a mechanism for the construction of consent because it constitutes a graduated hierarchical structure.[15]

This is expressed in Bolivia by a republican state that excluded the Indians, who were, nevertheless, the basic labour force for the production of wealth in this territory. The excluded indigenous population had, however, a history of resistance and rebellions. Despite the denial of the plurality of identities and cultures and of the logic of those who would be dominated by the seigneurial elite, to be an Indian had meant for a long time a kind of complex and dual identification determined by the seigneurial position through the act of exclusion. But it would also be reassumed at some point as an identity by those who had been denied or excluded.

First, in an analysis of how indigenous political presence influenced the configuration of the ideology of the seigneurial pole, Zavaleta establishes that the cycle of indigenous rebellions in 1780, indigenous resistance to the expropriation of their land during the nineteenth century, and, in particular, the

---

of mixed European, Andean and/or African origin. The Indians were described as 'of tributary caste', referring to a head tax or tribute paid by all those who occupied land in rural communities, a use which carried on into the republican or post-independence period, while the creoles supposedly of European descent and the mixed-race *mestizos* were subject to different tax regimes. In fact the tax regime or fiscal category into which a person fell and one's economic position and occupation had more to do with being assigned to one of these groups than their ancestry or 'race'. Hence, when Zavaleta refers to the 'seigneurial caste', he is really referring to the social group of upper class landlords who also monopolized government posts and claimed to incarnate European culture. Thus, they were similar to European aristocracies, although in English terms they would have been denominated as 'gentry', that is landlords who did not belong to titled and thus properly so called seigneurial lineages; there were and are no titled families in Bolivia. [Trans.]

15 Zavaleta, *Towards a History of the National-Popular in Bolivia*, p. 138.

presence of Willka in the Bolivian federal revolution[16] (which were modes of reaction to and rebellion against colonial denial) ended up reinforcing the social Darwinist component in the seigneurial ideology of the dominant caste. Its republican continuation was the ideological denial of the Indians, in which it identified and homogenized the dominated groups as the object of political exclusion and economic exploitation, through various forms of indigenous tribute to the Bolivian state and to local landlords.

But the Indians were also perceived as a great existential threat, as that which the seigneurial elite denied but could not exterminate because in that case they themselves would have had to work. It was a population that could not be tamed and that rebelled from time to time, in a way that constantly raised the possibility that they would seize the position of the dominant. Here Zavaleta demonstrates how the incorporation of one of the histories of this motley society, that of indigenous rebellions, had powerful effects in the way in which the ideology of the dominant group in society was configured, with negation, exclusion and exploitation of the Indians on the one hand, and fear or loathing of the Indians and their rebellions on the other.

Zavaleta understands this process as a particular history (that of Aymara rebellions) within a motley society, which implies a certain degree of autonomy and social and cultural differentiation, that plays a major part in determining the ideology of the class that ought to give apparent political unity to this society.

He also considers how the seigneurial relation or articulation influences the consciousness of the dominated. He writes:

> [...] there is a dissolution of popular identity based on this loyalty or spiritual submission to the seigneurial, a loyalty that clearly permeates all levels of society. Here, therefore, one who cannot claim the title of Spanish lord at least claims that of pre-Spanish lord, but the seigneurial reasoning remains intact [...]. It is perhaps the most consistent conservative element of all those that exist in Bolivian society, the most general reactionary feeling.[17]

---

16 In nineteenth-century Bolivia, any violent change of government—what would today be called a 'military coup' in most cases—was referred to as a 'revolution'. The 'federal revolution' was a civil war won by the Liberal faction which proclaimed a vague 'federal' ideology as its banner, although once it took power it maintained a unitary and more or less centralized system of government. [Trans.]

17 Zavaleta, *Towards a History of the National-Popular in Bolivia*, p. 139.

Zavaleta also thinks the Indians through Hegel's conception of the dialectic of master and slave, or lord and serf. I will cite a couple of complementary passages:

> The truth is that to oppress is to belong to the oppressed, and the more personal the relation the more the slave contaminates the master with his servitude. The slave is the sickness of the master and not his freedom.
>
> [...]
>
> The Indian, in turn, and we are still referring the level of the quotidian, will wish not to be Indian but to be Spanish or will think that he can be Spanish, that is, he will dream as the oppressed dream rather than identify as oppressed. This is the conservative ground or spirit of the of the history of the country, its most precapitalist and general essence. The persecuted thus take on the permanence of their persecution. After all, this is not incompatible with a popular history.[18]

This internalization of the consciousness of the master in the dominated—part of the mutual determination of the components of the relation of domination—is what is referred to as overdetermination in Marxism.

It is an analysis in terms of totality and, above all, of intersubjectivity. Zavaleta does not think of the formation of the identity of the indigenous and that of the seigneurial in isolation, to then see how they come together. He thinks of how they determine each other within the existing relations of domination and their unfolding.

For Zavaleta, the seigneurial articulation was the cement of Bolivian society, at least until the beginning of the twentieth century, and continued to be the strongest and broadest articulation until the 1952 revolution. It did not disappear after that re-constitutive moment. Thinking through the Indian problem in this Hegelian mode but as part of a structural Marxist matrix of explanation, Zavaleta continued, under new conditions, a tradition of thought concerning alienation in the country.

To recall a couple of previous moments in this tradition: First, nationalist historical revisionism proposed to create a de-alienating local history to substitute the seigneurial oligarchic version, which was how part of the nation thought of itself. Then there were the works of Sergio Almaraz and Marcelo Quiroga Santa Cruz on the alienation of natural resources, which also ended

---

18 Zavaleta, *Towards a History of the National-Popular in Bolivia*, p. 139–40.

up (above all in the case of Almaraz) incorporating, as part of their explanation, the new type of ideological alienation produced by imperialist penetration.

In *Lo nacional-popular en Bolivia*, Zavaleta goes further back to recognize the deepest and most continuous structures in the seigneurial articulation. The strongest new elements appear with the conquest, continue during the republic, survive the nationalist revolution and even persist in the articulation of the contemporary left.

It can be said that the persistence of the Indian as a component of the ideological structure of present day society is an index of the persistence of the seigneurial, in so far as the indigenous component does not become the pole of articulation of a separatist or autonomous identity but rather forms part of the identity of the dominated and of the non-recognition of equality among Bolivians.

Considering the diversity of histories within a motley social formation allows for thinking the problem of intersubjectivity not only in terms of individual and collective subjectivities within a single cultural matrix but also the confrontation of collective subjectivities from diverse cultural matrices.

Zavaleta does not analyse the Indian as part of a dialogue but rather as part of processes in which negation as well as resistance and rebellion strongly mark the consciousness of contrary poles.

Seigneurial articulation expresses this in the history of Bolivian society. The idea of motley social formation is a way to synthesize the Zavaleta's study and explanation of the complexity present in a society like Bolivia.

Conceiving of Complexity

The elaboration of this theory implies a change in Zavaleta's conception of what Bolivia is as a society and a history. In the 1960s, like other nationalists of his time, Zavaleta thought that Bolivia was a nation in practice, against those who denied it, the anti-nation, and that it needed above all to overcome internal obstacles which did not allow it to unfold as a sovereign nation-state. This is what at one point I called dualist ontology, a conception favoring simplification.

With the notion of motley social formations and other ideas developed in *Lo nacional-popular en Bolivia* and 'Las masas en noviembre' [The masses in November], he develops a new understanding of the problem, conceiving Bolivia as a highly complex society, with structural, temporal and historical diversity, partially articulated and apparently unified.

In several steps, Zavaleta shifts from nationalist simplification to a vision of the internal structural differentiation of the nation and the country, above all in terms of the analysis of social classes, which at a certain moment in the 1970s became the cognitive strategy of proletarian centrality. This position was his way of beginning to recognize social division in historical and genetic, and, therefore, temporal terms, as something that could be overcome through critical knowledge and the development of a collective subject that creates the conditions for another type of society. From this perspective that serves to explain social differentiation within a homogenized or capitalist society, Zavaleta began to take up the recognition of social diversity not contained by capitalism or its margins of totalization.

Zavaleta reflects on the complexity that comes, on one hand, from the growing differentiation generated by the capitalist mode of production as the irradiation of a time that introduces constant change and its resulting uncertainty, while also bringing about homogenization of the society through a process of concentration. On the other hand, he considers the complexity that comes from the coexistence of diverse temporalities, histories and political and social forms which are apparently unified through political dominion, first during colonialism, then in the republican period and even after the national revolution.

In the stage of the nationalist conception, Bolivia was thought of as a nation that was something like its essence, easy to recognize. It was enough to focus on the working people, the nation made up of peasants, workers and middle classes in particular, or to narrate their struggles, rescuing them from oblivion or obscurity, in order to produce national consciousness. This implied a kind of ideological substitution or de-alienation, which is not easy to do, but it is a straightforward operation of critique and substitution of the alienating ideology.

In the 1970s and 1980s, Zavaleta went on to think that Bolivia was a society difficult to know, or that faced great obstacles to self-knowledge, not due to the lack of education or theories, but rather due to the lack of conventional unity of its social reality. His notion about the limits to knowledge of Bolivian society is not the result of mysticism, or due to an inherent inaccessibility of the object of thought. They come rather from the difficulty of explaining its social heterogeneity and complexity by means of a single and general model.

In these decades Zavaleta develops a complex idea of Bolivian society, one that replaces the more simplistic image he held of the country and its history. He does not just recognize this complexity, but goes on to elaborate an explanation of it, not only in terms of the structures actually in existence but also of Bolivia as a historical totality, a set of determinations and processes that continue to condition the way we live today. He thinks the complexity of the present on the basis of thinking the complexity of the past.

Motley Society and Baroque Theory

Zavaleta carries out all his analyses of Bolivia, above all those of his mature period, in a style that is quite peculiar and unique in Bolivian social science. Here I want to consider the correspondence between, on one hand, the type of social science or theoretical thought and the mode of construction of historical explanation and, on the other, the type of society which he conceptualized with the notion of the motley.

To this end I will refer to some of Alejo Carpentier's ideas on the baroque and marvellous realism. Carpentier says that Latin America is a baroque continent, basically stemming from the mixture (*mestizaje*) it has experienced in various ways. This is because: '[. . .] every symbiosis, every mixture generates baroqueness.'[19]

This is another way of thinking the composite and heterogeneous nature of Latin American realities, in this case in terms of its art. Carpentier characterizes the baroque as follows:

[. . .] we have, in contrast, the baroque, a constant of the spirit that is characterized by a horror of the void, the naked surface, linear and geometric harmony, a style where, around the central axis—not always manifest or apparent (in Bernini's Santa Teresa it is very difficult to determine the presence of a central axis)—what we could call 'proliferating nuclei' multiply, that is to say, decorative elements which completely fill the space occupied by the construction, the walls, the whole architectonically available space, with motifs endowed with their own expansion and which hurl, project the forms with an expansive force outwards. That is to say, it is an art in movement, a propulsive art, an art which goes outward from a centre, in a certain sense breaking through its own borders.[20]

---

19 Alejo Carpentier, 'Lo barroco y lo real maravilloso' in 'Razón de ser' in *Ensayos* (Havana: Letras Cubanas, 1984), p. 119.

20 Carpentier, 'Lo barroco y lo real maravilloso', p. 112.

I do not propose to equate the baroque with the motley, because the baroque implies a higher level of fusion which is precisely what the motley lacks; but the baroque is a type of cultural production carried out in conditions of social heterogeneity. I intend to use these ideas of the baroque to characterize Zavaleta's work, which is also a kind of cultural production.

One feature of Zavaleta's work is the vitality of his writings, in various senses. On the one hand, there is what he called the intellectual wear and tear (*desgaste*) of producing articulated categories and explanations about the history of Bolivia and modern times in general. There is vitality as creation, not as a mere intellectual exercise but as a vital act in which his life was spent.

His writings have the force of the events that are his object of reflection and analysis, above all because this is a thinking that intervenes actively in that history and that reality, creating ideas and articulating explanations for them. Other features mentioned by Carpentier are also present. There are no empty spaces in Zavaleta's texts, perhaps not due to a horror of emptiness but rather because in general there are no superfluous parts. There is a density in his texts which give the impression of an explosion of everything he has worked out almost artistically, as intellectual creation.

This does not mean that his texts, especially his mature ones, are complete or without holes, problems, insufficiencies or limitations, which exist in every text. There are no spaces in which nothing is composed and mere information is presented without creating anything. There is density in the sense of a thought in movement, which, in the articulation of almost every term it incorporates, produces a particular kind of synthesis, which, on thinking something specific, incorporates what it has been thinking about the totality of its history. It is a density of continual syntheses, in which more and more elements are incorporated, not merely as information but as creative fusion.

This is a density with proliferating nuclei. A major proliferating nucleus is the theory of the law of value, which Zavaleta translates into the explanation of the state, ideology and the complexity of motley societies, to produce other nuclei more relevant for the explanation of this type of society. On the basis of this more general point of reference, Zavaleta produces concepts such as those of the constitutive moment, crisis as knowledge, motley social formation, on an intermediate level. Ideas such as seigneurial paradox and articulation, the state of 1952 and a vast set of specific ideas about Bolivia at the same time follow this dynamic of expansion around an architectonically available space, to paraphrase Carpentier.

Zavaleta designs his intellectual space in such a way that, while at the beginning it appears to have a clear centre, which is the theory of the law of value, this quickly becomes a group of proliferating nuclei as it is placed in movement in order to explain other dimensions of reality and their degrees of correspondence. Perhaps it would be better to say that Zavaleta has no single centre, but rather what Carpentier called a set of proliferating nuclei in an architectonically available space under construction.

At a certain point this space was thought with the idea of the horizon of visibility. Its architectonic organization began around the idea of proletarian centrality and continued with the idea of the masses. These ideas, after being centers of intellectural construction for a time, diffused into another series of proliferating nuclei such as the ideas of primordial form, constitutive moment and several others which in turn through intellectual creation tend toward becoming another set of proliferating nuclei.

Abstraction that Subsumes, Abstraction that Universalizes

It is in this sense that produces density in his explanatory work. He does not work with general models of subsumption, that is, with models with pretensions to general validity, which would be used to organize local data and thus explain them as one more case of the operation of universal laws. He works with abstractions and even produces a good number of them, but with the following difference: they are not abstractions that subsume but what I would call abstractions that universalize.

Abstractions that subsume are part of a general model that operates via the reduction of the object of study to an a priori logic of explanation. Its application ends up selecting all those elements which the model of subsumption can contain and leaves aside all that which is particular or local.

Universalizing abstractions pay attention to the particularities of local reality or historical specificity and tries to explain them with elements or categories that situate them on a level of potential universalization, which implies the possibility of communicating the explanation of that specificity or local reality to other subjects with other specificities.

This universalizing abstraction gives rise to vitality in thought, because it is elaborated from the guts of the problem, seeking and producing its theory, that is, its level and form of abstraction. This provides the vitality and density of Zavaleta's work, which cannot be found in a conventional use of models of subsumption, more common in social science today in Bolivia.

From the heart and movement of things, Zavaleta practices abstraction not by induction, but by what he calls the production of concrete thought, following the Marxist tradition. To elaborate concrete thought is to produce particular syntheses in light of the principle of totality, which is not at all compatible with an empiricist or inductivist conception of knowledge.

Speaking of literature and art, Carpentier said: 'Description is unavoidable, and the description of a baroque world necessarily has to be baroque.'[21]

I consider Zavaleta to be the baroque in Bolivian social science, that is, the author of a description, so to speak, adequate or corresponding to the world he thinks and tries to explain. In general, in Bolivia social thought has been simpler than the type of reality that it contemplates. This displays a degree of backwardness or non-correspondence in relation to other cultural expressions, such as the arts.

Some of Sergio Almaraz' writings have characteristics described by Carpentier—those of vitality and of thought in movement that produces proliferating nuclei—but they do not approach the richness, complexity and density of Zavaleta's work.

If it can be said that Bolivia is a baroque reality, product of symbiosis and mixture (as Carpentier would say) but also baroque in its cultural expressions due to it being a motley society (as Zavaleta would say), Zavaleta's is the only baroque oeuvre in the sphere of social science. It is the kind of political and historical thought that corresponds to the reality in which it exists. It does not operate via reduction and simplification with the consequent impoverishment of the self-image of Bolivia; it is thinking that, by conceiving of complexity in its understanding of Bolivian history, enriches our image of the country.

The Necessity of Incorporating Several Conceptions of the World

I will now comment on another of Alejo Carpentier's ideas, that of marvellous reality (*lo real maravilloso*), in relation to Zavaleta's idea of motley society. Carpentier's idea of marvellous reality contrasts with that of magical realism, above all with respect to Latin American literature. Some of his ideas allow comparisons which clarify the notion of motley society. Carpentier says: 'Everything unusual, everything astonishing, everything that falls outside the established norms is marvellous.'[22] Later he adds: '[. . .] and our marvellous

---

21 Carpentier, 'Lo barroco y lo real maravilloso', p. 124.

22 Carpentier, 'Lo barroco y lo real maravilloso', p. 119.

reality is what we find in a brute, latent, all-pervading state in everything Latin American. Here the unusual is everyday; it was always everyday.'[23]

Reinterpreting this in Zavaleta's key, I would say that both for foreigners and for locals the marvellous or unusual character of many of our realities comes precisely from that which Zavaleta thinks of as motley, that is, the lack of homogeneity of the social substance. This is also because there are no common norms with which to recognize and think all the things of the continent. There are no such norms because there is a diversity of historical times, modes of production, local structures of authority and political life. There are different languages, which are at the same time different conceptions of the world. Since there are no complete fusions, symbioses or articulations, the unusual or marvellous is the product of the way we live with different codes of interpretation and recognition of reality and, in large part, also because we ignore those other codes that exist beyond our own.

This poses the problem of the limits that language places on social knowledge. While Spanish is the language we generally use as a mode of translation and appropriation of the general theories of our time, it is insufficient for understanding or explaining all that which has not yet been transformed by the canons of historical time of capitalist modernity and what is more loosely called Western culture.

Carpentier relates how Bernal Díaz del Castillo, when he arrived in Tenochtitlan,[24] felt that he did not have a vocabulary to feel and explain that immense reality, and in his report to the King of Spain said that for lack of words and names he ended up not expressing it. Zavaleta begins to articulate a matrix of explanation of social diversity on the basis of a language and a theoretical tradition that belong to the historical time of capitalist modernity. His merit consists precisely in that on that basis he produces a nucleus of reception for other histories. On the basis of what he achieved, one could think that this language is or will be insufficient, although at present it is a condition of possibility and a necessary step.

Following Carpentier in the idea of correspondence between description-expression and the type of reality, it may be thought that in the future we will have to elaborate a more composite language, as the dialogue across social differences develops a broader horizon of visibility, which implies a conception of the world that is also more complex and diversified.

---

23 Carpentier, 'Lo barroco y lo real maravilloso', p. 122.

24 The Nahuatl language name of the Mexica (or Aztec) capital, sited in the centre of what is now Mexico City or the Federal District (translator's note).

This composite language may perhaps not have to do so much with the necessities of recognizing and describing what is new, for which it will probably be sufficient to develop the same framework, but rather with the recognition of the old, the past, the excluded. It would be a composite language that, while it aims to better think about ourselves in the present and the future, will only be achieved in so far as it enables a better recognition of the realities of the past.

Perhaps this implies that we also have to internalize various conceptions of the world, many of them incompatible among themselves at several points or taken as a whole, and begin to establish a kind of hermeneutic dialogue inside each of us. A composite language of this kind is not produced by introducing vocabulary from other cultures in an atomistic manner and almost, so to speak, folklorically, into the dominant language, but rather by establishing a dialogue and a cultural construction that entails the incorporation of various conceptions of the world in each one of us and in the culture of the country in which we live.

Today several theories of complexity or paradigms of the complex are being developed,[25] but they have more to do with the high degree of differentiation and uncertainty within one type of society. In Zavaleta's thought we confront another type of complexity, that of the heterogeneity or diversity of social substances. To think in the world today, both types of theories of complexity are equally necessary.

---

25 In social science, in the work of Niklas Luhmann; concerning nature, above all the work of Ilya Prigogine and that of Edgar Morin.

CHAPTER SEVENTEEN

Nationalization of Marxism

René Zavaleta's work is oriented toward the production of local knowledge, above all in terms of history. Local knowledge is not a documented description of local events, but rather a historically and theoretically articulated explanation. I will present two arguments on the production of local knowledge, the first on the production of theory and the second on what I will call the nationalization of Marxism. They are two aspects of the same intellectual process.

A process of producing local knowledge which fully accounts for the specificity of historical articulation of a society cannot be successfully achieved through the exclusive use of general theoretical models, commonly used as models of subsumption to explain specificity as a case of general laws. Theory must be produced at different levels, based on the cognitive problems and specificity of the local social articulation.

This production cannot simply be the utilization of general models that explain, essentially, the causal nuclei of social reality, plus the description of details of local reality; nor can it be the simple description of local phenomenology, whether in the specific language which corresponds to it or in a more or less universalizable and communicable language that is capable of translation into the experiences of other societies and, hence, also into their general theories in the last instance.

The production of local knowledge must always have a component of production of theory, if it is to contribute something new to the explanation of that reality. If the aim is to do social science, it is necessary to have recourse to theories, that is, to concepts that claim some level of generality with reference to the scope of its validity. This process gives rise to what I would call the appropriation of general theories, since not everyone produces the theory necessary to explain the objects they study.

In the specific case of Zavaleta, this occurs via what I call the nationalization of Marxism, which consists in an appropriation via internalization. In so far as this becomes an internalized view of the world, it becomes the daily way of thinking of the set of relations and experiences in everyday life, and of reflection on the society in which one lives.

Formal and Real Subsumption of Theories

In order to analyse this process, I use two categories that Marx proposed for the analysis of the phases of development of the capitalist mode of production, and extrapolate them to treat the process of appropriation of general theories. These categories are formal subsumption and real subsumption, which Zavaleta made much use of. It can be said that there are processes of formal subsumption in the appropriation of theories when one appropriates one or several more or less general theories and uses them as general models on various levels of analysis in order to explain specific or local cases, directly applying them without a process of revision or modification and without producing additional theory that would be compatible with or reform the general theory. The explanation arises basically from the type of problematization and intellection already prepared by the general model and not from a cognitive problematization constructed on the basis of the specific moment.

Real subsumption of theory is practiced by knowing subjects when the theory has been incorporated in such a way that there is a transformation of the subjectivities that internalize it, with the result that the appropriated theory is converted into a means of production of more theory, of the revision of the theory itself on the basis of the problems posed in the process of its appropriation; that is to say, when it becomes a means of transformation or intellectual production that achieves a significant degree of self-referentiality or rootedness.

Real subsumption of theory occurs when this theory does not function as an instrument or model that is basically external, but when it has undergone the process of internalization and, thus, the movement of this theory also becomes a development of one's own thought and, therefore, becomes theoretical production. This creation generally arises at the level of a broad theoretical strategy or of a program of research that corresponds to a type of theory of society and its epistemological perspectives. When one not only uses theories, but also develops this kind of internal movement, it constitutes a form of intellectual self-development.

In Zavaleta's case, I think this occurs as the nationalization of Marxism, since it is not an individual appropriation but rather is done in the context of what Zavaleta previously called a national self. It is a process of appropriation and internalization of a general theory of an era (the historical time of capitalist modernity) in order to think and explain a local reality that is quite complex and composite. This occurs not by subsuming the Bolivian case within a model of general validity, but through a process of experience and reflection on the limits of validity of what Zavaleta calls models of regularity, in the production of a system of categories that could account for the specific problems of knowledge and explanation of the social reality configured through local history. At the same time, the general theoretical matrix—in this case Marxism—is reformed and developed.

In Zavaleta's words, the aim is to participate in the general debate of the era, in this case on the basis of a local history that is composed of a group of partially articulated and apparently unified histories and temporalities.

In order to produce this local knowledge, as structured and causal explanation, there has to be production of theory on some level. If one only applies general models via the subsumption of the specific case, what results is an explanation of what is common to local history and to the rest of the histories that have been explained by this general theory, and not the specificity of the local situation, although this application of the general model may be accompanied by a phenomenological description of local details.

If local history is not to be a mere filler or complement to an explanation on the basis of the simple application of a general model through subsumption, it is necessary to produce additional theory, with certain degrees of generality on the basis of that specific problematic and that reality.

This is what Zavaleta does. On the one hand, he appropriates a general theory of epochal character, that is, Marxism, and internalizes it. He makes it into an intellectual movement that, in order to explain the specificity of the problems of the history he studies and make it more intelligible, produces additional theory, and reforms the matrix of Bolivian intellectual history in which he is working.

Zavaleta is the only one to do this in a systematic and radical fashion. There are other, much more partial and weaker attempts. Social science in Bolivia has existed and exists mainly in the modality of formal subsumption of theories; in this sense, it has not undergone what I am calling a process of intellectual nationalization. Social science and research in Bolivia generally oscillates between the formal subsumption of general theories and rich phenomenological descriptions of Bolivia's cultural and social configurations.

The works of the Andean Oral History Workshop (Taller de Historia Oral Andina, THOA) is a significant counterpoint. The group proposes to think on the basis of the specific history of the Aymara peoples and the decoloniza-tion of Bolivian history, not through what I call here the appropriation and nationalization of general theories, but rather through the recuperation and unfolding of their own conceptions of politics, history and society.[1]

Gustavo Rodríguez' historical research[2] tries to follow Zavaleta's pattern with a stronger emphasis on documented historical research than on theo-retical production, but with this documentary work organized around a the-oretically structured explanation.

These are the most significant exceptions to the more generalized practice of social science, which, I have argued, still follows the mode of formal sub-sumption of general theories, or else lacks any theoretical explanation beyond the description of a specific case. The works of Raúl Prada and Álvaro García Linera also follow the pattern of appropriation of general theories in processes of internalization that lead to the production of more theory and, to some extent, to its nationalization.[3]

Nationalization of a General Theory of the Era

I have said that this process of real subsumption of general theory, in Zavaleta's case, is in large part a nationalization of Marxism. To my mind, the most significant developments in the history of Marxist theory arose through other great nationalizations of Marxism, such as those carried out, in their

---

1 See above all Silvia Rivera's works: 'Oprimidos pero no vencidos' and 'La raíz. Colo-nizadores y colonizados' in Xavier Albó and Raúl Barrios Morón (eds.), *Violencias encu-biertas en Bolivia* (La Paz: CIPCA/Aruwiyiri, 1993); and those of Carlos Mamani, *Metodología de la historia oral* (Chukiyawu: THOA, 1989) and *Los aymaras frente a la historia. Dos ensayos metodológicos* (Chukiyawu: Aruwiyiri, 1992).

2 See Gustavo Rodríguez, *El socavón y el sindicato. Ensayos históricos sobre los traba-jadores mineros: Siglos XIX y XX* (La Paz: ILDIS, 1991); Gustavo Rodríguez, *Estado y municipio en Bolivia* (La Paz: Ministerio de Desarrollo Sostenible y Medio Ambiente, Secretaría Nacional de Participación Popular, 1995); Gustavo Rodríguez, *Poder central y proyecto regional. Cochabamba y Santa Cruz en los siglos XIX y XX* (Cochabamba: ILDIS, 1993); Gustavo Rodríguez and Humberto Solares, *Sociedad oligárquica, chicha y cultura popular* (Cochabamba: Editorial Serrano, 1990).

3 See Raúl Prada Alcoreza, *La subversión de la praxis* (La Paz: Episteme, 1989); Álvaro García Linera, *Reproletarización. Nueva clase obrera y desarrollo del capital industrial en Bolivia (1952-1998). El caso de La Paz y El Alto* (La Paz: Muela del Diablo, 1999).

separate ways, by Lenin, Gramsci and Mariátegui,[4] to mention only the most relevant for this discussion.

The production of a new set of categories within Marxism has occurred in societies in which there was an intellectual appropriation of this tradition and general theoretical matrix for the modern era, and when this body of thought has rooted itself in local problems and processes. At the same time, the Marxist tradition on an international level has been enriched by contributions which are not limited to the explanation of the society within which they were generated, but rather have acquired a universalizable character in so far as they have been converted into categories or theory.

Theory so produced might in turn be directly applied to new contexts, that is, once a new set of categories is created it tends to be used as a general model of explanation through subsumption, but this is not the fault of those who produced the theory but rather of those who use it in a formal or instrumental way.

Marxism did not arrive in Bolivia with Zavaleta. It was present from the beginning of the twentieth century or even earlier; but in general, even in its most fertile moments, such as in the work of Arze or Lora,[5] it has existed in the modality that I call formal subsumption of general theory. This is clearest in Guillermo Lora, who focuses exclusively on Bolivian political processes. Precisely here, in dealing with the specificity of Bolivian history, the events of local history are organized according to a model determined by a general Marxist theory.

This occurs above all in the periodization of the phases of development of the workers' movement, paradoxically via a study of the particular political processes of the Bolivian working class, through a simplified version of Marxism as explanation of the most varied aspects of historical and social life on the basis of the development of the forces of production, without a set of mediating categories.

---

4 See above all José Carlos Mariátegui, *Siete ensayos sobre la realidad peruana* (Lima: Amauta, 1928) and Gramsci, *Cuadernos de la cárcel*.

5 The most relevant works of José Antonio Arze are *Ensayos filosóficos* (La Paz: Roalva, 1980); *Sociografía del incario* (La Paz: Fénix, 1952); and *Sociología marxista* (Oruro: Editorial Universitaria, 1963). We have commented in a previous chapter on Lora's most outstanding work, *La revolución Boliviana* and the four volumes of *Historia del movimiento obrero Boliviano*.

While Lora's is a radical discourse that aims to ground a critique of bourgeois domination in the scientific explanation of Bolivian history, with a focus on political processes and struggles, it is nevertheless an economistic Marxism in terms of the structure of the explanation. It explains the political life of local history on the basis of what Zavaleta called a model of regularity, that is, around the theory of a determined sequence of modes of production, the class structures that accompany it and a conception of class struggle linked to the dynamic of development of the forces of production.

This is not accompanied by a theorization of the state and the group of mediations and intermediate levels of organization of society that would allow for an explanation of, for example, politics, in a way that is not highly determined by the model of regularity but rather responds to its local historical specificity.

When there is no development of a theory of the superstructure, it is unlikely that a process of nationalization of Marxist theory will occur, since this is the level in which the diversity of the world is expressed, as Zavaleta himself wrote in 'Las formaciones aparentes en Marx' [Apparent formations in Marx].

Antonio Gramsci's work is the principal mediator or facilitator in the process of nationalization of Marxism that took place with Zavaleta, since Gramsci developed a complex theory of the operation of the superstructure in the mediations of the productive moment. Gramsci founded the contemporary development of theory concerning the construction of politics and thereby the political construction of reality, especially hegemonies and historical blocs as the articulations of historical totalities. Gramsci also theorized the construction of the nation not merely as the result of the organization of internal markets and, in consequence, of the demarcation of territories of sovereign capital nationalized by the configuration of political states. Rather he proposed to think the national question as a process of organization of culture and also as the modern form of articulation of the state and civil society, that is, as a problem of the historical and political articulation of social totality in modern times.

Gramsci provides a principle set of concepts, such as hegemony, historical bloc, passive revolution and moral and intellectual reform, that Zavaleta uses to devise his own concepts, such as constitutive moment, primordial form, accumulation within the class, the self-determination of the masses. Marx is the other basic referent, from whom he takes the ideas of formal subsumption, real subsumption, and the categories that make up the law of value.

These elements are used to produce the new constellation of categories for explaining Bolivian history, thereby contributing to Marxism in general and to Latin Americans in particular. The production of local knowledge which Zavaleta's work offers articulates the ideas of Marx and Gramsci to elaborate new materials that add to and partly reform the general theory, but from within it. His work is also based on an ample study of the historiographic knowledge of Bolivia's diverse histories.

Local Knowledge Equals Theoretical Production Plus Logic of Place

Theoretical production is done on the basis of cognitive accumulation, in the double sense of successive developments and appropriations on the level of theoretical production as well as the study of historiography and other descriptive, analytical and narrative materials of Bolivia's histories.

With this I do not mean to say that the only form of local knowledge is that produced by the appropriation or nationalization of general theories, and in particular of Marxism, but rather that this was Zavaleta's method, and that for his time or even until today, it is the most consistent explanatory strategy and its results are still the most profound with respect to the explanation of the historical process of the totality in the local conditions of motley society.

The explanation for Zavaleta's production of local knowledge is presented throughout this study. I have here only sought to focus on the idea that to have local production of knowledge there must by theoretical production in order to really account for the specificity of local history and for this specificity not to be seen simply as the proof or one more case of general theories.

In Zavaleta's intellectual development, there was what I call an appropriation or interiorization, a process of taking root in which Marxism was nationalized. There took place a process of real subsumption of general theories which resulted in intellectual production that explained the data of his reality in theoretically articulated concrete notions, at the same time transforming the intellectual matrix itself.

The production of local knowledge is a process of appropriation and internalization of general theories, the production of additional theory, and the articulation of data and facts of local history in such a way that the explanation produced is carried out on the basis of the production of concrete thought or the logic of the specific object, but in terms that can be universalized.

The production of local knowledge is a synthesis in Marx' sense—an articulation of multiple determinations in a double sense. It is an articulation of the multiple determinations of reality and the multiple determinations of the process of intellectual production. It is, hence, a complex process, because it implies accounting for social and historical specificity and diversity via the articulation and production of a group of theoretical abstractions, in such a way that it is not limited to proving general truths in a particular case, which would be a sort of false or apparent totalization between local history and theory. There must be vitality on both sides, that is, theory has to have grown roots in the local history from which it flourishes, and local history also has to do so on the basis of those roots.

The organic totalization of historical and social explanation occurs through the real subsumption of theory, which means precisely theory's generation and regeneration on the basis of thinking historical specificity. This is what Zavaleta's work has done for Bolivia.

In brief, it can be said that local knowledge is achieved in the fusion of the production of new or more theory with the logic of the place.

CHAPTER EIGHTEEN

The Explanatory Structure of Lo Nacional-Popular en Bolivia

All the elements of Zavaleta's mature theoretical and historical work are present in *Lo nacional-popular en Bolivia*. This text, which remained unfinished, was published posthumously in Mexico in 1986, after his death in November 1984.

In the last years of his life, Zavaleta had proposed to study modern Bolivian history, in particular the period from 1952 to 1980. But, in the course of his reflections on the conditions of knowledge in a motley society like that of Bolivia, he decided that it was necessary to go further back in history, at least as far back as the War of the Pacific (1879–1884).[1]

To this end, he managed to write three chapters, which were published as *Lo nacional-popular en Bolivia*. The first chapter, 'La querella del excedente' [The struggle for the surplus] focuses on the analysis of the War of the Pacific. The second, 'El mundo del temible Willka' [The world of the fearsome Willka], is an analysis of the Federal Revolution at the end of the nineteenth century. The third chapter, 'El estupor de los siglos' [The torpor of centuries][2]

---

1 Zavaleta, *Towards a History of the National-Popular in Bolivia*, p. 1. This war was started by Chile, which invaded first the coastal territory immediately adjacent to what was then its northern frontier, which was part of Bolivia, and then the south of Peru including the capital, Lima. Bolivia in fact soon retired from active conflict while Peru was ravaged until the formal end of hostilities. Both Peru and Bolivia lost territory to Chile, but for Peru this was only a portion of its extreme south coast while Bolivia lost its only direct access to the Pacific and has been land-locked ever since. Nationalist history (or myth) represents this loss as traumatic and a significant cause of Bolivia's posterior economic difficulties, although the lost coast was inaccessible and lacked any adequate sea-ports; the closest and most used port, Arica, belonged to Peru before the war. Nevertheless, Bolivia has never ceased to demand that Chile restore its access to the sea, so far without success (translator's note).

2 This chapter was edited in mimeographed form as one of the publications of the Postgraduate Studies Division of the UNAM Faculty of Economics, as the third volume of something titled *Elementos de historia social de Bolivia*.

continues the analysis of the repercussions of Willka's presence, but focuses on the analysis of the Chaco War (1931–1935) and its aftermath.

Zavaleta did not live to write about the period that was to be the focus of the book, that of the 1952 national revolution and its process up to 1980; he perished of a terrible illness late in 1984.

In one of his notebooks there is an outline of this work in which he includes a fourth chapter, to be called 'La canción de María Barzola' [María Barzola's song], for which, however, no other mention been found. The title suggests that it would have dealt with the 1952 revolution, taking stock of all the social struggles that led up to the revolutionary moment as another landmark that was constitutive or reconstitutive of Bolivian society.

'Las masas en noviembre' [The masses in November], a text that deals with events decades after the point at which *Lo nacional-popular en Bolivia* leaves off, may be taken as covering the functions of the chapter that Zavaleta meant to write on the post-1952 period. In it, with the aim of explaining the crisis of the state in 1979, he traces its causes back to the history of the state of 1952.

Zavaleta wrote *Lo nacional-popular en Bolivia* in Mexico, where he occupied various academic posts. From 1976 to 1980, he was director of the Facultad Latinoamericana de Ciencias Sociales (FLACSO, Latin American Faculty of Social Sciences). From 1980 to 1984, he was professor of postgraduate studies in the School of Economics at the National Autonomous University of Mexico (UNAM) and professor in the Department of Social Relations at the Autonomous Metropolitan University—Xochimilco. Though outside the country, he was a member of the Bolivian Communist Party from 1978 until his death in 1984.

Research Programme

In the introduction to *Lo nacional-popular en Bolivia* Zavaleta presents his program of research as follows:

> The problem that this study seeks to investigate is that of the formation of the national-popular in Bolivia, that is, the connection between what Max Weber called social democratization and state form. By this we mean the different patterns of socialization as they existed and their indices of power, as well as the so-called mass projects. In other words, the relation between programme and reality.[3]

---

3 Zavaleta, *Towards a History of the National-Popular in Bolivia*, p. 1.

This is the nucleus of the strategy of explanation—the study of the relations of articulation between the state and civil society, not in a static way but in terms of process. This is the way of proceeding that Gramsci and Marx founded and developed, although the idea of social democratization, as Zavaleta recognizes, is Weber's.

The analysis of the social and state connection is a Marxist strategy of explanation. In this chapter, my thesis is that *Lo nacional-popular en Bolivia* has Marxist foundations, a Marxism that is not the simple application of general theory to Bolivian history, but rather the development of that theory of the era on the basis of the specific problems posed by the historical process of that society.

Zavaleta structures the history of the connection between social democratization and state form in accordance with the following criteria. In the introduction, he presents his methodological point of view: 'From a methodological perspective, we will proceed by isolating certain events, circumscribed in time, or regional situations, circumscribed in space. This is a response to a scarcity of information and it undoubtedly entails a symbolic selection.'[4]

These circumscriptions in space and time correspond, above all, to periods of crisis. These are what Zavaleta has called constitutive moments. His representative moments are those of crisis and reconstitution of society. The chapters he managed to write deal with the principal crises of the last hundred years of Bolivian history. He writes: 'The history of these hundred years in Bolivia will therefore necessarily be the history of a series of crises or pathetic social agglutinations.'[5]

From the start, he poses the problem of the adequacy of the way of knowing the society whose historical explanation is sought:

[...] although certainly there is not a single way of knowing each thing, crisis acquires a special connotation in relation to those societies like the Bolivian that are incalculable and incognizable. Each mode of being necessarily engenders a form of knowledge, and therefore we maintain that it would be wrong to speak of a general method of knowing common to all societies. In this society specifically, moments of crisis operate not as a form of violence against the routine order, but as a pathetic manifestation of the points within society that would otherwise remain submerged and gelatinous.

4 Zavaleta, *Towards a History of the National-Popular in Bolivia*, p. 2.

5 Zavaleta, *Towards a History of the National-Popular in Bolivia*, p. 18.

Later he writes:

> [...] it is at the moment of crisis or its equivalent (a moment of intensity) that, in its results or synthesis, for this constitutes the only phase of concentration or centralization, a formation that otherwise would appear only as an archipelago can be seen [...] and here the degree of revelation is also proportional to the degree of generality of the crisis [...].[6]

Zavaleta's basic idea is that crises are the moments best suited to study motley societies, those not constantly articulated, much less uniform in terms of their substance and temporality. In the moment of crisis, there is a sort of totalization which depends on the degree of movement of the society. Zavaleta assembles his study and explanation of Bolivian society and history around the nuclei of these crises.

In the first chapter, 'La querella del excedente', Zavaleta focuses on the crisis of the War of the Pacific. To explain the conjuncture of the war, he proceeds to analyse the social equation or axis in each of the countries that took part in the conflict, that is, Bolivia, Peru and Chile. Once the representative moments have been selected, he goes on to analyse the historical formation of what in other writings he called the primordial form, that is, how state and civil society have been articulated in each of these societies. He also refers to this as social axis or equation.

His treatment of the war is not focused on military questions. Zavaleta explains why Chile won the war and Peru and Bolivia lost by looking at how the state was organized in each one of these societies and how it was connected to its civil society. For him, Chile had constructed a social optimum, more or less strong and organic relations of correspondence between the state and civil society, where the state predominated over society (since independence, with its roots in the conquest and the colonial period). This gives it superiority over Bolivia and Peru, where, since independence and the organization of the republics and especially due to colonial past, they had only managed to construct weak articulations between the state and society.

Zavaleta studies how each of these societies was historically prepared, or not, for the conflict. Chile's superiority did not consist in its military power, but rather in the strength or superiority of its social equation, which the Chilean oligarchy had produced in the construction of its nation-state, in a significant case of an optimum correspondence between state and society,

---

6 Zavaleta, *Towards a History of the National-Popular in Bolivia*, pp. 17–18.

despite its limitations. The strength of the quality of the Chilean primordial form was greater than the quantity of the Bolivian and Peruvian societies with their poor and weak social equation. He writes: '[...] the general foundation of modern societies is determined by the way in which they achieve their totalization. That is, totalization plus the qualitative form in which totalization is realized.'[7]

This means that an analysis of the conjuncture, for example, that of a war, cannot be done without reviewing its prior history, that is, its process of totalization; the components have a different weight in the history of totalization of each of these societies. Zavaleta says:

> The War of the Pacific, then, was a confrontation between three historical accumulations or, rather (although this requires some qualification), the apex or end of each—which is the state. It must be noted that there are wars that are more properly a matter of the state and more popular wars, by which we mean to designate the different degrees of penetration in the collective ideological formation. [...] In any case, the central quality or feature of the war is its interstate character. In Peru and Bolivia, it was purely an affair of the state; in Chile, the state had the capacity to mobilize the people psychologically and administratively.[8]
>
> [...]
>
> [...] the conflict is between different types of social equations or the degree to which each of them is the bearer of an optimum. We must explain what it is that we mean by what we have reiteratively called the social equation or optimum, which is nothing but the relational quality of a society.[9]

First of all, Zavaleta studies the history of the articulation or articulations of the social equation in each of the countries. He goes on to analyse the war or confrontation, not in terms of clashes between armies but rather between different social equations. His explanation is sociological and historical, not military and conjunctural.

He studies the social equation of each society, tracing its constitutive moments. The starting point is the organizing analytical axis, the state–civil

---

7 Zavaleta, *Towards a History of the National-Popular in Bolivia*, pp. 41–2.

8 Zavaleta, *Towards a History of the National-Popular in Bolivia*, pp. 58–9.

9 Zavaleta, *Towards a History of the National-Popular in Bolivia*, p. 60.

society relation in each society. From there he goes on to a comparative analysis between societies, how each dimension of social reality (the state and civil society) was formed, and then brings in the relations between states and between nations, and the effects that these have on the state–civil society articulations inside each country.

He proceeds from the simple to the complex, just as Marx[10] describes his own approach and as Novak formulates what he called cognitive idealization.[11]

He thinks each society from within, from a certain level of belonging, knowledge and experience. He only speaks with conviction of those societies in which he had lived, which he knew from the inside. His years of exile, from the military coup of 1964 onwards, led him to live in Uruguay, Chile, Mexico, Argentina and Great Britain, and to travel to other countries. Exile functions as a universalizer and relativizer of experiences and ideas.

In the confrontation of different social equations, the weaknesses and strengths of each appears with more clarity. In analyzing a sole primordial form, it is possible to establish the type of force that the state has over civil society or vice versa, but it is difficult to assess the magnitude of this force; this is what is revealed when a society confronts another or others.

In his discussion of the War of the Pacific, Zavaleta takes the problematic of surplus as a focal point for the analysis of the social equation. Chile made war in order to take over resources that would allow it to appropriate the greatest surplus in its history. It did so making use of the optimal condition of its social equation. Peru lost the war at its wealthiest moment, that is, when it had a high internally generated surplus. According to Zavaleta, this shows that what determined the outcome of a war is not the relative scale of each country's surplus, but rather how this surplus is appropriated and used to organize internal mediations in the composition of its primordial form. In making this argument, he challenges a famous claim of Marx: 'Marx wrote that wars are not waged between countries but between gross products. Today we can affirm that this betrays a certain—necessary—economistic bias.'[12]

To do so is to understand a general conflict exclusively on the basis of a single moment of social reality. To think of war as a confrontation between

---

10 See *Grundrisse: Foundations of the Critique of Political Economy* (*Rough Draft*) (London: Penguin, 1973).

11 Leszek Novak, *The Structure of Idealization: Towards a Systematic Interpretation of the Marxian Idea of Science* (Dordrecht, Holland: D. Reidel Publishers, 1980).

12 Zavaleta, *Towards a History of the National-Popular in Bolivia*, p. 60.

social equations is, on the other hand, to think in terms of the epistemological or explanatory principle of totality.

In Bolivia, the dominant landlord caste basically appropriated the agricultural and mining surplus via indigenous tribute, that is, the exploitation of indigenous labour, which supported both the state or and the local landlords. The Bolivian state did not attempt to contain its society but, on the contrary, tried to deny it ideologically and in large measure to exclude it politically. Bolivia had not attempted the construction of a nation-state as had occurred in Chile. In this sense, it had an endemic weakness in terms of social and political organization. Zavaleta analyses the surplus in relation to its role in the formation of the ideology of the dominant classes in each of the countries in conflict, and in relation to the articulation of each social totality:

> If by mediation we understand the transformation of the fury of the oppressed into part of the programme of the oppressor, which is after all a hegemonic relation, it's obvious that mediation is all the more possible the greater the surplus because to represent the state to society and society to the state is something that involves money, concessions or privileges. Still, the concept of surplus is, in the first place, a relative concept because it must refer to a surplus relative to a given moral-historical norm [. . .].[13]

Peru and Bolivia did not use the surplus to construct mediations through which the state could attempt to contain civil society, such that in the conjuncture of the war its surplus could be transformed into the form of power that it needed to confront the enemy.

One of the veins or dimensions that Zavaleta explores most is how surplus circulates on the level of the construction of politics. Strictly speaking, he does not discuss the peculiarities of the forms of exploitation or the production and appropriation of surplus in the economic sense, but rather how this surplus is converted into state spending and in particular into structures of mediation between the state and civil society. He is also concerned with how the use of surplus value determines the ideology of, above all, the dominant class, but also of the dominated.

In the course of his analysis of the conflict of the War of the Pacific, Zavaleta presents a wide range of reflections on the capitalist state and the law of value. The central and most general hypothesis in this chapter is that at the base of the complex analysis in *Lo nacional-popular en Bolivia* is the

---

13 Zavaleta, *Towards a History of the National-Popular in Bolivia*, p. 40.

theory of value as it was formulated and developed by Marx. He does not expound nor does he explain the law of value, but it is present almost everywhere and at the same time invisible, translated or transformed, in the analysis of the most diverse aspects of Bolivian social reality and history. This is precisely his contribution: he does not present a new exposition of the law of value, but rather makes productive use of it as the articulating axis of what lies outside its scope.

The Model of Separation

To take the relation between state and civil society as the axis or nucleus of the explanatory strategy provides an approach, in terms of the social totality, to the outcome of the process of social transformation which gave rise to the implantation of the capitalist mode of production.

A synthetic way to explain this point is found in a twofold idea of separation. First is the separation obtained through the process of primitive accumulation, that creates the conditions for free men, freed from the means of production and juridically free. Upon this state of separation at the base is another separation, that of politics as a state form.

Within this universe of theoretical explanation, the state can only be understood based on the law of value, which is not to say that the law of value should be an exclusive or self-sufficient referent. The separation between state and civil society is a historical distinction that strictly speaking is produced with the development of capitalist society. In terms of methodology, it is a strategy appropriate to think such societies.

Drawing from this methodological schema, Zavaleta begins to explore the processes of separation in Bolivian society and the degree to which it has or has not been produced. This is one of the features of the social heterogeneity or diversity that he calls motley society.

His analysis of the production of the state of separation relies on the set of categories that come from Marx. Two categories stand out: formal subsumption and real subsumption.[14] Studying formal subsumption reveals the changes in the social relations of production at the juridical level; but only with real subsumption is there a change in historical time, that is, in the modality of transformation of nature, both internally and externally.

---

14 Karl Marx, *Capital* 1.4

The processes of real subsumption are the most important marker, determining the change at the deepest level of the quality of the social substance, which is historical time.

Zavaleta combines Gramsci's idea of moral and intellectual reform with Marx's idea of real subsumption. From his standpoint, real subsumption is what allows moral and intellectual reform in a society. It creates the conditions and the need for hegemony at the political-ideological level.

These ideas, which correspond to a moment of maturity in the structural and genetic explanation of capitalist society, serve Zavaleta in discerning the margins of expansion and implantation of the states of separation economically and politically, that is, to think the limits of the historical time in Bolivia and its past. He then thinks that which has not been totalized by capitalism except partially or apparently.

In this, he is similar to Marx, whose idea it was to start from the knowledge of more complex and developed societies (which implies an evolutionary concept) in order to extrapolate some of the elements for explaining earlier societies, which would not have created the conditions for knowing or explaining themselves.

Zavaleta operates in the same fashion. Employing categories that apply to modern capitalist society, he begins to explain aspects of other realities with other organizing principles, but especially ones which enter into contact with capitalist society, at the level of local structures as well as the world system.

Different aspects of the societies and communities which have not internally produced states of separation in the productive moment and the political moment—which means there persist ancestral modes of the transformation of nature in the agrarian world and a set of local structures of authority—are explained using the model of separation. For Marx and his successors, this means that the movement of civil society provides the explanation and origin for state formation.

Zavaleta synthesizes the relation in this way: 'the state as the sum of all aspects of power and civil society as the set of material conditions in which power is produced'.[15]

One can begin with a theory that attempts to explain the state of separation according to the following chain of development: primitive accumulation—formal subsumption—real subsumption—moral and intellectual

---

15 Zavaleta, *Towards a History of the National-Popular in Bolivia*, p. 58.

reform—capitalist hegemony. One can then analyse aspects of societies in which that separation did not occur.

Zavaleta analyses each country in the War of the Pacific in terms of these processes of separation of the productive and the political and in terms of the relation between state and civil society, as well as the mediations that constitute the social equation or axis in each local history.

He analyses the way in which the problem of surplus shaped the ideology of the respective dominant classes and their society and the degree to which the surplus was or was not converted into a state form and system of mediations. He then goes on to explain why, in the confrontation between these historical totalizations, some societies were historically prepared to lose and others to win, given the strength and composition of the articulation between the state and civil society.

The Law of Value as Nucleus

As a whole, Zavaleta's procedure in methodological and theoretical terms is thoroughly Marxist. I want to emphasize three aspects of this.

First, this is an investigation and an explanation articulated around an invisible but all-pervading nucleus, which is the law of value: a law of value thought from the perspective of totality, as an articulation of social processes that start with the production of the state of separation and primitive accumulation, followed by formal subsumption and then real subsumption. This continues in parallel with the separation of politics, which become the state form, which, in so far as it corresponds to a strong process of real capitalist penetration in society, creates the conditions for a state constructed as hegemony via moral and intellectual reform on the level of the social totality.

This is the central point. *Lo nacional-popular en Bolivia* is an explanation of Bolivian history around and on the basis of the law of value.

The second point is that this is an analysis in terms of totality, or rather, in terms of historical totalization. It is an analysis in terms of a totality differentiated by historical processes. It is a double differentiation, on the one hand a differentiation that comes from history and produces the state of separation in the productive moment and in politics, and on the other hand a type of theoretically elaborated differentiation, that which Zavaleta himself expresses through the metaphor of base and superstructure, but which he goes on to think about in an elaborate way by considering how its articulation comes

about via concepts such as socio-economic formation, motley social formation, primordial form and historic bloc.

Zavaleta conceives of differentiation in the articulation of the social totality in historical and theoretical terms. This is characteristic of a Marxist
explanatory strategy, in particular of an axis which runs from Marx to Lukács
and Gramsci, and which Zavaleta continues through the tasks he sets out to
explain Bolivia.

Specific Logic (Complex and Composite)
of the Specific Object (Complex and Composite)

This leads me to the third point, which I want to propose by recalling Marx's
idea of developing the specific logic of the specific object. Zavaleta's work is
Marxist in this sense, a development of Marxism on the basis of the specific
problems of the reality he studies. This has several implications, in the first
place, that the reality that constitutes the object of thought has a complex
character, owing not only to diversification within one and the same social
and historical matrix, but also to the existence of a social diversity in the form
of the coexistence of different historical times, political forms and productive
moments. Hence the specific logic of the specific object has to be, to continue
using these terms, a complex logic in which the set of theoretical and methodological elements appropriated within the Marxist tradition can only be a part
of that logic, even if they are the core of articulation and reception of the other
elements.

Zavaleta's Marxist explanatory strategy is the mode of articulation and
reception of other histories of Bolivian society within the complexity of the
specific logic of this specific object, which emerges from the insertion of those
other histories and from the fact that there is no fusion that would give rise
to a new time or unity of reality, but rather a motley coexistence.

The explanation therefore takes the form of a composite logic because it
deals with a composite object. It might be better to speak of complexity and
composition to distinguish two things: the complexity of a reality that corresponds to differentiation within one and the same type of social substance,
and the type of theoretical complexity that one has to develop to explain it;
and another problematic that consists in the diversity or social heterogeneity
coexisting in a society which is composite. A logic of the specific object is
both complex and composite because it responds to these two characteristics
of the social reality under consideration.

Zavaleta uses the elements of an explanatory strategy or program like Marxism as a theoretical nucleus around which to articulate, almost in artisanal fashion, the specific logic of the specific object. This corresponds to the type of local historical and superstructural accumulation by which the theoretical nucleus can be modified or revised.

Zavaleta's work does not employ Marxist theory as a set of general models of explanation via subsumption, but instead draws on this idea of the articulation of the specific logic (complex and composed) of the specific object (complex and composed) which is motley.

The National-Popular

Zavaleta's final work proceeds from the expansion of the epistemological and historical horizon of proletarian centrality. The horizon of democracy as the self-determination of the masses is only possible on the basis of proletarian centrality which overcomes its corporative limits and also becomes intersubjective and a composite object.

It is with the idea of the national-popular that Zavaleta proposes the study and explanation of Bolivian history starting with proletarian centrality and extending it to the totalizations that the proletarian subject has achieved in the country's history.

From this point of maturity, it is possible to go back and review the country's historiography, including that which Zavaleta had previously produced. New historical moments, such as that which Zavaleta discusses in 'Las masas en noviembre', allow one to see the past with a greater explanatory ability, that is to say, in an expanded horizon of visibility. The national-popular, in turn, becomes a type of identity that is theoretically, politically and historically articulated by Zavaleta's work and grounded in a more collective effort.

It is a position that Zavaleta produces towards the end of the 1970s and the beginning of the 1980s, considering the contemporary processes unfolding in Bolivia. On that basis, he undertakes a new project of revision of Bolivian history and thus the production of a new explanation that does not necessarily negate all the preceding work, his own and that of others, but rather articulates it in a wider, more diversified and complex explanatory structure.

The object of study—the national-popular as a connection between social democratization and the state form—is defined by a horizon of visibility brought about by the movements of Bolivian society in the late 1970s, when the 1952 state enters into crisis, and by Zavaleta's intellectual work. His writings express as social science and political thought a wider horizon of visibility that articulates the new tendencies in Bolivian society. They create a fuller and more complex program for study of the past and produce the conditions for revision and development of his own thinking.

The Symbolic Selection of Constitutive Moments

In the second chapter of *Lo nacional-popular en Bolivia*, 'El mundo del temible Willka', Zavaleta analyses a civil war, that is, an internal conflict, the Federal Revolution at the end of the nineteenth century (1899), which was the confrontation between two factions of the dominant caste, which in schematic terms corresponded to, on the one side, the Conservative silver mining and large landlord bloc, highly pre-capitalist, and on the other, a group known as the Liberals, more centred on the new commercial networks of the period and the increasingly capitalist tin mining, although its ideology was not free of seigneurial elements.

In this confrontation, which became a civil war, the Liberals exploited an autonomous mobilization of the Aymaras in the north of the country, mainly in the department of La Paz, whose leadership was in the hands of Zárate, 'the fearsome Willka', until they felt that the indigenous mobilization could do away with the whole of the dominant caste; they then made a new pact of unity with the Conservatives, so that both could join forces against the greater threat of the Indians.

Zavaleta argues that at the moment when some conditions for a broader process of nationalization were arising in Bolivia, that is, the incorporation of the indigenous population around a more democratic program, the dominant bloc reacted by reinforcing its strong seigneurial component, which was reconsolidated in the face of a greater threat than it had ever faced. The outcome of the Federal Revolution was a social Darwinist ideology that denied and excluded the Indians much more powerfully than before.[16]

Zavaleta analyses how, in a moment of crisis, some aspects are revealed that do not appear fully under normal conditions of domination. One of these is precisely the strong seigneurial character of the dominant bloc, which was

---

16 Zavaleta's analysis can be compared to the works of Marie-Danielle Demélas: *Nationalisme sans nation? La Bolivie a la fin du XIXe siècle* (Paris: Éditions du C. N. R. S., 1980); and 'Darwinismo a la criolla. El darwinismo social en Bolivia, 1880–1910', *Historia Boliviana* 1 (1981): 55–82.

not overcome in this crisis, but rather was deepened through the transformation of the groups of which it was composed. He analyses this conjuncture on the basis of the same criteria of his general program of study of the articulation between the process of social democratization and state form. In the case of the Federal Revolution, it was once more resolved by excluding the Indians, and in consequence by the reconstitution of a highly apparent state in Bolivian territory.

He also incorporates another history (here simplified in order to focus on his methodology)—the political history of the indigenous peoples who intervene and who come with their own conceptions of territory and of war, their political program and their social organization. If the nucleus of that social organization is the *ayllu*, the indigenous rebellion headed by Zárate Willka is 'the *ayllu* in action';[17] it is an autonomous intervention in Bolivian politics.

The Federal Revolution is a reconstitutive moment for the dominant caste in the country, which intervenes with all the weight of its seigneurial past in order to renew itself through an internal re-composition of the dominant bloc, in a new conjuncture of danger produced by the ascent of the Indians. For that reason, Zavaleta wrote at one point that Bolivia was a sort of walled-in society, in which what the seigneurial articulation wanted to recognize conceived itself as besieged from outside by what it had excluded, the Indians.

The Federal Revolution is a conjuncture in which the principal political forces existing in the country—Conservatives, Liberals and Indians—are mobilized. This is a sort of constitutive moment, in reality strongly reconstitutive, because it restores, for a new period, the old conditions of conflict and social composition of the country. The type of seigneurial articulation that would characterize the social life of the country for another half-century would emerge from this, although it would persist with the same strength for only thirty years, until the Chaco War.

In the third chapter of *Lo nacional-popular en Bolivia*, 'El estupor de los siglos', Zavaleta turns to the Chaco War, covering the period from 1930 to 1935. Once again, this is a conflict between states. Zavaleta analyses how the state and civil society had been articulated in Paraguay and Bolivia up until that moment. In Bolivia, the Chaco War began as purely a matter of the state; in contrast, the reaction in Paraguay managed to mobilize its society, since it felt that its very existence was in danger. Part of Bolivian society initially felt a sig-

---

17 An expression that Zavaleta used to speak of *katarismo* in 'Las masas en noviembre'.

nificant degree of alienation with respect to the Chaco War, since the territory in dispute was not socially or politically incorporated in the historical core of the country.

Once again, Zavaleta explains the defeat in war, and not only the defeat but also the process as a whole, as a result of the weak state-society relation in Bolivia. This was a situation in which a good part of its people did not feel that they belonged to the Bolivian state; nevertheless, in the course of the war, some things were transformed. Above all those who entered the combat zone ended up producing a new kind of intersubjectivity, which the dominant class and the state had not previously been able to produce. In war—as in situations of crisis in general—there was an encounter between social groups that did not meet in daily life because they were excluded and separated, that is, they were not hegemonically integrated.

The elements of the country's social diversity, represented in the flesh by the men mobilized by the war, encountered one another and began to articulate within society a new type of intersubjectivity. This is precisely the kind of intersubjectivity that, as it matured, would put the oligarchic state in crisis, since on the basis of this historical moment a powerful precedent was created for the development of an ideological process in which the construction of the national would undermine the narrow scope of legitimacy of seigneurial ideology. A national movement began to organize itself and would precipitate a political crisis over the next two decades until its culmination in the 1952 revolution.

In analyzing the Chaco War Zavaleta once again thinks of the weak political and national construction in the relation between the state and civil society in Bolivia, above all in the leadership of the state, and how the war, in the beginning basically an affair of state, generated a new social movement that sought a new type of articulation between the state and civil society, proceeding from the grass roots. In this sense, it also becomes another constitutive moment.

Composition of Proliferating Nuclei

The other component of the explanatory structure of *Lo nacional-popular en Bolivia* is the idea of constitutive moments. Zavaleta organizes his study of Bolivian history around a representative selection of moments of crisis—the most general and intense—which are at the same time constitutive or reconstitutive moments.

There are two criteria for the selection of these moments. The first is that the horizon of visibility of a society must broaden in the crisis. There is a moment of fluidity and totalization, that is, of communication, which in the moments of normality of a motley society does not occur, since such a society is made up of different temporalities and social substances that cannot be represented in a single code, let us say, the dominant one. The other criterion is that of the constitutive moment as a kind of matrix of articulation and condensation of what will be a program for the life of a society for a good while. It determines the basic structures and the direction in which history will tend.

In the text the process tends to be presented the other way around, that is, first, the constitutive moment is determined, and after that the period that it inaugurates is narrated. Zavaleta retreats in time until he determines the constitutive moment and on that basis, gives an account of both what followed and what preceded it.

The structure of *Lo nacional-popular en Bolivia* is organized around these two nuclei, the idea of crises as moments of knowledge and constitutive moments. Around them unfolds the ensemble of the Marxist strategy whose nucleus in turn is the theory of value. This is a center that moves accompanied by a constellation of intermediate-level concepts such as the historical bloc, the socio-economic formation, the primordial form and others.

The structure of *Lo nacional-popular en Bolivia* is that of a set of proliferating nuclei. This is not a reflection on historical processes in Bolivia that follows the sequence of events, but rather the importance that each of them has acquired in the conjuncture and in collective memory over time.

This is a structured way of thinking Bolivia and, therefore, is a way to rationalize the image we have of our country or our reality. It works not through reduction or simplification under a schematic formal monologue to which a national identity adheres, but rather through the elaboration of an image or self-image of Bolivia which has a structure of rationalization that organizes the complexity that produced our history and the histories that constitute us today. This is carried out via a series of proliferating nuclei which end up producing a baroque image of Bolivia, an image that is rational and baroque, dense and in reflexive movement.

Diversity Explained by a Major Abstraction

Finally, in conclusion, I would like to propose a hypothesis about this work and its implications for what I would call the production of local knowledge.

Zavaleta thinks that backward societies are more complex because they are composed of a social diversity that is in contrast with the greater homogeneity of the societies considered to be developed in world history. Zavaleta seeks to understand the complexity, heterogeneity and motleyness of Bolivian society from the perspective of the greatest theoretical abstraction of the era, the law of value, which corresponds to the greatest abstraction produced in modern times, that is, the abstraction of labour time.

It may seem paradoxical to explain a particular society made up of diverse historical temporalities, productive moments, and political forms or a heterogeneity of local authority structures, only apparently unified by a partially modern state, with a theory that thinks the greatest abstraction of modernity, which implies a homogenization of social substance; but it so happens that this type of work has produced the best results in the explication of Bolivia.

Zavaleta develops this strategy in the broadest and most radical way in *Lo nacional-popular en Bolivia*, which is where he also incorporates with greatest care the social diversity of Bolivian history. It is in this sense that I consider it to be his most Marxist work, since it is where he applies most fully and deeply or radically the program of inquiry and the explanatory strategies contained in the law of value, which is at the core of the theoretical identity of Marxism.

In applying this program all the way to the root, he ends up producing a reflection on its limits, on the relativity or margins of its pretensions to explanatory validity. In this way he carries out an internal critique and conceptual reform that allows the inquiry to continue to be productive via the production of new categories, the re-articulation of the conceptual system and the recognition of the determinative weight of the dimensions of reality explained by each of these categories. It is a mode of thought that produces consciousness of the world as it produces local knowledge.

Where many people see a distancing from Marxism in Zavaleta's work, I would argue that in fact it constitutes a process of radicalization in Marx' sense, that is, it seizes things at their roots. The theoretical roots are in Zavaleta himself as he not only uses Marxism but produces it and does so in relation to the historical roots of the society he is examining. It is a radicalization that grows roots, that is, it creates conditions not only for him to think with a high degree of self-referentiality, but also for others of us to be able to think this society within this tradition that he has created.

When a type of cognitive strategy and conception of the world has been radicalized, that is, when it has been extended to think all problems on the basis of the same core, however complex it may be, there are also more conditions for a dialogue with other conceptions on the basis of an identity. In this work, while Zavaleta thinks on the basis of a particular theoretical identity, he maintains a dialogue with other major theories of our time, in particular with Weber and Tocqueville.

When a theoretical identity is consistent and rooted, the dialogue with other frameworks can involve the incorporation of the ideas of others without their modifying the general quality of the primary theoretical identity, although they transform and enrich it. This is what occurs with the inter-theoretical dialogue in Zavaleta's work. The configuration of his own identity does not occur before or after, but is something that is ripened in integration; the more advanced the process of development of identity, the richer the dialogue.

Lo nacional-popular en Bolivia is thus the study of the diversity and complexity of Bolivian history through the major theoretical abstraction of the era, the law of value, which becomes a nucleus of articulation and reception for other histories. It becomes the nucleus for the articulation of the social totality, in an intellectual process of rational-artisanal production of the specific, complex and composite logic of a specific object, motley Bolivian society.

CHAPTER NINETEEN

Knowledge and Self-Determination

Construction of Concepts

One may ask what it is to know in the context of Zavaleta's reflections, which establish a whole theoretical strategy to think societies like ours. I start with a passage from Zavaleta: '[. . .] to know in any case is not a mere composition of concepts; it is a vital act, a struggle, and, therefore, a dangerous affair, an organizational act.'[1]

Nevertheless, Zavaleta worked hard to construct concepts. Here I distinguish at least three levels of work. First, on the level of Marxist theory, Zavaleta worked on the reconstruction of some ideas; he also constructed new ones in entering the debate on the relation between base and superstructure, and in his consideration of the limits of the validity of what he called a model of regularity, in order to account for what he called the special accumulation of the superstructures in the context of diversity. These texts work on the level of the specific, local accumulation of each society, producing a series of concepts related to the problematic of ideology, the state and politics, with the aim of circumscribing the validity of a model of regularity. At the same time that Zavaleta explains the law of value in depth, as the nucleus of the model of regularity, he produces other categories of analysis, which take into account the determination of the productive moment but do not subsume the explanation of politics, ideology and the history of nations under the model of regularity. He explains how this determination continues, in a specific way, in other spheres of life.

Zavaleta makes use of other concepts, such as those elaborated by Gramsci. There is an intellectual process in which the model of regularity acquires greater explanatory force when it is more rigorously delimited, that is, when it is not applied to explain everything outside the context for which it was produced, but rather its limits of validity are determined in order to produce other concepts where the existing ones are insufficient.

---

1 Zavaleta, 'Las formaciones aparentes en Marx': 17.

This is a reconstruction of concepts, that is, a re-articulation in which the limits to the value of general models become clear. With the law of value, produced for the time of the introduction of the capitalist mode of production, the idea of the moment of production as the primary determinant is maintained; but since in Zavaleta everything is located in a horizon of analysis that follows the epistemological principal of totality, the categories through which politics is thought must be reconstructed to account for the practices through which the social totality is articulated and the productive moment is reproduced.

This is a re-composition of elements already developed by Marx, and in particular of one Marxist tradition, developed by Lukacs and Gramsci, which consists in a complex theory of social reality and which recognizes different levels of generality of the available explanatory models. This provides an opening to the history that it has to account for at each point in its specific local articulation.

This reconstruction of elements already existing in the Marxist tradition, with the introduction of some new ones, gives rise to a Marxism with better knowledge of the limitations of the models it has produced and their horizons of validity, which correspond not only to the historical time of capitalism but are also configured within differentiated spheres of that same reality. What results is a series of more or less general ideas about the state, ideology, politics and the nation, which do not serve for presenting a general model of the superstructure, but are rather a basic axis for the ad hoc articulation of a specific explanation of each history.

Categories such as historical bloc and hegemony have a general content and refer to a historical time that can serve to articulate thinking about the different local histories. They do not configure a model of subsumption of the specific histories. They form part of one level of work in the construction of concepts, supplementing the previous concepts with greater specificity.

Theory as Object of Desire

On a second level, Zavaleta carries out his own construction of concepts which respond in a more specific way to the problems posed by the knowledge of complex, heterogeneous and backward societies such as the Bolivian. These include the concepts of the primordial form, the constitutive moment, crisis as knowledge, the ideas of accumulation within the class and the masses, and his four concepts of democracy and self-determination.

These are developed within the Marxist tradition, but with a high degree of creativity and freedom. This creative freedom is possible when one has a thorough knowledge of the material one works with. A process of appropriation has taken place, that is, a certain way of thinking has become part of oneself, so that it is no longer simply utilized, as if it were an external tool used to make things. It becomes a part of oneself, a part that has to be developed just as one has to live.

The freedom in intellectual creation comes from this process of appropriation and internalization in which theory becomes a vital part of our being, in such a way that self-development is linked to the development of the theory which has been appropriated. In this sense, theory becomes what I would call an object of desire, of the desire of construction of one's own subjectivity. Our subjectivity generally begins to form in an involuntary and unconscious manner, through different forms of socialization. At some point, we begin a deliberate process of self-development, selecting the elements we incorporate and directing the development of that which we have already assimilated or appropriated. Theory thus becomes an object of desire, at least in two senses or phases that I have indicated with reference to Zavaleta.

First, one can desire theories that we ourselves have not made, but that we consider useful or good for the constitution and development of our subjectivity. Later, in a stronger sense, theory becomes an object of desire in the sense of desiring oneself, in the development of one's own thought, in the unfolding of a self that organizes its ideas of the world and of its life, that reflects on that world, its actions, its feelings. It is the object of desire of a consciousness that aims to understand and dialogue with its world on the basis of its own structuration, the way in which it receives the live discourses and representations that exist in its world, and also on the basis of the expression and communication of the movement of its thought.

In this sense, knowing is a vital act, it is an aspect of self-development, since, in order to know, one has to produce theory and construct concepts. Via this construction, that which does not fit into general categories, the specific composition of the moment in which we are living or that we are studying can be made intelligible for oneself and possibly for others. It is also a vital act in the sense that it implies beginning to think for oneself or for ourselves, not for another or others.

Intellectual Self-Referentiality

To know, in the strongest sense, must always be an internal act. Otherwise all we have is information. This is what is meant when it is said that to know is to live for oneself, for ourselves, or both at once, since the processes of knowledge are generally also collective processes. Thus, increasing degrees of self-referentiality are implied in the recognition, understanding and explanation of the world. This does not mean that on the basis of oneself, whether individually or collectively, one can think and begin to think everything, without information or theories.

We can organize realities as remote or abstract as society or the world system around our own nucleus of reception. This nucleus of reception or self-reference is the knowledge of our own society. Since we are all differentiated products of the movement of our society and of its horizons of visibility and political programs, knowing ourselves implies knowing our society. This idea was proposed by Marx. What Zavaleta did was to elaborate this nucleus of self-reference of knowledge of Bolivian society.

In the process of studying or understanding Bolivian society or of making it intelligible, Zavaleta incorporates general theories in order to create this self-referentiality, but he does not convert them into it. As he achieves higher degrees of organization of his thought and of the explanation of that reality, he produces a nucleus of reception of knowledge that others have acquired of other realities, and even constructs his own mode of knowledge, not only of Bolivia but also in order to think other societies, in order to account for local accumulation in the configuration of reality.

Knowing in this way, elaborating one's own self-referentiality, is the practice of a degree of self-determination, since it implies organizing and directing the ideas that we produce and also those that we receive. This is a first implication of conceiving of knowing as an organizational act, as the construction of concepts but also as an organization of intellectual self-referentiality, which implies belonging to a reality not for having been born in a certain territory, but as a result of the intellectual and affective appropriation of it. Intellectual appropriation of reality occurs when we can produce a constellation of ideas that constitute a frame of intelligibility and a coherent organization of consciousness, and when this constellation offers to the self that elaborates it a direction for action within that reality through that appropriation.

Thinking Self-Development

I continue this reflection with some words of Maria Zambrano: 'In any case knowing is a form of love, also a form of action, perhaps the only one that we can exercise without regrets today, the only one whose responsibility is in proportion to our strength.'[2]

Knowing is a form of love, which is a way of being, a way to belong to oneself, to belong freely to other people. It is a way to create spaces of understanding and interpretation of the possibilities of individual and collective development. To know is to think the conditions of self-development, to think the obstacles, normally hidden, that prevent us from advancing and making possible the recognition of the potentialities that are being generated in our world.

Knowing is a form of love, because it is thinking the conditions of self-development, including those of others. Knowing is not the imposition of norms on what is, what cannot be and what could be. Knowing is also a form of love in so far as it implies recognizing—recognizing others on the basis of what they say and what they think, processing this via our nucleus of self-reference and returning it as a dialogic reflection.

Knowing is a form of action in various senses. It is action in the sense of construction of a structure of understanding of the experiences of the world. Knowing is action in so far as it is intellectual production, not mere capture and reception. It is action in so far as it is the production of concepts and theories, and the explanation of specific histories on the basis of those concepts.

Knowing is also a form of action in so far as it defines reality as it aims to explain it, in that it affects other actions of men as it directs them in one or another direction.

The other sense in which knowledge is an organizational act is on the level of relations between men. The aim in this case is to know societies that are dominated on a regional and world level, societies that have an internal history of domination by a few, which are restructured time and again through independence, reforms and revolutions.

Knowing, then, is to explain the causes and nature of domination. In this sense is it a political act and an organization, to begin with, of the collective consciousness that can partially, and later fully, resist the reproduction of those structures of domination and substitute them with democratic structures of self-determination.

Zavaleta said that without knowing the past we are more or less condemned to incessantly repeat it. There are only two ways to overcome it: by destroying it or by knowing it. It could be said that something can only be

---

2 Maria Zambrano, *Pensamiento y poesía en la vida española* (Madrid: Endymión, 1987), p. 91.

destroyed if it is known. Here, Zavaleta linked the idea of social science and that of the workers' movement in a double sense. The constitution of the working class as a movement, that is, structural location plus history, establishes the condition of possibility of self-knowledge of a society, that is, social science in modern times. At the same time, social science potentiates that same workers' movement as a political force of transformation, that is, social revolution, socialist revolution, which would be a moment of broad democratic self-determination of the masses, which would in turn be a condition of possibility of the development of social science.

For that reason, knowing as an organizational act is also a dangerous thing, since it implies a social force that separates itself from the dominant ideology, which means questioning the structures of domination within society. It begins to suspend the reproduction of those authoritarian and exploitative relations. Knowing can be dangerous because it implies the possibility of organizing in another way, and more so if that knowledge is something produced, socialized, accumulated, appropriated and developed within the world of the workers, since they are those who in the last instance transform the world and, through knowing, themselves as well.

Knowledge or social science practiced in the way Zavaleta conceived it is a dangerous affair for the dominant pole of society, and for the state, because knowledge is the core of a political project; according to what society is believed to be or what is believed to be known about this society, one imagines what one wants to do in it in the future, and what can be done individually and collectively.

Organization of National Consciousness and the Collective Self

The third level on which Zavaleta constructs concepts is in the explanation and characterization of Bolivian society and its history. Here he produces, or modifies for this specific context, concepts such as the seigneurial paradox, the national-popular, motley society, oligarchic phase of the state, Bolivia as a society in a state of error, and above all the general articulation, the analysis of Bolivia and its history from the perspective of the totality.

This can be conceived as an act organizing what can be called national consciousness, in a new phase beyond or after the nationalist moment. More generally, the aim is the organization of total social consciousness, as a relative consciousness that involves local self-reference and self-determination, that tries not to accept the definition of our society imposed from outside or by the dominant pole of the society.

This implies that the acts of self-determination are complex; they are acts of organization of ideas and of men. Up till now I have commented more on the organization of ideas, but if the forms of organization among men and their intersubjectivity are conditions of possibility for an organization of ideas, then the moments of greatest possibility for knowledge are those moments of self-determination of the masses in the history of the country. This is above all because the masses suspend or break with the dominant ideology in these moments of self-determination, making possible new networks of communication within society, and the revelation of structures of reality that the normal conditions of domination do not allow to be seen and known.

This corresponds to his idea of crisis as a method of knowing. But what it is interesting to think of here is the relation between knowledge and self-determination, which unites two things: the idea of knowledge as a condition for the exercise of freedom, and the idea of individual knowledge via the roundabout route of the explanation or understanding of social totality.

The first idea has a Hegelian aspect that is present in Zavaleta. It combines Hegel's dialectic of master and slave with Marx's idea that every individual is the product of the whole set of social relations. On the side of the dialectic of master and slave, this implies that knowledge is something developed on the part of he who labours, who assumes self-consciousness through this labour, that is, knows how the world is materially transformed and knows himself; in consequence, the servile relation can be overcome.

Zavaleta analyses this dialectic in Marx's theoretical horizon, as a process in which the first acquisition of the individual self comes about through the development of capitalism, which implies the loss of the collective pre-capitalist self; in a second step, there is another loss of the self in the productive moment, in the moment when the worker sells his labour power and his freedom is consumed as the productivity of capital. In this process, the possibility of a new recuperation of the self appears, but on the basis of the type of subject produced by the new mode of production, that is, on the basis of the collective worker. This intersubjectivity is the historical and social condition of recognition and knowledge of the new reality and of oneself in that world.[3]

To know oneself has, then, a double and even triple implication. One has to know within the horizon of the social totality or know social totality as a

---

3 Ideas developed by Zavaleta in 'Las formaciones aparentes en Marx', 'Antropocentrismo en la formación de la ideología socialista' and 'Cuatro conceptos de democracia'.

collective being, through the forms of intersubjectivity that the modern world has produced, or, finally, through a process of breaking with the ideology or the apparent forms produced by the organization of social relations that correspond to the capitalist mode of production. That is, one must exercise some degree of self-determination on the basis of the new condition of the collective subject, which at times aims to convert the abstract and formal equality of capitalism and its liberty for itself into democracy for us.

In this line of conception of historical processes, Zavaleta thinks first of how anthropocentrism arises, then how this is converted into proletarian centrality and social science, and finally, how this becomes democracy as self-determination of the masses. That is, he conceives of how men first of all create their self-reference on a general level; then how this is historically translated into a series of structural positions with different capacities of cognitive exploitation within the horizon of visibility of their time and society. First, he thinks how self-reference is structured on a general level as anthropocentrism and then how this is developed in political history, that is, in the confluence, fusion and specific action of subjects in the conjunctures of self-knowledge and self-determination.

One should recall, in parallel to this, what Zavaleta called representative democracy as a state method of knowing. But precisely because this is representation and not self-determination, it is not social self-knowledge but rather a knowledge that is articulated by the state in order to govern better. In the last instance, it is in order to dominate better.

In the 1960s, Zavaleta talked about a collective self and how the individual self could not be saved where the national self was in danger or did not manage to organize itself. The collective self was the nation, that is to say, a subject that is ideologically constructed and organized, and only partially constituted.

In the 1970s and 1980s Zavaleta continued to concentrate on the collective self, but this collective self was no longer the nationalist nation, but rather in the first instance it corresponded to the collective worker. The collective worker is the type of productive force that results from the development of capitalism; and the collective worker becomes what he calls the total worker, which is the history of the workers' movement, the accumulation within the class, lived as a collective head and body and not merely as individuals.

National-Popular Identity

Finally, it can be said that the other dimension of this collective self is a product of the kind of intersubjectivity that is produced in moments of crisis, which is what he calls the national-popular.

The idea of intersubjectivity as such is not equivalent to a collective self, since various alternative and contradictory identities circulate within it; but one of the results of the intersubjectivity that is constituted above all in those moments that Zavaleta calls the 'masses' is the national-popular identity, that is, the feeling of belonging to a broad collectivity, which is above all a community forged through historical and political struggles of all the workers. There is a common matrix of local identification and thought, although this is heterogeneous because, as Zavaleta says, they live in a motley society. The national-popular is the type of identity or collective self that arises in a motley society, and in particular in Bolivian history and society.

The motley cannot be the defining feature of each of the heterogeneous parts that compose Bolivian society; that is to say, the motley is not being Aymara or being Quechua in the first instance, but rather it serves precisely to refer to the moment in which, at the same time, various temporalities and forms of economic and political organization coexist in an unequal and incompletely articulated manner, under relations of domination.

The national-popular is the type of intersubjectivity and identity that is produced in incomplete and fractured processes of construction of the nation, or in the production of political, economic and cultural self-reference. It is not only a type of intersubjectivity or identity, but rather it is basically a type of history, that is, of social materiality.

Returning to the terms in which Zavaleta framed his analysis, this the national-popular deals with the relation between social democratization and state form, or the relation between the state and civil society in terms of processes of equality.

It can be said that the national-popular in Bolivia is what has remained or has solidified as social substance and identity, that is, the complex and unequal degrees of self-reference that this society has achieved in different periods, in political, ideological and economic terms; it can also be said that the national-popular is the measure of belonging that has been produced by social struggles in the country and the attempts to construct a nation.

The national-popular in Bolivian history is a product of the level self-determination with which the primordial form has been configured, above all in its constitutive moments and their successive restructurations.

CHAPTER TWENTY

The Conception of Politics

Politics as Synthesis, Constitution and Government

In this chapter I want to focus on Zavaleta's conception of politics. Zavaleta was a political thinker, and he thought politics on the basis of history. He thought that history was the *longue durée* of politics.[1] This means that he thought of politics in terms of its process of formation, as well as its projects and desires. Politics is also a form of producing history, which is the movement of societies.

Zavaleta thought politics from what he called a total perspective, following Goethe. He understands the state as the synthesis of each society, and politics as the specific modes of relation between the state and society through the systems of mediation; he therefore thinks of politics within civil society.

In particular, Zavaleta is concerned with the process of formation of politics in modernity, that is, the process of separation of the political sphere, which is the condition of possibility for considering the state as an analytical level separated from civil society, because such a separation has historically occurred.

To explain this process, Zavaleta draws on Marx, whose ideas he reconstructs or incorporates in the development of his own thought. What is peculiar in his work is that he reflects on the most general structures of politics in the modern world, and at the same time works on analyzing specific or local conjunctures or histories, in which there are relations of interdependence.

The study of conjunctures in local histories is what allows him to revise and develop general theory, and vice versa—the development of general theories serves to produce the specific explanation of conjunctures and histories. Zavaleta's distinctive strength lies in that these are not separate tasks, that is, divided between purely theoretical texts and others that analyse the conjuncture without referring to more general moments, but rather in the analyses

---

1 Zavaleta, *Towards a History of the National-Popular in Bolivia*, p. 151.

of conjuncture he also reflects on the structuration of the most general forms of power, such as the state.

In politics, societies culminate the process of production of their general form, that is, the organization of collective political power and the social order, which is how relations between men will be reproduced and thereby other forms and dimensions of social life, including the economic structures and the direction of that society.

Regarding politics in general, Zavaleta writes: '[. . .] politics is but the mode of appearing of a certain efficient relation between the power structure and man as a group, between the form that power has assumed and the real distribution of those men in those circumstances.'[2]

And regarding government: '[. . .] If it's true that to be is to choose oneself, as André Gide once wrote, the production of politics has to do with the logic of ends without which the state would respond only to the instinct of self-preservation of the strongest.'[3]

This implies that while politics is a form of totalization or of production of the unity of a society, political construction is conceived as always local. Hence, politics must always be thought together with history, on the basis of local histories, in the context of broad human diversity. In this sense, it is difficult to speak of a general theory of the state, even in the modern era.

In so far as the state is considered to always be a synthesis of its society and thus of a local history, states are or would be the expression of the different political results produced by different local histories. That diversity is expressed with more force when the states in question are more organic and representative or correspond to their society, that is, in Zavaleta's language, when they express an optimal equation; that is to say, when they do not adopt a common or general political model imposed by imperialist powers in various regions of the world. In those situations, states only present a partial synthesis of their society and rather express, more than their own society, the realities of regional and world power.

In modern times, something apparently paradoxical occurs with politics: it is responsible for unifying that which has been separated by the capitalist mode of production and the modern form of separation and concentration of politics in modern society, which is the state. It is charged with the task of unifying the society that has produced that state of separation, but in a way

2 Zavaleta, *Towards a History of the National-Popular in Bolivia*, p. 53.

3 Zavaleta, *Towards a History of the National-Popular in Bolivia*, p. 72.

that does not reverse that separation but rather seeks unification via repre-sentation, that is to say, a unity that maintains the state of separation and reproduces it as the form of modern social development.

Politics also has to do with the movement of societies, in so far as they propose certain ends, that is, a politically oriented movement. In this sense, history is the *longue durée* of politics, the movement of societies in accordance with the ends proposed by the power structures that result from the organiza-tion of men. The quality of totalization is important in this movement of soci-eties, that is, what kind of organization has arisen among men and what ends have been put forward via the organization and the exercise of its political power, and in consequence, what kind of intersubjectivity has been produced.

With reference to this quality of totalization, we can return to Zavaleta's idea of the constitutive moment from the perspective of the production of politics. Constitutive moments are moments of political and ideological foun-dation that arise with the constitution or reform of social and economic struc-tures. The fluidity that characterizes moments of crisis contributes to these re-foundations of the general structures of society. In their successive consti-tutive moments, they are re-composed through a political construction in the conjuncture of crisis. There is a re-organization among men and, therefore, a shift of direction, of social ends. They are moments in which a society, or a part of a society, defines its programme of life, and this is basically a political act on the basis of socio-cultural elements.

Politics does not constitute societies, but it is the social and collective practice through which men define in their constitutive moments, which are complex and composite events, the direction of their final organization in that conjuncture of social change.

In so far as politics is a logic of ends, it is also a dimension in which men exercise choice in the movement of their society, that is to say, that moment in which men's freedom intervenes in the determining forces of history, as the product of one of them conditioned by the rest.

I now turn to some general features of politics on the level of the con-ceptualization of the state. The state, in particular in Marxist theory, is, in the first instance, a form of domination in societies divided into classes, that is, it is a form of organization among men that results in an asymmetrical power structure through which part of society, in particular the dominant class, maintains the rest in subordinate positions, which generally implies that they are integrated into the state as the governed, without participating in deci-sion-making or leadership.

This is another element of the state: the political direction of society, that is to say, the production and implementation of ends, which generally follow the pattern of expanded reproduction within a capitalist society, around which it is necessary to organize other tasks of political construction. One of these is nation formation, which can be considered together with the construction of hegemony.

The state produces political identity, the sense among all the citizens of belonging to the same political unit, fundamentally on the basis of the homogenization and articulation of social and economic structures. Another dimension of nation formation (nationalization, in Zavaleta's sense) is the production and exercise of sovereignty within society and between states and societies. This implies that politics is a form of collective differentiation; via the construction of the nation, politics is also a form of exercise of collective freedom.

The development of the modern state generally implies the construction of hegemony in Gramsci's terms, that is, the organization of culture or simultaneity of domination and direction through the organization of state apparatuses and through ideological production for the direction of that society, that is, through institutions plus the concentration of politics in them and ideological direction produced via those structures.

This implies that politics is part of culture, in at least two ways. First, politics is part of culture in so far as it is organization; politics culminates the series of processes of organization of social life in different contexts in the form of the general power of the state. Secondly, it is part of culture in that it defines general and specific social ends.

Politics has a strategic and tactical relation to culture. On the strategic level, it plays a part in the definition of the general ends of a society. On the tactical level, politics is the mode in which that society thinks about how to achieve those ends.

The state is the principal form of development of political autonomy and strategic rationality in society. It is a form of concentration of politics and of rational organization of power, which implies that politics is more than a rationalization and instrumentalization of ends linked with the development of specific structures, in terms of institutions and subjects of reason and political action. The state is just one way to carry this out. One of the features of modern politics is the development of its autonomy, which produces a differentiated system of political structures—the internal structure of the state and its acting subject, the bureaucracy.

Politics is also a system of articulation of social totalities. From the perspective of the state, this is a system of mediations with civil society. The state is a form of political unification that maintains internal differentiation and the separation of politics. Mediations are the form of unification and maintenance of differentiation. Politics is also the set of specific forms of composition or articulation of the differentiations of the social totality. Politics is not the substance of the social totality; it is its form of unification, the logic of its ends and, in consequence, its government. It is a movement of accumulation and local causation.

Politics and Local Knowledge

I would like to propose a general hypothesis on the relation between politics and knowledge in Zavaleta's work, in order to fill out the conception of politics elaborated in his work with another element. In several of his analyses of the state, Zavaleta recalled an often-overlooked idea of Marx's—that the form of the community is the principal productive force. Here I want to use that idea in order to present my conception of the way in which Zavaleta links politics and knowledge.

Just as Marx thought the form of the community was the principal productive force, Zavaleta thought the form of the community was the principal condition of social self-knowledge. What Zavaleta called a total perspective is present in both formulations. When Marx conceives the form of the community as a productive force, he is translating something from the analytical level of the simplest of his abstractions to the level of articulation and composition of the totality, the level on which the whole of social relations of production plus the political forms of their reproduction are considered at the same time as a productive force, that is to say, as an element that corresponds to a simpler level of abstraction.

The most complex unit is the form of the community, which is reconsidered in its relation to a category that corresponds to a simpler level of abstraction and, as such, to a partial reality. Here there is a flux of categories that, while they possess a specific location in the general conceptual system, once they are placed in movement, can serve, without losing their specificity, to complete the conceptualization of other levels or other concepts. This is the case of the idea of the form of community as the principal force of production.

In Zavaleta's proposal there is the idea that the form of the community is the principal condition of the possibilities and impossibilities of social self-knowledge; the total perspective, or the idea that things are known via their generalization, is also present. If this idea is developed from the perspective of politics, it means that the form of politics, through which society is totalized, synthesized, articulated, directed and governed, is what conditions the possibilities of self-knowledge.

How a society is divided and once again unified, how it is organized, to what ends and how it is directed, determines what it can know about itself. The way in which a society is organized on the level of its basic social and economic structures, which are the mode of production and the social classes, determine what Zavaleta called the horizon of visibility or the conditions of possibility of local social self-knowledge. And the way in which a society is synthesized on the political level—how it is directed and to what ends—determines the forms of cognitive exploitation of that horizon of visibility.

Society does not always explicitly propose self-knowledge as an objective. Organization, political direction and the political ends of society condition self-knowledge.

Zavaleta thinks that one can only know from inside, from what he called the internal horizon. Politics is always a local construction, the most local part in the configuration of that internal horizon. The base of the internal horizon has more features in common with world time, and politics is what constitutes its specificity.

Politics is not only present in the processes of formation of the local horizon of visibility but also in the practices of cognitive exploitation of that horizon, that is, what is known, how it is known and how deeply. It also depends on the interaction of men, their objectives and the degrees of generalization attained in their thought or in the explanations of the historical processes that they have been able to produce. It depends on the types of intersubjectivity that have been produced.

A dictatorship, which is a wholly authoritarian form of political intersubjectivity, breaks communication within its society and, therefore, also blocks its organic unification. It produces blindness, that is to say, a great incapacity of recognition of the movement of society and hence of self-knowledge.

A democratic intersubjectivity, in contrast, as state policy, in the first place allows for a reading of the movement of its society, which converts it into basic and necessary adjustments between the state and civil society. In the case of a democratic intersubjectivity beyond the state, as politics within civil society, the internal horizon broadens still further, as society is no longer only an object of knowledge of the state, but also the subject and object of knowledge constituted by the whole network of intersubjectivity politically activated around the task of reflecting on its reality and collective aspirations.

This leads us to the problematic of the relations between freedom and knowledge. Zavaleta writes:

> [. . .] [in] the interaction between free men ... one is created in the image of the other; they penetrate one another, but the freedom of one advances the freedom of the other and is in some measure its precondition. We must differentiate therefore between an oppressive solidarity and an organic and civil solidarity. The quality of the inter-action naturally has much to do with the social optimum.[4]

If the social structure is characterized by relations of extreme inequality and domination, the internal horizon is also restricted in self-knowledge because there is no common and generalized intersubjectivity. The image and knowledge that that society can have of itself is partial and distorted, as a result of the need to conceal and justify those social inequalities.

Equality between men, the generalization of freedom among them, is what extends the internal horizon and at the same times makes it possible to achieve a total perspective in practices of knowledge, because the exercise of existing freedoms expresses the most diverse elements of the social formation.

Equality and freedom are the best conditions for self-knowledge; that is, politics as the mature self-consciousness of human action on social structures permits the best exercise of social science.

Political Thought, Freedom and Self-Determination

If history is the *longue durée* of politics, political self-consciousness is achieved through the study of local history and its processes of causation. If politics is also considered to be a local construction, political thought as reflection on reality and not projection is thus historical critique. It is a genetic explanation of its conditions of existence, of the formation of structures and ends, which are at the same time the space in which it thinks itself.

Political discourse can also be, and very often is, a discourse that justifies the form of domination and government, which selectively reconstructs history to that end. Zavaleta's political thought in the last two decades of his life is of the first type—reflexive thought, historical critique—oriented by a desire for self-knowledge, which also implies self-criticism.

---

4 Zavaleta, *Towards a History of the National-Popular in Bolivia*, p. 126.

His political thought was also interested in the collective construction of a vision for the future, starting from historical explanation and critique, in the production of a new logic of ends rooted in national-popular history, that is to say, on the basis of the experiences of the local construction of politics proceeding from social struggles in Bolivia.

While a large part of Zavaleta's work consists in a theoretically sustained historical inquiry into Bolivian history, the whole of his thought acquires meaning in the light of a collective project encapsulated in the notion of self-determination. If there is one idea that represents the orientation of all Zavaleta's thought, it is precisely that of self-determination, which unites freedom and self-knowledge. I quote two eloquent passages:

> Self-determination in any case cannot mean the disappearance of external constraints; it means, rather, the elaboration of one's own objective or will within a set of external constraints, that is to say, these can be eluded insofar as they are known. Knowledge of the world and a realistic view of oneself are the absolute prerequisites of self-determination.[5]
>
> [. . .]
>
> The underlying problem is that of self-interest or the instinct of self-preservation in the realm of thought. It must be said that to reason against one's life is a grave sin. All men are indebted first of all to themselves, to their identity. To fully possess oneself, that is, to determine oneself, enables one to think of other things. First one has to be oneself in order then to contribute something, if possible. A certain degree of healthy selfishness is the key to sovereignty, but also to class consciousness or to personality, to all forms of self-determination.[6]

Zavaleta's work is a process of realization of self-determination, belonging to oneself by exercising more and more extensive freedoms, which imply the freedom of others, that is to say, the general democratization of the society that one belongs to. In this sense, an early concern of Zavaleta's with the connection between the fate of the personal self with the national self reappears; he had said that there was no personal salvation where the national community was lost. Zavaleta's work draws a powerful connection between a personal conception of destiny and the collective destiny.

5 Zavaleta, *Towards a History of the National-Popular in Bolivia*, p. 69.

6 Zavaleta, *Towards a History of the National-Popular in Bolivia*, p. 194.

The written works analysed in this book are part of the necessary task of elaborating self-knowledge for self-determination. Zavaleta's thought also proposes that personal self-determination is a difficult and complex task that begins with a process of knowing one's own society and, afterwards or at the same time, intervenes in it to create the conditions of collective freedom which are those that make possible the development of one's own freedom.

In Zavaleta's intellectual work there is a process of personal construction and self-development that was conceived as part of a national process of development in Bolivia, emphasizing the correlation between sovereignty and self-knowledge. The lucidity of his thought corresponds to the degree of self-referentiality produced; but his is also a fragmented thought because it recognizes, historically and politically, the disarticulation of its society, that is to say, it feels and expresses what he himself called oppressive solidarity. However, it is not a thought defeated by the history of its society, since he also extracts from it the referent for thinking the possibilities of democratization, nationalization and local self-determination, on the basis of the history of the workers' movement and the construction of the masses produced by the irradiation of proletarian centrality in the crisis of the state of 1952. That was the time in which he lived and what I have selectively presented here is the consciousness that it produced.

PART E

The Current Relevance of Zavaleta's Thought:
A Comparative Analysis

CHAPTER TWENTY-ONE

On Zavaleta's Thought Today

Concerning the Evaluation of Past Theories

The analytic route taken so far has consisted in relating intellectual production to its historical context, the political and intellectual conditions of its moment of production. Its explanatory capacity has been contrasted with some other contemporary modes of explaining history and thinking politics. My project has been informed by a strong conviction of the historicity of theories and intellectual production.

The aim of this chapter is to evaluate the potential that Zavaleta's work may possess to continue thinking and explaining Bolivian history and other processes in the world today.

In evaluating this body of work focused on historical explanation and on thinking politics in history, two dimensions can be distinguished: one that concerns specific explanations of different periods of Bolivian and Latin American history, and another that concerns the mode of elaborating such explanations, which is the theoretical and methodological framework. The current relevance of Zavaleta's thought can be evaluated in both dimensions, but with different criteria.

The present relevance of historical explanations of periods before the author's time must be evaluated with reference to the alternative explanations of same historical events produced since Zavaleta's.

The historical potential of his methodological and theoretical strategies must be evaluated in with reference to their capacity to produce knowledge, with respect to other current alternatives. The task of evaluation consists essentially in contrasting theories and, strictly speaking, a good evaluation is done in a process of production of new knowledge rather than in the mere formal comparison of theories and methodologies independently of the investigation and explanation of a given object.

Another dimension of evaluation on this level is carried out within a given theoretical matrix and its methodologies, in relation to the new problems that have appeared and must be faced in the realities one aims to explain. History is the movement of everything. Theories must be evaluated and developed in relation to the history of which they are part, its reflexive part.

If one evaluates theories historically, it is possible to think of processes and degrees of cognitive accumulation, without necessarily positing a linear progression. This means that theories that served to explain other events and historical moments but that are problematic or insufficient today do not for that reason cease to have any value. They had explanatory capacity in their time. The past reemerges in studies of the present with the theories of its time, or in the way in which it was thought and explained in that moment. In this sense, we do not only have historical memory, as a product of previous research, but one can also have a kind of theoretical memory.

In this sense, it is possible to link cognitive accumulation and theoretical memory. When one does social research and explanation with recourse to history, the historical events one works with might have been produced in the first place by other theories, which play a part in constituting historical memory. If we revise and reform this historiographic production and use it to advance new explanations, then we are not only working on these historical events, but also on the theoretical and methodological mode in which they were produced and articulated. Here there is a process of cognitive accumulation under the modality of development.

When one critiques the articulation of those historical events and not only the accuracy of information or reliability of sources, one also enters the critique of the way in which that history was elaborated, that is, on the level of its theoretical-methodological premises. Even in this case I believe that there is cognitive accumulation, although under the modality of substitutive critique, which does not necessarily substitute everything; it can combine revision and correction with substitution, which is always partial.

The group of theories and methods that have been used to study and explain the history of a society, even if they have been abandoned and substituted, remain as a kind of theoretical memory for the attentive student of his or her society. The past reemerges in current studies that theorize the period.

Even if Zavaleta's work turns out to be useless to understand current problems (which is not what I argue here), its value would remain as the thinking that probed most deeply and widely in the explanation of the twentieth century and its historical roots in Bolivia.

Finally, I want to propose a central criterion in the evaluation of work like Zavaleta's. It is not adequate to evaluate a mode of explanation and its theoretical foundations by subsuming new historical events and processes to something which, one supposes, ought to function as a formal model of regularity; and in so far as there are things that remain outside it or can only be partially included, to suppose the model and thought are invalidated.

In the first place, I think this sort of evaluation is inadequate because it is based on the assumption that history can be sufficiently explained on the basis of general theories or models of regularity, and that a researcher's work ought to ultimately configure such a model, which can then be used for the simple practice of subsuming new events.

Zavaleta's critical work argues precisely that this procedure is inadequate. He reflected on its limits and developed the idea of using general theories, within the relative limits of their validity, as cores that function as starting points around which one has to elaborate the particular articulation that accounts for each historical specificity. This may imply articulating several models of regularity, different levels of analysis and, above all, the articulation of movement of the social diversity in each conjuncture, time, and process.

In this sense, I would like to evaluate the potentialities and current relevance of Zavaleta's ideas and mode of proceeding. It seems to me inadequate to judge whether his theoretical models and categories can subsume new events; it seems more pertinent to ask if his ideas as a whole, or some of them in particular, are still good starting points and guides to think the specific historicity of what we have lived through after his death as a result of developments internal to our society and on a world level.

To this end, I will first briefly evaluate the relevance of Zavaleta's work in relation to contemporary social processes in Bolivia and the tendencies or currents in social sciences in the country. I will then contrast these with some historical and intellectual processes on a world level which pose new problems for the work of historical explanation and interpretation.

The Current Local Intellectual Horizon

After Zavaleta died at the end of 1984, significant processes of change and reform in the country began, from 1985 onward. The role of the state in economic and social regulation was reduced and state mining companies were closed and privatized. There was, therefore, a gradual loss of the power of the miners' unions which had been the axis of proletarian centrality in the history of Bolivia.

I mention this change because it raises the question of the relevance of intellectual work that argued for the possibility of knowledge of a society on the basis of the idea of proletarian centrality, which persists in underlying form in its expanded version which is the idea of the self-determination of the masses.

The deterioration of the centrality of the workers has been accompanied by some changes in the most characteristic features of the social sciences.

In general, there is a shift from macro to micro, in history, sociology and political analysis. There are gains and losses in this. In the panoramic, macro-historical narratives presented as histories of the country, there is a tendency to include those events selected by certain conventional criteria of the macro-historian. In recent years there have been advances in the study of many areas that had not previously been developed. Important work has been done on regions[1] and subjects who were not central to nationalist historiography, such as artisans, Indians and peasants.[2]

Historical research has developed to include previously excluded subjects and events, but I would argue that Zavaleta's form of synthesis and articulation of historical knowledge has not been surpassed. I think this is because there have been no historical moments in Bolivia that have articulated a horizon of visibility greater than that of Zavaleta's time, nor have subjects been constituted that could produce and exploit them. The constitution of the subjects themselves is a condition of the expansion of the horizon.

The life of the social sciences and historical inquiry does not depend only on their internal dynamic and their theoretical and methodological choices, but also on the global social conditions and configurations in which they are practiced. There are moments more propitious for broad syntheses and for deep penetration. And there are periods and moments that rather favour study of the micro, the partial, the conjunctural, rather than national history, the entire society, the world.

---

1 See the work of Gustavo Rodríguez Ostria, *Poder central y proyecto regional. Cochabamba y Santa Cruz en los siglos XIX y XX* (Bolivia: ILDIS/IDAES, 1993); *Estado y municipio en Bolivia. La Ley de Participación Popular en una perspectiva histórica* (La Paz: Ministerio de Desarrollo Sostenible y Medio Ambiente, 1995); *La construcción de una región. Cochabamba y su historia, siglos XIX-XX* (Cochabamba: Universidad Mayor de San Simon, Facultad de Ciencias Económicas y Sociología, 1995).

2 I refer above all to the work of Silvia Rivera, Carlos Mamani and the investigations of the Aymara Oral History Workshop (*Taller de Historia Oral Aymara*, THOA).

Today we are in a period of inquiry that is dispersed, micro, in parts; important but insufficient. One of the cultural and political obstacles to internally articulating global macro- and historical explanations is that our self-image and aspirations as a society come to us from outside. The incapacity of explaining oneself totally as a country, in turn, reinforces the definition and direction of the country from outside or by others.

An exception, and therefore an alternative model for articulating a global historical horizon from the life of local subjects, is the work of Silvia Rivera and the THOA collective—Carlos Mamani, Roberto Choque and other Aymara historians. Their perspective is one of moral and intellectual decolonization, and the privileged mode of doing it is oral history, which, at the same time as it produces memory, is a process of personal and collective decolonization of the subjects who work on their history and identity in this way.

I would argue that this type of work elaborates histories that cannot be explained by the law of value and, in consequence, are the cause of the motley quality that Zavaleta speaks of. It is the history of historical times and in historical times other than that of capitalism.

I think that this type of work can be complementary to Zavaleta's in the following way. Zavaleta works on a conceptual network in order to think history and diversity on the basis of the margins of expansion of the law of value, which is an important (but not the only) index of national homogenization, above all because it is the index of homogenization on a world scale. At the same time, Zavaleta produced a consciousness of the diversity of historical times. He prepared the general matrix for the reception of the alterity of the histories of other historical times.

The decolonizing history of Rivera and other Aymara historians works with the contemporary memory and identity of that cultural alterity, but it is not yet an alternative that accounts for the national and the world in our history and in our country, which is what Zavaleta provides, with the advantage of being conscious of that subaltern diversity.

This is why I think they can be complementary without being identical in their premises and modes of proceeding. An understanding of the motley must be achieved through the composition of various modes of thought, corresponding to the underlying diversity, not in a single mode.

I return to my initial concern about the current relevance of proletarian centrality in questions of knowledge, once this centrality has been weakened. My answer is simple. I believe that the moments in which new knowledge has been produced and cognitive strategies articulated can continue to be points of reference or even points of departure, even when the social config-uration has changed, as long as there are no alternatives with a greater capac-ity for explanation and articulation of different levels of analysis.

Using Zavaleta's language, I would say that the cognitive strategies of the moment of configuration of a broad horizon of visibility can serve further investigation and thinking when their social conditions no longer exist, in a reduced horizon of visibility.

It can be said that societies sometimes regress with respect to their capac-ities for global self-knowledge, although at the same time they may know some parts of themselves better. Perhaps what Habermas[3] says is true: that societies never cease to learn, but they may do so in uneven ways. At times they achieve a global awareness and reflexivity; at times they lose it and learn in the meanders of the multiplicity of processes of daily life.

Despite the deterioration of proletarian centrality, the cognitive strategy articulated as a form of exploitation of that moment in Bolivian history can still serve for social inquiry today, because it was on that basis that the most complex and complete method of explaining and understanding local history and the society that produced it was developed.

The historical centrality of the Bolivian proletariat existed because it became national and at the same time made its society national; it articulated the broadest network of intersubjectivity in the country. In the absence of a broader substitute, that previously existing configuration can still be used, as long as the new intellectual and social realities are incorporated; that is, if the configuration revises, corrects and completes itself with new concepts and directions in social and historical research.

Nevertheless, I have a criticism of the pretensions to validity of this dis-course of proletarian centrality. I think that at the same time as sustaining its usefulness and relevance, as I have just done, one can also relativize it in sev-eral ways. Zavaleta himself took the first steps in this direction. The first is to substitute the proletariat, as a kind of transcendent subject in the elaboration of local knowledge, by historical subjects. Proletarian centrality existed in Bolivia and it produced an intersubjectivity which permitted the margins of self-knowledge that were achieved.

The second step consists in extending this nucleus to the idea of self-determination of the masses, which means that the proletariat does not know alone, but rather on the basis of the conditions of articulation and circulation

---

3 Jürgen Habermas, *La reconstrucción del materialismo histórico* (Madrid: Taurus, 1983).

that it created. The third step is the idea that Zavaleta developed over the years, that of the motley. This contains the affirmation of proletarian centrality, which becomes exclusivity in affirming that what has not been touched and transformed by the law of value is unknowable in modern terms; the lack of homogeneity or the motley quality of Bolivian society makes it unknowable. At the same time, his notion recognizes the limits of the applicability of Marxist theory to the historical time and social space transformed and organized by capitalism. Generality and centrality are affirmed within temporal limits. Social quality is differentiated in terms of historical time.

This relativization in terms of limits of validity in accordance with historical times seems to me to be a virtue of this thought. But at the same time, it poses its great problem. How can one know, think and explain what is outside capitalist historical time? Who can know those things, and when? A partial answer contained in Zavaleta's work is that it can be known within the margins of articulation with totalities predominantly organized by capitalist principles and in spaces where some type of intersubjectivity with a proletariat has been constituted. The proletariat introduces the possibility of self-knowledge as it partially overcomes the apparent formations that legitimate this type of society.

Another answer is that it cannot be known, that there is no one who could know it. Societies that have not been dissolved, disorganized and reorganized by capitalism of course think of themselves, but they do not know themselves. Knowledge passes through articulation with capitalism and its subaltern marrow, the proletariat.

Hence, these societies only know themselves when they are disorganized from without, which generates self-reflection in the moment of rupture and articulation with what is foreign, which is generally dominant. These social processes facilitate the task of analytic abstraction or analysis of social facts.

Here is it clear that this is a modern and Western notion of knowledge, which is identified with science; it is the de-personalization and de-communalization of knowledge.

This is what I understand to be the problem in Zavaleta's work. His lucid consciousness of the limits of what he considers the best cognitive framework, Marxism, ends up denying the possibility of knowledge outside modern capitalist historical time and its margins of motley articulation and coexistence.

What is upheld is not only proletarian centrality in problems of knowledge, but the centrality and virtual exclusivity of one historical time, that of capitalist modernity, for knowledge and social science.

Zavaleta opened the way for thinking the limits of modern civilization and social science in relation to questions of social knowledge. I think we need to push this still further by suspending or relativizing the centrality of modern historical time and its modes of thought in order to imagine knowledge outside it, a task that can begin with recognizing other forms of reflexivity.

Zavaleta did not have an answer for these problems, nor do I. But the first thing one can do is argue for this opening without giving up.

I think that one should work towards elaborating a composite thought, heterogeneous but coherent, above all if one lives in a motley society. Zavaleta helps us to think what is modern in our history, but to think the rest one has to qualify or relativize, and in some cases eliminate, some powerful assumptions, such as the epistemological centrality of modern historical time in relation to other times and cultures.

Like Zavaleta, I choose Marxism as the principal, but not sole, strategy for thinking modernity and its limits, which Zavaleta has illuminated. From that point one has to begin to listen to and recognize other knowledges or forms of knowing.

Another shift in Bolivian social sciences is worth commenting on. The focus of the social sciences has moved from an interest in self-knowledge to an interest in governability; this implies the substitution of an emancipatory project by a conservative one. This orientation, of course, is more evident in political analysis and economics.

With respect to this passage from a focus on self-knowledge to a concern with governability, I want to present a series of comparative analyses, centered on the characteristics of the structure of the explanations that are produced from each perspective.

This turn towards the concern with governability in the social sciences has generally occurred through the adoption of models of social and political analysis of representative democracy, modernization and the system of political parties. These theoretical models are accompanied by beliefs and criteria of evaluation of a liberal character. This group of ideas is developed together with the predominant political discourse, which at present articulates and complements the objectives of the reform of the state. This consists in liberalizing the market and allowing it to regulate itself, and in governability as the objective of the processes of consolidation of democracy.

These are models that function through subsumption. They order local events according to the predominant Anglo-Saxon political model, which thus serves to present a systematic, ordered description rather than an explanation. It serves as a model of description via subsumption and also as a normative model, since that which remains outside or is not practiced in accordance with the necessities of the model and its governability becomes the object of political criticism in the voice of social science. Hence, many works of political analysis today are full of criticism of those subjects who have not modernized themselves, rather than explanations of the reality of these subjects.

This is a political model that functions as an instrument of analysis (basically a model of description) in social science and in its application becomes a normative model, although it is often presented as if it were impartial scientific analysis. Governability becomes a regulative idea that overdetermines the labour of explaining why things are as they are and not as the model dictates.

This type of standard work in social science displays what this country has in common with others, which can be obtained through the simple application of general models; but local specificity and its historical density remains unstudied, or rather, only superficially studied.

The institution of a system of political parties and a representative regime from the 1980s onward and the neoliberal reforms of the economy and the state made it possible to use general models to account for part of Bolivian reality, as models that were being implemented on a normative level in various countries around the world. But Bolivia's historical depths, its complexity and specificity, its motley quality remained outside, poorly investigated or not at all; it became a residue.

In these tendencies, the normative dimensions of the social sciences are superior to their degree of reflexivity and desire for self-knowledge. This discourse works for liberal reform rather than for social explanation, that is, it aims to order or re-order society rather than to know it.

This type of practice of social science formulates an impersonal discourse, with pretensions to greater scientificity and to de-ideologization. There is an attempt to wipe away subjectivity and positioning, which is easier when one works with models that one has not produced and are merely applied, subsuming the facts analysed. The aim is to explain things from a distance, with the models in use on an international level and without ideology.

Finally, with respect to Bolivia, I want to comment on Zavaleta's thought with respect to the problematic of the nation and nationalism today. One type of argument to disqualify Zavaleta's ideas as irrelevant is that in this age of globalization, de-nationalization and reduction of national sovereignties, a nationalist and socialist thought no longer serves to think about the present.

In the first place, it can be said that Zavaleta's mature works are not the formulation of a nationalist doctrine but rather a historical and social explanation of the processes of construction of the state and of ideological production. The nationalist triumph is explained by the type of ideological substitution that it carries out. The liberal reforms of the present can be explained in the same way, as a new process of ideological substitution. This can be understood as a process of passive revolution without a constitutive moment; for that same reason one may suspect that it is shallow or superficial, which does not mean that it is not effective and real.

I consider that the set of categories that Zavaleta produced and articulated (from Marx to Gramsci) and that served to explain the nationalist construction can also serve to explain its crisis and de-constitution or disorganization and substitution, and the attendant institutional and ideological reform. In fact, Zavaleta was the first to begin to study and explain the crisis of the 1952 state or the synthesis of the nationalist period. Present-day liberal discourses, including that of the social sciences that accompanies the political discourse, do not explain the crisis and the historical process of deterioration, but describe social reality without historical explanation. They are discourses of ideological substitution that think on the basis of a fragment of the present which denies that past. Liberalism does not explain the process of decomposition of nationalism and the socialist left. It is a discourse that judges the failure of those projects; it is a model of social and political re-ordering, not a model of explanation.

I think that the notions of primordial form, motley society and others proposed by Zavaleta, not exclusively but together with other contemporary ideas and developments, still serve as part of the theoretical materials that we can use to think current social and political changes.

One cannot use the explanation of one historical moment to account for the configuration of another historical moment. What one can do is to use the mode of thinking, the cognitive strategy, or some of its concepts. What is fundamental is the way of setting up the explanation and attending to accumulated and articulated historical knowledge.

Current Problems in the International Intellectual Context

Analytical Marxism

In this section I contrast Zavaleta's thinking with some current lines of thought, the problems they propose and their explicatory strategies and levels of reflexivity.

First, I consider Marxism, and specifically what is known as analytical Marxism, which has been one of the most prolific theoretical modalities over the last two decades, together with another subject that interests me: the specificity of the history of politics.

I think that one of the merits of Zavaleta's Marxism is to have worked toward a better explanation of the specificity of history and politics within the general theory of history which Marxism claimed to be, although it generally worked on the basis of the abstraction of supposedly historical subjects. Social classes—the proletariat, the bourgeoisie—tended to become transcendental subjects within the framework of the historical time of modernity.

Zavaleta worked on the basis of the recognition of historical subjects, not only assumed in theory with their potentialities and limitations, but effectively constituted in local histories. This kind of focus allows for a better explanation of the specificity of local histories.

In order to make room for politics and historical specificity, Zavaleta developed the idea of the margins of or limits to the validity of the models of regularity, so as to elaborate, around and beyond them, an account of historical specificity that could not be subsumed by such models.

If we compare this thought to analytical Marxism, above all that based on the theory of rational choice and game theory, he latter assumes the rationality of an abstract subject, while Zavaleta examines the processes of constitution and de-constitution of historical subjects. Analytical Marxism works on the basis of the supposition of a type of rationality in individual and political actors.

This is a return to the predominance of subsumption in explanation, both in the version informed by theories of rational choice and game theory, such as the works of John Elster[4] and John Roemer,[5] and the technological version

---

4 See, in particular, John Elster, *Making Sense of Marx* (Cambridge: Cambridge University Press, 2000).

5 Above all John Roemer, *Analytical Foundations of Marxian Economic Theory* (Cambridge: Cambridge University Press, 1981); and John Roemer, *A General Theory of Exploitation and Class* (Cambridge: Harvard University Press, 1982).

of G. A. Cohen,[6] which follows, in accordance with the logic of contemporary analytical philosophy, the idea of the supremacy or centrality of the development of the forces of production in social and historical explanation.

The problem with Cohen's analytical and technological Marxism is that, despite the rigorous labour of analytical reconstruction of historical materialism, there is no valuation of politics, of its capacity to construct social realities. There is a tendency to explain politics through an analysis of the movement of the productive forces.

The problem with analytical Marxism based on the theory of rational choice is that it is not useful to explain genetic processes of the construction of subjects, ideas and strategies. These are models of social interaction where what matters most is individual action and the reasons for that action. A previously constituted structure of choices and consequences is taken for granted. Rational choice theory is not very useful to explain processes of constitution; it explains situations with already established conditions and with a rationality of action which is, in most cases, presupposed.

Both in the technological school of Cohen and the micro-analysis of Elster, Roemer and their school, there is a significant process of formalization of theory around a nucleus. In the first case, this is the dynamic of development of the productive forces, and in the second, it is rational choice (which is generally micro-economic rationality) as the foundation of the interaction of individuals and collectivities.

This theoretical sophistication of formal rationality, which appears in the various modalities of analytical Marxism, can be contrasted with the sophistication of Zavaleta's historical explanation; a complementary contrast is that between the formalization around a sole nucleus and the baroque proliferation of nuclei in Zavaleta's work.

The sophistication—and vitality—that introduces complexity through various nuclei that refer to diverse configurations of the duration and density of historical time is capable of giving a better account of the specificities of local histories. It does not formalize through reduction, but rather designs a network of proliferating nuclei, their mode of synthesis and expansion, so that the form of thought does not eliminate what cannot be formalized but rather gives it the room it deserves.

---

6 See Gerald Allan Cohen, *La teoría de la historia de Karl Marx. Una defensa* (Madrid: Siglo XXI de España, Editorial Pablo Iglesias, 1986).

With this I do not mean to argue for the uselessness of analytical Marxism. But despite its contributions, I find Zavaleta's theoretical baroqueness more adequate for thinking our societies.

His work revitalized Marx and Gramsci and brought them up to date for historical inquiry in Bolivia; his is a legacy that we can use to orient our work, adapting it to new questions, redeploying these authors to address our local intellectual context.

Problems of Globalization

The group of processes that have come to be known as globalization also modify, in part, the tasks of social research and explanation. The growing interpenetration of the productions of some societies in others and the speed at which this happens poses new epistemological challenges at the same time as it provides new tools to account for the new configurations, including new technologies and networks of communication.

There is now a considerable level of consensus as to the general nature of globalization, although there is still some debate as to its implications. What rather becomes problematic is thinking local culture, politics and history at its margins.

I think that work like Zavaleta's can allow us to understand what is local, that which remains outside the processes of globalization, and also how these processes of globalization are received or occur within local histories. Since globalization does not mean general homogenization on a world level, local diversity still has to be explained. In this sense, I consider that Zavaleta's work can be a supplement, even a necessary one, to theories formulated around the idea of globalization.

There are also elements in his work that can serve as a nexus, such as the concepts of the primordial form and dependent determination, which shed light on the limits of the determining force of world processes and in particular of externally imposed policies through the study of the internal composition and history of the state and civil society. We must study both sides—local history and world history. Theories of globalization must include theories that integrate what is local into the macro-process, not as a mere afterthought or secondary detail but as processes with autonomous capacity for the production of social reality.

Today, with good reason, there is an emphasis on processes of internationalization and globalization. The emphasis on what is national and local comes from another era, that of the projects of national and social liberation. Zavaleta's work is of that era.

The appearance of new theories that respond to new configurations of reality does not necessarily substitute or annul the preceding ones; they can complement and mutually correct each other.

We might recall that Marxism was one of the principal methods of study of previous phases and forms of a world system, which, in so far as they were of an economic nature, could well be explained from a framework centred around the law of value, which indeed explains the broadest processes of homogenization of social reality on a world scale. In so far as globalization embraces culture, consumption, and politics, a more complex theoretical framework is necessary, which must not obviate the intersection of the local and the global.

In the face of these processes, one can think in two ways. One can think from outside or from the world, from the processes of globalization, which can provide a lucid consciousness of the broad tendencies of the age; but if one stays at this level, it becomes a subordinate kind of thought—well informed, up to date and sophisticated, but in the end subaltern, if one belongs to a corner of the world like Bolivia.

This is why I think it is also necessary to think from inside, starting from the composition of the local primordial form, its internal history and that of its articulation with the world. Thought from within can give us the possibility of a certain degree of sovereignty or freedom in the composition of our own consciousness.

In social science and personally, one must think at the same time from outside, from the world, and also from inside or from the local primordial form and its history. Our thought must be constructed with the dimensions that constitute us, without reducing one to the other.

Postmodernism and Modernist Baroque

One of the components of our current intellectual space is the postmodernist critique of general theories and their pretensions to general validity.

Here I am interested in comparing the manner in which Zavaleta relativizes general theories with the postmodern critique that seeks to move out of the logic of modernity. I think there are several points of convergence and at the same time serious differences. Without reconstructing the varied spectrum of postmodern thought, I will make comparisons on the basis of its most general aspects.

In the first place, I think Zavaleta seeks to abandon political and historical teleologies (present in Marxism and other modern theories of history) through the production of knowledge of local histories and the explanation of their specificity, rather than through a general critique of metanarratives.[7]

I think the advantage of this consists in working on the relativization of general theories without losing historical depth, since the attention to local history does not fragment historical time in order to value the present by itself. To avoid this, Zavaleta combines what is general in the era (given by the law of value) with what is specific to the conjuncture and the special accumulation of each local history. The principle of totality is used methodologically, but it is also relativized. This can be seen in the use of a theoretical core deemed proper to the modern era, which is the law of value, and the production of other proliferating nuclei which aim to account for the configuration of the special accumulation of each history; these are not reduced to the global centre.

In contrast to the postmodernism that criticizes metanarratives and decentres theories and subjects, Zavaleta's is a kind of modernist baroque, which maintains parts of the evolutionism, vanguardism and teleology of political and aesthetic modernism—the ideas of totality, emancipation, self-determination, sovereignty, self-knowledge—but within a thought that relativizes all these components, not through their negation and substitution, but through their insertion in complex theoretical solutions.

There is a relativization of the pretensions to validity and explanatory and emancipatory power, by way of increasing complexity, or the articulation of all of these components in a conceptual constellation that corrects and reconfigures each of them, illuminating its limits and serving to think the specific complexity of each history.

To this is added the critique of the transcendent subject, through the recognition of the constitution and proliferation of historical subjects. This leads to the revision of the pretensions to general validity of the centrality of the proletariat and its identification as the subject of social science, as the part that understands the whole. Zavaleta started from this centrality and began to revise it. I discussed the limits of this task or process at the beginning of this chapter.

Finally, it is worth contrasting the postmodern practice of collage with the idea of the motley. The former is linked to the fragmentation and coexistence

---

7 See Jean-Francois Lyotard, *La condición posmoderna* (Madrid: Cátedra, 1989).

of styles. In the postmodern aesthetic and existential or social sensibility, fragments of diverse conceptions, practices and works of art are brought together, their meaning given by their partial present coexistence for those who experience this encounter. These fragments do not carry the whole history of the totalities to which they belong; they are not holographic. The postmodern collage is not problematic in itself. It is not primarily concerned with problems of knowledge of diversity; it serves to recycle parts of civilizations, works, ideas, feelings, in heteroclite configurations for the present.

The idea of the motley, as elaborated by Zavaleta, serves not only to think diversity but also everything problematic in its social co-existence, and what is problematic in the knowledge each of the parts has of the others and of itself. The motley is not the collage or co-existence of fragments but rather the co-existence of incomplete social totalities. This may appear as the co-existence of superimposed fragments of different types of societies in the same place or country, but this is a result of the epistemological obstacles implicit in this idea of the motley.

Here there may be a point of contact with the idea of the incommensurability of cultures and of the relevant knowledge of and in each culture, which is present in some postmodern thought, although it is an idea that preceded it.

The idea of the motley is not a postmodern idea, in terms of theoretical structure or in terms of sensibility. It has in common the aim of thinking the limits of modernity and of the processes of modernization, above all in the periphery, but it is nevertheless thought on the basis of one of the principle modernisms, Marxism, although a Marxism relativized and secularized from the standpoint of local histories.

The motley is a mode of thinking from within that which remains outside of modernity, which results in a recognition of what is unknowable in and from that position and, therefore, it is rather a consciousness of its limits.

It is good to have at one and the same time a vision from within and one that aims to think from outside, as does postmodernism, so as to locate and orient our inquiry with greater consciousness of the horizon of our own thought.

Hermeneutics and Reflexivity

In contemporary philosophy and social sciences, hermeneutics have constituted one of the principal modes of development and renovation, although in various forms. I am interested in commenting on Zavaleta with reference to two aspects of this current: interpretation and reflexivity.

Zavaleta never wrote about hermeneutics, but he did practice interpretation, with the difference that he did not assume it as an alternative to explanation but rather as complementary to it and continuous with it. First of all, he articulates a core structure of causal explanation, selecting constitutive moments and crises in the history of a society, through which it is possible to reconstruct the principal structures configured in a specific history. On the basis of this framework he begins to interpret particular events and actions, which acquire meaning within general social processes. At the same time, he interprets on the basis of local history and its wealth of meanings, to which he adds the meanings that result from a consideration of events and actions in the reconstructed historical background.

Zavaleta's process of historical explanation takes what is general in the period as a starting point, and then transforms it as he begins to articulate local history through a series of intermediate categories until he arrives at a narrative in which the specific accumulation of that history predominates, on the surface of the narrative, while the theoretical elements persist as a backdrop or skeleton. This is a form of theoretical reflexivity from the perspective of local history, since it not only applies what is general and subsumes the particular, but through the investigation and explanation of the latter, leads to the revision and modification of the theoretical starting points, their margins of validity, their consistency and the explanatory capacity of their categories.

Another dimension where reflexivity appears in Zavaleta's work is through the inclusion of an element of dialogue in his form of Marxism, in particular in the idea of intersubjectivity. This appears above all in the idea of accumulation within the class, where history and intersubjective dialogue substitute the rational monologue and the kind of transcendental subject present in certain vulgar formulations of Marxism.

The reflexive dimension in Zavaleta appears most forcefully in the following three aspects. First, it is found in the question about the social and intersubjective conditions of possibility of knowing this society. Second, it is present in the fact that these works of historical and political explanation contain a constant reflection on the limits of knowledge, that they constantly interrogate their own margins of validity, their theoretical frameworks and their structures, necessities and tasks. Third, this reflexivity gave rise to a process of increasing relativization of theory, but not by its abandonment but rather through a more precise delimitation of its sphere of validity, which gives rise to a pluralization of the theoretical universe in order to account for historical specificity. The production of local knowledge is at once a reflection on society and a form of reflection on the theory that one uses.

Micro-level interpretation of individual and collective actions, in Zavaleta, does not have the cultural community as its principal referent, but rather the explanatory linkages of macro-processes, elaborated in terms of causality. In this sense, while what he does is interpretation, strictly speaking it perhaps should not be called hermeneutics, given the other implications of that conception.

At present, to interpret generally means to think the meaning of micro-events in relation to partial totalities or communities of culture, which implies giving considerable importance to the past. When one interprets on the basis of a causal framework, the past has a weight of structural historical accumulation, but the power of the present is greater than in a hermeneutic practice whose dialogue is rather with the cultural horizon of the past. The other extreme is intentionalist understanding in the style of Von Wright,[8] which focuses on the present.

A composite method of study and composite answers (explanation plus interpretation, for example) seem to be more adequate since they are better able to think the diverse dimensions of our social lives.

Validation, Contrast, Currency

It often happens that theories are not validated by their explanatory capacity, their results and their potential to continue producing other theories, but rather for their degree of participation, or not, in the predominant language games of a discipline,[9] of the wider intellectual space, at a particular moment. Something like this is happening with Zavaleta's work at present, in Bolivia and elsewhere.

Zavaleta's work is produced and presented in languages that are not part of the predominant games of the moment. This is the primary reason for denying the current relevance of his work. Nor does it take part in the concerns and questions of the present moment, such as: How is Bolivia to be made governable? How to enter the world market? How to reform the economy and the state so that we obtain the consensus of world powers?

8 Georg Henrik von Wright, *Explicación y comprensión* (Madrid: Alianza, 1987).

9 See Ludwig Wittgenstein, *Philosophical Investigations* (New York: John Wiley, 2010).

Zavaleta's work is composed with a combination of a Marxist language and other elements that he produces and incorporates, although within a theoretical tradition. At that time, the 1970s and early 1980s, Marxism was one of the predominant language games in many Latin American countries and their respective academic contexts. Today this is no longer the case. In the social sciences in Bolivia, there is a process of moving away from Marxism, and in this process Zavaleta's work also tends to be invalidated, not through the presentation of intellectual alternatives with greater explanatory capacity, but as the result of a political and intellectual shift towards new language games that have greater currency in the new networks of economic and political power.

For this reason, it is difficult to work with Zavaleta's ideas in the networks that are more institutionalized and in tune with the project of developing the social sciences in Bolivia as apprenticeship in and application of the theoretical models that predominate in the Anglo-Saxon academic world and international institutions.

For that reason, I think that any new project engaging Zavaleta's ideas will have to evaluate his thought in relation to these new theoretical currents, considering its margins of validity and explanatory capacity in that process of evaluation. It is not a discourse whose assumptions, concepts and structure would already be recognized as a generally accepted framework, or as a language game in which today's community of researchers in social science in the country takes part. There is, however, a group of intellectuals who make use of Zavaleta's ideas in a heterodox manner, including Luís H. Antezana[10] and Fernando Mayorga.[11]

The rhetoric of proletarian centrality and the self-determination of the masses seems a thing of the past, something out of date, to most people today. Indeed, they are things of the past, because they were also the organizing core of the central form of intersubjectivity of an era. But, as Baudelaire might say,[12] modern things in their great expressions are configured in such a way that they show us the strength and beauty of what is transitory, what is contingent,

---

10 Above all his books, Luis H. Antezana, *La diversidad social en Zavaleta Mercado* (La Paz: CEBEM, 1991); and *Sentidos comunes* (Cochabamba: CESU-UMSS, 1995).

11 See Fernando Mayorga, *Discurso y política en Bolivia* (La Paz: CERES, 1993); and *La política del silencio* (La Paz: ILDIS, 1991).

12 Charles Baudelaire, *El pintor de la vida moderna* (Bogota: Áncora Editores, 1995). Published in English as *The Painter of Modern Life and Other Essays* (Jonathan Mayne trans.) (London: Phaedon, 1964).

at the same time as they contain what is permanent. In contemporary Bolivia the self-determination of the masses and proletarian centrality have been interrupted, but I believe that we are now in a situation in which the great modern expressions of the recent past can provide more self-knowledge than the productions of the present. The modernity of that time was more reflexive than the current projects, processes and ideas of modernization.

Today, many are living the passage from the disenchantment of that time and its emancipatory beliefs to the pragmatic illusions of the present, which has not yet reflected on its own limits.

I do not mean to say that what we had, and in particular Zavaleta's work, is enough to continue thinking the present. What I am suggesting is that there are previous achievements that have not been totally exhausted and that are not yet obsolete. Some can be reanimated, in the way in which Walter Benjamin thought that fragments of the past that had not been realized could be retrieved in order to carry out the tasks of the present. I think the projects of self-knowledge and self-determination, and their theorization, are things that we can and must articulate in our work in the present.

Synthesis–Conclusion

With this brief review of the present conjuncture, I have not tried to show that Zavaleta's ideas can solve the problems we face today. I have tried, rather, to show how he took on some of the challenges of his time in the conditions that existed then, and that his work still has intellectual potential even in the current conditions, especially the local ones.

Zavaleta's ideas are fundamentally useful or relevant to begin to account for local histories in successive phases of processes of globalization. He remains a good starting point, not an endpoint. The achievements of the past are valuable to us in beginning new projects and formulating new questions, not in repeating the old ones. In this lies the vitality of works of the past.

Bibliography

WORKS BY RENÉ ZAVALETA MERCADO

50 años de historia. Cochabamba: Los Amigos del Libro, 1992.

The Agrarian Problem and the Formation of the State: The Cases of Mexico, Argentina and Bolivia. Series: 'Le problème agraire en Amérique Latine'. Latin American Research Workshop, February 1977.

'Allende y Pinochet. La democracia de clase en Chile'. *El Excelsior*, 9 September 1975.

'Ambivalencia de la clase media'. *La Nación*, 1 August 1959.

'Ante las elecciones, Falange prefiere el camino del golpe'. *La Nación*, 26 May 1959.

'Antropocentrismo en la formación de la ideología socialista'. *Dialéctica* 8(13) (1983): 61–74.

'Augusto Céspedes y una historia chola'. *Marcha*, 7 December 1956.

'Barrientos. Realmente parece un norteamericano'. *El Día*, 15 January 1966.

'Bolivia. Algunos problemas acerca de la democracia, el movimiento popular y la crisis revolucionaria' in *América Latina 80. Democracia y movimiento popular.* Lima: DESCO, 1981, pp. 373–80.

'Bolivia. La crisis de 1971'. *El Excelsior*, 26 August 1975.

'Bolivia. La división trotskista'. *El Excelsior*, 4 November 1975.

'Bolivia. Las luchas mineras'. *El Excelsior*, 2 March 1975.

'Bonapartismo y nacionalismo'. Unpublished manuscript, c. 1970s.

'Caciques enriquecidos adoptan para el campesinado una tesis rosquera'. *La Nación*, 27 January 1963.

'Campaña sin sentido favorecida por equivocados y extremistas'. *La Nación*, 20 August 1959.

'Chile y Perú. Los motivos militares'. *El Excelsior*, 8 October 1974.

'Chile, Kissinger, libertad. Sobre idiotas y ratones'. *El Excelsior*, 25 November 1974.

'Church y el fascismo chileno. Cómo sucedieron las cosas'. *El Excelsior*, 2 December 1975.

'Cinco años de revolución en Bolivia'. *Marcha*, 26 April 1957.

'Clase y conocimiento'. *Historia y Sociedad* 7 (1975): 3–8.

'Cuatro conceptos de democracia'. *Dialéctica* 7(12) (1982): 11–30.

'Detrás de las fuerzas armadas. La crisis nacional en Chile'. *El Excelsior*, 25 February 1975.

'Dilemas argentinas. El tiempo no se detiene'. 18 November 1975.

'Dogmas y paradojas que anulan a la ayuda norteamericana'. *La Nación*, 15 November 1959.

El assalto porista. El trotskismo y el despotismo de las aclamaciones en los sindicatos mineros de Bolivia. La Paz: n.p., 1959.

'El Che en el Churo'. *Marcha*, 10 October 1969.

'El derrocamiento de Paz'. *Marcha*, 29 January 1965.

'El estado en América Latina'. *Ensayos* 1 (1984): 59–78.

'El fascismo en Chile. La provocación inminente'. *El Excelsior*, 3 December 1974.

'El fascismo y América Latina'. *Nueva política* 1 (1976).

'El largo viaje de Arze a Banzer'. *Bases. Expresiones del pensamiento marxista boliviano* 1 (1981): 101–24.

'El peor enemigo de la Gulf'. *Marcha*, 9 January 1970.

El poder dual. Problemas de la teoría del Estado en América Latina. Mexico City: Siglo XXI, 1974.

'El porvenir de América Latina y su papel en la elaboración de una nueva humanidad'. La Paz, 4 April 1954.

'El sangriento domingo onomástico. Tema para la calumnia y el absurdo'. *La Nación*, 1959.

'Elijamos un presidente y no un prisionero. Militantes del MNR exigen todo el poder para el jefe del partido'. *La Nación*, 22 April 1959.

Estado nacional o pueblo de pastores. La Paz: E. Burillo, 1956.

'Falange o la caída de un estilo político'. *La Nación*, 29 April 1959.

'Fascismo, dictadura y coyuntura de disolución'. *Revista Mexicana de Sociología* 12(1) (1979): 75–85.

'Forma clase y forma multitud en el proletariado minero en Bolivia' (1983) in René Zavaleta, *La autodeterminación de las masas*. Bogota: CLACSO/Siglo del Hombre Editores, 2009, pp. 263–88.

'Formas de operación del estado en América Latina'. Unpublished manuscript, *c.* 1970s.

'Funambulesca teoría expónese en nombre del sindicalismo'. *La Nación*, 1959.

'Golpes tranquilos. El sueño del pasado'. *El Excelsior*, 15 June 1976.

'Imposibilidades de alto nivel'. *La Nación*, 25 May 1958.

Introduction to *Bases. Expresiones del pensamiento marxista boliviano* 1 (1981).

'Joven deshabitado culpa al país por sus desgracias personales'. *La Nación*, 17 March 1960.

'Juan José Torres. El sistema de mayo'. *El Excelsior*, 5 June 1976.

'Juegos de Banzer. El nuevo orden'. *El Excelsior*, 19 November 1974.

La caída del MNR. Manuscript, 1970.

'La dictadura de Banzer. Desacato de los obreros'. *El Excelsior*, 14 November 1976.

'La estructura democrática del MNR no admite imposición de fórmulas'. *La Nación*, 23 August 1959.

'La explotación del petróleo'. *La Nación*, 11 January 1957.

La formación de la conciencia nacional. Cochabamba: Los Amigos del Libro, 1990.

'La fuerza de la masa'. *Cuadernos de marcha* 3 (1980): 29–42.

'La huelga de masas'. *El Excelsior*, 29 June 1976.

'La razón de la soberanía'. Unpublished manuscript.

'La reforma del estado en la Bolivia posdictatorial'. *Cuadernos de marcha* 5(26) (March–April 1984): 3–8.

'La revolución boliviana y el doble poder'. *Marcha*, 20 July 1962.

La revolución boliviana y la cuestión del poder. La Paz: Dirección Nacional de Informaciones, 1964.

'La subversión armada de la rosca cruceña, un atentado contra la unidad nacional'. *La Nación*, 27 May 1959.

'La zona conflictiva. Balanza de una intriga'. *El Excelsior*, 16 December 1975.

'Las costumbres militares'. *El Día*, June 1979.

'Las dos caras de la violencia más brutal'. *El Día*, 25 September 1965.

'Las formaciones aparentes en Marx'. *Historia y Sociedad* 18 (1978): 3–25.

'Las ideas de Leigh. La fascistización en Chile'. *El Excelsior*, 29 August 1975.

'Las luchas antiimperialistas en América Latina'. *Revista Mexicana de Sociología* 27(1) (January–March 1976).

'Las masas en noviembre' in René Zavaleta (ed.), *Bolivia, hoy.* Mexico City: Siglo XXI, 1983, pp. 1–30.

'Las muertes de abril'. *El Día*, 25 June 1966.

Lo nacional-popular en Bolivia. Madrid: Siglo XXI, 1986. Available in English as: *Towards a History of the National-Popular in Bolivia, 1879–1980* (Anne Freeland trans.). London: Seagull Books, 2018.

'Los ciclos históricos y la aptitud creadora del individuo' (1954). *Presencia*, 2 February 1957.

'Los crímenes de Ovando'. *Marcha,* 2 April 1971.

'Los fracasos del terror'. *Marcha*, 28 May 1965.

'Los idus de marzo. El golpe en la Argentina. *El Excelsior*, 23 March 1970.

'Los idus de marzo. El golpe en la Argentina'. *El Excelsior*, 23 March 1976.

'Los muertos que no han vivido'. *La Nación,* 1959.

'Los orígenes del derrumbe'. *Marcha*, 22 January 1965.

'Mayo minero. Riesgo que vale un destino'. *El Excelsior*, 5 May 1976.

'Militares y campesinos. Crisis en Bolivia'. *El Excelsior*, 6 June 1974.

'Movimiento obrero y ciencia social. La revolución democrática de 1952 en Bolivia y las tendencias sociológicas emergentes'. *Historia y Sociedad* 2(3) (1974): 3–35.

'Muerte de los mineros de Catavi'. *El Día*, 8 October 1965.

'Notas sobre la cuestión nacional en América Latina' in Juan Enrique Vega (ed.), *Teoría y política en América Latina.* Mexico City: CIDE, 1982.

'Notas sobre la cuestión nacional en América Latina' in Marcos Palacios (ed.), *La unidad nacional en América Latina. Del regionalismo a la nacionalidad.* Mexico: El Colegio de México, 1983, pp 87–98.

'Opónense al predial rústico dirigentes mal informados y explotadores bien informados'. *La Nación*, 27 February 1963.

'Ovando el bonapartista'. *Letras Bolivianas* 9 (June 1970): 14–25.

'Perón y López Rega. Desventura de una mediación'. *El Excelsior*, 17 July 1975.

'Perspectivas de la represión. El terror ineficaz'. *El Excelsior*, 28 January 1975.

'Peruanizar al Perú. De Mariátegui a Morales'. *El Excelsior*, 1 June 1976.

'Problemas de la determinación dependiente y la forma primordial' in Susana Bruna et al., *América Latina. Desarrollo y perspectivas democráticas*. San José de Costa Rica: FLACSO, 1982, pp. 55–83.

'Recordación y apología de Sergio Almaraz', prologue to Sergio Paz Almaraz, *Bolivia. Réquiem para una república*. La Paz: Biblioteca de Marcha, 1969, pp. 1–30.

'Reflexiones sobre abril'. *El Diario*, 11 April 1971.

'Todo lo que Bolivia es hoy no es sino el desplegamiento de 1952'. Interview with Mariano Baptista Gumucio, *Ultima Hora*, 1983.

Towards a History of the National-Popular in Bolivia, 1879–1980 (Anne Freeland trans.). London: Seagull Books, 2018.

Unified Approach to Development Analysis and Planning. Case study: Chile. United Nations Research Institute for Social Development, June 1972.

OTHER SOURCES

AGUILUZ, Maya. *Una lectura sociológica. El caso de un pensador boliviano. Carlos Medinaceli y su época*. México City: FCPyS-UNAM, 1991.

ALBARRACÍN MILLÁN, Juan. *El gran debate. Positivismo e irracionalismo en el estudio de la sociedad boliviana*. La Paz: n.p., 1978.

——. *Geopolítica, populismo y teoría sociotriconopanorámica*. La Paz: Universo, 1982.

——. *Orígenes del pensamiento social contemporáneo en Bolivia*. La Paz: Empresa Editora 'Universo', 1976.

——. *Sociología indigenal y antropología telurista*. La Paz: Universo, 1982.

ALBÓ, Xavier. '40 naciones en una'. *Cuarto intermedio* 6(1) (1988): 19–44.

ALMARAZ PAZ, Sergio. *Bolivia. Réquiem para una república*. La Paz: Biblioteca de Marcha, 1969.

——. *El poder y la caída. El estaño en la historia de Bolivia*. Cochabamba: Los Amigos del Libro, 1967.

——. 'Lo básico. No perder el gas y ganar el mercado argentino para YPFB' in Julio Rojas Arajo (ed.), *Foro nacional sobre el petroleo y gas*. Cochabamba: Editorial Universitaria, 1968, pp. 83–111.

——. *Petróleo en Bolivia*. La Paz: Editorial Juventud, 1958.

ALTHUSSER, Louis. *On the Reproduction of Capitalism: Ideology and Ideological State Apparatuses* (Etienne Balibar pref., Jacques Bidet intro., G. M. Goshgarian trans.). London: Verso Books, 2014[1971].

———. 'Philosophy as a Revolutionary Weapon'. 1968. Available at: https://bit.ly/2xYJCuN (last accessed on 12 December 2019).

ANDERSON, Benedict. *Imagined Communities: Reflections on the Origin and Spread of Nationalism*. London: Verso Books, 1983.

ANTEZANA, Luis H. *La diversidad social en Zavaleta Mercado*. La Paz: CEBEM, 1991.

———. *Sentidos communes*. Cochabamba: CESU-UMSS, 1995.

———. 'Sistema y procesos ideológicos en Bolivia (1935–1979)' in René Zavaleta (ed.), *Bolivia hoy*. Mexico City: Siglo XXI, 1983, pp. 60–84.

ARZE, José Antonio. *Ensayos filosóficos*. La Paz: Roalva, 1980.

———. *Sociografía del incario*. La Paz: Fénix, 1952.

———. *Sociología marxista*. Oruro: Editorial Universitaria, 1963.

AYALA, Ernesto. *¿Qué es la revolución boliviana?* La Paz: Burillo, 1956.

BAKHTIN, Mikhail M. *Speech Genre and Other Late Essays* (V. W. McGee trans., C. Emerson and M. Holquist eds). Austin: University of Texas Press, 1994.

BARCELLI, Agustín. *Medio siglo de luchas sindicales en Bolivia*. La Paz: SPI, 1956.

BAUDELAIRE, Charles. *El pintor de la vida moderna*. Bogota: Áncora Editores, 1995.

———. *The Painter of Modern Life and Other Essays* (Jonathan Mayne trans.) (London: Phaedon, 1964).

BENJAMIN, Walter. *Selected Writings*, 4 VOLS. Cambridge, MA: Harvard University Press, 2004–06.

BLOCH, Ernst. *Sujeto-objeto*. Mexico City: Fondo de Cultura Económica, 1985.

BRAUDEL, Fernand. *La historia y las ciencias sociales*. Madrid: Alianza Editorial, 1968[1958].

BURKE, Kenneth. *A Rhetoric of Motives*. Berkeley: University of California Press, 1969.

CARPENTIER, Alejo. 'Lo barroco y lo real maravilloso' in 'Razón de ser' in *Ensayos*. Havana: Letras Cubanas, 1984.

CÉSPEDES, Augusto. *El dictador suicida. 40 años de historia de Bolivia*. Santiago de Chile: Editorial Universitaria, 1956.

———. *El presidente colgado*. La Paz: Juventud, 1966.

CHATTERJEE, Partha. *Nationalist Thought and the Colonial World: A Derivative Discourse*. Minneapolis: University of Minnesota Press, 1993.

CISO. *El pensamiento de Sergio Almaraz*. La Paz: Centro de Investigación de Sociología, 1993.

COHEN, Gerald Allan. *Karl Marx's Theory of History: A Defence*. Princeton, NJ: Princeton University Press, 2001[1978].

———. *La teoría de la historia de Karl Marx. Una defensa*. Madrid: Siglo XXI de España, Editorial Pablo Iglesias, 1986.

CONDARCO MORALES, Ramiro. *El escenario andino y el hombre*. La Paz: Imprenta y librería Renovación, 1971.

———. *Zárate, el "temible" Willka. Historia de la rebelión indígena de 1899*. Santa Cruz de la Sierra: Editorial El País, 2011.

CRN (Coordinadora de Resistencia Nacionalista). *El nacionalismo revolucionario contra la ocupación norteamericana.* La Paz: CRN, 1967.

DEMÉLAS, Marie-Danielle. 'Darwinismo a la criolla. El darwinismo social en Bolivia, 1880–1910'. *Historia Boliviano* 1 (1981): 55–82.

——. *Nationalisme sans nation? La Bolivie a la fin du XIXe siècle.* Paris: Éditions du C. N. R. S., 1980.

ELSTER, John. *Making Sense of Marx.* Cambridge: Cambridge University Press, 2000.

FESTINGER, Leon. *A Theory of Cognitive Dissonance.* Stanford, CA: Stanford University Press, 1957.

FLISFISCH, Ángel. 'La polis censitaria. La política y el mercado' in Francisco Rojas Aravena (ed.), *Autoritarismo y alternativas populares en América Latina.* San José: FLACSO, 1982, pp. 107–40.

GARCÍA LINERA, Álvaro. *Reproletarización. Nueva clase obrera y desarrollo del capital industrial en Bolivia (1952-1998). El caso de La Paz y El Alto.* La Paz: Muela del Diablo, 1999.

GRAMSCI, Antonio. *Cuadernos de la cárcel.* Mexico City: Juan Pablos, 1975.

HABERMAS, Jürgen. *Legitimation Crisis* (Thomas A. McCarthy trans.). Boston, MA: Beacon Press, 1975.

——. *La reconstrucción del materialismo histórico.* Madrid: Taurus, 1983.

——. *Theory of Communicative Action,* 2 VOLS (Thomas A. McCarthy trans.). Boston, MA: Beacon Press, 1984 and 1987.

——. 'Towards a Reconstruction of Historical Materialism' (Robert Strauss trans.). *Theory and Society* 2(3) (Autumn 1975): 287–300.

HEGEL, G. W. F. *Phenomenology of Spirit* (Peter Fuss and John Dobbins trans). Notre Dame, IN: University of Notre Dame Press, 2019.

——. *The Science of Logic* (George di Giovanni trans.). Cambridge: Cambridge University Press, 2015.

HOLLOWAY, John. 'Debates sobre el estado en Alemania occidental y en Gran Bretaña'. *Críticas de la economía política* 16–17 (1980): 223–50.

——. *Fundamentos teóricos para una crítica marxista de la administración pública.* Mexico City: INAP, 1982.

HOLLOWAY, John, and Sol Picciotto (eds). *State and Capital: A Marxist Debate.* London: Edward Arnold, 1978.

JESSOP, Bob. 'Recent Theories of the Capitalist State'. *Cambridge Journal of Economics* 1(4) (December 1977): 353–73.

JUSTO, Liborio. *Bolivia. La revolución derrotada.* Cochabamba: Ediciones Ryr, 1967.

LACLAU, Ernesto. *Politics and Ideology in Marxist Theory: Capitalism–Fascism–Populism.* London: Verso, 1979.

——. 'Teorias marxistas del estado. Debates y perspectivas' in Norbert Lechner (ed.) *Estado y política en América Latina.* Mexico City: Siglo XXI, 1981, pp. 25–59.

LAKATOS, Imre. *The Methodology of Scientific Research Programmes, Volume 1: Philosophical Papers* (John Worrall and Gregory Currie eds). Cambridge: Cambridge University Press, 1978.

LIJPHART, Arend. *Democracias contemporáneas.* Barcelona: Ariel, 1998.

———. 'El enfoque del poder compartido para sociedades mutiétnicas'. *Autodeterminación* 12 (1994): 159–83.

———. 'The Power-Sharing Approach' in J. V. Montville (ed.), *Conflict and Peacemaking in Multiethnic Societies* (New York: Lexington Books, 1991).

LORA, Guillermo. *Historia del movimiento obrero,* 4 VOLS. Cochabamba: Los Amigos del Libro, 1967.

———. *La revolución boliviana.* La Paz: Difusión, 1964.

LUKACS, Georg. *History and Class Consciousness: Studies in Marxist Dialectics* (Rodney Livingstone trans.). Cambridge, MA: MIT Press, 1971.

LYOTARD, Jean-Francois. *La condición posmoderna.* Madrid: Cátedra, 1989.

MALLOY, James. *Bolivia. La revolución inconclusa.* La Paz: Centro de Estudios de la Realidad Economica y Social, 1989.

MAMANI, Carlos. *Los aymaras frente a la historia. Dos ensayos metodológicos.* Chukiyawu: Aruwiyiri, 1992.

———. *Metodología de la historia oral.* Chukiyawu: Ediciones del THOA, 1989.

MARIÁTEGUI, José Carlos. *Siete ensayos sobre la realidad peruana.* Lima: Amauta, 1955.

MAYORGA, Fernando. *Discurso y política en Bolivia.* La Paz: CERES, 1993.

———. *La política del silencio.* La Paz: ILDIS, 1991.

MAYORGA UGARTE, José Fernando. *El discurso del nacionalismo revolucionario.* La Paz: CIDRE, 1985.

MITRE, Antonio. *Los patriarcas de la plata.* Lima: Instituto de Estudios Peruanos, 1981.

MNR. *Un llamamiento para la constitución del frente de liberación nacional.* La Paz: MNR, 1964.

MONTENEGRO, Carlos. *Las inversiones extranjeras en América Latina.* Buenos Aires: Coyoacán, 1962.

———. *Nacionalismo y coloniaje.* La Paz: Ediciones Autonomía, 1944.

MURRA, John. *Formaciones económicas y políticas del mundo andino.* Lima: Instituto de Estudios Peruanos, 1975.

O'CONNOR, James. *The Fiscal Crisis of the State.* New York: St. Martin's Press, 1973.

O'DONNELL, Guillermo, Philippe C. Schmitter and Laurence Whitehead (eds). *Transitions from Authoritarian Rule: Comparative Perspectives.* Baltimore, MD: Johns Hopkins University Press, 1986. Available in Spanish in four volumes: *Transiciones desde un gobierno autoritario. Volumen 1: Europa meridional; Volumen 2: América Latina; Volumen 3: Perspectivas comparadas; Volumen 4: Conclusiones tentativas sobre las democracias inciertas.* Barcelona: Oniro, 1994.

OFFE, Claus. *The Contradictions of the Welfare State* (John Keane ed. and intro.). Cambridge, MA: MIT Press, 1984.

PERELMAN, Chaïm, and L. Olbrechts-Tyteca. *The New Rhetoric: A Treatise on Argumentation* (John Wilkinson and Purcell Weaver trans.). Notre Dame, Indiana: University of Notre Dame Press, 1969.

PEREYRA, Carlos. *Configuraciones. Teoría e historia*. México: Edicol, 1979.

POULANTZAS, Nicos. *State, Power and Socialism* (Patrick Camiller trans.). London: Verso Books, 1980.

PRADA ALCOREZA, Raúl. *La subversión de la praxis*. La Paz: Episteme, 1989.

QUIROGA SANTA CRUZ, Marcelo. *La victoria de abril sobre la nación*. La Paz: Burillo, 1964.

RIVERA, Silvia. 'La raíz. Colonizadores y colonizados' in Xavier Albó and Raúl Barrios Morón (eds), *Violencias encubiertas en Bolivia*. La Paz: CIPCA/Aruwiyiri, 1993.

———. 'Luchas campesinas contemporáneas en Bolivia. El movimiento katarista, 1970–1980' in René Zavaleta (ed.), *Bolivia, hoy*. Mexico City: Siglo XXI, 1983.

———. 'Memoria colectiva y memoria popular. Notas para un debate'. *Bases. Expresiones del pensamiento marxista boliviano* 1 (1981).

———. 'Oprimidos pero no vencidos'. *Luchas del campesinado aymara y qhechwa de Bolivia, 1900–1980*. La Paz: HISBOL/CSUTCB, 1984.

ROBERTS BARRAGÁN, Hugo. *La revolución del 9 de abril*. La Paz: n.p., 1971.

RODRÍGUEZ, Gustavo and Humberto Solares. *El socavón y el sindicato. Ensayos históricos sobre los trabajadores mineros, Siglos XIX y XX*. La Paz: ILDIS, 1991.

———. *Estado y municipio en Bolivia*. La Paz: Ministerio de Desarrollo Sostenible y Medio Ambiente. Secretaría Nacional de Participación Popular, 1995.

———. *Poder central y proyecto regional. Cochabamba y Santa Cruz en los siglos XIX y XX*. Cochabamba: ILDIS, 1993.

———. *La construcción de una región. Cochabamba y su historia, siglos XIX-XX*. Cochabamba: Universidad Mayor de San Simon, Facultad de Ciencias Económicas y Sociología, 1995.

———. *Sociedad oligárquica, chicha y cultura popular*. Cochabamba: Editorial Serrano, 1990.

ROEMER, John. *Analytical Foundations of Marxian Economic Theory*. Cambridge: Cambridge University Press, 1981.

———. *A General Theory of Exploitation and Class*. Cambridge: Harvard University Press, 1982.

ROJAS ORTUSTE, Gonzalo. *Democracia en Bolivia. Hoy y mañana. Enraizando la democracia con las experiencias de los pueblos indígenas*. La Paz: CIPCA, 1994.

RUSCONI, Gian Enrico. 'Intercambio político' in *Problemas de teoría política*. Mexico City: Instituto de Investigaciones Sociales, UNAM, 1985.

SAYER, Derek. *The Violence of Abstraction: The Analytical Foundation of Historical Materialism*. London: Basil Blackwell, 1987.

SCHMITT, Carl. *The Concept of the Political* (George Schwab trans.). Chicago: University of Chicago Press, 1996.